# The Principles of New Ethics

From Descartes to Spinoza, Western philosophers have attempted to propose an axiomatic systemization of ethics. However, without a consensus on the contents and objects of ethics, the system remains incomplete. This four-volume set presents a model that highlights a Chinese philosopher's insights on ethics after a 22-year study. Three essential components of ethics are examined: metaethics, normative ethics, and virtue ethics.

This volume is the second part of the discussion on normative ethics. The author analyzes humanity, liberty, justice, happiness, and systems of moral rules. He puts forward 26 value standards that construct a system of measuring state instruction; reveals the relationship between humanity, liberty, and justice; puts forward three objective laws of happiness; and discusses the goodness of important moral rules, such as honesty, self-respect, and courage.

This set is an essential read for students and scholars of ethics and philosophy in general.

**Wang Haiming** is a professor at the Department at Philosophy at Peking University, China, mainly pursuing the study of ethics and political philosophy. He has published ten academic monographs, including *New Ethics, The Methods of Ethics, A Theory of Human Nature, The Ideal State, Justice and Humanity*.

# China Perspectives

The *China Perspectives* series focuses on translating and publishing works by leading Chinese scholars, writing about both global topics and China-related themes. It covers Humanities and Social Sciences, Education, Media and Psychology, as well as many interdisciplinary themes.

This is the first time any of these books have been published in English for international readers. The series aims to put forward a Chinese perspective, give insights into cutting-edge academic thinking in China, and inspire researchers globally.

Titles in philosophy currently include:

**Secret Subversion II**
Mou Zongsan, Kant, and Original Confucianism
*Tang Wenming*

**The Development Trajectory of Eastern Societies**
*Zhao Jiaxiang*

**Historical Evolution of the Eastern Mode of Production**
*Zhao Jiaxiang*

**Skipping the Caudine Forks of Capitalism**
*Zhao Jiaxiang*

**Theories and Practices of Scientific Socialism**
*Zhao Jiaxiang*

**The Principles of New Ethics**
Volume 3: Normative Ethics II
*Wang Haiming*

For more information, please visit https://www.routledge.com/series/CPH

# The Principles of New Ethics
Volume 3: Normative Ethics II

# Wang Haiming

LONDON AND NEW YORK

This book is published with financial support from the Chinese Fund for the Humanities and Social Sciences

First published in English 2020
by Routledge
2 Park Square, Milton Park, Abingdon, Oxon OX14 4RN

and by Routledge
52 Vanderbilt Avenue, New York, NY 10017

*Routledge is an imprint of the Taylor & Francis Group, an informa business*

© 2020 Wang Haiming

Translated by Peiling Zhao
Proofread by Yang Aihua

The right of Wang Haiming to be identified as author of this work has been asserted by him in accordance with sections 77 and 78 of the Copyright, Designs and Patents Act 1988.

All rights reserved. No part of this book may be reprinted or reproduced or utilised in any form or by any electronic, mechanical, or other means, now known or hereafter invented, including photocopying and recording, or in any information storage or retrieval system, without permission in writing from the publishers.

*Trademark notice*: Product or corporate names may be trademarks or registered trademarks, and are used only for identification and explanation without intent to infringe.

English Version by permission of The Commercial Press.

*British Library Cataloguing-in-Publication Data*
A catalogue record for this book is available from the British Library

*Library of Congress Cataloging-in-Publication Data*
A catalog record has been requested for this book

ISBN: 978-1-138-33163-1 (hbk)
ISBN: 978-0-367-49709-5 (pbk)
ISBN: 978-0-429-44719-8 (ebk)

Typeset in Times New Roman
by codeMantra

# Contents

1 Humanity and liberty: the highest value standards of state institutions 1

2 Justice, humanity, and increasing or reducing the quantum of interests of everyone—the system of value standards of state institutions 100

3 Happiness: the moral principle of self-regarding 151

4 The system of moral rules 223

*Index* 273

# 1 Humanity and liberty
## The highest value standards of state institutions

### Humanity

The so-called "humanity" (*ren-dao* 人道) in ancient China, also known as "the ways of humans," refers to "the proper ways people behave," which means the sum of norms for all human behaviors. Thus, "humanity" comprises all the ethical norms and rules of law. It includes a set of ethical norms, such as the three cardinal guides (for the emperor-official, father-son, and husband-wife relationships); the five constant virtues, such as benevolence (*rén* 仁), righteousness (*yì* 义), propriety (*lǐ* 礼), wisdom (*zhì* 智), and fidelity (*xìn* 信); and a series of basic legal principles, such as death penalty for murder and credit in paying back debt. Thus, Sima Qian says,

> The ways of humanity are multifarious, and the rules for humanity are all pervasive; nonetheless, indoctrinating people with moral virtues of benevolence and righteousness and disciplining them with penalty prove to be the most basic principle of humanity. From this principle, it follows that people with good moral virtues are rewarded with esteemed social status and those with abilities and achievements are endowed with graces and honors. Ultimately, governing the nation with this principle unifies millions of people all over the nation into an entity of one mind.[1]

However, the denotation of the concept of "humanity" (*ren-dao*) in today's Chinese language, as we can see, has become rather narrow and refers only to "humanity" as defined by the concept of "humanism." Thus, the narrowed concept of humanity now functions merely as a moral principle: namely, a moral principle of humanism; as a result, "humanity" and "moral principle of humanism" have become the same concept.

This narrowed concept of humanity is congruent with the Western concept of humanity because the Western concept contains neither the "ways of humans" nor the rules of law; like the concept of humanism, it retains only the moral meaning and remains a moral term referring to certain moral principles. The concept of humanity problematized through these comparisons and contrasts appears to be rather specific and complicated.

Therefore, in order to define the term "humanity," we must, first, define the most ambiguous and controversial term of "humanism."

## Humanism: a social and thought system that regards humans as the highest value

As Arsenas Jorge says, the origin of humanism can be traced back to ancient Greece and Rome:

> Humanists are inspired by ancient thoughts and arts, because the latter itself is a manifestation of humanism and a historical stage.... The progressive thoughts and arts of Greece represented by Heraclitus, Democritus, Aristotle, Epicurus, Phidias, Euripides, and other masters precisely form a glorious stage of humanism.[2]

As a systematic theory, humanism was undoubtedly formed during the Renaissance and became the leading thought of the time. According to its birth and development, its historical process can be divided into three major stages.

The first stage is the humanism of the Renaissance from the 14th century to the 16th century, which is represented by Dante, Lorenzo Valla, Giovanni Pico della Mirandola, Pietro Pomponazzi, Juan Luis Vives, Desiderius Erasmus, Luther, Thomas Moore, Michel de Montaigne, and Bruno.

The second stage is the humanism of the Age of Enlightenment from the 17th century to the 18th century, which is mainly represented by Bacon, Descartes, Hugo Grotius, Pascal, Spinoza, Locke, Anthony Ashley Cooper of Shaftesbury, Montesquieu, Voltaire, Rousseau, Denis Diderot, Claude Adrien Helvetius, Baron d'Holbach, Jean Meslier, Étienne-Gabriel Morelly, Gabriel Bonnot de Mably, Adam Smith, Bentham, and Goldwin.

The third stage is the humanism of the 19th and the 20th centuries, which is represented by the utopian socialists Henri de Saint-Simon, Charles Fourier, and Robert Owen; by the German enlightenment thinkers and classical philosophers Johann Gottfried Herder, Kant, and Feuerbach; by the Russian revolutionary democrats Aleksandra Ivanovich Herzen and Nikolay Gavrilovich Chernyshevsky; and by other numerous liberalists and socialists. All liberalists are surely humanists, and almost all socialists are humanists.

Humanism may thus be considered the largest school of thought in the history of human thought. Most of the great philosophers in human history may be considered humanists. So, what is humanism? The systematic theory of humanism was formed during the Renaissance, but the word did not exist then. Instead, there existed only the word *humanitas*, a Latin word which means the secular education of human beings; this originated from the word *humanus* (meaning human, humane, humanistic, or civilized). The word *humanitas* evolved into the term *humanism* around the early 19th century. *Humanismus* is its equivalent in German, and "humanism" is its equivalent in English.

It thus becomes clear that the term humanism came into being as late as the 19th century. Etymologically speaking, humanism coincides with humanitarianism, a humanistic and secular educational and thought system, in that both are the kind of social system and thought system that seeks to maximize the development of human intelligence through the revival of classical humanistic education. In this sense, the etymological meaning of humanism is identical with humanitarianism. This might explain why the word humanism can be translated into Chinese as *ren-dao zhu-yi* (humanism) or *ren-wen zhu-yi* (humanitarianism). Nonetheless, the definitions of humanism and humanitarianism differ in their etymological meaning; they are not the same concept.

Humanism, by its definition, is not confined to its etymological meaning—the revival of a classical humanistic education and thought system—but instead refers to a revival of the new spirit, the new attitude, and the new belief in the classical humanistic education: namely, a social system and a thought system that regard humans as the highest value.

"Humans are the highest value and valuable social wealth. This principle has been an enduring principle for humanism-oriented philosophy in the past and the present."[3] So, why are humans the highest value? This question can be approached from the following two perspectives.

On the one hand, as many sages, such as Holbach and Spinoza, have said, humans are the highest value to humans because what humans need the most are humans. Therefore, humans are the highest utility and value to humans. "Of all things, what man needs most is man."[4] What humans need the most are humans because, as Alfred W. Adler and many other sages have claimed, the interests of every man are provided to him by human society—human society is the highest utility and value to every man. Human society is merely the sum of every man. So, it can be concluded that human society is the highest value to every man, that every man is the highest value to every man, and ultimately that humans are the highest value to humans.

On the other hand, humans are the highest value to humans because humans themselves are the end (purpose) of human society, while human society is only a means that serves the interests of every man. The most systematic and profound exposition of this truth is the famous formula for humanity by Kant that "man is an end in itself."

> Man and generally any rational being, exists as an end in himself, not merely as a means to be arbitrarily used by this or that will, but in all his actions, whether they concern himself or other rational beings, must be always regarded at the same time as an end.[5]

As the end of human society, a human is the value standard of measuring if the human society is good or bad and the value standard of measuring all the things in society; thus, the value of humans transcends the value of all things in society: humans are the highest value or dignity. As Kant says, "Whatever has a value can be replaced by something else which is equivalent; whatever, on the other hand, is above all value, and therefore admits of no equivalent, has a dignity."[6]

Since humans are the highest value, it is plain that any man, no matter how bad he is, ought to be punished for his bad deeds and the damage he inflicts on society and others, and regarded as a bad man; nevertheless, above all, as he is a human, and is the highest value, he ought to be loved, treated, and regarded as a human. This is the highest moral principle of treating humans. This truth is articulated by Feuerbach: "If the essence of man is the essence deemed supreme by man, then, in practice, the highest and first principle must also be the love from man to man."[7] Thus, expressions such as "fraternity," "treating humans as humans," and "humans as the highest value" are generally listed on par with each other as the fundamental features of humanism when people try to define it:

"Humanism means that humans should be regarded as humans. Man himself is the highest end, and the value of man lies in himself."[8] "Generally speaking, humanism, in its constant endeavor to restore human nature, is most concerned with regarding humans as humans, not as inhumans."[9] "Humanism includes philanthropism of a certain form."[10]

To sum up, humanism is the social and thought system that regards humans as the highest value and thus deems "treating all humans with goodness, loving all humans, and regarding all humans as humans" as the highest principle of treating others.

### Humanism: a social and thought system that regards humans' creative potential as the highest value

Upon closer scrutiny, "humans" as the highest value is a rather ambiguous and general concept. The inherent defects, sense of inferiority, jealousy, illnesses, pains, and other human traits also belong to "humans," so these qualities, if they have value at all, are only negative values and are not worthy of the highest value at all. Because of this, Pascal exclaims:

> Let man respect his own values, let him love himself, for there is a good enough nature in him, but do not let him love the base things in him... It is as dangerous to show the bestiality of a man without showing his greatness as to show his greatness without showing his baseness. It is even more dangerous for people not to know that there are two sides in a man. So it will be beneficial for people to know how a man can be both base and great at the same time.[11]

Then it follows that "humans" as the highest value does not refer to all of the things in humans; it means only some part of humans. Perry notices this too: "Humanism regards people as objects worthy of praise. What, we then

*Humanity and liberty* 5

ask, in humans can be regarded as praiseworthy?"[12] What is it? Let's listen to the reply of Pico, the Renaissance humanist:

> God recognizes that man is a creature of uncertain nature, and gives him a place in the middle of the world, and says to him: 'Adam, we have not given you a fixed place to live, nor have we given you our own unique form or function, so that you may attain your residence, form and function according to you own desire and judgment. The nature of all other creatures is restricted within the limits of our laws. But we give you a free will, and you are not bound by any limitation; your own free will determines the limits of your nature. We have placed you in the center of the world, making it easier for you to observe everything in the world from now on. We make you neither heaven nor earth, so that you are neither mortal nor immortal, so that you may be a shaper of yourself, free to choose, glorious to make yourself whatever you like.'... Who does not envy our chameleon? Who can envy anything more?[13]

Such wonderful elaboration unveils the truth of humans as the highest value: humans as the highest value refers to their development and perfection, self-choice, and self-cultivation, that is, the realization of man's inherent creative potential. Ultimately, it refers to man's self-realization, wherein "self-realization" and "realization of creative potential of the self" are the same concept: man becomes the worthiest individual possible through self-realization. In this regard, Buyeva well sums up the fundamental characteristics of humanism: "The 'human thing' usually covers a wide spectrum... But the most important thing is the growing demand for self-fulfillment and creativity, especially for developing creativity."[14]

However, one may wonder about the truth to the claim that self-realization and realization of the creative potential of the self is the highest value. The answer is positive since, according to humanists, self-realization and self-perfection is the highest human feature that makes humans 'humans' and distinguishes them from animals:

> Although humans and animals are similar in some aspects, there is one feature that is unique to humans, that is, humans can improve themselves while animals cannot. Since the beginning of human history, humans have known such a difference between themselves and animals. Therefore, the concept that humans can perfect themselves is as old as the world itself.[15]

These words are very true but not profound enough. Ultimately, the question of why self-realization is the highest value can be approached from two aspects.

First of all, modern psychology, especially Maslow's psychology, confirms the great discovery of the Renaissance humanist thinkers that every man is born with creative potential. However, qualitatively speaking, each man has a different type of creative potential. For example, some people have the creative potential of painting, while others have that of speculation. Quantitatively speaking, the creative potential of each man differs in degrees, that is, people with the same creative potential may have different degrees (different amount, different capacity, or different level) of this. But it is not this simple. According to Maslow's psychology, humans have five basic needs which can be arranged hierarchically as such: physiological needs, security needs, social belonging, self-esteem, and self-realization. As this psychological hierarchy shows, the realization of man's creative potential satisfies man's highest need, namely, the need for self-realization, and thus becomes man's highest happiness and highest value. After all, is not the highest value the value of satisfying man's highest need? Is not the highest happiness the psychological experience of realizing man's highest need?

Furthermore, humans' self-realization can maximize the satisfaction of all the needs of the whole society as well as those of everyone in society. The wealth of any society, whether material or spiritual, is nothing but the product of human activities, nothing but the result of the exertion of human abilities and the realization of human potential, and ultimately nothing but the result of the realization of human creative potential. Therefore, the fuller one's self-realization and the greater the realization of one's creative potential, the richer the material and spiritual wealth the society will have, the more prosperous and progressive the society will be, and the fuller the satisfaction of everyone's needs will be. On the contrary, the more inadequate one's self-realization and the less the realization of one's creative potential, the less material and spiritual wealth the society will have, the more depressed and backward the society will be, and the more inadequate the satisfaction of everyone's needs will be. Therefore, as the source of all wealth, the self-realization of every man and the realization of every man's creative potential is the most fundamental, the most important, and the greatest wealth; it can meet the needs of both the entire society and every man in the society to the fullest extent, and thus has the highest value.

It can thus be concluded that the claim that humans are the highest value refers to humans with many negative values (shortcomings, cruelty, illness, jealousy, misfortune, etc.) and describes only the shallow, external, skin-deep, and basic side of the truth of humans as the highest value. The internal, deep, essential, and advanced side of the truth is that man's self-realization—the realization of man's inherent creative potential—is the highest value. If this is the case, it follows that we ought to make men realize themselves and make men become the worthiest humans possible—namely, make humans become humans. This is the highest moral principle of treating humans; this is the true essence of Renaissance humanism!

Therefore, Perry observes, "The ways of life and training so important to the humanists can unify all desires to produce a perfect and harmonious personality and are elevated by practical reason as the supreme moral principle governing human action."[16] Helda says,

> If one does not transform himself to what he can possibly be and ought to be, he will not make a contribution to humanity. Therefore, everyone must first plant and guard the flower beds in this 'humanist' garden, where he will grow as trees and blossom as flowers.[17]

Miyashima also says, "Humanism is the general term for the ideas that respect, support and realize the principle of allowing humans to be humans."[18]

In summary, it can be concluded that humanism is the social system and thought system that regards the realization of humans' creative potential as the highest value and thus regards "making man realize his creative potential and become the worthiest individual possible" as the highest principle of treating humans. In short, humanism is the social and thought system that regards man's self-realization as the highest value and thus deems "treating all humans with goodness, loving all humans, and regarding all humans as humans" as the highest principle of treating humans.

### *Humanity: a supreme value standard of state institutions*

Humanism, thus, takes on two definitions: a broad definition and a narrow definition. In the broad definition, it is the social and thought system that regards humans as the highest value, and thus deems "treating all humans with kindness, loving all humans, and treating all humans as humans" as the highest principle of treating humans. It can be called "philanthropic humanism" or the humanism of "regarding humans as humans." On the contrary, humanism in the narrow definition refers to the social and thought system that regards the realization of man's creative potential as the highest value, and thus regards "making man realize his creative potential and become the worthiest individual possible" as the highest moral principle of treating humans. It may be called "the humanism of self-realization" or "the humanism of making humans become humans." David Gorjkoch has remarked on the twofold definition of humanism:

> In the Age of Gellius of the Roman Empire, an important distinction was made between two types of humanism: one type refers to 'good deeds,' and the other means 'comprehensive physical and mental training'.... The notion of good deeds originated from Prometheusian humanism while the notion of comprehensive training of body and mind arises from the humanism of the sage.... The Renaissance humanism established the tradition of the humanism geared toward the comprehensive physical and mental training.[19]

So, what is the relationship between these two types of humanism? Given the discussions above, man as the highest value is only the external, shallow, skip-deep, and basic side of the truth of man as the highest value; the internal, deep, essential, and advanced side of the truth is that man's self-realization—the realization of man's inherent creative potential—is the highest value. Based on this understanding, philanthropic humanism is close to the shallow, external, skin-deep, and basic side of the truth of man as the highest value while the humanism with self-realization identifies with the internal, deep, essential, and advanced side of the truth. This connection has been articulated by Helda. In his book *Letters on Humanism*, Helda writes, "The tender sympathy for our human weaknesses, which we usually call benevolence, is not the whole content of humanity." Sympathy is not the whole content; it is not even the essential content. What, then, is the essence of humanism? Helda answers that it is to allow self-realization "to nurture man by all means possible and to perfect man. This is the ideal essence of humanism."[20]

From discussions on the broad and narrow definitions of humanism and their relationships, we can see that humanity, as a moral principle of humanism, namely, a moral principle of regulating what human behaviors ought to be, also has a broad sense and a narrow sense, correspondingly. On the one hand, in the broad sense, humanity is the behavior of regarding humans as the highest value, thus treating all humans with goodness, loving all humans, and treating all humans as humans. It is the behavior of loving all without distinction based on the belief that humans are the highest value. It is, ultimately, the behavior of "regarding humans as humans." This is the highest moral principle of treating humans. On the contrary, inhumanity and un-humanity are behaviors of ignoring humans as the highest value and thus abusing humans, the behaviors of treating humans with cruelty. They are, ultimately, behaviors of "regarding humans not as humans." This is the highest immoral principle of treating humans. What has been presented so far is the moral principle and the immoral principle in the broad sense—the shallow, skin-deep, and external sense. Take treating captives as an example.

If we treat captives as humans before we treat them as prisoners, we will provide them with food and clothing, without abusing them. This treatment is called humanity. On the contrary, it is inhumanity and un-humanity if we treat prisoners as prisoners, not as humans, and abuse them cruelly. In a more general sense, anyone, no matter how bad he is, should be punished for his bad behavior; but first of all, he should be treated kindly because he is human and the highest value. This is humanity. On the contrary, it is inhumanity and un-humanity if we punish him only as a bad person without treating him kindly as a human. This is what humanity and inhumanity mean in the shallow and broad sense.

On the other hand, in the narrow sense, humanity is the behavior of regarding the realization of human creative potential as the highest value and thus allowing humans to realize their creative potential. In other words, it is the behavior of regarding human self-realization as the highest value and allowing human self-realization, and ultimately the behavior of "making humans become humans." This is the highest moral principle of treating humans. On the contrary, inhumanity and un-humanity is the behavior of not allowing humans to realize their creative potential, the behavior of not allowing self-realization, the behavior of "not allowing humans to become humans." This is the highest immoral principle of treating humans. What has been presented so far are the principles of humanity and inhumanity in the narrow sense—thus also the deep, internal, essential, and advanced sense. Here is an example.

A father who loves his children very much would spare nothing from his fortune for the sake of their future. However, he would not allow his children to live according to their own will; he would force them to live according to his design. As a result, his children would not be able to make their own choice and achieve their self-realization. What this father did is the behavior of inhumanity in the deep and narrow sense. On the contrary, there is another father who, while nurturing and educating his children all the time, respects their freedom and allows them to choose and realize themselves according to their own will. So, what this father did is the behavior of humanity in the deep and narrow sense.

Nevertheless, ultimately, "humanity" is fundamentally different from other moral principles, such as "kindness" and "benevolence," and, similarly, "humanism" is fundamentally different from other moral theories, such as "egoism" and "altruism" since humanism, like these moral theories, is not only a moral theory concerning certain moral principles but also, like capitalism, socialism, and communism, a theory of a certain social system. Socialism and communism are both theories of an ideal social system within which the means of production are public. Humanism is the theory of the ideal social system that "treats humans with goodness"; it is the theory of the ideal social system that regards humanity as the supreme principle of state institutions; it is the theory of the ideal social system that sets "regarding humans as humans" and "making humans become humans" as the supreme principle of state institutions. This theory of an ideal social system, on the one hand, allows everyone to be treated as humans and of the highest value; on the other hand, it allows everyone to realize their creative potential and become the worthiest individuals possible.

This is fantastic, indeed! The state institution which "regards humans as humans" and "makes humans become humans" can be called the most beautiful ideal state institution. This ideal social system is indeed the most beautiful! Especially, its principle of "making humans become humans" is the best! Just try to imagine a country whose social system allows everyone to realize their creative potential and become the worthiest individual possible: on the one hand, everyone in the country would enjoy the highest happiness (happiness of self-realization is the highest happiness); on the other hand, the country enjoys material and spiritual wealth enriched by the realization of everyone's creative potential, and everyone's needs will thus be met to the greatest extent. Is not this the ideal country that all generations of thinkers have ever dreamed of?

State institution and social system are decisive, fundamental, and global factors. In general, whether the national moral character is good or bad depends on whether the state institution and the social system are good or bad. As long as the state institution and the social system are good, the moral character of the vast majority of nationals will be good; if the state institution and the social system are bad, the moral character of the vast majority of nationals will be bad. Therefore, what the humanist thinkers of the past have striven to pursue is not really the moral problem of how everyone treats others, but the realization of a kind of ideal state institution and social system, a kind of humanistic state institution and social system, a kind of state institution and social system that regard humans as humans and make humans become humans.

Renaissance humanism from the 14th to the 16th centuries, as Miyajima says, was essentially not a moral theory of how everyone treated others, but a kind of state and social system that opposed feudalism and theocracy by reviving classical culture, thus "becoming a principle of a social innovation that opened up a new era in human history and a new society."[21] The humanism of the Enlightenment in the 17th and the 18th centuries, as we all know, was the bourgeois revolutionary theory of abolishing feudal despotism and replacing it with "freedom, equality, and fraternity" in the new capitalist society. Humanism in the 19th and the 20th centuries, especially the socialist humanism, is a new theory of the human social system to overcome the abuses of capitalism.

Humanism, as we can see, is a theory of moral principles, yet it is, in essence, a theory of ideal state institution and social system, a theory of state institution and social system on humanity, and ultimately, a theory of a social system in which humanity is regarded as the supreme value standard for state governance and state institutions. Correspondingly, humanity is a moral principle of how to treat humans, yet it is, in essence, the highest moral principle of how the ruler ought to treat the ruled, the highest value standard of how the ruler ought to govern the country, and, ultimately, the supreme value standard for state governance and state institutions. Therefore, Helda writes,

> The sole purpose of all human institutions, of all science and art, if they are reasonable, is to humanize us, that is, to transform the barbarians and semi-barbarians into human beings, so that a small part of us will first attain the form that is recognized by reason, required by duty, and envied by our wishes.[22]

Panzaru further clarifies this point for us, "humanism has gained the meaning of a political program... a standard, and a rule for organizing and managing society."[23] Thus, as Miyajima says, where there are state and social systems, where there are rulers and the ruled, there will be humanism.

> No matter in what historical age or what form of society, as long as there is such a social organization as the state, from which a certain degree of academic culture is formed, we can generally see the signs of this

form of humanitarian. For, as we must admit, once the various systems of the state and society arise, the opposition and difference between the ruler and the ruled, between the objective system and the individual desire will arise, and distortion and repression of the human nature will inevitably follow to some extent.[24]

However, humanity as the supreme value standard of state institutions, just like justice as the fundamental value standard of state institutions, refers not merely to a couple of principles but to a system of principles consisting of a series of principles. Among these principles, "regarding humans as humans" is the general principle of humanity in a broad sense while "making humans become humans" is the general principle of humanity in a narrow sense. From these two general principles of humanity, it is easy to deduce a series of principles of humanity. It becomes apparent that humanism, in the narrow sense of "making humans become humans," is far more fundamental, profound, and advanced than humanism in the broad sense of "regarding humans as humans." Nonetheless, humanism in the narrow sense can only demonstrate, in its best sense, that self-realization ought to be realized and humans ought to be treated as humans, but it fails to specify on how we can make humans become humans and make them realize themselves. The humanist answers to this question can be summed up in two major aspects.

The positive answer is that each man ought to be free because liberty is the fundamental condition for each man to realize his creative potential to become the worthiest individual possible and the fundamental condition for each man to attain his own self-realization; thus, liberty is the positive fundamental principle of humanity and the most fundamental humanity. The contrary answer is that alienation ought to be eliminated because it is the fundamental obstacle to the realization of each man's creative potential to become the worthiest individual possible and the fundamental obstacle to everyone's self-realization: thus, alienation is the negative fundamental principle of humanity and the most fundamental inhumanity. Liberty and alienation are the positive and negative fundamental principles of humanity, respectively, and are the two most important and most complex specific principles of humanity, both of which are composed of a series of more specific sub-principles.

## Liberty: the most fundamental humanity

What is liberty? Hu Shi answers, "'Liberty' in ancient Chinese means 'because of oneself,' that is, not because of external forces; it means 'self-determination'."[25] Its equivalent in the European language is thus "'liberty' means 'liberation,' which is liberation from external sanctions in order to 'make one's own decisions.'" What Hu says rings true: liberty is a behavior that can be carried out according to one's own will without external obstacles. In this sense, liberty is a rather simple and clear concept. However, upon leafing through the voluminous history of human thoughts, we are astonished to find that almost all thinkers in the past have extolled liberty but have never settled on an exact definition. According to Acton's statistics, there are over 200 definitions of liberty: "Freedom is a concept with 200 definitions."[26] Thus, in the words of Sartori, liberty is a "chameleon-like concept."[27] So, the debate among theories of liberty is ultimately the battle over the concept of liberty. So, Alan Ryan writes, "What has happened among those who try to persuade us to adopt their preferred understanding of the nature of freedom is nothing but an endless battle over concepts."[28] However, this battle is, as Berlin puts it, not simply a battle over academic concepts "with a great deal of human history behind them."[29] Lincoln's remarks help explain it better:

> The world has never had a good definition of the word liberty, and the American people just now are much in need of one. We all declare for liberty; but in using the same word, we do not mean the same thing.[30]

Therefore, the analysis of the concept of liberty has great theoretical and practical significance. So, what is exactly liberty? What debates have been made about the concept of liberty?

## *The concept of liberty: liberty and the ability to exercise liberty*

If we want to know what liberty is, then it is natural that we must know where liberty is. As it is known to all, there is no such thing as liberty in the abiotic world because it is impossible to state whether a mountain or a river is free or not. Similarly, there is no such thing as liberty in the plant world, for it is impossible for us to claim whether a tree is free or not. Apparently then, liberty exists only in the animal kingdom because animals, by definition, are creatures that can move freely. However, not all movements of animals are free. Is heartbeat free or not? Is blood circulation free or not? Obviously, in these movements, there is no such thing as liberty or non-liberty. So exactly, in what sphere of the animal world does liberty exist? The answer is that liberty undoubtedly exists in the field of activity dominated by psychology, consciousness, and will. Therefore, Locke says:

> Liberty presupposes understanding and will. A tennis-ball, whether in motion by the stroke of a racket, or lying still at rest, is not by any one taken to be a free agent. Once we inquire into the reason, we shall find that it is because we conceive not a tennis-ball to think, and consequently not to have any volition, or preference of motion to rest... and therefore has not liberty, is not a free agent; but all its both motion and rest come under our idea of necessary, and are so called.[31]

Liberty, it can be concluded then, is an activity controlled by mind, consciousness, or will. In this sense, liberty belongs to the category of behavior which, by definition, means the actual activity controlled by the consciousness of an organism. So, what kind of behavior is liberty? Liberty is the behavior that can be carried out according to one's own consciousness, that is, according to one's own cognition (knowledge or understanding), emotion (desire or ideal), and will (purpose); non-liberty is the behavior that cannot be carried out according to one's own consciousness, that is, according to one's own cognition, emotion, and will. However, in general, we tend to say that liberty is a behavior that can be carried out according to one's own will, instead of saying that liberty is a behavior that can be carried out according to one's own thoughts or wishes. Why is that?

This is because liberty is necessarily related to will, but not necessarily related to cognition or emotion. Just imagine the situation in which a person is unable to do something but is very eager and willing to do that something. As we can see, if he cannot do something according to his own thoughts or wishes, it may not be because he is not free, but it may be because he is incapable. For example, if my leg was broken, even if I wanted to play football when I saw someone else playing it, I would not be able to. Obviously, I cannot say that I couldn't play because I had no liberty to play football, but I can say that I couldn't play because I was unable to play. Conversely, a person will have the will to do something only when he thinks he has the ability to do that something. Then it follows that if he cannot do something according to his will, it is, in general, not because he is incompetent, but because he has no liberty.

Imagine this: if I broke my leg, I would only have the desire to play football, but never have the will to play football. Only when my leg is healed and I can play football will I have the will to play football. If I can't play football according to my will, I can't say that I have no ability to play football; I can only say that I have no liberty to play football. So, it is fine to say that liberty is a behavior that can be done according to one's own understanding and wishes, but it is more precise to say that liberty is a behavior that can be done according to one's own will. That's why we often say that "liberty is the behavior that can be carried out according to one's own will instead of one's own wishes and desires."

However, upon closer scrutiny, the definition of liberty as a behavior that can be carried out according to one's own will needs further refinement. That a person can act according to his will is obviously because there is no obstacle to acting according to his will. Therefore, Feinberg says, "freedom is without restriction."[32] Berlin says, "The fundamental sense of freedom is freedom from chains, from imprisonment, from enslavement by others. The rest is extension of this sense, or else metaphor. To strive to be free is to seek to remove obstacles."[33] Rawls says:

> Therefore I shall simply assume that any liberty can be explained by a reference to three items: the agents who are free, the restrictions or limitations which they are free from, and what it is that they are free to do or

not to do.... The general description of a liberty, then, has the following form: this or that person(or persons) is free (or not free) from this or that constraint (or set of constraints) to do (or not to do) so and so.[34]

Liberty, then, is the behavior carried out according to one's own will as a result of the absence of coercion or obstacles. The problem is, however, that the obstacles that prohibit one from acting according to one's own wishes or will, as Feinberg puts it, may exist either outside one's own body, as external obstacles or restrictions, such as pressure from others, laws, public opinions, and society, or within one's own body, as internal obstacles or restrictions, such as poverty, ignorance, poor health, and uncontrollable feelings. Does the existence of these two kinds of obstacles mean that they are not free?

When the obstacle or constraint that prevents a person from acting according to his will is an internal one, then we cannot say that this person is not free; we can only say that he is incapable or that he does not have the ability to exercise liberty. Only when the obstacle or constraint that prevents a person from acting according to his will is external can we say that this person is not incapable but not free. For example:

In a country that allows its citizens liberty to travel abroad at will, the obstacle that prevents a citizen from travelling abroad according to his will does not exist outside himself, which means it is not because the country does not allow him to travel abroad; it exists, rather, within himself for the obstacle might be that he has no money to travel abroad. We cannot say, then, that he has no liberty to travel abroad, but we can say that he has no ability to travel abroad. The truth is that he has complete liberty to travel abroad, but he simply does not have the ability to take advantage of the liberty to travel abroad.

On the contrary, if the obstacle that prevents a citizen from travelling abroad according to his will lies not within himself (he is rich, healthy, and has leisure and interest) but outside himself, say, in the country that does not allow this person to travel abroad, then we cannot say that he is not capable of going abroad, but we can say that he has no liberty to go abroad.

Therefore, whether a person is free or not has nothing to do with his own internal obstacles to the exercise of his own will, but it has everything to do with external obstacles only. Liberty, then, means there is no external obstacle to the exercise of one's own will; the absence of internal obstacles does not mean liberty but means the absence of ability or condition to use liberty. Such distinction between "liberty" and "the condition to use liberty" is stressed by Berlin,

> It is important to discriminate between liberty and the conditions of its exercise. If a man is too poor or too ignorant or too feeble to make use of his legal rights, the liberty that these rights confer upon him is nothing to him, but it is not thereby annihilated.[35]

However, as Berlin puts it, many people equate "condition to use liberty" with "liberty"; thus, they assert that those who do not have the "condition to use liberty" due to such internal obstacles as poverty are not free. Berlin writes,

> It is argued, very plausibly, that if a man is too poor to afford something on which there is no legal ban—a loaf of bread, a journey round the world, recourse to the law courts—he is as little free to have it as he would be if it were forbidden him by law.[36]

Admittedly, liberty is of no value and no meaning to those who do not have the ability or condition to use it because of their own inherent obstacles, but this does not mean that they are not free. The following is an example.

When the Yuquan Mountain in Beijing is open, and everyone can climb the mountain at will, I am unfortunately suffering from severe arthritis, which is an inherent obstacle that prevents me from climbing the Yuquan Mountain in accordance with my desire. In this case, it is not that I do not have the liberty to climb the Yuquan Mountain but that I do not have the ability or condition to use this liberty. Though this case may, of course, result in the same fact as when I do not have the liberty to climb the Yuquan Mountain, we cannot say that in my case I do not have the liberty to climb the Yuquan Mountain; we can only say that this liberty to climb the Yuquan Mountain is of no use to me. Having no liberty is fundamentally different from having liberty that is of no use.

Imagine I have a computer. I don't know how to use it, so it is of no use to me. In this case, whether I have this computer or not results in the same thing: that I do not use the computer. However, I cannot conclude that I do not have a computer. Similarly, freedom of thought and political liberty might be worthless and meaningless to those who are illiterate and destitute, and having these freedoms result in the same thing as not having them. However, we cannot say that they have no freedom of thought or political liberty, or that their thoughts and politics are not free, or that they are subjected to ideological and political slavery.

It can be seen that liberty is not identical to the removal of obstacles to the exercise of self-will. Liberty means only the removal of external obstacles to the exercise of self-will while the removal of internal obstacles to the exercise of self-will does not mean liberty but the ability or condition to use liberty. In other words, having liberty or not is a matter external, not internal, to oneself. What is internal to oneself belongs only to the category of having the ability to use liberty, but not to the category of having liberty or not.

The argument of distinguishing between liberty and the ability or condition to use liberty is of great theoretical as well as practical significance. In a society where the masses do not have the ability or condition to take advantage of liberty because of their own inherent obstacles such as poverty and ignorance, liberty is of no use to them. So, of course, we are obliged to strive for material wealth and education for the masses so that justice and equality can be realized.

Nevertheless, we must neither regard these abilities and conditions that make useless liberty into useful liberty as liberty itself nor go to the other extreme to ignore liberty. Liberty is the most fundamental and necessary condition for the realization of individuals' creative potential of the self and social progress, and thus the most fundamental and necessary condition for the prosperity of a society. It then follows that in the long run only by living in a free society can people truly get rid of poverty and ignorance. While justice and equality is a question of how to distribute a cake, liberty is a matter of how to make that cake bigger.

However, even in the West, for many years, many political parties, reformers, and revolutionaries have only considered about how to rid the people of poverty and ignorance and mistaken the ability and condition that make useless liberty useful as liberty itself, consequently making liberty an abandoned concept. This abandonment is particularly worrisome to Berlin, who writes,

> And, finally, the need to create conditions in which those who lack them will be provided with opportunities to exercise those rights (freedom to choose) which they legally possess, but cannot, without such opportunities, put to use. Useless liberties should be made usable, but they are not identical with the conditions indispensable for their utility. This is not a merely pedantic distinction, for if it is ignored, the meaning and value of liberty of choice is apt to be downgraded. In their zeal to create social and economic conditions in which alone liberty is of genuine value, men tend to forget liberty itself; and if it is remembered, it is liable to be pushed aside to make room for these other values with which the reformers or revolutionaries have become preoccupied.[37]

In short, it is not accurate to say that non-liberty means being unable to act according to one's own will. That the act cannot be carried out according to one's own will may be due either to the existence of the intrinsic obstacle within the person or to the existence of the external obstacle of the person himself. The person is not free in the latter case, but in the former case, he simply does not have the ability or condition to use liberty. Therefore, to put it in precise language, non-liberty is an act that cannot be carried out according to one's own will because of external coercion, while liberty is an act that can be carried out according to one's own will without external coercion. This precise definition of "liberty" and "non-liberty" shows the differences between "liberty" and "the ability or condition to use liberty." On this puzzle, Hobbes has made an amazingly clear comment:

> Liberty, or freedom, signifieth properly the absence of opposition (by opposition, I mean external impediments of motion).... But when the impediment of motion is in the constitution of the thing itself, we use not to say it wants the liberty, but the power, to move; as when a stone lieth still, or a man is fastened to his bed by sickness.[38]

Unfortunately, nowadays, scholars, both Chinese and Western, almost unanimously regard Hobbes' definition of liberty as a definition of "negative liberty" and believe that there is a "positive liberty" beyond the liberty so defined. The representative of this theory of the concept of liberty is Berlin's well-known theory of "two concepts of liberty."

## Two concepts of liberty: liberty as self-restraint

The so-called theory of "two concepts of liberty" by Berlin has a rather long history and inherited the intellectual tradition of Western philosophers about the concepts of liberty over the past 2,000 years. Among the Western masters of this intellectual tradition, there are Socrates, Plato, Spinoza, Voltaire, Kant, Fichte, and Hegel. According to the great masters of these ideas, liberty is different from the good of humanity, such as justice and benevolence, because justice and benevolence are pure good and pure good things, while liberty is not pure good or a pure good thing. Therefore, they are keen on discriminating different concepts of liberty in order to establish the so-called "true liberty."

However, these masters go astray in their attempts to seek true liberty as they have gone so far as to concur with each other that true liberty is autonomy, or, more precisely, rational autonomy, which means that reason governs one's desire so that one is able to do what one ought to and refrain from what one ought not to. True non-liberty is non-autonomy, or more precisely, rational non-autonomy, which means that one's desire governs one's reason so that one does what one ought not to do but fails to do what one ought to do. On this definition of liberty, Spinoza's statements are most explicit: "There are those who are controlled by emotions or opinions and those who are guided by reason... I call the former slaves and the latter freemen."[39]

> I call humans' weakness in controlling and restraining their emotions enslavement, for when a man is governed by his emotions, he will lose the autonomy of his actions, subject himself to fate, and thus be occasionally compelled to do bad things even though he knows what is good for him.[40]

Berlin fully embraces the intellectual tradition of this so-called "true liberty" and calls it "positive liberty," which means one's own rational autonomy or the domination of one's reason over one's emotions. He writes:

> But the 'positive' conception of freedom as self-mastery, with its suggestion of a man divided against himself, has, in fact, and as a matter of history, of doctrine and of practice, lent itself more easily to this splitting of personality into two: the transcendental, dominant controller, and the empirical bundle of desires and passions to be disciplined and brought to heel.[41]

If this so-called definition of true liberty or positive liberty—reason governing emotions—holds true, then liberty is indeed the elimination of an inherent obstacle of its own—unreasonable emotions—and can thus be called positive liberty, and the liberty to eliminate external obstacles can only be called negative liberty. So, Berlin moves on to say: "Freedom is self-mastery, the elimination of obstacles to my will, whatever these obstacles may be—the resistance of nature, of my ungoverned passions, of irrational institutions, of the opposing wills or behavior of others."[42]

This obviously means that if the obstacle to the exercise of self-will is the existence of "the resistance of nature," "irrational institutions," "the opposing wills or behavior of others," then the liberty gained through eliminating the obstacle is negative liberty; if the obstacle is the existence of "one's own ungoverned passions" within oneself, the liberty gained through removing this obstacle is positive liberty.

However, the domination of rationality or the domination of reason over desire is not liberty but self-restraint or continence, because self-restraint or continence is the domination of reason over desire while the mastery of desire and passion over reason is not non-liberty, but non-self-restraint or indulgence. Therefore, Spinoza and his successor Berlin's assertion that the domination of reason over desire is liberty, while the governing of desire over reason is non-liberty is erroneous as it mistakenly equates self-restraint with liberty and non-self-restraint with non-liberty.

As it has been hardly recognized, "self-restraint" and "liberty"—"non-self-restraint" and "non-liberty"—are fundamentally different from each other. Obviously, whether a man acts out of self-restraint, with his reason governing his desires, according to his "rational mind," or acts "out of non-self-restraint, with his desires governing his reason, or according to his desires," he acts, in both situations, according to his own will. The only difference between the will in these two kinds of situations is that he acts according to his rational will in the former situation and according to his irrational will in the latter. The following is an example.

A man knows that drinking is harmful, so he stops drinking. He acts according to his will, so his behavior is liberty. But if he is addicted to alcohol and cannot refrain from drinking, even though he knows it is harmful to drink, isn't he acting according to his will (his will to drink) as well? His self-indulgence in continuing to drink simply means that he acts not with the control of his rational mind over his desire, but with his desire governing his rational mind. Therefore, we can see that he makes decisions according to his own will, not according to the will of others. In this sense, if a man indulges himself because he is governed by his desire, he is not un-free but self-indulgent, for what he lacks is not liberty but self-restraint.

In conclusion, Plato, Spinoza, Kant, and Hegel, and their successor Berlin are wrong to claim that true liberty is the governing of one's own reason over one's desires: the domination of reason over desire is self-restraint but absolutely not liberty; self-restraint is fundamentally different from liberty. Thus, on the one hand, Berlin deduces from an incorrect premise that "the domination of reason over emotion is positive liberty," a conclusion that this kind of liberty is positive liberty; the claim that positive liberty is the elimination of internal obstacles—namely, irrational emotions—is thus untenable. On the other hand, his argument that there are two kinds of liberty, positive liberty—elimination of internal obstacles—and negative liberty— the removal of external obstacles—is equally untenable. The revelation of Berlin's mistakes further demonstrates the validity of Hobbes' distinction between "liberty" and "the ability or condition to use liberty": liberty is merely the removal of external obstacles to the exercise of self-will, while the removal of internal obstacles to the exercise of self-will is not liberty but the ability or condition to use liberty.

## *Values of liberty: liberty as the most fundamental necessary condition for achieving the creative potential of individuals*

**The Intrinsic Value of Liberty: liberty is the most profound need of humanity.** "Liberty, love! /These two I need./For my love I will sacrifice life, /For liberty I will sacrifice my love." Who does not know this poem by Sandor Petofi? What poem can be more widely popular than this one? There are few people, whether ancient or modern, who fail to love, pursue, or praise liberty. Berlin, however, poses these interesting questions about the value of liberty: "Finally one may ask what value there is in liberty as such. Is it a response to a basic need of men, or only something presupposed by other fundamental demands?"[43]

Liberty is, indeed, a basic need of human beings. The reason is that as Pavlov says, any form of matter that can maintain its own existence depends on the balance between its internal factors as well as the balance between the complex of internal factors and the external environment. The more advanced and complex the form of the matter is, the more difficult it is for it to maintain the balance between its internal factors and the external environment, and the more complex and advanced the conditions for maintaining this balance.[44] The balance of stones can be maintained under almost any condition. Plants need sunlight, water, and nutrition to maintain the balance. Animals are more advanced than plants in form, so what basic condition do they need for maintaining balance and survival? It is their ability of free movement. Animals are free moving creatures, but plants are not creatures that can move freely. Plants do not have the ability to be free, because they can live without the ability to be free; therefore, plants do not need liberty as their basic condition. In contrast, if animals are not free, they will not be able to survive. Let's take a stupid pig as an example. Would it survive if it were stupid enough to lose all its liberty and be fixed like a tree in a certain place and left to the mercy of the wind, the sun, and the rain? Therefore, for survival, animals need liberty; liberty is the fundamental condition and need for the survival of animals. Pavlov says:

> Free reflex is surely a common characteristic of animals, a general response, and one of the most important innate reflexes. Without this reflex, every tiny obstacle that an animal faces will completely obstruct its life process. This is well known to us: all animals, when deprived of their usual liberty, strive to free themselves; it is especially so with wild animals, when captured for the first time.[45]

As humans possess that which is inherent in animals, liberty must also be the basic need of humans. Moreover, their need for liberty is greater than that of animals as liberty is far more basic and important to humans than it is to animals. Matters of lower form have no need for liberty or the ability to use liberty. Liberty is an advanced need or ability developed only when matters evolve to the form of an animal. It can be concluded that the lower the animal is on the evolutionary ladder, the lesser its need for liberty, the less important and the less basic its need for liberty; the more advanced the animal is, the greater its need for liberty, the more important and more basic its need for liberty. The human is the most advanced animal, so its need for liberty is the most important and the most basic need; thus liberty is the most profound human need.

So, in particular, what profound and basic level does liberty occupy on the spectrum of human needs? Maslow says: "There are at least five goals, which can be called five basic needs, namely needs for physiology, safety, love, respect, and self-realization."[46] The basic degree of needs for liberty is roughly the same as that of the needs for safety and love. In a gist, the need for liberty is roughly as basic as the need for safety or the need for love, but not as basic as physiological needs. Berlin says, "The Egyptian peasant needs clothes or medicine before, and more than, personal liberty."[47] However, the need for liberty is more basic than the need for respect and the need for self-realization, as a man can still live even if he has lost respect and accomplishes nothing. But if he loses liberty and exists like a plant, then it is absolutely impossible for the man to survive. So, Toynbee says, "Man cannot live without a minimum of freedom, any more than he can live without a minimum of security, justice, and food."[48]

Liberty is a basic need of human beings. Where there is a need, there will be a desire; where there is a desire, there will be a purpose. Thus, desire is the awareness of need, and the purpose is the fulfillment of the desire. Therefore, from a comprehensive perspective, it should be said that liberty is a basic need, basic desire, and basic purpose of humans. In other words, one of the basic purposes of human activities is to meet the need for liberty, realize the desire for liberty, and achieve the purpose of liberty. This explains why in our human history, there are so many liberty fighters who sacrificed their lives just for liberty. This could also explain why even if liberty brings disaster and pain, liberty per se is still a happy thing; even if slavery brings happiness and joy, it is still a painful evil in itself. "Everyone is born to yearn for freedom and to hate slavery."[49] In a word, people often seek liberty for the sake of liberty per se: freedom is the end, not the means. Sartre even goes so far as to argue that all human activities should be aimed at liberty.

> When I affirm that freedom, under any concrete circumstance, can have no other aim than itself, and once a man realizes, in his state of abandonment, that it is he who imposes values, he can will but one thing: freedom as the foundation of all values. That does not mean that he wills it in the abstract; it simply means that the ultimate significance of the actions of men of good faith is the quest of freedom in itself. We will freedom for freedom's sake through our individual circumstances.[50]

Sartre's argument is rather narrow. Liberty cannot be the fundamental purpose of all human activities, because human beings have other basic needs. But liberty is indeed one of the basic purposes of human activities. Therefore, liberty is valuable, not essentially because it is the means to achieve other valuable and desirable things, but because liberty itself is valuable and desirable, can meet people's needs, and is, the purpose that people pursue. Hence, liberty has intrinsic value.

Intrinsic value, relative to the extrinsic value or instrumental value, stems from Aristotle's "intrinsic" and "instrumental good": "good obviously has double meanings, one is that things are good in themselves while the other is that things are good as a means to achieve their own good."[51] Therefore, intrinsic value can be called "value-as-an-end" or "value-in-itself." It is the value-in-itself or value-as-an-end, rather than instrumental value, that is desirable, that meets the needs of individuals and achieves the purpose. For example, health and longevity are desirable; they're the purpose people pursue; they're of value-in-itself and therefore have intrinsic value. On the contrary, the so-called extrinsic value, that is, the instrumental value, is valuable only because its result is desirable, can satisfy the needs, and thus is the purpose pursued by people. For example, the result of winter swimming—health and longevity—is desirable and valuable, and is thus the purpose that humans pursue, so winter swimming has extrinsic value and is of instrumental value. In this sense, liberty is not only an intrinsic value because it has value in itself and is the purpose humans pursue, but also an extrinsic value: liberty is also a means to achieve many other valuable things.

**The extrinsic value of liberty: liberty is the most fundamental necessary condition for achieving the creative potential of individuals and social prosperity and progress.** The valuable things that can be achieved through liberty are beyond enumeration. In more precise language, liberty is the most fundamental necessary condition for achieving all valuable things. As stated in earlier passages, liberty is a behavior that can be carried out without external obstacles, according to one's own will. Liberty is an enabling and possible behavior, a possibility of behavior, an opportunity for behavior. That is to say, the value of liberty lies in the opportunities and possibilities it provides. Therefore, Hayek says, "Liberty can give individuals only opportunities."[52] H. B. Phillips also writes, "In an advancing society, any restriction on liberty reduces the number of things tried and so reduces the rate of progress."[53] Therefore, if there is liberty, there will be opportunities to acquire all the valuable things, and there will be possibilities to acquire all the valuable things; if there is no liberty, there will be no opportunity to acquire all the valuable things, and there will be no possibility to acquire all the valuable things. Hence, liberty is the most fundamental necessary condition to acquire all the valuable things. Therefore, Locke writes, "Liberty is the foundation of all others."[54] So does Hayek: "Liberty is not just one of the numerous values, but the root of all values."[55]

Liberty is the most fundamentally necessary condition for all valuable things; among them, the most important, as the Renaissance humanism discovered, is self-realization. The so-called self-realization, that is, self-improvement and self-fulfillment, is to realize potentials within individuals so that they can become the worthiest individuals possible. Maslow writes:

> It refers to man's desire for self-fulfillment, namely, to the tendency for him to become actualized in what he is potentially. This tendency might be phrased as the desire to become more and more what one idiosyncratically is, to become everything that one is capable of becoming.[56]

Although according to modern psychology, creativity is an inherent potential of everyone, most people lose it gradually after birth.[57] Therefore, each individual's self-realization is, in fact, the realization of his creative potential.

The point is that creativity is originality as creativity means being original and unique, and if it is not original and unique, it will be imitation, not creation. In this sense, the realization of a person's creative potential demands, in fact, the development of his unique personality as its most fundamental necessary condition. These two are positively related to change: the more fully an individual's personality is developed, the more fully his creative potential will be realized, the greater the degree of his self-realization will be; the more his personality is bound, the more difficult it is to realize his potential, the lower the degree of his self-realization will be. That's why most of the great scholar, great inventors, great artists, and great literati in China and abroad are Independent monsters. The more intolerant of unique personalities a society is, the less pioneering zeal it will have. "The number of independent-thinking individuals in a society is in general in positive proportion with the number of geniuses, the number of individuals with spiritual strength and moral courage."[58] Mill laments, "Only the cultivation of personality makes—or can make—a fully developed human being."[59] Maslow also writes enthusiastically,

> Self-fulfilling people, though not lacking in any basic need, are still motivated to fight, to explore, and to get ambitious. This is quite unique, for their sole motivation is just to develop their personality, realize, mature, and develop their personality; in a word, it is self-realization.[60]

So, how can a person's personality be fully developed? Obviously, the degree of the development of one's personality depends on the degree of liberty he has. The personality a man has and who he is are the results of his own actions, just as this existentialist belief says: "He is what he does."[61] Thus, only when one has liberty to act according to one's own will can he create a self with his own unique personality; on the contrary, if he loses his liberty, subjects himself to others, and acts according to the will of others, then the personality he has created is what others chose for him and thus will not be his own unique personality.

Given this, the most fundamental necessary condition for self-realization is the development of personality, and the most fundamental condition for the development of personality is liberty. So, ultimately, liberty is the most fundamental necessary condition for self-realization, and they are in positive correlation with each other: the freer a person is, the more fully his personality will be developed, the more his creative potential will be realized, the higher the degree of his self-realization will be; the less free a person is, the less fully developed his personality will be, the less his potential will be realized, the lower the degree of his self-realization will be. Therefore, Humboldt writes in the book *The Role of the State*,

> The true purpose of man, not the capricious appetite but the eternal purpose set for him by reason, is to cultivate his strength to the fullest and to the most balanced as a whole person. Freedom is the most important and indispensable condition for such cultivation.[62]

Moreover, as Maslow has repeatedly stressed, "self-fulfilling individuals have more free will and less subordination to others than ordinary people,"[63] and "these people are less willing to yield to repression, restriction, and restraint, and, in a word, less subservient to socialization."[64] "They can be called self-governing individuals who are governed by rules of their own personality rather than by social rules."[65] "A good environment, whether for the sake of promoting self-fulfillment or health, should be like this: supply all the necessary materials, then step aside and let the organism finds its wishes and demands and make its own choices."[66]

However, some liberal thinkers, such as Berlin, doubt that liberty is a necessary condition for the realization of everyone's creative potential because they believe that in an un-free society, there is no shortage of talented people. Berlin then says, "And if this is so, Mill's argument for liberty as a necessary condition for the growth of human genius falls to the ground."[67] Indeed, there are many talented people who are not free. However, these people are able to realize their creative potential, not because they are allowed to be at the mercy of others and lose their liberty, but because they have the courage to resist and fight for liberty. Based on the fact that there are often talented people in an un-free society, Berlin denies that liberty is a necessary condition for the realization of everyone's creative potential. Such an argument by Berlin is therefore untenable.

In any given society, there exist some talented people, because it is possible that people in any society may have liberty. However, in a free society, people get liberty without resistance and sacrifice, so everyone has liberty, and it is thus possible for everyone to develop their creative potential and achieve self-realization. On the contrary, in an un-free society, if people want to be free, they must resist and sacrifice, such as sacrificing health, happiness, personality, love, and even life. In such a society, therefore, only a very small number of people are likely to fight for liberty and self-fulfillment—the few are the singing Pedophian liberty fighters, who, by their own actions, prove that life is precious, love is dearer, and both can be thrown away for liberty's sake.

Liberty is the most fundamental necessary condition for everyone to realize and develop their creative potential. Meanwhile, it is also the most fundamental necessary condition for social prosperity and progress because society is the sum total of everyone. The more fully individuals realize their creative potentials, the more creative the society will be. The more fully individuals develop their abilities, the more prosperous the society will be. The fuller the self-realization of individuals is, the more progressive the society will be. Thus, Dewey says: "Freedom is important because it is a condition for the development of personal potential and society."[68] Admittedly, liberty is not the sole element of social progress. The development of science, the invention of technology, the improvement of tools of production, the democratization of politics, and the improvement of morality are all essential elements of social progress. However, all the elements of social progress are nothing more than the product of human activities and the result of the realization of human potentials. Ultimately, as liberty is the most fundamental and necessary condition for the realization of creative potential, liberty is the most fundamental and necessary condition for all of these elements.

Therefore, it can be said that liberty, though not the sole element of social progress, is the most fundamental element of and condition for social progress. In this sense, Mueller calls the spirit of liberty "the forward spirit" or "the progressive spirit" and repeatedly says: "the only infinite and permanent source of progress is freedom."[69] Given this, if we want to make social progress, we ought to make people fundamentally free; if we suppress liberty, we will fundamentally hinder social progress. In other words, a free society is bound to prosper and progress; an un-free society is bound to stagnate. If an un-free society can progress, it is not because it is not free, but because in this un-free society, there are liberty fighters who are brave enough to resist society and willing to sacrifice their lives.

There is more to it! That liberty is the most fundamental necessary condition for self-realization also means that liberty is the fundamental principle of humanity. For the so-called humanity, as a humanistic moral principle, regards self-realization as the highest value and is thus the behavior of self-realization. Ultimately, liberty is the behavior of "making humans become humans": namely, the behavior of making humans realize the creative potential of the self and become the worthiest humans possible. In this sense, the statement that "liberty is the most fundamental necessary condition for self-realization" clearly means that liberty is the fundamental principle of self-realization, that is, to make humans become humans. Ultimately, we can say that liberty is the fundamental principle of humanity or that liberty is the most fundamental humanity. Therefore, Paul Kurtz, a famous contemporary humanist thinker, stresses this point once again in the following statements: "Among the value standards protected by humanism, individual freedom is the most basic";[70] "the basic principle of humanism is to safeguard individual freedom";[71] "the first principle of humanism is to strive for freedom";[72] "the core value of humanism is personal freedom."[73]

Liberty is not only the fundamental principle of humanity but, more importantly, the highest value standard of state institutions. This argument can be deduced in two ways. First, because humanity is the highest value standard of state institutions, and liberty is the fundamental principle of humanity, we can conclude that ultimately liberty is the highest value standard of state institutions. Second, as self-realization is the highest value of humanity, and liberty is the most fundamental necessary condition for self-realization, liberty as the highest value is the highest value standard of state institutions. It, then, follows that liberty and humanity are both the highest value standards of state institutions. However, these two values are of different depths: humanity is the highest surface value standard of state institutions, while liberty is the highest deep value standard of state institutions.

If the idea that justice is the value standard of state institutions is the great discovery of the ancient Greek thinkers and, ultimately, Plato's great discovery, then liberty as the value standard of state institutions is the great discovery of Renaissance humanism and, ultimately, Dante's great discovery. Dante stresses the importance of liberty again and again: "A good nation is free."[74]

> This principle of freedom for all of us is God's greatest gift to mankind. As long as we depend on it, we can enjoy the happiness of human beings; as long as we depend on it, we can enjoy the happiness of heaven. If that's the case, then when people can make full use of this principle, who would say that human beings are not in their best position?

"When human beings are most free, they are best destined."[75]

With these insights, liberal thinkers such as Acton and Hayek have systematically demonstrated the principle that liberty is the highest value standard of state institutions. From their demonstration, they conclude that "the idea of freedom is the noblest idea of value—it is the supreme law in the life of human society,"[76] that "freedom is not the means to achieve a higher political purpose because it is the highest political purpose in itself,"[77] that "freedom is the highest good of a nation."[78]

Apparently, liberty as the highest value standard of state institutions is definitely not a simple, single moral principle or value standard. It is a rather complex system of moral principles or value standards composed of a variety of moral principles or value standards. In more specific terms, this system of moral principles or value standards is originally composed of two major types and six principles: three general principles of liberty—the principle of rule of law of liberty, the principle of equality of liberty, the principle of limit of liberty—as well as three specific principles of liberty—the principle of political liberty, the principle of economic freedom, and the principle of freedom of thought.

## Principles of liberty: general principles of liberty

### *The rule-of-law principle of liberty*

No society can be completely free without coercion. So, what kind of society is a free society? As society is a collective or a community formed by two or more people through certain associations, then the characteristics of free collectives are the characteristics of a free society. However, what kind of collective is a free collective? Evidently, a free collective is such a collective, in which all coercion is unanimously obeyed by all members. In this way, although the collective is coercive, everyone's obedience of it is obedience of their own will; therefore, no one feels the sense of non-liberty. For example, playing cards and playing chess both must conform to some mandatory rules, but players do not feel that they are not free. Why? Is it not because everyone agrees to obey these mandatory rules? The same is true of society. If all the coercive rules of society conform to the norms of conduct agreed upon or accepted by all members of the society, then each person's obedience of the coercion of the society is also obedience of his own will; therefore, this society is free.

However, how can we achieve consensus or approval in a society when the total of members in a society or a nation usually amounts to hundreds of millions of people? Undoubtedly, the only way to do this is to practice democracy and reach a consensus indirectly through the principles of "the representative system" and "the majority rule." Thus, on the one hand, many citizens may disagree with the codes of conduct formulated by the representatives; however, since these representatives are elected by these citizens, they indirectly agree with the codes that they directly oppose to. On the other hand, the norms established by the majority of representatives may be opposed by the minority of representatives; however, since they agree with the principle of "subordination of minority to majority," these norms, which the minority directly disagree with, have indirect consent from the minority. The code of conduct directly or indirectly agreed upon by every member of society—law and morality—is called "public will." Therefore, as long as democracy is practiced, the law and morality of a society, no matter how many members there are in the society, can be directly or indirectly agreed upon by each member and become a "public will." So, each individual's obedience of the public will is obedience both of others' will and of his own will; thus, each individual is free. As Rousseau says,

> Man is free, though he succumbs to the law. Here succumbing does not mean submitting to a certain individual, for in that case it means that I submit to the will of another individual; it means submitting to the law, because in this case we submit only to the public will that belongs both to me and to anyone else.[79]

It follows, then, that the so-called free society must have two conditions. The first condition is that the society must be ruled by law, not by man. That is to say, rulers must govern according to law and morality, not arbitrarily by deviating from law and morality. In this sense, Hayek says, "Nothing distinguishes more clearly conditions in a free country from those in a country under arbitrary government than the observance in the former of the great principles known as the Rule of Law."[80]

The second condition is that the laws and morals of the society must be enacted or approved by all of its members or their representatives, so that the laws and morals are the manifestation of public will, not the manifestation of the will of a few. Richard Price puts it well:

> Liberty is too imperfectly defined when it is said to be 'a Government of LAWS and not by MEN.' If the laws are made by one man, or a junto of men in a state, and not by common CONSNET, a government by them is not different from slavery.[81]

In summary, any coercion in a free humanistic society must be in conformity with the laws and morals of that society, and all the laws and morals of that society must be approved directly or indirectly by all of its members. This is the rule-of-law principle of liberty and the rule-of-law standard to measure whether a society or a country is free and humanistic or not.

### The equality principle of liberty

Is a society free and humane if all of its coercions conform to its laws and morals and all of its laws and morals are manifestations of public will? Not yet. A free and humane society must have another condition, that is, everyone must conform to coercions identically and equally, and enjoy liberty equally. Otherwise, this society will obviously not be a free society if some people must obey the laws while others do not, or if some can enjoy liberty while others cannot.

Therefore, Hobhouse says:

> When we assume that the rule of law guarantees freedom for all, we are assuming that the rule of law is impartial and selfless. If some laws are made for the government while others for the masses, or if some laws are made for the aristocracy while others for the common people, or if some laws are made for the rich while others for the poor, then the rule of law cannot guarantee freedom for all. In this regard, freedom means equality of freedom.[82]

Adam Ferguson says, "Freedom... It is to make the most effective application of all just restrictions to all members of a free society, whether they are dignitaries or civilians."[83] Hayek writes, "The great goal of the struggle for freedom has always been equality before the law."[84]

Liberty should be the basis for equal enjoyment by all, not only because liberty is the most fundamental humanity, the most fundamental necessary condition for realizing the creative potential of individuals so that they can become the worthiest persons possible, but also because liberty is a human right, the lowest, the bottom-line, and the most basic human right, to which each individual, as a shareholder in the human society, is entitled. Therefore, Article 2 of *The Declaration of Human Rights* states that "the purpose of any political union is to protect the inherent and inviolable rights of the human being. These rights are freedom, property, security and resistance to oppression." Since liberty is a human right, it should be equally enjoyed by all. Thus, we can say that everyone is equal in terms of liberty.

Hobbes was the first to reveal this principle. He writes, "A man should be contented with so much liberty against other men as he would allow other men against himself."[85] This principle is systematically expounded by the contemporary philosopher Rawls, and is described as "the first principle of justice:" "each person is to have an equal right to the most extensive scheme of equal basic liberties compatible with a similar scheme of liberties for others."[86] Enjoying liberty equally means equal obedience of coercion and the law. In Western terms, everyone is equal before the law; in Chinese terms, if the prince breaks the law and commits the same crime as the common people, he ought to be incriminated equally.

In short, everyone ought to enjoy liberty on equal footing: everyone is equal before liberty; everyone ought to obey coercion on equal footing; everyone is equal before the law. This is the equality principle of liberty, which is the equality standard of measuring whether a society and a country are free and humane or not.

## The limit principle of liberty

Is a society free and humane if it meets the standard of the rule of law and the standard of equality? To clarify this question, let us assume that there is a society in which all members are willing to live like soldiers and consent to enact and obey the most stringent laws on an equal footing. If so, this society does meet the rule-of-law standard and the equality standard of liberty, but it is obviously not a free and humane society, for its limit of coercion is too large while the limit of liberty is too small. Therefore, to create a free and humane society, we need another element, that is, the limit of coercion and liberty.

There is no doubt that a society cannot maintain its existence without a certain degree of coercion. However, there are two kinds of coercion. One is evil and bad, such as killing and robbing; the other is good, kind, and necessary, such as shooting murderers and punishing criminals. In terms of the value of liberty, the so-called good, kind and necessary coercion is good only when measured by its result. However, in terms of the nature of coercion itself, it cannot be anything else but bad because it deprives people of liberty. The only difference between these two kinds of coercion is that good coercion is a necessary bad. There are two things that might make it a necessary bad. The first is that it prevents a greater bad. For example, cutting open the belly for appendicitis surgery is bad and evil, but this bad is necessary because it can prevent a greater bad—death. The second is that it allows us to achieve a greater good. For example, swimming in the chilly winter is painful and evil, but this bad is necessary because it can achieve a greater good—health and longevity. One may wonder: does the necessity of social coercion, then, lie in the prevention of a greater bad, the pursuit of a greater good, or both?

The necessity of social coercion is only to prevent a greater bad, not to seek a greater good. Though social coercion can prevent the decay of a society and guarantee its existence, it cannot promote the development of society. As studies on the value of liberty show, liberty is the most fundamental necessary condition for the realization of everyone's creative potential and the progress of the development of society. Doesn't this mean that coercion and non-liberty are the fundamental obstacles to the realization of everyone's creative potential and the progress of social development? Thus, in summary, it can be asserted that, in the long run, coercion can only maintain the existence of human beings and society, and only liberty can promote the development of human beings and society.

Given this, under the premise that society can exist, the more coercion and the less liberty there is in a society, the less fully individuals can realize their creative potential, the slower the development and progress of society will be in the long run, the more unfortunate people will become. On the contrary, the less coercion and the more liberty there is in a society, the more fully individuals realize their creative potential, the faster the development

## 30  Humanity and liberty

and progress of the society will be in the long run, and the happier people will be. Therefore, we can conclude that the coercion of a society should be kept to the minimum necessary for its existence while the liberty of a society should be extended to the maximum permissible by its existence.

This is the limit principle of liberty, which is the standard of measuring whether a society and a country are free and humane or not. Hayek considers this to be the most fundamental standard and principle of a free state, so he writes at the beginning of *The Charter of Liberty*: "This book deals with the human condition that interpersonal coercion is reduced to the minimum possible. We call such a country a free country."[87]

However, what is the minimum and what is the maximum are relative and uncertain concepts. What is a minimum of coercion for some people may be too much beyond the minimum level of coercion for others, and vice versa. Therefore, some people, such as the so-called ultra-liberals, advocate a "night watchman" state and say that "the less governance the government offers, the better the government is." Others, such as the so-called neoliberals, argue that such a small amount of coercion is insufficient to guarantee the existence of the society, and that the minimum coercion necessary for the existence of the society is much stronger and wider. This requires that on the one hand, the coercion of a free society must follow the principle of an absolute and definite minimum, and, on the other hand, the liberty of a free society must also follow the principle of an absolute and definite maximum.

It is probably Humboldt who first expounded on this principle systematically. He summarized this principle as one of "using coercion only to prevent bad but not to obtain good" and regarded it as the first principle of the role of the state:

> The first principle must be that the state does not take any care of the positive welfare of its citizens, except to safeguard the security they need to deal with themselves and foreign enemies. A state should not take one step further than this, which means it must not restrict the freedom of citizens for other ultimate purposes.[88]

Mill agrees with Humboldt and regards the limit principle of liberty as representative of the aim of his work on liberalism, *On Liberty*.

> The object of this essay is to assert one very simple principle as entitled to govern absolutely the dealings of society with the individual via compulsion and control, whether the means used is a physical force in the form of legal penalties or the moral coercion of public opinion. That principle is, that the sole end for which mankind are warranted, individually or collectively, in interfering with the liberty of action of any of their number, is self-protection. That the only purpose for which power can be rightfully exercised over any member of a civilized community, against his will, is to prevent harm to others. His own good, either physical or moral, is not a sufficient warrant.[89]

Humboldt's and Mill's theory on the principle of the limit of liberty and coercion—the theory of applying social coercion only to prevent greater bad and not to seek greater good—seems, roughly speaking, very biased, but, when examined in detail, turns out to be incisive ideas full of logical force. Indeed, it can be deduced from the value of liberty, which is the most fundamental necessary condition for the realization of each person's creative potential and the progress of social development, that in the long run, coercion can only maintain the existence of society, and only liberty can promote the development of society. It can be asserted that in the long run, as long as society can exist, social coercion ought to be reduced to zero to allow complete liberty. In other words, coercion ought to be used only to maintain the existence of society, not to promote the development of society; only liberty ought to be used to promote the development of society. This is the absolute limit principle of liberty, the absolute limit standard of liberty of measuring whether a society and a country are free and humane or not.

To sum up, the three principles of liberty, the rule-of-law, equality, and limit principles, are the general principles of a free and humane society, and the universal standards of measuring whether any society is free or humane. If a society is in conformity with these three principles, it will be a free and humane society; if it violates any one of them, it will not deserve the good name of a free, humane society. With these universal principles, it is possible to solve the extremely complex and concrete problems of liberty in human society—political liberty, economic freedom, and freedom of thought, thus establishing three more important specific principles of liberty, namely, the principle of political liberty, the principle of economic freedom, and the principle of freedom of thought.

## Specific principles of liberty

### *The principle of political liberty*

Liberty is defined as an activity that can be carried out according to one's own will without external coercion; this means that political liberty should be defined as an activity that can be carried out according to one's own will without external coercion. For example, in a country ruled by the despotic monarchy, it is only the monarch who can make national politics work according to his will. Therefore, in such a country, as Rousseau says, only the monarch has political liberty, while any other person's political liberty is zero: "Here all individuals are equal, precisely because they are equal in enjoying zero freedom. The subjects have no laws to follow but the will of the monarch while the monarch has no rules to follow but his own desires."[90] On the contrary, in a democratic society, it is every citizen who can make national politics work according to his will. Therefore, in a democratic society, every citizen enjoys political liberty.

So, how can political liberty be carried out according to one's own will? There is no doubt that we must have political power, for the so-called politics, as mentioned before, means power management, power governance, and power domination. Given this, anyone who wants politics to proceed according to his will must have power. Without power, how can power be managed? Therefore, only when a person has political power can he make politics work according to his own will and thus have political liberty; if he does not have political power, he cannot make politics proceed according to his own will and cannot have political liberty. Have you wondered why in a monarchical state only one sovereign has political liberty and no one else has it? Is it not because what makes a monarchical state an autocracy of the monarch is that the supreme power of the state is in the hands of the monarch alone? Have you wondered why everyone in a democratic society has political liberty? Is it not because what makes a democratic state democratic is that the supreme power of the state is equally shared by every citizen?

The truth is that whoever has political power will have political liberty. Therefore, whoever has the highest political power will have the highest political liberty, whoever has lower political power will have lower political liberty, and whoever does not have political power will not have political liberty. Thus, to be precise, in a monarchical state, it is not that the monarch alone has political liberty but that only the monarch has the supreme political liberty. Beyond the monarch, officials at all levels have political power, so they have political liberty, though not the supreme political power of the monarch. The governor has political liberty to make the politics of a province proceed according to his will to a certain extent; the mayor has political liberty to make the politics of a city proceed according to his will to a certain extent; the county magistrate has political liberty to make the politics of a county proceed according to his will to a certain extent.

However, in any society, power is only owned by rulers and administrators; the ruled and the managed cannot have power; the ruled and the managed can only have rights but not power. The so-called power, as mentioned above, is a coercive force owned only by the rulers or administrators of the society and approved by the society to force the ruled or the managed to obey. In this way, only the rulers and administrators of the society have political liberty, and the ruled and the managed cannot have political liberty. This is no surprise. As politics is the rule of power and the management of power, political liberty is then the liberty of the rule of power or the liberty of the management of power. Ultimately, political liberty is only the liberty of rule and management. Hence, the liberty of rule and management can be owned only by the rulers and administrators, not by the ruled and the managed.

Political liberty is bound to be enjoyed only by those who have political power, so it is bound to be enjoyed only by the rulers of society. Obviously, what has been stated here is just the objective nature of what political liberty is, not the moral principle of what political liberty ought to be. Ought political liberty to be enjoyed only by rulers, not by the ruled? No! As we all know, every citizen, whether he is the ruler or the ruled, is entitled to political liberty. This is the moral principle of political liberty. Thus, on the one hand, the objective nature of political liberty dictates that political liberty can be enjoyed only by the ruler; on the other hand, the moral principle of what political liberty ought to be states that it ought to be enjoyed by every citizen and, ultimately, by the ruled. Is this not as self-contradictory and paradoxical as square-round or wood-iron? In fact, it is not.

Admittedly, political liberty can be owned only by the ruler, and the ruled cannot have political liberty; this is the objective nature of political liberty that cannot be bent according to the human will. But, suppose there is a society in which the ruled can, in turn, manage the ruler, and thus become administrators and rulers of the ruler, then will not the ruled in such a society have the same political liberty as the ruler? Yes, they will. Though it is impossible for the ruled to have political liberty as long as they are ruled, the ruled can have political liberty, not because they are ruled, but because they become rulers in a sense. So, how can a society make the ruled rulers?

To make this happen, there is only one way, which is democracy. As Cohen says, "democracy is the rule by the people"; "democracy is a system of people's self-governance"; "democracy means that the people themselves manage themselves and the people are rulers."[91] More precisely speaking, democracy is a regime in which every citizen—the ruler, officials, the ruled, or the common people—has an equal share in the supreme power of the state; democracy is a regime in which every citizen is equally the supreme ruler of the state; democracy is a regime in which every citizen is equally entitled to make the state politics move according to his own will. Thus, democracy is a regime in which every citizen has an equal share of the supreme political liberty. In this sense, democracy is a sufficient and necessary condition for every citizen to have the supreme political liberty in full equality.

In this way, democracy resolves, through turning the ruled into the ruler, the conflict between "the moral principle that every citizen—whether the ruler or the ruled—ought to have political liberty and power" and "the objective nature of what political liberty and political power are—they are owned only by the ruler"; thus, this moral principle is established. However, officials at all levels of any society must, in fact, possess more or less political power and political liberty. Therefore, as President Wilson says, political liberty, as a moral principle of what ought to be, entails the common people's liberty to make officials rule according to the will of the common people and the liberty of the ruled to make the ruler rule according to the will of the ruled; "political freedom is the right of the governed to make the government fit for their needs and interests."[92]

Apparently, the moral principle that every citizen ought to have political power to enjoy political liberty is founded on the dual bases of humanity and human right. From the perspective of human right, the reason why everyone, whether officials or common people, ought to have political power to enjoy political liberty is that political liberty is a human right. Marx says,

> As part of human rights, political right is a right that can be exercised only with others. The content of this right is to join the community, to participate in the political community and the state. These rights belong to the category of political freedom.[93]

Political liberty is a human right. Therefore, according to the principle that "everyone ought to enjoy human rights in full equality," everyone ought to enjoy political liberty in full equality, that is, hold the supreme power of the state in full equality so that state politics can be carried out in accordance with their own will. Thus, we can see that the principle of political liberty is based on the principle of human right.

From the perspective of humanity, political liberty is the most important social freedom, and is, thus, the fundamental feature of the humanistic society. This is not only because politics is the most important social coercion and thus political liberty gives every citizen the most important social freedom. More importantly, it is because every citizen has political liberty that the ruler must rule according to the will of every citizen, that is, ultimately according to the will of the ruled. In this way, the realization of the other social freedoms of every citizen, especially those of the ruled, such as freedom of speech, freedom of the press, and economic freedom, depends entirely on his will and is thus guaranteed.

On the contrary, when there is no political liberty, the ruler does not rule according to the will of every citizen, but according to his own will. Thus, as the realization of other social freedoms of every citizen, especially of the ruled, depends entirely on the will of the ruler, not on the will of the citizen, the realization of these freedoms will not be guaranteed. Therefore, as political liberty determines other social freedoms, it is the fundamental guarantee for other social freedoms and thus the fundamental guarantee for humanistic society—liberty is the most fundamental humanity. Sartori says, "Political freedom is not psychological, ideological, moral, social, economic or legal freedom. But these freedoms all take political freedom as their preconditions."[94] Thus, if a society is to become a humanistic society, it is essential that every citizen has political liberty. Hence, the principle of political liberty is based on the principle of humanity.

In a word, every citizen ought to hold the supreme power of the state in full equality so as to become the supreme ruler of the state in full equality so as to make the politics of the state proceed according to his own will in full equality so as to share the supreme political liberty in full equality. In other words, the politics of a country ought to be carried out with the equal consent of every citizen, in equal accordance with the will of every citizen, and, ultimately, in accordance with the will of the ruled. This is the "principle of political liberty"; this is the political liberty standard of measuring whether a society and a state are free and humanistic or not. Together with the "principle of political equality," this principle forms the basis of "principle of people's sovereignty" and democracy.

### Principle of economic freedom

The principle of economic freedom undoubtedly originated with Adam Smith, who called it the "natural freedom system:"

> all systems, either of preference or of restraint, therefore, being thus completely taken away, the obvious and simple system of natural liberty establishes itself of its own accord. Every man, as long as he does not violate the laws of justice, is left perfectly free to pursue his own interest his own way, and to bring both his industry and capital into competition with those of any other man, or order of men.[95]

Friedman summarizes these words into a famous saying, "The government should be an arbitrator, not an interested party," and then expounds it in this way:

> the existence of a free market does not rule out the need for government. On the contrary, the necessity of a government lies in that it can be both the forum for and the maker of 'the rules of the game' and the referee who interprets and enforces the rules.[96]

More specifically, economic activities should be regulated by market mechanisms and not by the government, because "government regulation" and "government management activities beyond the purpose of formulating and safeguarding economic rules" are the same concept. This means that government management should be limited to agreed economic rules in order to ensure their implementation. Within the scope of these economic rules, everyone ought to enjoy both the freedom to conduct economic activities in full accordance with his own will, and the freedom to engage in economic activities, such as production, distribution, exchange, and consumption, in full accordance with his own will.

This is the principle of economic freedom and the value standard of economic freedom used to measure whether the state institution and state governance is good or bad. To be more specific, this value standard is founded on four principles: humanity, justice, human right, and efficiency.

First of all, from the point of view of humanity, we can see that according to the limit principle of liberty, the coercion in a country ought to be maintained at the minimum necessary for the country to exist, while liberty in the country ought to be extended to the maximum possible for the country to exist. In other words, as long as the state can exist, the state's coercion ought to be reduced to zero to allow complete liberty. This is because coercion can maintain the state's existence, but only liberty can promote national development. This means that the rationale behind the government's regulation of economic activities is that economic activities cannot exist without government regulation. However, as Smith has discovered, on the one hand, with the invisible hand of free competition, the market economy is a kind of economy that can exist and develop spontaneously without government management, because free competition can lead to the highest efficiency in allocating resources; on the other hand, without government protection of economic rules, the market economy cannot exist or develop. Therefore, the market economy ought to exist and develop spontaneously, and the government's management ought to be confined to the implementing of economic rules that protect the market economy. Any government regulation that goes beyond the implementing of economic rules of the market economy means violating humanity's limit principle of liberty and is therefore unfair.

Second, from the perspective of justice, we can see that only economic freedom and free competition can realize the economic justice of equivalent exchange. As a result of its suppression and violation of free competition, government regulation creates monopoly; it creates monopoly prices and excess profits above marginal costs; it creates price differences above opportunity costs; it creates rent-setting, renting, and rent-seeking; and it, ultimately, creates injustice. Monopolies are bound to lead to non-equivalent exchange. This is because under the condition of free competition, in order to maximize profits, manufacturers are bound to set the output level above which the marginal cost equals the price.[97] That is to say, under the condition of economic freedom and free competition, the commodity prices are equal to marginal costs, that is, an equivalent exchange is necessary: it is the price law of free competition. Conversely, commodity prices under monopolistic condition are bound to be much higher than marginal costs. That is to say, monopoly prices are bound to be higher than marginal costs.[98] This means that that monopoly prices are higher than marginal costs, namely, non-equivalent exchange, is necessary: non-equivalent exchange is the price law of monopoly.

Furthermore, from the perspective of human right, economic freedom is undoubtedly only a prerequisite, a condition, or an opportunity for a person to acquire material wealth, not the acquisition of material wealth itself. It is possible that a person with economic freedom may still be an extremely poor person. Therefore, economic freedom is by no means a high-level economic right, but the most basic economic right of each individual; it is rather the necessary, minimum, and lowest economic right of each individual; it is the economic human right of each individual. Therefore, economic freedom belongs to the category of human right. Therefore, Smith writes,

> To prohibit a great people, however, from making all that they can of every part of their own produce, or from employing their stock and industry in the way that they judge most advantageous to themselves, is a manifest violation of the most sacred rights of mankind.[99]

Finally, in terms of efficiency, economic freedom is efficient while economic non-freedom is inefficient. As studies on the value of liberty show, liberty is the fundamental condition for everyone to realize their creative potential and for the development and progress of the society; on the contrary, coercion and non-liberty are the fundamental obstacles for everyone to realize their creative potential and for the development and progress of society. In view of this, under the premise that economic activities can exist, the more government regulation, the less economic freedom, the slower the economic development and progress will be in the long run; the less government regulation, the more economic freedom, the faster economic development and progress will be in the long run. This explains why nations with a market economy and economic freedom prosper and maintain a greatly enhanced standard of living for the common people, while nations with a controlled economy and less economic freedom suffer from a stagnant economy, and the living standard for the common people remains extremely low.

Given this, economic freedom is an extremely important value standard of measuring if state institutions are good or bad. It is not only a value standard of state institutions for measuring whether an economic system is free or not; because of this, it is also a standard of measuring whether an economic system has the human right and is fair, humanistic, and efficient or not. If an economic system conforms to the principle of economic freedom, it is not only a free economic system but also a humanistic, human-right, just, and efficient economic system. On the contrary, if it violates the principle of economic freedom, the economic system is not only un-free but also inhuman, human-right-less, unjust, and inefficient.

In this sense, it is apparent that since the start of civilized society, human society has had only one economic form and system without government control, that is, the market economy, which conforms to the principle of economic freedom and is therefore a free, human-right, just, humanistic, and efficient economic form and system; all other economic forms and systems—the market economy controlled by the government, the so-called mixed economy, and the planned economy—violate the principle of economic freedom to varying degrees and are therefore, to varying degrees, un-free, inhuman, unjust, human-right-less, and inefficient economic forms and systems. In a word, a market economy without government control is the only economic form and system that fully conforms to the value standard of state institutions, and is the only ideal economic form and system of human society.

## *Principle of freedom of thought*

What is the principle of freedom of thought? People often assume from its name that freedom of thought, as referred to in the principle of freedom of thought, means that everyone ought to enjoy the freedom to have thoughts, which ought not to be limited or prohibited. This is a wrong assumption.

On the one hand, the principle of freedom of thought is a moral principle, and therefore, like all moral principles, it can regulate only the behavior, not the thought, of each individual. Thus, the principle of freedom of thought is a principle about what behavior each individual ought to have, not about what thoughts each individual ought to have. On the other hand, as Bury says, apparently no society or nation can restrict or prohibit people from thinking anything: "No one can prohibit a man from thinking whatever he wants to keep secret in his belly."[100] Indeed, only behaviors—what we do and what we say—can be restricted or prohibited, but thoughts—what we think—cannot be restricted or prohibited.

So, in a word, the principle of freedom of thought is a principle of what behaviors ought to be, not a principle of what thoughts ought to be. What kind of behavior is freedom of thought as in the principle of freedom of thought? Bury believes that it refers to the freedom of behaviors in expressing thoughts, including the freedom of speech. He writes,

> The innate freedom of private thoughts is not valuable. If a man has thoughts about something, but if he is not allowed to pass it on to others, he will feel discontented and painful. In this case, his thoughts are worthless to others. Therefore, to have any value at all, freedom of thought must contain freedom of speech.[101]

To be precise, the so-called freedom of thought is the freedom to engage in acquiring and conveying thoughts. The main way to acquire and convey thoughts is undoubtedly speech and publication. Therefore, freedom of thought is mainly about freedom of speech and freedom of the press.

It is plain that anyone's thoughts cannot be developed under the conditions of coercion and slavery. Freedom of thought, as many sages have said, is a fundamental condition for the development of culture and is positively correlated with it: the more freedom of speech and press a society has, the more prosperous its culture is, the more prosperous its sciences—natural sciences, social sciences, and philosophy—are, the richer the truth it will have, and the more spiritual wealth it will acquire. The less freedom of speech and press a society has, the more depressed its culture is, the more backward its sciences—natural sciences, social sciences, and philosophy—are, the poorer the truth it will have, and the less spiritual wealth it will acquire. Therefore, Acton says, "Freedom is the condition for truth to come into being."[102] So, is the more the freedom of speech and press, the better, so that it will come to complete freedom without any restrictions? The answer is yes. Bury says:

> It has been historically proven that knowledge grew when Greece had complete freedom of thought. In modern times, as the laws that forbid thought had been completely abolished, knowledge grew at a magic rate suspected as tricks of devils by the eyes of those enslaved by the medieval

church. In this way, in order for social customary systems and methods to adapt to new needs and new environments, it is natural that people have complete freedom to refute and criticize social habits, systems and methods, and freedom to express the most unconventional ideas, without worrying about whether these ideas go against the grain or not. If the history of culture teaches us any lesson, it is that the supreme condition for spiritual and moral progress which can be obtained entirely by the power of men is the absolute freedom of thought and speech.[103]

Ultimately, speech and press should be completely free, not only because the development of thought is proportional to the degree of freedom, but also because any restriction on freedom of speech and freedom of the press violates the universal standards of a free and humane society. First of all, according to the "the rule-of-law principle of liberty," any coercion of a society must conform to the laws and morals of that society and ultimately must be agreed upon by all members of that society. In this sense, anyone, no matter how absurd and dangerous his ideas and opinions are, ought to be allowed to speak out; otherwise, what would the whole membership agree to? Therefore, no matter who is forbidden to express any opinion and idea, it violates the "the rule-of-law principle of liberty" standard of the humanistic society. Cohen says:

> If we want to maintain democracy, we must be completely free. The freedom to criticize, the freedom to express objections, though unpopular, perhaps harmful or unconventional, is indispensable in a democratic country. This absoluteness does not come from intuition or the need based on five senses, but from the need to work and participate in management. Free and open discussion of all issues of concern to society is a prerequisite for full and effective participation.[104]

Second, according to the "the equality standard of liberty," everyone ought to enjoy freedom equally and obey coercion equally. Therefore, everyone ought to be equal before the freedom of thought. That is to say, any person, no matter how low his status and how absurd and dangerous his thought is, ought to be allowed to express himself freely; allowing only some people to enjoy the freedom of thought violates the "the equality standard of liberty" of a humanistic society.

Finally, in accordance with the "the limit standard of liberty," a society's coercion should be maintained at the minimum necessary for the society's existence. Obviously, only behaviors can endanger the existence of society; no thoughts, speeches, or newspapers, however absurd and dangerous, can endanger it. So, Cohen says, "In a democracy you can speak and write as you like, but you can't do as you like."[105] Only freedom of behavior should be limited, while the freedom of speech and the freedom of the press should not be restricted; this would violate the "the limit standard of liberty" of a humanistic society.

40  *Humanity and liberty*

This explains why most of the well-known fighters and the classical documents of liberty and humanity advocate freedom of speech and press. Robespierre says: "The right to express ideas through language, writing or publication should not be hindered or restricted in any way... Freedom of the press should be complete and unlimited; otherwise there will be no freedom of press." Penn says, "Freedom of press and freedom of expressing ideas through other channels cannot be abolished, suspended and restricted."[106] Roosevelt takes the United States as an example and says, "This freedom is not restricted at all except by the conscience of the American people." The Virginia Bill of Rights of the United States has stipulated that "freedom of press is one of the important guarantees of freedom, and any government, unless it is a tyrannical government, should never restrict it."[107] Article I of the Bill of Rights of the United States of America states that

> Congress shall make no law respecting an establishment of religion, or prohibiting the free exercise thereof; or abridging the freedom of speech, or of the press, or the right of the people peaceably to assemble, and to petition the Government for a redress of grievances.

The declaration of the First National Congress of the Kuomintang convened by Dr. Sun Yat-sen of China also says, "It is determined that the people have complete freedom of assembly, association, speech, publication, residence and belief."

As can be seen, every member of the society ought to enjoy the freedom of gaining and conveying thoughts. In other words, every member of society ought not to be prohibited from gaining and conveying ideas. Ultimately, speech and press should be completely free, without any restrictions; otherwise, people would not enjoy real freedom of thought, and the country and society would not be a real free and humanistic country and society. This is the principle of freedom of thought, which is the standard of measuring whether a country and society are free and humanistic or not.

As it seems, the principle of freedom of thought is not as important as the principle of political freedom, nor as basic as the principle of economic freedom. But, as Mueller says, "all human welfare depends on mental well-being."[108] Freedom of thought is the fundamental condition for the prosperity of a society's sciences, including natural sciences, social sciences, and philosophy as well as for the prosperity of its culture. It is the fundamental condition for the development of a society's spiritual wealth; it is thus also the fundamental condition for the prosperity of a society's material wealth. It is, ultimately, the fundamental condition for every progress in a society. Given this, the principle of freedom of thought is far superior to the principle of economic freedom and the principle of political liberty; thus, freedom of thought is the supreme principle of liberty. Therefore, Karl Popper says: "freedom of thought and freedom of discussion are the highest values of liberalism." Bury says, "Freedom of thought is the highest condition for social progress."[109] Milton also writes, "Give me the liberty to know, to utter, and to argue freely according to conscience, above all liberties."[110]

Admittedly, complete freedom of speech and press often has some harmful consequences, such as the spread of misleading fallacies. The rationale behind opposition to freedom of speech and press is nothing more than prohibiting erroneous thoughts. However, this rationale, as many sages have said, is untenable: on the one hand, the one who forbids thoughts may not be right, and the forbidden thoughts may not be wrong, as the so-called wrong thoughts we forbid today are often the truth of tomorrow; on the other hand, even if the forbidden thoughts are wrong, they ought not to be forbidden because truth is born only in its struggle against wrong thoughts. Without this struggle, truth will lose its vitality and become a fixed dogma. So, as Mill says, "We can never ascertain that the idea we are trying to suffocate is a wrong one; even if we can be sure, suffocating it is still a sin."[111]

Therefore, if the freedom of speech and press is restricted because of the harm of complete freedom of speech and press, the harm caused by such restriction is far greater than the harm caused by complete freedom of speech and press. Nolan says,

> The price of freedom of expression is that there are many ideas that will come out: they are not only incorrect, but also conducive to harmful actions in the long run. We believe this is a dearly price. But if we don't pay that price, then we will have to allow a society or some powerful organizations in society the right to exclude at any time those views that they feel unacceptable. The abuse of such power may far exceed the abuse of the right to freedom of expression.[112]

As Tocqueville says, "If anyone could point out a credible middle ground between the complete freedom of thought and the submission or obedience, I would like to stand in that position. But who can find this middle ground?" "There is no middle ground between submission and permission as far as the press is concerned. In order to enjoy the great benefits of freedom of press, we must endure the inevitable suffering it has caused."[113] Well, compared with the great benefits it brings, the harm of the complete freedom of thought is almost nothing. Has it been rare that human beings have to seek big profits with minor harms? Bryce says, "All systems are imperfect."[114] With each advantage there is always a disadvantage. Why do we turn a blind eye to the evils of so many extremely bad national systems but fuss over and get infuriated about the harm of freedom of speech and press?

Moreover, liberal thinkers long time ago found out that there are some ways to prevent the harm of complete freedom of speech and press without restricting it. One way is to improve the discernment of listeners and readers. Nolan says, "Building a society with good communication channels and high critical thinking capacity is the best way to prevent the risks of freedom of expression."[115] Such a society can be established only through complete freedom of thought. Therefore, the harmful consequences of complete freedom of thought can be gradually prevented through freedom of thought itself.

Another way is to hold both the speaker and the publisher accountable: everyone must be held accountable for the harmful consequences of his or her speech and publication. Penn says,

> People don't need permission to say what they want to say, but they are responsible for the big mistakes they make afterwards. Similarly, if a person makes mistakes in a publication, he is as responsible for mistakes in the publication as he is for mistakes in his own speech.[116]

The fear of taking responsibility for the harmful consequences of one's own speech and publications is undoubtedly effective in preventing the harmfulness of one's own speech and publishing, without restricting the complete freedom of speech and publishing. Therefore, the French Declaration of Human Rights stipulates:

> The free communication of ideas and opinions is one of the most precious rights of man. Every citizen may, accordingly, speak, write and print with freedom, but shall be responsible for such abuses of this freedom as shall be defined by law.

This is an excellent expression of the principle of freedom of thought.

## Liberalism: a state institution and thought system that regards liberty as the highest value

### Liberalism: definition and objects

The term liberalism, as Lord Iakerton sees it, appeared in the 18th century: "Liberalism—the first use of the term by the Archbishop of Canterbury in 1707."[117] But the concept of liberalism preceded the term. Liberalism, as a state system and a systematic theory, began during the British Revolution in the 17th century, with Locke as its generally acknowledged founder. Over the next 400 years, liberalism became the dominant Western ideology, thus producing liberal thinkers as numerous as stars.

The representative figures of classical liberalism are Benedict de Spinoza, John Locke, John Milton, Montesquieu, Jean-Jacques Rousseau, Thomas Paine, Thomas Jefferson, Alexander Hamilton, Benjamin Constant, Tocqueville, Immanuel Kant, David Hume, Edmund Burke, Adam Smith, Jeremy Bentham, John Stuart Mill, Herbert Spencer, etc. The representative figures of neo-liberalism are Thomas Hill Green, Bernard Bosanquet, Francis Herbert Bradley, Leonard Hobhouse, John Dewey, etc.; representatives of contemporary liberalism are Friedrich Hayek, Milton Friedman, Michael Oakeshott, Sir Karl Raimund Popper, Berlin, John Rawls, Robert Nozick, Ronald Dworkin, James M. Buchanan, Giovanni Sartori, and so on.

These people are all widely acknowledged representatives of liberalism. However, these people's liberalism theories are so dizzily inconsistent, flexible, divergent, and abstruse that until today many scholars still find that there is no definite way to define liberalism and even believe that it is impossible to define liberalism. Sartori shares this belief and says: "If we compare the label 'liberalism' with those similar concepts, such as democracy, socialism and communism, then liberalism is unmatched in one respect: among all concepts, it is the most uncertain and difficult term to grasp."[118]

However, no matter how divergent the views of these liberals are, they cannot have nothing in common or universal, because there is no such thing that has nothing in common with other things. So, what is the unique common ground or universality of these liberal theories that distinguishes them from theories, such as totalitarianism and socialism?

Obviously, all liberalism theories share a common characteristic: they are, without exceptions, a thought system that advocates the realization of a free society, just like all communism theories are, without exceptions, a thought system that advocates the realization of a public ownership society. Liberalism is a theory that advocates the realization of a free society; this is the universality unique to all liberalism theories, namely, the differential and fundamental feature that distinguishes liberalism from other theories, such as totalitarianism and socialism. Therefore, this can be called the definition of liberalism. Implied in the definition that liberalism is a thought system that advocates the realization of a free society are three fundamental questions that liberalism must answer.

The first question is: what is a free society? This question concerns the "principle of liberty." The second question is: why should we achieve a free society? This question concerns the "value of liberty." The final question is: how can we achieve a free society? This question is one of "constitutional democracy." These are the objects for studies on liberalism. Therefore, liberalism, as a complete theoretical system, originally consists of three parts: the theory of value of liberty, the theory of principle of liberty, and the theory of constitutional democracy.

**The theoretical system of liberalism: the theory of value of liberty, theory of principle of liberty, and theory of constitutional democracy**

*Theories on the value of liberty*

The starting point of the theory of liberalism is undoubtedly the question of the value of liberty. In this regard, as Sapiro says, no matter how divergent the views of liberalists are, they all worship liberty, praise liberty, advocate liberty, and believe that liberty is of very great value: "Liberalism is a typical feature of all times, it firmly believes that freedom is indispensable to achieve any goal worth pursuing."[119] Hu Shi says, "Liberalism is the great movement in human history that advocates freedom, worships freedom, strives for freedom, enriches freedom, and promotes freedom."[120] Indeed, anyone who denies this point and that liberty is of great value is undoubtedly no longer a liberalist.

Great value is surely different from important value and maximum value, as well as from the highest value and the supreme value; these values, however, belong undoubtedly to the category of great value. All liberalists believe that liberty has great value, but they do not all agree that liberty has the highest value, nor do they all agree that liberty has the supreme value. However, from the perspective of the liberalism in the scientific and complete form of liberalism, liberty has supreme value: the liberalism in the scientific and complete form of liberalism is also called libertarianism. Therefore, David Spitz, a liberalist, wrote the first of the ten tenets of liberalism before his death: "Esteem liberty above all other values, even over equality and justice."[121]

Why is libertarianism the scientific and most complete form of liberalism? Because Renaissance humanitarianism found that human self-realization, that is, the realization of every individual's creative potentials of the self, has the highest value. Although there are many conditions and ways for self-realization, there is undoubtedly only one fundamental condition and route: liberty is the most fundamental condition and route for self-realization. Given this, liberty has, thus, the highest value. But the highest value is not necessarily the maximum value. Liberty is the highest value, so the value of liberty ought to be much higher than the value of bread. But, as Berlin reminds us, the value of liberty is not as great as that of food and clothing all the time, for example, "The Egyptian peasant needs clothes or medicine before, and more than, personal liberty."[122] Spitz's maxim that liberty is worth more than equality and justice is well said, but the value of liberty is not necessarily greater than the value of equality and justice.

However, since liberty has the highest value, it is obvious that people ought to be made free and that liberty ought to be the highest value standard of state institutions. Therefore, Acton stresses again, "The idea of freedom is the noblest idea of value—it is the supreme law in human social life";[123] "freedom is the supreme law and can be restricted only by greater freedom."[124] But, in fact, how can people be free? Man is a social animal, and the life he lives is social, so only when the society in which people live is free can people really achieve liberty. In this sense, Hayek says,

> But, once its advantages were recognized, men began to perfect and extend the reign of freedom and, for that purpose, to inquire how a free society worked. This development of a theory of liberty took place mainly in the eighteenth century. It began in two countries, England and France.[125]

But, after all, what is a free society? Or, what is the principle of a free society? This is the core issue of liberalism. Liberalism is mainly a system of a series of principles of liberty, as well as a system of a series of principles of a free society. Hayek writes,

> When one of the intellectual leaders of nineteenth-century liberalism, Benjamin Constant, described liberalism as *the systeme de principes*, he pointed to the heart of the matter. Not only is liberty a system under which all government action is guided by principles, but it is an ideal that will not be preserved unless it is itself accepted as an overriding principle governing all particular acts of legislation.[126]

This is why liberalism belongs to the object of ethics; liberalism, fundamentally speaking, is a system of a series of principles and value standards, namely, the system of value standards of state institutions. Therefore, Acton writes, "The urgency of freedom as a moral issue is far greater than that of freedom as a political issue."[127]

*Theories on the principles of liberty*

Upon closer scrutiny, the system of liberty principles established by liberalism—that is, the principles of a free society—actually consists of two series of principles: the general principles of a free society and the specific principles of a free society. The former mainly refers to the rule-of-law principle of liberty, the equality principle of liberty, and the limit principle of liberty; the latter mainly includes the principle of political liberty, the principle of economic freedom, and the principle of freedom of thought. No matter how different the views of liberalists are, they must all advocate or acknowledge these principles of liberty; otherwise, they will no longer be liberalists. Nonetheless, liberalists often disagree on the specific content of these principles. Our investigation of the principles of freedom is, of course, based on liberalism in the most complete form.

Any coercion of a society must conform to the laws and morals of that society; all of its laws and morals must be agreed upon, directly or indirectly, by all members. This is liberalism's "rule-of-law principle of liberty." On this principle, Hobhouse writes, "We have seen that the reign of law is the first step to liberty... the first condition of free government is government not by the arbitrary determination of the ruler, but by fixed rules of law."[128] Hayek further adds,

> The conception of freedom under the law that is the chief concern of this book rests on the contention that when we obey laws, in the sense of general abstract rules laid down irrespective of their application to us, we are not subject to another man's will and are therefore free.[129]

Everyone ought to enjoy liberty equally: everyone is equal before liberty; everyone ought to obey social coercion equally; everyone is equal before the law. This is liberalism's equality principle of liberty. On this principle, Hayek writes,

> In all these fields (and, as we shall see later, in that of contract) freedom does mean and can mean only that what we may do is not dependent on the approval of any person or authority and is limited only by the same abstract rules that apply equally to all.[130]

Therefore, "The great aim of the struggle for liberty has been equality before the law."[131]

The coercion of a society ought to be kept to the minimum necessary for its existence, and the liberty of a society ought to be extended to the maximum possible for its existence. This is liberalism's limit principle of liberty. In this regard, Popper clearly states, "The principle of liberalism dictates that the restrictions on everyone's freedom necessary for social life should be reduced to a minimum."[132] Liberalists have no objection to this principle; if they do, they are not liberalists. However, the minimum and the maximum are relative and uncertain concepts. Therefore, what is minimum coercion to some liberalists may seem to be coercion of a high order to other liberalists, and vice versa. Therefore, some liberalists advocate a "night watchman" type of country, asserting that "the least the government governs, the best the government is." Others, on the contrary, argue that such a small amount of coercion is not enough to guarantee the existence of society and that the minimum coercion necessary for the existence of society is much more powerful and complex than these. Therefore, they argue that the state should actively intervene in economic and social life.

The politics of a society ought to obtain the direct or indirect consent of every citizen; it ought to be carried out directly or indirectly according to the will of every citizen; ultimately, it ought to be carried out according to the will of the ruled. This is liberalism's principle of political liberty. Jefferson summed up this principle in *The Declaration of Independence* in a sentence: "The legitimate power of the government depends on the consent of the ruled." President Wilson, who Berlin calls "an absolute liberalist," wrote, "Political freedom is the right of the governed to make the government fit for their needs and interests."[133] Acton believes these statements are the liberalism's policies on the government, "In *The Declaration of Independence*, Madison, Adams, Franklin, Jefferson, Hamilton and others expressed the view of constructing a new theory of government: in practice, the ruled decide the policy of the government."[134]

Economic activities ought to be regulated only by market mechanism, not by government's coercive command; the government's management ought to be limited only to establishing economic rules and guaranteeing their implementation; within the scope of these economic rules, everyone ought to enjoy the freedom to conduct economic activities in full accordance with their own will. This is the principle of economic freedom of liberalism. The discoverer and founder of this principle, as we all know, is Adam Smith, who calls it a "system of natural freedom":

> All systems, either of performance or of restraint, therefore, being thus completely taken away, the obvious and simple system of natural liberty establishes itself of its own accord. Every man, as long as he does not violate the law of justice, is left perfectly free to pursue his own interest his own way, and to bring both his industry and capital into competition with those of any other man, or order of men.[135]

Every member of society ought to enjoy the freedom to obtain and convey any idea; in other words, every member of society ought not to be prohibited from obtaining and conveying ideas. Ultimately, speech and press ought to be completely free and ought not to be subject to any restrictions. This is liberalism's principle of freedom of thought. On this principle, Penn writes, "Freedom of the press and the freedom to use other means of expression of ideas cannot be abolished, suspended and restricted."[136] Roosevelt went on to take the United States as an example and said, "This freedom is not restricted at all except by the conscience of the American people."[137] The Virginia Bill of Rights of the United States has stipulated that "freedom of the press is one of the important guarantees of freedom, and any government, unless it is a tyrannical government, should never restrict it." Article I of the Bill of Rights of the United States of America states that "Congress shall not enact laws on the establishment of freedom of religion or prohibition of belief and deprivation of the freedom of speech or publication of the people."

There are six major principles of liberty that liberalism holds for a free society: three general principles of freedom—the rule of law, equality, and limit of freedom—and three specific principles of freedom—political freedom, economic freedom, and freedom of thought. So, how can we achieve these principles and make a society a free society? This is a question of the way to realize the principles of freedom, namely, the way to realize the free society. This is the research object of the third part, also the last part, of liberal theory. The relatively complete and scientific theory of liberalism on this issue, as we all know, is the so-called "constitutional democracy theory": "constitutional democracy" is a sufficient and necessary condition for the realization of a free society.

### Theories on constitutional democracy

Liberalists believe that democracy is the only regime to realize political liberty and thus guarantee the realization of all other social freedoms. Therefore, Acton said, "freedom is considered to be a product associated with the elected government."[138] Hayek stressed again and again, "Democracy itself is not freedom, but it is the most important guarantee of freedom."[139] However, liberalists are well aware that democracy is only a sufficient and necessary condition for the realization of political liberty or a politically free society, but not a sufficient and necessary condition for the realization of a free society. Democracy is simply a necessary but insufficient condition for the realization of a free society. The reasons are the following:

On the one hand, democracy, in its essence, is the politics in which all citizens hold the supreme power on an equal footing, but in terms of its realization, it is bound to be the politics in which most citizens hold the supreme power. In this way, most citizens may abuse all their supreme powers to get the better of their opponents:

> If the majority does not unite to act like one person to oppose the views and interests of the so-called minority who acts like one person, then why do we call it the majority? But if you admit that a person with unlimited authority can abuse his power to oppose his opponent, on what ground can you deny that the majority can do the same?[140]

Tocqueville calls this kind of abuse of the supreme power held by the majority "majority tyranny." Democratic societies with majority tyranny are clearly not free societies.

On the other hand, even if democracy does not lead to tyranny by the majority over the minority, it may still lead to tyranny: a tyranny that infringes on the individual freedom and right of everyone. The supreme power is, by nature, linked with the infinite power and can thus easily evolve into the infinite power, so Tocqueville points out that the supreme power of society, whether in the hands of the monarch or in the hands of the people, may become infinite power and degenerate into tyranny:

> Whenever I see any authority, whether it is called the people or the king, whether it is called the democratic government or the aristocratic government, or whether it is exercised in the monarchy or in the republic, is granted the power and capacity to decide on everything, I would say that it sows the seeds of tyranny.[141]

In short, the reason why democracy is a necessary condition rather than a sufficient condition of a free society is that the political power of a democratic regime may be infinite, thus violating the value standards of state institutions such as liberty, and finally leading to democratic tyranny. In this sense, if the democratic regime can be forced to abide by the value standards of state institutions such as liberty, then this democratic society is a free society. Therefore, the democracy whose supreme power is effectively restricted by the value standards of state institutions such as liberty is a sufficient and necessary condition for the realization of a free society. This kind of democracy whose supreme power is effectively restricted by the value standards of state institutions such as liberty is nothing but the "constitutional democracy" advocated by liberalism. Constitutional democracy is the democracy that is effectively restricted by the value standards of state institutions such as liberty, equality, justice, and humanity, the democracy that takes these values standards of state institutions as the guiding principles of the Constitution, the democracy that follows the Constitution and is restricted by it.

Admittedly, the constitutions of various countries follow or violate the value standards of state institutions such as liberty, but, as is well known, in terms of the tradition of the constitution, the documents' main acts, namely, the acts of governmental organizations—emphasizing the principle of decentralization—and the bill of rights—emphasizing the principles of human rights—embody and follow the principle of liberty. Therefore, as far as the tradition of constitutional thought is concerned, constitutional democracy is the democracy that restricts the power of democracy and makes it follow the free constitution, which is the sufficient and necessary condition of a free society. All constitutional democratic societies are free societies; all free societies are constitutional democratic societies. As Sartori repeatedly says, "The constitutional system is in fact a liberal system, both in the past and in the present. It can be said that liberal politics is constitutionalism."[142]

## *Theoretical categorization of liberalism: the most fundamental humanism*

Synthesizing the liberalist theories on the value of liberty, principles of liberty, and constitutional democracy, we can see that liberalism, as far as its general form is concerned, is a thought system of a free society, of the value and principles of liberty, and of ways of realizing liberty. In other words, liberalism is the thought system about the principles of a free society and the ways to achieve it, and the theory about a free society. In this sense, any theory advocating the construction of a free society belongs to the category of liberalism. However, liberalism, as far as its complete form is concerned, is a state institution and thought system that regards liberty as the highest value. As it regards human liberty as the highest value, liberalism, on the one hand, regards liberty as the highest value standard of state institutions, which means that it regards "the rule-of-law principle of liberty," "the equality principle of liberty," and "the limit principle of liberty," as well as a series of principles of liberty, such as economic freedom, political freedom, and freedom of thought, as the highest value standards of state institutions. On the other hand, it regards constitutional democracy as the way to realize these principles, that is, the way to realize a free society.

From this point of view, liberalism obviously belongs to the category of humanism: liberalism is the humanism of a free society. As mentioned earlier, the humanism discovered in the Renaissance is the social and thought system that regards the realization of a human's creative potential of the self as the highest value, thereby regarding "the realization of creative potential of the self" as the highest value standard of state institutions. The most fundamental necessary condition for the realization of creative potential of the self is liberty. Therefore, so-called humanism is, ultimately, the social and thought system that regards human liberty as the highest value—and thus regards liberty as the highest value standard of state institutions: liberalism is the most fundamental humanism. Therefore, Paul Kurtz calls liberalism "liberal humanism."[143] John Jevinsbo simply calls liberalism "free humanism."[144] Berlin and other liberal thinkers often equate liberalism with humanism and call it "humane and liberal tradition" and "humanitarian liberalism."[145]

In the course of its historical development, humanism has evolved, through narrowing down and deepening its senses and shifting from describing its symptoms to probing its causes, into three major forms. The ancient fraternity humanism regards man as the highest value; the Renaissance humanism of self-realization regards the realization of man's creative potential as the highest value; the liberal humanism of the Western mainstream ideology since the 17th century—liberalism—holds that human liberty is the highest value.

As liberalism is not only the most fundamental humanism, but also the institutionalized and organized humanism, it is the humanism that can be realized through some realistic route. As far as its complete and scientific form is concerned, liberalism, like all theories about an ideal society, such as socialism, is not only a theory, a doctrine, an ideology, or a political thought but also a movement, an organization, a political party program, a system, and a form of state organization. Liberalism is a state institution and thought system that regards liberty as the highest value. Through his inspection on the history of European liberalism, Ruggiero finally concludes, "Various definitions of liberalism have been given. It can be called a method, a political party, an art of rule, a form of state organization."[146]

Sartori writes: "It can be concisely asserted that liberalism is the theory and practice of providing individuals judicial protection of their political freedom and individual freedom through constitutional state."[147] Collingwood makes a similar observation: "The word 'liberalism' has long been used in the name of constitutional freedom and representative government principles in the country of its origin, and all political parties in the English-speaking have shared this wealth."[148] Essentially, liberalism is the most profound form of revolution, because, as Popper says, "the transition from closed society to open society can clearly be described as the most profound revolution that mankind has experienced."[149]

## Alienation: the most fundamental non-humanity

### *The concept of alienation*

Alienation comes from the Latin word *alienatio*, which means alienation, separation, transfer, and otherness. It mainly refers to someone who becomes the other, someone who entrusts himself to others, and someone who transfers his own things to others.[150] From this, the term has gradually been fixed as a scientific term and divided into two parts: one is taken as an ordinary general scientific term; the other is taken as a special specific scientific term, that is, as a basic concept of the thought system of humanism.

*Alienation as a general scientific term*

Alienation, when used a general term in science, means that things change into other things, that things change into alien things, or that things change into other things alien to themselves. The concept of "alienation," which Hegel uses to construct his philosophical system, has the same meaning: the natural world is the self-alienation of absolute spirit. The core concept of "alienation" which Feuerbach reveals as the essence of Christianity shares this meaning as well: God is the alienation, externalization, and objectification of human nature; "God's personality is the means, by which man can make his own essential stipulations and appearances another being, stipulations and appearances external to his being. God's personality is nothing but the alienation and objectification of human personality."[151]

In fact, the typical concept of alienation as a general scientific term is, nevertheless, also the "alienation" in biology, a term relative to "assimilation." Biology explains this concept as follows:

> Metabolism is one of the basic characteristics of life. Its general definition refers to the sum of all chemical actions in organisms, including assimilation (or anabolism) and dissimilation (or catabolism). Assimilation is an energy absorption process in which organisms absorb substances from the outside world and transform them into their own constituents through complex chemical changes. Alienation is the process in which organisms decompose their own constituents and release energy.[152]

That is to say, both alienation and assimilation are changes. However, while assimilation is the change of life toward itself, alienation is the change of self toward the other.

It can be thus concluded that as a general scientific term, "alienation" is only a specific concept of change, totally subordinated to and dependent on the scope of change, so it has no independent value for scientific research and cannot be independently studied as a subject of research by any science. The kind of "alienation" that has scientific research value and becomes the special research object of science is the "alienation" as a special and specific scientific term, that is, the "alienation" as a basic concept of the thought system of humanism. What is, then, the meaning of this kind of alienation?

52  *Humanity and liberty*

*Alienation as a basic concept of humanism*

Alienation in Hegel's and Feuerbach's works mainly refers to a change from one thing to another, while alienation in Marx's and Engels's works mainly refers to people's behavior of being un-free, enslaved, and coerced. In *Das Kapital*, Marx states, "The worker himself constantly regards objective wealth as capital, and produces it as his dissimilated domination and exploitation of his power."[153] Half a century after the initial publication of Marx's *Manuscript of Economics and Philosophy* in 1932, the "alienation fever" that had been flourishing in Western academia also interpreted it in this way: "Alienation mainly refers to the feeling that people's destiny is not dominated by themselves, but controlled by external forces, by other people's destiny, by other people's luck or by a certain system."[154] Alienation refers to people's behavior of being un-free, enslaved, and coerced; this is the kind of alienation which is the basic concept of the thought system of humanism. As the fundamental principle of humanism is liberty, which represents the positive side of humanism, does not alienation, understood as behavior of being un-free, enslaved, and coerced, represent the negative side of humanism? But the question is: is it right to define alienation as "the behavior of being un-free, enslaved or coerced"? The answer is no. If the answer is yes, does it not mean that alienation is the same concept as behavior of being un-free, enslaved, or coerced? If the answer is yes, does it not mean that alienation will lose its need of independent existence? If it is, we may wonder why the concepts of non-freedom, slavery, and coercion are so simple and clear, while the term alienation is so confusing and divergent. Moreover, the etymological origin of non-freedom, enslavement, and coercion are rather distant from that of alienation. So, what is the definition of alienation? Let us go back to Marx's analysis of alienation.

> Its alien character emerges clearly in the fact that as soon as no physical or other compulsion exists, labor is shunned like the plague. External labor, labor in which man alienates himself, is a labor of self-sacrifice, of mortification. Lastly, the external character of labor for the worker appears in the fact that it is not his own, but someone else's, that it does not belong to him, that in it he belongs, not to himself, but to another.[155]

This is to say that the so-called alienated labor is such a kind of labor done by the laborer under coercion and, thus, has the following characteristics: it is labor done by the laborer, but it belongs not to the laborer but to the coercer; it is labor made by the laborer, but it is not belonging to himself, is not owned by himself, is estranged from himself, and is alien to himself. "Labor done by the self but not belonging to the self" is the fundamental characteristic that distinguishes alienated labor from non-alienated labor; "coercion" is the cause of this kind of alienated labor.

Therefore, being coerced, enslaved, and un-free is not alienation but the cause of alienation. Alienation is a behavior in which the individual does something not belonging to himself, something alien to himself; it is a behavior that is alien to the individual himself. Just try to imagine why a person would alienate himself from his own behaviors. Is it not bcause people must behave not according to his own will but according to others' will as a result of non-freedom and enslavement under external coercion? Here is an example.

During the War of Resistance against Japanese Aggression in China, Japanese soldiers forced an old Chinese man to rape his daughter-in-law in front of everyone and threatened to shoot him if he did not obey the order. The old man had to act accordingly. His behavior occurred under coercion and non-freedom. Therefore, the behavior, though done by the old man himself, is not a behavior done out of his own will, but a behavior that is done under the domination of the will of the Japanese soldiers; this behavior thus belongs to the Japanese soldiers. This behavior is done by the old man, but it does not belong to him and is alien to the old man himself. This behavior is ultimately the alienation of the old man.

As the example illustrates, non-freedom, slavery, and coercion are the causes of alienation; alienation is the behavior of an individual under un-freedom, enslavement, and coercion, behavior which does not belong to the individual himself but to others, namely, the coercers; behavior which is done by the self but is estranged from the self and alien to the self; behavior which is done by the self but is not his own. As far as the doer of the behavior—the individual himself—is concerned, the behavior is done by the individual; however, the will behind this behavior is not that of the individual himself; this is not his own behavior but a behavior which does not belong to his self and is alienated from his self. This is the definition of alienation as the basic concept of humanism.

In this sense, alienation as a basic concept of humanism may also refer to the change of a thing (John's behavior) to something alien to itself (Peter's behavior), which means that the behavior is done by John, but it belongs not to John but to Peter. Thus, alienation as a basic concept of humanism belongs to the concept of alienation as a general scientific term (the change of the thing to something alien to the thing itself). However, as a general scientific term, alienation means that its alienator can be anything, that the change can be about anything, and that alienation is the change from one thing to another; as a basic concept of humanism, alienation means that its alienator can only be humans, that the change can only be about human behaviors, that alienation is the behavior that an individual human does but this behavior is alien to the individual himself and belongs to others.

As demonstrated above, alienation as a basic concept of humanism is a concrete deduction of alienation in human behavior as a general scientific term. Ultimately, it is a concrete extension of the etymological meaning of alienation (estrangement, separation, transfer, and otherness). In this regard, the *Encyclopedia of Philosophy* in the United States clearly states:

> The term alienation has many different meanings in daily life, science and philosophy. Most of these meanings can be regarded as a modification of a broad meaning proposed by semantics and etymology. In this sense, alienation is an activity, as a result of which something or someone becomes estranged from something or someone.[156]

*Popular definitions of alienation*

Alienation, studied both in China and in other countries, is widely known as a basic concept of humanism rather than as a general scientific term. Their definitions, though various and divergent, are fundamentally identical in that they all believe alienation to be the process of change in which one's own behavior becomes an alien force of dominating, controlling, and enslaving oneself.

"Alienation is a philosophical sociological category that reflects the objective transformation of human activities and their results into the independent forces that govern and antagonize human beings."[157]

> Alienation is a way of experiencing, in which an individual feels like an alien or he feels he is estranged from himself; he does not experience himself as the center of his own world, the creator of his own actions, and the results of his actions and actions become his masters. He submits to them, and even worships them.[158]

This is the popular definition of alienation. This popular definition is, however, untenable, for two reasons. On the one hand, what this definition suggests is not a concept of alienation but a concept of slavery or, more specifically, a concept of a specific type of slavery. There are no more than two kinds of slavery: one kind refers to enslavement by one's own activities and the results thereof, as workers are enslaved by the capital they create; the other refers to enslavement by forces other than one's own activities and the results thereof, such as that of nationals enslaved by despots. What the popular definition of alienation describes is the type of slavery in which humans are enslaved by their own acts and the results thereof. As mentioned before, slavery is evidently not alienation, but the cause of alienation, for alienation means that the behavior, which is done by the individual himself under the condition of being enslaved, belongs not to the individual himself but to the enslaver.

On the other hand, the popular definition of alienation is one-sided. According to this definition, only the behavior that is enslaved by one's own activities and products thereof is alienation, but the behavior enslaved by others' activities and products thereof is not alienation. From this definition it can be then deduced that whether workers are alienated by capitalists or not depends on the source of the capital that enslaves the workers: if the capital is created by workers themselves, then we can say that it is alienation; if the capital is not created by workers but, say, is accumulated by capitalists themselves, then we can say that it is not alienation. But, does this deduction make sense at all?

In fact, the opposite is true. An individual's behavior of being enslaved is considered as alienation, precisely because the enslavement is not done by the individual himself but by others.Enslavement is not alienation but the cause of alienation. Only the behavior done under enslavement can be called alienation. Why? It is because, in the condition of being enslaved, the behavior of an individual does not belong to the individual himself but to the enslaver: alienation is the behavior of the individual himself but does not belong to the individual himself. Evidently, only when the enslaver is another person will the behavior by the individual under enslavement become a behavior that is alien to the individual himself and belong to the enslaver; this behavior, then, is alienation. If the enslaver is the individual himself, then the behavior of the individual under enslavement is the behavior that is done by the individual himself and belongs to the individual himself; this behavior is not alienation. Imagine a miser. By whom is he enslaved? He is enslaved by himself, by his own desire to save money. In his case, the behavior under enslavement is the behavior which is carried out by the miser himself and belongs to the miser himself; then, this behavior is not alienation.

However, can we venture further to conclude that "the behavior of being enslaved by one's own activities and products thereof" is absolutely not alienation? No, we can't. "The behavior of being enslaved by one's own activities and products thereof" may be alienation, but it must be based on the premise that "one's own activities and products thereof" have become external forces—such as other people or other things—which are independent of oneself and therefore do not belong to oneself. For example:

The capital is created by workers and is the product of workers' surplus labor. That the labor performed under the enslavement of the capitalists goes through the process of alienation is entirely based on the premise that "the capital is independent of workers and belongs instead to capitalists." Only under the premise that the capital belongs to capitalists can we say that the labor that workers perform under enslavement of capitalists is the alienated work that "does not belong to workers themselves but belongs to capitalists." On the contrary, if the capital belongs to workers, then the work that they do under the enslavement of their own desire for capital, like the behavior of "misers," "money slaves," "house slaves," and "car slaves," is "the work which is done by the workers themselves and belongs to workers themselves," and is therefore not an alienated labor.

It becomes clear that alienation does not occur in self-enslavement, but can occur only in the enslavement by external forces (other people or things, such as capital, which belong to others, etc.). However, this external force that enslaves one may be the result of one's own activities, such as the capital created by enslaved workers, or it may not, as in the Japanese invasion of China. In accordance with this distinction, alienation can also be divided into two categories: one is the alienation which is being enslaved by one's own activities and the results thereof, such as workers' alienated labor; the other is the alienation due to being enslaved by forces other than one's own activities and the results thereof, such as the old man being forced by Japanese soldiers to rape his daughter-in-law. The popular definition of alienation recognizes the former kind but not the latter, thus committing the fallacy of mistaking a part for the whole. The difference between "alienation enslaved by the product of one's own activities" and "alienation enslaved by forces other than the product of one's own activities" can facilitate a classification of alienation, but its main significance is not in classifying alienation but in defining it. So, what is the classification of alienation which is of great significance to the division of alienation?

*Forced alienation, voluntary alienation, and unconscious alienation*

Alienation, according to the nature of "non-freedom," its cause, can be classified into three types: forced alienation, voluntary alienation, and unconscious alienation. Forced alienation originates from "forced and absolute non-freedom," which is unchangeable, involuntary, and inescapable. For example, the old man is forced to rape his daughter-in-law under the bayonet of Japanese soldiers, prisoners are forced to work under the custody of the prison, and children are forced by their parents to go to school. In these examples, their behaviors are all alienated behaviors done by them in the condition of unchangeable, involuntary, and inescapable non-freedom. These behaviors originate from "forced and absolute non-freedom," so they are called "forced alienation": forced alienation is alienation in which one is forced to abandon one's own will and submit to the will of others.

Voluntary alienation is the alienation that one voluntarily abandons one's will and follows others' will. This alienation stems from "voluntary non-freedom." The so-called voluntary non-freedom is the non-freedom that can be avoided but one does not avoid, is the non-freedom that one is willing to accept and even actively strives for. For example, for wages, workers voluntarily abandon their own will, surrender to the will of capitalists, and work under the supervision of capitalists; for their own future, people voluntarily abandon their own will, surrender to the will of leaders, and act according to the will of leaders; to earn money, prostitutes voluntarily abandon their own will, surrender to the will of their clients, and put their bodies at the mercy of their clients. All of these behaviors are alien to individuals who do these behaviors themselves; all of these behaviors are voluntarily carried out by individuals themselves under the circumstance, in which they can avoid no-freedom, but they do not. Thus, all of these behaviors can be called voluntary alienation.Therefore, voluntary alienation, as Marx says, is, ultimately, a kind of alienation that takes place when the non-freedom, enslavement and coercion are used as means. In his words, "alienated labor degrades voluntary activities and free activities as means."[159]

However, people tend to think that "voluntary non-freedom" is a paradox: voluntary and self-consenting non-freedom is no longer non-freedom; voluntary and self-consenting enslavement is no longer enslavement. Regarding this view, Berlin makes a very witty and convincing refutation:

> Nor does universal consent to loss of liberty somehow miraculously preserve it merely by being universal, or by being consent. If I consented to be oppressed, or acquiesce in my condition with detachment or irony, am I the less oppressed? If I sell myself into slavery, am I the less a slave? If I commit suicide, am I the less dead because I have taken my own life freely?[160]

Voluntary non-freedom is not only non-freedom but also further away from freedom than involuntary non-freedom. If people's non-freedom and enslavement are not voluntary, they will strive for freedom and will eventually achieve freedom. If their non-freedom and enslavement are voluntary, doesn't this mean that they give up freedom and therefore never have it? So McFallon says, "Knowing where the shackles are is the first step toward freedom. If a person ignores the shackles or likes them, he will never see the day of freedom."[161] Therefore, as far as the feeling of alienation is concerned, the pain of voluntary non-freedom and voluntary alienation is lighter than that of forced non-freedom and forced alienation, but as far as the degree of alienation is concerned, the former is greater than the latter.

Unconscious alienation is the alienation that the individual who, as a result of his self-forgetting, self-loss, and self-degradation, loses his own will and mistakes others' will as his own will. This alienation stems from "unconscious non-freedom." There is some difference between unconscious non-freedom and voluntary non-freedom. People in voluntary non-freedom only suppress and give up their own will, but they still have their own will, and thus feel that they are un-free. Although they give up their freedom, they may still have the possibility to strive for freedom and get rid of alienation. On the contrary, the individual in unconscious non-freedom has lost his own will and regards the will of others as his own, so he does not feel he is un-free. Thus, it is unlikely that he will fight for freedom and get rid of alienation. In this sense, unconscious alienation is the deepest alienation, an extreme and total alienation. Allow me to take the old Chinese saying "a square hole inside a circle" as an example to illustrate this difference.

If a person is "a square hole inside a circle," it means that he acts according to the will of others (i.e. the circle) but still has his own opinions (the square hole). So, this person still has his own will, so his act is under voluntary non-freedom and thus a voluntary alienation. On the contrary, if he loses his will, becomes a circle within a circle, acts according to the will of others, and follows the trend, but still enjoys being in such a state, then he reaches the state of unconscious non-freedom, and his behavior is thus unconscious and total alienation.

Though the pain of voluntary alienation and non-freedom is less than that of forced alienation and non-freedom, there is still a sense of alienation and non-freedom after all, and therefore the pain is still felt by individuals. On the contrary, individuals with unconscious alienation and unconscious non-freedom have completely lost their sense of alienation and non-freedom, and thus feel no pain at all. Therefore, the degree of alienation is inversely proportional to the feeling of alienation: the lighter the degree of alienation, the more pain individuals will feel; the greater the degree of alienation, the lesser the pain individuals will feel. Total alienation means that there is no pain; forced alienation is the most painful and is a primary and basic alienation; voluntary alienation is less painful and a middle-level and local alienation; unconscious alienation is a painless, advanced, and total alienation. There is a good analogy to illustrate these three kinds of alienation: forced alienation is an acute disease, voluntary alienation a chronic disease, and unconscious alienation an incurable disease.

## *The value of alienation*

From the concept of alienation, there emerges a question: is alienation something that ought to be and that is benevolent, good, and of positive value, or something that ought not to be and that is evil, and bad, and of negative value? The answer to this question depends, first, upon the moral value of the will of the alienated person. If the alienated person is bad, what he wants to do is a bad thing, that is to say, his will is harmful to others and has negative value, then the alienated behavior of forcing him to give up his own will and to submit to the altruistic will of others is obviously of positive value. In short, depriving a bad person of his freedom to do bad things and thus making him alienated is "ought to be." For example, it undoubtedly ought to be moral and of positive moral value to force criminals to reform through labor to make them act not according to their harmful will but according to the altruistic will of others. On the contrary, allowing criminals the freedom to harm others to eliminate their alienation is of negative moral value and is thus something that ought not to be and that is immoral.

However, if an alienated person is a good person, and his own will is harmless to others, does his alienation still have positive value? Yes, such alienation may still have positive value. We often see that adults are often unable to convince their children and have to force their children to give up their irrational will and submit to the adult will. We also often see that the wise and the excellent sometimes cannot persuade the foolish and the ignorant and have to force the ignorant and the foolish to give up their wrong will and submit to the right one. The alienation of children and ignorant and foolish people is undoubtedly of great benefit to them and their society, and is therefore of great positive value.

Nonetheless, the benefits and value of alienation, however great, can only be temporary, local, and non-fundamental. Seen from a fundamental, long-term, and global perspective, alienation can only have negative value. Alienation is the behavior which is carried out by the individual himself under enslavement and non-freedom, which is done not according to his own will but according to the will of others, and which is alienated from the individual himself and not belonging to him. It is, therefore, obvious that alienation is the fundamental obstacle to self-realization, and there is a negative correlation between the two. The more alienated a person is, the more alienated acts dominated by other people's will he will be, the less personality he will have, the less he will develop his creative potential, and the lower his level of self-realization will be. The less alienated a person is, the fewer the alienated acts dominated by others he will carry out, the more personality he will have, the more he will develop his creative potential, and the higher his level of self-realization will be. So, Lukacs says, "Alienation means, first of all, an obstacle to the formation of a complete human being."[162] Alienation is "one of the biggest obstacles that prevent a person from becoming a real person and having a real personality."[163] Alienation is the fundamental obstacle to self-realization, and it has the highest and the greatest negative value for the country and its people. This point can be explained in two aspects.

On the one hand, self-realization satisfies the highest need of each individual. Modern psychology, especially Maslow's psychology, shows that human beings have five basic needs, which are, in the hierarchal order from the lowest level to the highest level, physiological needs, safety needs, love needs, self-esteem needs, and self-realization needs. Since alienation hinders the satisfaction of each individual's highest need, it also has the highest negative value for each individual and is thus everyone's biggest misfortune. Does the highest negative value not hinder the satisfaction of the highest needs? Is the highest misfortune not the misfortune that the highest need cannot be realized?

On the other hand, self-actualization can satisfy all the needs of the whole society and each individual because the wealth, whether material or spiritual, of any society is nothing but the product of human activities, the result of the exertion of human abilities, and the realization of its creative potential. Therefore, the more the self-realization and creative potential of human beings are realized, the richer the material and spiritual wealth the society will have, the more prosperous the society will be, and the more fully everyone's needs will be met. On the contrary, the less self-realization and human potential is realized, the poorer the material and spiritual wealth of the society will be, the more depressed the society will be, and the less fully everyone's needs will be met. Hence, self-realization is the source of all wealth, and the most fundamental, the most important, and the greatest wealth; therefore, it can meet the needs of the whole society and everyone to the greatest extent, thus having the greatest value. Given this, doesn't alienation, as a fundamental obstacle to self-realization, cause the greatest damage to the interests of the whole society and everyone? Is it not the greatest misfortune of the whole society and everyone? Does it not have the greatest negative value?

It can be concluded that alienation has the highest and greatest double negative value for the country and every citizen in it, which means that, for the whole country and every citizen, the positive value of alienation can only be temporary, local, and non-fundamental, while the negative value is definitely long-term, global, and fundamental. Therefore, eliminating alienation is a very important value standard of state institutions and state governance. So, how is this standard positioned in the value standard system of the state institutions?

Our research on humanity and liberty shows that "making human self-realization possible" is the general principle of humanity and liberty as the fundamental condition for self-realization is the most fundamental humanity. "Making humans free" is thus the fundamental principle of humanity. From this point of view, on the one hand, alienation is the most fundamental inhumanity because it is the fundamental obstacle to self-realization; on the other hand, "eliminating alienation" is the same as "making people free," so it is also the fundamental principle of humanity. Making people free is the positive fundamental principle of humanity and the highest positive value standard of state institutions, while eliminating alienation is the negative fundamental principle of humanity and the highest negative value standard of state institutions.

But how can we eliminate alienation? Non-freedom, enslavement, and coercion are the causes of alienation: alienation is nothing more than the alienated behavior which the individual does under the circumstances of non-freedom, enslavement, and coercion, which does not belong to the individual himself. Therefore, the abolition of enslavement, coercion, and non-freedom is the basic principle of eliminating alienation. However, how should we abolish non-freedom, enslavement, and coercion to eliminate alienation? This is a very complicated problem. To tackle this problem, we should first determine the specific type of alienation we are facing by asking ourselves these questions: is it secular alienation or religious alienation? Is it economic alienation, political alienation, or social alienation?

### Economic alienation

*The concept of economic alienation: the labor by which the laborer creates material wealth does not belong to the laborer himself*

What exactly is economic alienation? The answer to the question is twofold. On the one hand, the so-called economy, as we all know, is about the production, exchange, distribution, and consumption of material wealth, that is, the sum of material wealth created by the activities of people. Therefore, economic alienation or alienated economy must be a kind of alienation about material wealth. On the other hand, the so-called alienation, as mentioned before, is the behavior which an individual carries out which does not belong to the individual himself. So, in a word, it can be concluded that the so-called economic alienation or alienated economy is the behavior of making material wealth that does not belong to oneself, the labor of creating material wealth that does not belong to oneself but belongs to others, or the labor that creates the material wealth that is alien to the individual himself. Given this, economic alienation, alienated economy, labor alienation, and alienated labor are the same concept.

Marx defines economic alienation in this way:

> Productivity and creation of general wealth, knowledge and so on is manifested in the alienation of the individual engaged in labor himself. He does not regard what he creates as a condition for his own wealth, but as the condition for other people's wealth and his own poverty.[164]

Therefore, what makes it economic alienation is that it separates the creator of material wealth from the owner of material wealth, which means that the creator is not the owner, and the owner is not the creator. So, the basic manifestation of economic alienation is that the more material wealth they create, the poorer they become; thus the creation is inversely proportional to ownership. On this regard, Marx stresses again:

> The laws of political economy express the estrangement of the worker in his object thus: the more the worker produces, the less he has to consume; the more values he creates, the more valueless, the more unworthy he becomes.[165] The worker becomes all the poorer the more wealth he produces, the more his production increases in power and range.[166] It is true that labor produces for the rich wonderful things-but for the worker it produces privation. It produces palaces-but for the worker, hovels.[167]

Evidently, economic alienation belongs to the category of labor; its species difference (basic nature) is that the wealth created by one's own labor is seized by others, that is, his labor is "exploited." In this sense, "being exploited" and "economic alienation" are actually the same concept. Therefore, economic alienation, like other alienations, is also caused by coercion and is thus a coercive behavior. Therefore, Marx says, "His labor is therefore not voluntary, but coerced; it is forced labor.... Its alien character emerges clearly in the fact that as soon as no physical or other compulsion exists, labor is shunned like the plague."[168] So what is the coercion that generates economic alienation? In other words, what is the root cause of economic alienation and exploitation?

*Root causes of economic alienation: monopoly of economic power and monopoly of political power*

The monopoly and the imbalance of power—economic power and political power—are the root causes of oppression, exploitation, and alienation. The root causes of economic alienation or exploitation lie in power monopoly and power imbalance. This is because groups with a power monopoly or excessive power are bound to rely on power and other coercive means to seize the surplus value created by groups with no or too little power and make them perform alienated labor to create wealth that does not belong to them.

Economic power monopoly can be divided into two types: seller's monopoly in the product market and buyer's monopoly in the labor market. The reason these two monopolies are the sources of exploitation and economic alienation, as Samuelson says, is that monopoly, whether it is the seller's monopoly in the product market or the buyer's monopoly in the labor market, means that the monopolist controls the price to a certain extent, which inevitably leads to the deviation between price and value, and to non-equivalent exchange. Non-equivalent exchange is the law of monopoly price, just as equivalent exchange is the law of free competition. However, the seller's monopoly in the product market, whose monopoly leads to the deviation of the product price from product value, is bound to offer a higher price than the value or the marginal cost.

> "The greatest bane of monopoly is not that it extracts monopoly profits, but that the monopoly price stipulated by it is far higher than the price determined by society according to marginal cost.... The real bane of monopoly is the deviation between price and marginal cost caused by human beings."[169] "The separation of price and marginal cost caused by monopoly means the exploitation of labor... Trade Unions' actions to raise wages in monopolistic enterprises eliminate such exploitation. As the whole society is exploited, changing this situation becomes a mission for the antitrust policy."[170]

The buyer's monopoly in the labor market, whose monopoly leads to the deviation between labor price and labor value, is bound to make labor price lower than labor value, that is, labor price or wage is lower than labor value and lower than marginal products of labor. The difference between wages and labor value or marginal products is undoubtedly the surplus value created by laborers and seized by capitalists and landlords. This is the exploitation of laborers by capitalists and landlords. In his definition of exploitation, Robinson writes, "Exploitation usually refers to that wages are lower than value of marginal material products."[171] Therefore, the exploitation of workers by landlords and capitalists, that is, the difference in wages below the value of labor or the marginal products of labor, is the inevitable result of the buyer's monopoly in the labor market, as Samuelson says: "The exploitation comes from the monopolized power of employers when they buy laborers (so-called 'buyer's monopoly')."[172]

It can be concluded that exploitation originates from the monopoly of economic power, that is, the buyer's monopoly in the labor market and the seller's monopoly in the product market. Therefore, Roemer says, "under the capitalist system, any commodity is exploited, not just the labor force." So, can we attribute the main source of exploitation to the seller's monopoly in the product market and the buyer's monopoly in the labor market? Samuelson's answer to this question is positive.[173]

In fact, as exploitation originates from power monopoly, it is bound to be proportionate to the level, strength, and size of the monopolized power, which means that the higher, stronger, and greater the power is, the stronger and deeper the exploitation will be; the lower, weaker, and smaller the power is, the weaker and lighter the exploitation will be. The supreme power of a country or society undoubtedly belongs to the category of political power. Therefore, political power dominates and controls economic power and is higher, greater, and stronger than economic power. In this sense, political power is the highest, greatest, and strongest power. Therefore, if economic power monopoly is bound to lead to exploitation, then political power monopoly is bound to lead to deeper exploitation. As Ma Yongjun has already observed, "Lack of a civil society, lack of democracy, as well as political power monopoly by some people, is the social basis for the continuation of political exploitation."[174]

So, what is the exploitation mode of the monopoly of political power? Ma Yongjun replies, "Political exploitation is concentrated on privileges, which means the monopoly of public resources. A privileged individual, through his monopoly of public resources, seizes the work of other individuals without compensation."[175] How true these words are! However, the control of public resources, that is, the control of tax revenue, state-owned resources, and public resources, is only one aspect of the exploitation due to a monopoly of political power; on the other hand, the government's control of the market economy is another aspect: government's control is the most fundamental means for the group with a political power monopoly to oppress and exploit the group without political power.

Admittedly, it is common that political power controls tax revenue and the state-owned and public resources in any country. The control of political power on tax revenue, state-owned resources, and public resources does not necessarily lead to exploitation. This is because in a country with a universal electoral democracy, everyone holds the supreme power equally, so everyone controls tax revenue, state-owned resources, and public resources equally. If individuals share equal control of taxes and state-owned and public resources, then control of political power will obviously not lead to exploitation. On the contrary, in non-democratic countries, such as those under despotic rule, some people monopolize the supreme power and political power, while others do not have any power, so there emerge two major groups: those who monopolize political power and those who do not have political power. In this way, only the group with a political power monopoly can control tax revenue, state-owned resources, and public resources, and this group is, therefore, bound to seize the interests of the group without political power for free by controlling tax revenue, state-owned resources, and public resources. Thus, controlling tax revenue, state-owned resources, and public resources is the main mode of exploitation by political power monopoly.

Therefore, Wright says, "The ability of the national bureaucratic elite to seize the surplus is based on their effective control over the productive resources of society."[176] Ma Yongjun further points out that this kind of exploitation mode of a political power monopoly existed universally in the West, but in China, it encompasses all other forms of exploitation:

> Where there is a collective existence, there is possibility of political exploitation, but only in the hierarchical collective is political exploitation institutionalized. In a democratic collective, any abuse of political power will be immediately pointed out and then corrected. Both ancient Greece and ancient Rome had populace politics, and Rome even set up a system of civil servants. In contrast, the ancient hierarchy in China maintained or even glorified, in the name of collectives, the domination of superiors over subordinates, which led to the politics of "concealment" and "deception." There was a permanent gap between officials and ordinary people in ancient Chinese society. Although political exploitation exists universally in the west, there are always resources to counter against it; however, political exploitation in China has been continuously improved and strengthened and become a mode of exploitation that encompasses all other forms of exploitation.[177]

So, exploitation and economic alienation can be divided into two categories. One is that the group with power monopoly relies on the economic power monopoly, mainly the monopoly of means of production, to seize the surplus value of the group without economic power or means of production. The other is that the group with political power monopoly relies on the political power monopoly, that is, the monopoly of the supreme power and political positions, to seize the surplus value of the group without political power or political positions. Therefore, in the so-called popular Marxist concept of exploitation, exploitation refers to the fact that the monopoly group of means of production relies on its monopoly to seize the fruits of the group of laborers without means of production. The exploitation in Marxism is only a specific kind of exploitation or economic alienation, namely, exploitation or economic alienation through the monopoly of economic power. In fact, there is another fundamentally different type of exploitation or economic alienation: exploitation and economic alienation through the monopoly of political power.

## The root of economic alienation: power imbalance

At a global level, the root of economic alienation or exploitation is not just power monopoly, but both power monopoly and power imbalance. This can be understood from two aspects. On the one hand, only class exploitation and class oppression originate from power monopoly because class exploitation and class oppression are the exploitation and oppression of the powerless group by the power monopoly group. On the other hand, an imbalance of power, with the monopoly of power as the extreme imbalance of power, will inevitably lead to exploitation and oppression. The only difference is that the power monopoly leads to class exploitation and oppression, while power imbalance without power monopoly leads to non-class exploitation and oppression.

Because power is a legitimate—approved by the general consent of members of society—dominating, and coercive force, there is actually no need for some people to monopolize power while some other people are totally deprived of power. As long as there is an imbalance of power, then those who have too much power will inevitably exploit and oppress those who have too little power.

> People are naturally ambitious, and their rights and desires can never be satisfied. If a class of people can plunder all other classes in pursuit of their own interests, they will certainly do so and make themselves as domineering and unrestricted as possible.[178]

The exploitation and oppression caused by this power imbalance, rather than by power monopoly, can be called "exploitation and oppression of strata," as Hume would like to put it. Since the implementation of universal suffrage democracy in Europe and the United States in the early 20th century, the exploitation and oppression that exist in those societies belong to the category of exploitation and oppression of strata rather than class exploitation and oppression. On the one hand, the capitalist countries in Europe and the United States have implemented universal suffrage democracy, which means everyone is in charge of the supreme power of the country on an equal footing, thus eliminating the monopoly of political power.[179] On the other hand, the universal suffrage democracy makes the supreme power of the state entirely and equally accessible to everyone, and the supreme power ultimately, according to the principle of majority rule, belongs to the people but is exercised by deputies elected by the people, namely, government officials. The political power, means of production, and economic power of the state and the government all belong to the people but are governed by government officials.

Given this, universal suffrage democracy eliminates not only the monopoly of political power, but also the monopoly of means of production and economic power. Furthermore, since universal suffrage democracy in capitalist countries in Europe and the United States, especially since the end of World War II, employee stock ownership has prevailed; "people's stock" ownership has been vigorously issued; participatory economic democracy, cooperative ownership, and welfare state system have been established. As a result, not only does every citizen have a share of economic power, but the vast majority of people also gradually become capital owners. Even in European and American countries where the polarization between the rich and the poor is the most serious, such as in the United States, the percentage of stockholders in the total population has risen from 60% in 1980 to 70% at present.

Clearly, European and American capitalist countries have eliminated, since the implementation of universal suffrage democracy, the monopoly of power—the monopoly of political power and economic power, thus eliminating class, class exploitation, and class oppression. However, the capitalist countries in Europe and the United States have not eliminated the exploitation and oppression of strata. In particular, the development of transnational corporations and global capitalism has made the economic power of the capitalist stratum more and more unbalanced with that of the working stratum and the masses. As far as the degree of exploitation and oppression of the working stratum by the capitalist stratum is concerned, it is much greater in the era of global capitalism after the 1970s than it was in the age of monopoly capitalism before the 1970s.

On the one hand, the turnover and profits of transnational corporations have increased substantially:

> The turnover of the 500 largest companies in the world increased by 11% in 1995. Their growth rate is four times faster than that of the world economy. In terms of profits, these transnational corporations have increased even more, reaching almost 15% in 1995, even up to 62% in the previous year.[180]

On the other hand, the real wages of workers and the masses in various countries have not increased correspondingly, but have shown a long-term downward trend:

> In the era of neoliberalism, the real wage growth rate of every country showed a long-term downward trend. The gap between real wages and labor productivity growth has expanded rapidly. From 1979 to 1995, the real wages of the 40% of the lowest wage workers in the United States decreased by 12% on average, while the real wages of the 60% of the lowest wage workers decreased by 9.8%. In other words, at the end of the 16 years, the average real wage of the 60% minimum wage workforce in the United States dropped by 10% compared with the beginning year. Figure 6-4 (in volume 2) also shows that the real wages of productive workers in the United States reached their post-war peak in 1972 and

have been declining since 1995, and have not yet returned to their peak levels. By contrast, CEO earnings were 42 times higher than the average worker's wages in 1982 and 411 times higher in 2005.[181]

Power imbalance is the root of oppression, exploitation, and economic alienation, so the degree of oppression, exploitation, and economic alienation is proportionate to the degree of power imbalance; however, class exploitation and class oppression caused by power monopoly is undoubtedly much more serious than exploitation and oppression of stratum caused by power imbalance alone. Therefore, in the era of global capitalism after the 1970s, the degree of exploitation and oppression of the working stratum by the capitalist stratum is much greater than that of the monopolistic capitalism before the 1970s but much less than that of the class exploitation and oppression of the proletariat by the bourgeoisie in the era of free competition capitalism in the 18th and 19th centuries.

In the age of the free competition capitalism of the 18th and 19th centuries, the class exploitation and oppression of the proletariat by the bourgeoisie were so serious—even Kelso and Adler, the authors of *The Capitalist Declaration*, who vigorously defended capitalism, admitted it—that it invited criticism not only from Marx and Engels and socialists in general, but also from Pope Leo XIII and Pius XI, as well as various social philosophers and reformers: "What all these men were criticizing was nineteenth-century capitalism that existed in England and the United States, the two countries in the world most advanced industrially. That nineteenth-century capitalism was unjust, no one can question."[182]

**State institutions that eliminate economic alienation: "democracy of universal suffrage by sortition;" "economic democracy of co-determination;" "welfare state system;" and "shareholder capitalism"**

Then the question is: can the elimination of the monopoly of power and the imbalance of power guarantee the elimination of oppression and exploitation of class and stratum, as well as of economic alienation? The answer is yes. There seems to be no doubt that public ownership of the means of production can eliminate the state system of power monopoly and power imbalance. Only with the public ownership of the means of production can everyone have the means of production and their economic power completely and equally, thus eliminating the imbalance of the means of production and economic power, as well as the oppression, exploitation, and economic alienation that inevitably result from them. In fact, it is not the case. As mentioned before, "the different degrees of love" as the law of human nature means that, in any society, no matter how noble his moral character, a man is always concerned with his own interests and only occasionally with interests of others; otherwise, he would deviate from "the different degrees of love" as the law of human nature and would not be human.

Given this, in any society, only private ownership can be efficient, while public ownership is bound to be inefficient. In a private society, the assets used by the private owners are owned by themselves, and their losses or gains are entirely borne by themselves, which means they will fully bear losses when there are losses and seize profits entirely when they make profits. This will undoubtedly motivate people to maximize profits at the lowest cost, as everyone would be eternally concerned with their own interests and only occasionally with the interests of others. Therefore, private ownership economy is an efficient economy.

On the contrary, public ownership does not possess this kind of efficiency mechanism. In public ownership, the assets used by everyone do not belong to themselves, and they neither bear the losses caused by themselves, nor gain the benefits from their improved efficiency. When they improve their efficiency, the benefits of their efficiency are shared by many people, so they can get very little from their improved efficiency. In a word, people are neither responsible for the losses they have caused nor accessible to the profits created by themselves. In this way, the public economy is doomed to be inefficient in any society, as everyone must be eternally concerned with his own interests and only occasionally with the interests of others.

In any society, public ownership is bound to be inefficient, so it violates the ultimate value standard of state institutions of "increasing the quantum of interests of everyone," and is thus a bad state institution. Only private ownership is efficient, so only private ownership meets the ultimate value standard of state institutions of "increasing the quantum of interests of everyone." It is thus a good state institution. This is not just the whole story. Abolishing private ownership and replacing it with public ownership also violates the value standards of state institutions, such as justice and freedom.

The private ownership of means of production and capital itself, just like the private ownership of means of livelihood and wealth, is not the root of oppression, exploitation, and economic alienation; only the private ownership that leads to monopoly and unbalanced private ownership of means of production or capital is the root of oppression, exploitation, and economic alienation. Today, the cooperatives in capitalist countries in Europe and the United States are still the private ownership of means of production and capital, but they have realized the equal ownership of capital and economic power among members; eliminated the monopoly of power and imbalance of power; and thus eliminated oppression, exploitation, and economic alienation and polarization between the rich and the poor. Therefore, as Kelso and Adler put it, it is only the concentration, monopoly, and imbalance of means of production and capital that should be eliminated, not the private ownership of means of production and capital:

> The root of the trouble was not the private ownership of capital, but the highly concentrated private ownership of capital. That being the cause, the remedy lies not in abolishing private property in capital, as Marx recommended, but rather in diffusing the private ownership of

*Humanity and liberty* 69

capital by bringing into existence new capitalists at a rate commensurate with the shift in the burden of production from human toil to capital instruments.[183]

In this way, if individuals own the means of production and capital, and if they do not exploit and oppress others, like the people in the European and American countries who now hold shares and have become the owners of capital, the means of production and capital they own become sacred and inviolable rights, just like their other private property. Or to use the welfare states, such as Sweden, as an example, although its per capita GNP ranked first in the world in 1974, Sweden is the country with the smallest gap between the rich and the poor. The pre-tax income of the people with the highest income, 10% of the population, is 144 times that of the people with the lowest income, 60% of the population. However, this gap is reduced by the high progressive tax and other tax policies adopted by the government, which has reduced the absolute average difference between the highest income and the lowest income in after-tax income to only three times. This means that the capitalist class and the working class have almost realized the just principle of distributing the value of marginal products according to production factors provided by them, such as labor, capital and land, thus almost eliminating oppression, exploitation, and economic alienation.

Undoubtedly, if systems such as "universal suffrage democracy," "economic democracy of co-determination," "welfare state system," and "shareholder capitalism" in Sweden and other European and American countries are further improved, the principle of justice in distribution according to production factors will be fully realized, thus eliminating oppression, exploitation, and economic alienation. In this way, the means of production and capital owned by these capitalists and the masses are as sacred and inviolable as their other private property. If we deprive them of their means of production and capital and implement public ownership, we will not only violate the principle of justice because of infringement of rights, but also violate the principle of liberty. We will deprive a person of the economic freedom to use and accumulate his own capital and become rich, just as ideological control and the lack of freedom of speech and press deprive a person of the freedom of thought to write and publish books, and become a greater thinker. This explains why Hayek once confessed, "I myself should certainly prefer to be without property in a land in which many others own something, than to have to live where all property is 'collectively owned' and assigned by authority to particular uses."[184]

As shown, in order to eliminate exploitation, economic alienation, and polarization between the rich and the poor, as well as the economic crisis of overproduction in capitalist countries in Europe and the United States today, we should never abolish the private ownership of means of production or capital and replace it with public ownership. Public ownership is not only inefficient but also runs counter to the ultimate value standard of state institutions of "promoting the quantum of interests of everyone." It also deprives everyone of their private property, which is against the value standards of state institutions, such as justice and liberty. Therefore, it is not the private ownership of means of production and capital that ought to be eliminated but the power imbalance between the capitalist stratum, the working stratum, and the masses: exploitation and economic alienation originate from the power imbalance rather than from private ownership.

To abolish exploitation and economic alienation, we don't need to abolish private ownership or capitalism. Capitalism is the most efficient state-owned system so far, and is thus most in line with the ultimate value standard of state institutions of "increasing the quantum of interests of everyone." It mainly relies on technological innovation, improved labor productivity, and reduction of production costs to increase the value of capital. Failing to increase value means the death of capitalism; thus, the persistent acceleration of technological innovation becomes part of the nature of the capitalist system. Therefore, what will replace the current global capitalist society in Europe and the United States must still be a capitalist society, of course, with no exploitation and economic alienation.

So, is this kind of society the cooperative capitalism? No! A cooperative system is a good system of mutual help and reciprocity among the masses. If it is regarded as the dominant economic system of a country, it will be an abominable system of injustice and non-freedom. On the one hand, the cooperative system, by restricting the share price and guaranteeing similar shares of each member, obviously violates the principle of economic freedom; on the other hand, no matter how much the share price of each member is, it is one vote per capita, which obviously violates the principle of economic justice. If we abide by the principles of justice and liberty, one share and one vote, and no restriction on equity, then it is no longer a real cooperative but a genuine capitalist joint stock company.

Indeed, whether from the development trend of capitalist means of production and capital ownership in Europe and the United States today or from the perspective of eliminating power imbalance and its exploitation and oppression, a capitalist society without exploitation and economic alienation would certainly implement the basic principle of cooperatives, that is, everyone is a shareholder, a private owner of capital, and a true owner of some capital in the future. This society is a kind of national capitalism, which is ultimately the so-called people's capitalism in the true sense. In this society, every individual has labor income and owns capital profits so that he can live a well-fed, well-heeled, truly free, and dignified life of "he who disobeys shall also eat"; he can also accumulate capital to realize his ideal of becoming a rich man.

However, the nature of things is that they are not homogeneous. Each individual is different from others in terms of talent, effort, luck, and family, and, thus brings different wealth, capital, and means of production to society. All of this wealth, capital, and means of production, however unequal, makes up their individual rights, and no one else has the right to interfere with, infringe upon, or deprive them; otherwise, it would violate the value standards of state institutions such as justice and liberty. Therefore, in a better capitalist society in the future, there will still exist social strata with varying wealth, capital, and means of production, with upper, middle, and lower social strata, just as there are upper, middle, and lower social strata in people's talents and efforts, but there will be no exploitation and economic alienation.

Given this, the imbalance of capital and economic power between the capitalist stratum and the working stratum or the masses in the European and American countries today should not be eliminated by depriving the capitalist stratum of capital and economic power; otherwise, it would violate the principles of justice and liberty. However, the power imbalance due to the greater economic power of the capitalist stratum can be counterbalanced by the power imbalance due to the greater political power of the working stratum or the masses in order to achieve the balance of power between the capitalist stratum and the working stratum or the masses, and ultimately eliminate exploitation and economic alienation. So, how on earth can we make the working stratum or the masses have greater political power to compete with the capitalist stratum's greater economic power, and thereby eliminate exploitation and economic alienation?

Clearly, first, like the European countries, Britain, Germany, France, and Sweden etc., we should establish strong trade unions and other popular political parties of the people, such as the Social Democratic Party, or the Socialist Party, or the Labor Party, who should then strive to become the ruling party so that the working stratum and the masses not only hold the supreme power of the state, but also hold important official positions of the government. This way they can gain the main political power of the state with a government that is strong enough to compete with the massive economic power of the capitalist stratum. And second, once the political parties of the masses, such as the Social Democratic Party, attain power, they should put the masses in charge of the supreme power of the state and institutionalize main government posts to ensure that the opposition party cannot abolish it if they come to power, as they would be ousted by the votes of the masses if they do so.

So, what is the system that enables the masses to take charge of the supreme power of the state and the main official positions of the government? The answer is undoubtedly that every citizen enjoys both full equality in their right to elect and be elected. This means that the answer can only be the system of "the universal suffrage democracy of sortation." The sortition election system not only guarantees that the majority of government posts must be held by the masses, but also ensures that every citizen enjoys full equality in their right to elect and be elected, thus making it possible for every citizen to have a voice in the supreme power of the state on an equal footing. In this sense, this system conforms to the principle of justice of

72  *Humanity and liberty*

full equality in political liberty and political power, and ultimately to the principle of people's sovereignty; this is just an electoral system. It is not just the revival of the sortition democracy of ancient Greece, but a revival with advanced forms such as the universal suffrage.

To sum up, the state institutions for eliminating exploitation and economic alienation are "democracy of universal suffrage by sortation," "economic democracy of co-determination," "welfare state system," and "shareholder capitalism." These state institutions undoubtedly have the following fundamental characteristics: they conform to the value standards of equality, liberty, and justice; this can only be realized in democratic countries. Therefore, the state institution for eliminating exploitation and economic alienation is ultimately constitutionalism, which conforms to the value standards of state institutions, which includes "humanity and liberty" as the highest value standard; "justice and equality" as the fundamental value standard; and "increasing the quantum of interests of everyone" as the ultimate value standard. Constitutionalism is a kind of democracy that holds the value standards of state institutions—such as liberty—as the guiding principles of the constitution and is governed by them.

### *Political alienation*

#### *The concept of political alienation*

Coercion means non-freedom and alienation. Politics, it goes without saying, is not only a kind of coercion, but also the most important, the most serious, and the highest-degree of coercion in any country and society, as politics is a kind of power rule that must be obeyed. So, can we say that the obedience of the ruled to any political power is a kind of political alienation where the ruled abandon their will and submit to the will of the ruler? No. Whether the obedience of the ruled to political power can be considered as political alienation or not depends entirely on whether the said political power reflects the will of the ruled. If the politics of a country embodies the public will and the will of every citizen, and then when the ruled obey that political power they are also obeying their own will. This means that they enjoy political liberty rather than suffer political alienation. On the contrary, if the politics of a country embodies only the will of the ruler, not the will of the ruled, the public will, or the will of every citizen, then the obedience of the ruled to this political coercion is political alienation, in which the ruled abandon their will and submit to the will of the ruler.

The reason is that under the political coercion that reflects one's own will, one's behaviors can be considered as political liberty. In contrast, political alienation is one's behavior under political coercion that does not reflect one's own will, and thus, it is the behavior that doesn't belong to one's self but to the political coercer. This means that political alienation includes a wide range of behaviors, as it not only belongs to the category of political behaviors, but also includes all behaviors governed by politics, such as economic behaviors, cultural behaviors, and social behaviors, ultimately all behaviors of social importance. For example:

Whether farmers work according to the system of fixing farm output quotas on the household basis or whether they follow the system of collective labor is part of the economic behavior category. However, if the dictator does not allow the system of contract production on the household basis and instead enforces the system of collaborative labor, then the labor of collective farmers, though an economic behavior, belongs to the category of political alienation. The work of scholars—writing and publishing—belongs to the category of cultural behavior. However, if the dictator does not allow these scholars to expose the dark side of the country but forces them instead to praise the merits and virtues of the country or write some love stories and funny tales which have nothing to do with state affairs, then their writing, which has nothing to do with state affairs, though a cultural behavior, belongs to the category of political alienation. The ethicists' behavior of establishing an ethics association belongs to the social behavior of assembly and association. However, if the dictator orders that the ethics society must be run by officials rather than the ethics scholars, and that only one ethics association can be established in the whole country, then the ethicists' behavior of establishing such an ethics association, which is run by the officials rather than by themselves, belongs to the category of political alienation.

It can be concluded that political alienation is not only the most coercive and serious alienation, but also the most extensive and almost all-inclusive alienation involving a wide range of behaviors. Therefore, it is an alienation with the most serious and extensive negative value and thus the fundamental obstacle for citizens in realizing their creative potential in all aspects, such as politics, economy, culture, and society. However, the way to eliminate political alienation is rather simple: if the state's politics embodies the will of all citizens, political alienation will be eliminated. Under what circumstances, then, does politics embody the will of all citizens in order to avoid political alienation? And under what circumstances does politics not embody the will of all citizens, allowing political alienation to occur?

*The root of political alienation*

Apparently, the key to the problem lies in whether the supreme power of the state is in the hands of all citizens or not. As mentioned earlier, whether one can make politics embody one's own will and proceed according to one's own will to enjoy political liberty or not depends entirely on whether one holds political power or not. Only when a person has political power can he make the politics proceed according to his will, enjoy political liberty, and avoid political alienation. If he does not have political power, he can neither make the politics proceed according to his will, nor enjoy political liberty, which means political alienation is bound to occur. In this way, as Marx points out, the root of political alienation lies entirely in the system of government that is followed: "monarchy is the complete manifestation of political alienation while a republic is the negation of political alienation within its domain."[185]

To be precise, only when democracy is practiced can every citizen enjoy political liberty and avoid political alienation; if non-democratic systems, such as despotism, are practiced, only a few people will enjoy political liberty, while the vast majority of citizens will inevitably suffer from political alienation. Since the times of Plato and Aristotle, the political system has been divided into four categories; monarchy, which is the system in which one person holds the supreme power; the republic is a system that allows a number of people to share the supreme power equally; monarchy is further divided into two major types: one type is despotic monarchy, despotism, unlimited monarchy, or absolute monarchy, in which one single individual holds the supreme power alone, that is, one individual holds the supreme power without the restriction from others and their organizations; the other type is called limited monarchy, decentralized monarchy, or incomplete monarchy, in which one single individual shares the supreme power unequally with others and their organizations, such as parliament, parliament of hierarchical councils, churches, nobles, lords, or local separatist regimes. A republic can also be divided into two types: one is oligarchy, an oligarchical or aristocratic republic, in which a few people share the supreme power equally; the other is called democracy or democratic republic, in which all people share the supreme power equally.

Non-democratic regimes, such as monarchy, limited monarchy, and oligarchical republic, are not the system that allows the supreme power of the state to be shared by all the people; they are the system that allows the supreme power of the state to be held by one person (monarch) or by a very few people (oligarchy). As a result, in the oligarchical republic, one the one hand, very few people hold the supreme power of the state equally and make politics proceed according to their own will, thus enjoying political liberty and avoiding political alienation. However, the overwhelming majority of the people obey politics not according to their own will, but only according to the will of the oligarchy. Thus, what the majority of people do is not the behavior which is done according to their own will and belonging to the people themselves, but the behavior done according to the will of the oligarchical ruler, which then reflects political alienation.

On the other hand, both the monarchy, which allows one individual to hold supreme power of the state without any restriction from others and their organizations, and the limited monarchy, which allows one individual to share the supreme power of the state unequally with others and their organizations, force the politics to proceed according to the will of the monarchy, though they may differ in their degree of enforcement. Therefore, as long as a country implements a monarchy, whether despotic or constitutional, then all people, except the monarch, obey politics not by their own will, but by the will of the monarch, therefore, what they do is not their own behavior according to their own will, but according to the will of the monarch. Their behavior is done according to the will of the monarch, and it is thus the monarch's behavior, not their own behavior, and thus is political alienation. This is the political alienation Marx talked about when he said, "Monarchy is the complete manifestation of this alienation."[186]

Indeed, on closer scrutiny, non-democratic systems, such as despotism, do not mean that only one individual or a few oligarchs in power have political liberty, it means that only one or a few oligarchs have the highest political liberty; officials at all levels, other than the monarch or a few oligarchs, do not have the highest political power, but they have some political power at other levels, so they also enjoy political liberty at some level except the highest level of political liberty; for example, the governor has the political liberty to conduct the politics of his province according to his will to some extent, similarly the mayor has the political liberty to conduct the politics of a township according to his will to some extent. Therefore, in non-democratic countries under a despotic regime there exists a monopoly of political power which creates two groups and two classes; the group that monopolizes political power (the official class), and the group that has no political power (the common people class). The common people class has no political power, so it has no political liberty and is in a state of total political alienation and enslavement. The official class monopolizes political liberty through monopolizing political power. The despot or a few oligarchs with the supreme power of the state enjoy the highest and complete political liberty and can thus completely avoid political alienation and enslavement. Officials at all levels have political power at all levels except the supreme state power, so they have political liberty at all levels except the highest political power. Therefore, each official is enslaved by only a few people, that is, his superiors, the despot, or a few oligarchs, and thus are in the state of political alienation only under the coercion of these few people. But they are also the masters who enslave an extremely large number of slaves (i.e. the common people) and thus enjoy extensive political liberty of varying degrees.

It can be concluded that political alienation mainly comes from the monopoly of political power: the monopoly of political power in non-democratic state systems, such as despotism, is the main source of political alienation. This means that democracy is the only state institution that can eliminate political alienation; a democracy eliminates the monopoly of political power, which means all citizens hold the supreme power of the state equally. In a democracy, both the ruled and the ruler hold the supreme power, which means both the ruled and the ruler are the supreme rulers; the ruled can make the state politics proceed according to their own will. As a result, every citizen, whether the ruled or the ruler, can enjoy political freedom equally and thus avoid political alienation.

## Consultative democracy and constitutional democracy of universal suffrage: state institutions for eliminating political alienation

On closer scrutiny, democracy takes many different forms, therefore not every democracy is a sufficient condition to eliminate national political alienation. First, democracy can be divided into a democracy of universal suffrage and a democracy of limited suffrage. A democracy of universal suffrage means that all the people in the country are considered citizens, while democracy of limited suffrage means that only some people in the country are considered citizens. In this way, if a country implements the system of democracy of limited suffrage, only a part of its people who are considered as citizens have political power and political liberty and can thus avoid political alienation, but the part of its people who are not considered as citizens have no political power or political liberty and are thus in a state of political alienation and enslavement.

The Athenian democracy in ancient Greece was a typical system of limited suffrage because slaves and women in Athens were not considered citizens and had no political power at the time; thus, they were in a state of political alienation and enslavement; only about one-tenth of the people in Athens were considered citizens, enjoyed political liberty and thus avoided political alienation. Only when a democracy of universal suffrage is practiced can every individual be considered a citizen and hold the supreme power equally, enjoy political liberty, and avoid political alienation. After World War II, citizenship is gradually owned equally by every individual in a democratic country, and democracy of universal suffrage has gradually been implemented which allowed every citizen to enjoy political liberty and avoid political alienation.

However, to be more precise, democracy of universal suffrage is only a necessary condition, not a sufficient condition, for every citizen to enjoy political liberty and avoid political alienation. Although democracy of universal suffrage allows all citizens to hold the supreme power equally, it also, realizing universal suffrage, must follow "the principle of majority rule." As a result of this principle, most people hold the supreme power, which may lead to the tyranny of the majority over the minority, cause the minority to lose their political liberty, and put the minority in a state of political alienation. So, how can we guarantee equal political liberty for both minority and majority to avoid political alienation? The only way is to implement deliberative and constitutional democracy: deliberative and constitutional democracy of universal suffrage is a necessary and sufficient condition for every citizen to enjoy political liberty and avoid political alienation. The reasons are as follows:

On the one hand, the deliberative democracy of universal suffrage system was created to solve the contradiction between the most profound nature of democracy (democracy is the regime in which all the citizens hold the supreme power equally) and the only way to realize democracy (the principle of majority rule). It is thus the most important way to realize equal supreme power for all citizens by both adhering to majority rule and protecting minority rights; it is a democracy that achieves its democratic legitimacy through equal consultation between the majority and the minority to hold the supreme power together and equally. It is a state institution in which all citizens, both the majority and the minority, both the dominant group and the marginalized groups, hold supreme power on an equal footing and avoid political alienation.

On the other hand, deliberative democracy, like the democracy of majority rule, may still possibly lead to democratic tyranny by violating the value standards of state institutions, such as liberty. The only difference between them is that the democracy of the majority rule is tyranny by the majority, whereas deliberative democracy is tyranny by all. As Lord Acton says, power, by its very nature, tends to be abused and corrupted, and the supreme power is absolutely bound to be corrupted: "Power leads to corruption, and absolute power leads to absolute corruption."[187] This is why deliberative democracy may still degenerate into tyranny: deliberative democracy may infinitely violate the value standards of state institutions, such as liberty.

Therefore, the way to avoid the degeneration of deliberative democracy into tyranny to guarantee the equal enjoyment of political liberty by every citizen and avoid political alienation is to subject deliberative democracy to the guidance and restriction of the value standards of state institutions, which include humanity and liberty as the highest value standards of state institutions, justice and equality as the fundamental value standards of state institutions, "increasing the quantum of interests of everyone" as the ultimate value standard of state institutions. This means that the supreme power which is held by the majority, the minority, and their equal participation is subject to the guidance and restriction of these value standards of state institutions. This kind of democracy, in which all citizens and the supreme power they hold equally are effectively restricted by the value standards of state institutions, is called a constitutional democracy. Constitutional democracy is a democracy that regards the value standards of state institutions such as liberty as the guiding principle of the constitution and subjects itself to the control of these value standards.

In this way, the state institution for eliminating political alienation is exactly the same as that for eliminating economic alienation. This state institution is a constitutional democracy. As constitutional democracy is a democracy that makes the value standards of state institutions, such as liberty, the guiding principle of its constitution and subjects itself to the restriction of these value standards, it must not only follow the principle of political equality, but also follow the principle of majority rule and protection of minority rights. Finally the majority and the minority groups hold the supreme power through consultation on the basis of equality. In a word, constitutional democracy must be consultative democracy. Therefore, Rawls says, "A good constitutional democracy, the term I used at the beginning, can also be understood as deliberative democracy."[188] Simon Chambers also wrote, "Almost everyone agrees with negotiation theory in some form (it's hard not to). More and more people regard constitutional democracy as a need for consultation in some fundamental ways."[189]

## Social alienation

### The concept of social alienation

Social alienation, as its name implies, is the behavior of subordinating to the social will against one's own will; it is not the behavior which is done out of his own will and therefore, does not belong to the individual himself; it is the behavior that is done according to the social will and thus belongs to the society. Then, one may wonder, does society have a will, too? Yes, it does. The so-called society, namely, an organized group of people, is a group of people or a community of more than two people joined together by certain interpersonal relationships. Therefore, the so-called social will is the will of the crowd, the will of the collective, and the will of others. In this sense, the so-called social alienation is the behavior of subordinating one's own will to the will of the crowd, the collective, and the will of others. Therefore, compared with the concept of economic alienation, whose extension is rather simple and narrow, the concept of social alienation has an extension that is not only broad and complex, but also pervasive, through its multifarious manifestations, in daily life. Therefore, Georg Lukacs says,

> An excellent, wise, and self-sacrificing fighter, although he can see the alienation in his labor and will naturally resist it, does not even think of getting rid of the chain of alienation in his personal relationship with his wife. Therefore, only in the activities of personal daily life can we finally overcome social alienation.[190]

Given this, submissions, ranging from the submission to the will of one's spouse, parents, and friends, to the submission to the will of colleagues, the crowd, and the leaders of the work unit, belong to social alienation. Social alienation is the behavior that one does, which does not belong to oneself, but belongs to one's spouse, parents, friends, colleagues, the crowd, and the leaders of the work unit. So, among such multifarious manifestations of social alienation, are there some types that are more important and representative than other types of social alienation? Yes. First of all, as society is a group of people, the basic expression of social will is undoubtedly the so-called will of the general public, public opinions, and ordinary demands. Therefore, the basic manifestation of social alienation is the submission of one's own will to the public will, and behavior that one does, which does not belong to oneself but to the public. What the existentialist philosophers, such as Rousseau, Nietzsche, Heidegger, and Sartre, have tried to reveal, as presented in the following, is this type of social alienation:

> Barbarians live their own lives, while people in society are always in a state of panic, always aware that they live in the opinions of others. In other words, they derive their judgment of the meaning of their own existence totally from the judgments of others.[191]

"Among the people, I live like the people, but do not think like myself thinking; and gradually I feel that people want to expel me from myself and rob myself of my soul."[192]

> It is not he who exists; others take his existence away from him. Other people… It's a neutral thing and means ordinary people. Ordinary people launched dictatorship over us: we enjoy the pleasures ordinary people enjoy; we judge literature and art the way how ordinary people judge literature and art; we even retreat from 'the public' the way how ordinary people retreat from 'the public'; we feel angry about what ordinary people are angry about.[193]

To summarize all of these arguments in one sentence: "Hell is other people."[194]

Second, since society is a crowd and a collective, what the social will represents is obviously the will of leaders or senior officials, because leadership is often the spokesman of the collective. Therefore, the typical manifestation of social alienation is that one subordinates one's own will to the will of one's superiors, or the will of the leaders, and carries out behavior that belongs not to oneself but to the leaders. For example, I don't want to attend those boring meetings, to write those popular articles, or even to glorify reality and praise the virtues of the country, but the leaders want me to do so, therefore, fear of offending the leaders, makes me follow these orders. This behavior is a typical manifestation of social alienation—submitting to the will of leaders. In fact, as Confucius already remarked on it a long time ago, "If the rulers favor courtesy, then the common people dare not be rude; if the rulers favor integrity, then the common people dare not disobey; if the ruler favors good faith, then the common people dare not be ungrateful."[195] These "dare nots" of the common people are submission of their own will to the will of their superiors and are thus a typical manifestation of social alienation.

As a representation of social will, the will of leaders and the will of the public have a common weakness: their will is neither permanent nor universal and is a rather fickle and specific thing. Therefore, these two kinds of will are not the standard expression of social will. Then, what is the standard manifestation of social will? Obviously, the standard manifestation of social will are the standards, norms, and rules of conducts formulated by society, which are essentially laws and morals. Laws and morals are permanent and universal, and thus are the standard manifestation of social will. If the laws and morals are not the manifestations of the will of every citizen—hence not the manifestation of my will—my submission to these norms will be a standard social alienation. The standard manifestation of social alienation means that I subordinate my will to the social norms and obey the rules which do not embody the public will. Take the morality of altruism that is prevalent in an autocratic society as an example. This morality demands me to devote myself selflessly to others and society: I will be a villain if I am not altruistic and a gentleman if I am altruistic. I know this morality is abominable. However, if I violate it, I cannot survive in the society. So, I have to abide by this morality and even fabricate some lies about how altruistic I am, thus making myself a hypocrite. These behaviors constitute a standard social alienation.

*The root of social alienation and ways to eliminate alienation: existentialist theories*

Conformity to the public, subordination to the superior, compliance with social norms, obedience to the social will, as we know, all belong to the category of the so-called "socialization." Therefore, social alienation primarily originates from socialization: social alienation is the socialization of social will that does not embody the public will. Then, what is the cause of this alienation? A systematic study of this question has been done, I am afraid, only by the existentialists. However, their conclusion is rather radical: social alienation is the nature of social life.

Nietzsche's argument on this conclusion is his "last man theory." This theory holds that the root of alienation is society; as long as a person lives in society and with others, he cannot help letting society and others dominate him, take away his freedom of choice, and alienate him into a mediocre "last man" without his own personality: "All contacts between people—'social'—always fall into an inevitable non-innocence. The whole society always causes people to become mediocre in some way, somewhere and sometimes."[196]

Heidegger's argument on this question can be called "the average man theory." This theory expounds that the essential relationship between people is to eliminate the differences and prominence so that the relationship between everyone becomes the relationship between people who are same and average.

> Being average is a kind of existential nature of ordinary people. Ordinary people exist essentially for the state of being average.... Being average predetermines what is possible and what is permissible to take risks, and it guards any exceptions that rush in. Any superior state is

quietly suppressed. Everything original has been smoothed overnight. Everything that has been striving is at hand. Any secret has lost its power. This annoyance of the average state also opens up an essential tendency of being here, which we call the smoothness of all possibilities of existence. Keeping distance, averaging state and leveling effect are the ways of ordinary people's existence. These ways form what we call 'public opinion.'[197]

In this way, as long as a person lives in a society and is part of the crowd, he cannot but lose his liberty and be at the mercy of the ordinary people, thus creating the selfhood that the ordinary people choose for themselves, that is, the selfhood that does not have a unique personality and is not his own selfhood, but rather the selfhood that he chooses for himself; it is not his own unique personality, without his own and true self. Clearly, ordinary people, others, and society are the root causes of social alienation.

Sartre's argument on this issue is his famous "gaze theory." According to this theory, as long as I live in society and among other people, I am under the gaze of others, and will lose the freedom of choice and become a being-in-itself according to the will of others. In this way, no matter what others do to me, the gaze and existence of others objectively deprive me of freedom of choice and bring me alienation; on the other hand, my existence and my gaze also objectively deprive others of freedom of choice and cause alienation to others: "Therefore, respect for others' freedom is an empty word, because even if we can assume that we can respect others' freedom, every attitude we adopt towards others is also a trample on the freedom we intend to respect."[198] Moreover, the fact is that I subjectively try to make others submit to my will while others subjectively try to make me submit to their will. Therefore, the essential relationship between me and others is a tricky relationship aimed at depriving each other of their freedom of choice and alienating each other: "My constant concern is to keep others' objectivity, and my relationship with the object-other is essentially caused by tricks designed to keep them as objects."[199] Therefore, in any case, others are always the root cause of my alienation, and thus my hell: "Hell is other people."[200]

In short, from the existentialist perspective, society and others are the root cause of social alienation. Then, to eliminate social alienation, I must escape from society and others. Nietzsche is more radical, believing that in order to eliminate social alienation, one must be a transcendental hermit: "Live in seclusion! Then you can live your own life."[201] On the contrary, Heidegger and Sartre are more moderate, advocating for a secular loner. Sartre uses the protagonist Roquentin in *Nausea* to demonstrate his structure of life. Roquentin is not a hermit away from the secular world, but a loner living in the secular world: "I am alone in this happy and normal voice of people."[202] As Heidegger points out earlier, it is impossible to escape society and stay away from the secular world.[203]

This is the existentialist perspective of alienation. It is neither a theory of economic alienation nor a theory of political alienation, but a theory of social alienation. Existentialism is actually the first theory that describes the phenomenon of social alienation, reveals its root causes, and explores ways to eliminate it, and thus achieves epoch-making significance in the history of studies on alienation. However, existentialism overgeneralizes when it asserts that social alienation is the nature of social life and that society is the root of social alienation. Social alienation is not the nature of all kinds of social life, but the nature of some kind of social life. In fact, social alienation is the nature of the kind of social life without the rule of law, without democracy, and without human rights. Therefore, the root of social alienation is not society, but the society without rule of law, democracy, and human rights.

*Roots of social alienation and ways to eliminate alienation: realizing the society of the rule of law, democracy, and human rights and cultivating individuals who pursue self-realization*

First of all, if a society is ruled by law, then any coercion of the society, as Hayek says, must conform to its social norms (laws and morals): "Under the rule of law, government can infringe a person's protected private sphere only as punishment for breaking an announced general rule."[204] Secondly, if a society is democratic, then all citizens of that society can hold the supreme power of society equally so that social management can be carried out according to their own will, and social norms can be consented to as a manifestation of the public will.

> Only when society is managed democratically can social autonomy be fully realized, that is, the autonomy of individuals living among people who are interrelated with each other. Only in a democracy can all members of society come up with their own rules to govern general affairs and place themselves under the constraints of these rules.[205]

Thus, in a democratic society ruled by law, any coercion imposed on me by the will of society, the will of the leadership, or the will of the public must conform to the social norms agreed upon by all members of society, and thus embody the public will that includes my own will. Therefore, when I obey the social will, I am also obeying my own will; when I obey social norms, I am obeying my own will; when I follow the will of the crowd, I am also following my own will; when I socialize, I reveal my personality. Therefore, my behavior is done out of freedom and is thus not social alienation.

On the contrary, in a society without the rule of law or democracy, social management can only be carried out according to the will of the ruler, not the will of all members of society. This is because the social will embodies only the will of the ruler, not the will of all the members of society; the social norms embody only the will of the ruler, not the public will of all members in the whole society. Therefore, when I obey the social will, I am giving up my own will; when I obey the social norms, I am suppressing my own will; when I follow the crowd, I am violating my own will; and when I socialize, I lose my own personality. In this way, what I do does not belong to myself, but belongs to society and others, and is, thus, social alienation.

As demonstrated, the reason why people suffer social alienation is not that they create the society and live in the society, as existentialism insists, but because they create and live in a society not governed by rule of law and democracy; thus, a society not governed by rule of law and democracy is the root cause of social alienation. Therefore, the way and the route to eliminate social alienation is not to escape from the society as advocated by existentialism—neither to be a transcendental hermit nor to be a mundane loner—but to realize the rule of law and democracy.

However, is the realization of governing by rule of law and democracy sufficient for eliminating social alienation? No! Because even in a society ruled by law and democracy, one cannot help having a behavior that cannot be explicitly regulated by the vast number of social norms or cannot help having behavior that deviates from social norms. Thus, in a democratic society governed by law, there are still many conflicts among self-will, others' will, will of leaders, and the public will, and it is inevitable that they cannot be all compromised. In such a case, how can a person carry out his own will and avoid social alienation? To achieve this, there must be two conditions: one is the objective condition that he must enjoy human rights, and the other is the subjective condition that he must ardently pursue self-realization.

Why is the enjoyment of human rights necessary for eliminating social alienation? The reason is that according to Maslow's theory of psychology, on the one hand, people's basic needs can be divided into five categories arranged from low to high level: physiological needs, safety needs, love needs, self-esteem needs, and self-fulfillment needs; on the other hand, relatively low-level needs take precedence over and are stronger than relatively high-level needs while high-level needs emerge after low-level needs are satisfied. Although the need for liberty is the basic need of human beings, it is obviously not more basic, lower, stronger, or of higher priority than the physiological need. So, Harold Laski says,

> Those who understand the daily lives of the poor, those who understand their acute sense of catastrophe at all times, those who understand their vain pursuit of good things from time to time, will well realize that freedom is not worth a penny without economic security.[206]

In a general sense, when a person's own will conflicts with other people's will (leadership will, people's will, or social will), and he is in a dilemma where he cannot achieve both ends, which means he is a situation of "he who does not obey, neither shall he eat," then he will have no choice but to obey the will of others and suffer from social alienation. Only when he is in a situation where "he who does not obey shall also eat" can he choose to disobey and to persist in his own will to avoid social alienation.

But what kind of society is a society where "he who does not obey, neither shall he eat"? It is a society without human rights. On the contrary, a society with human rights is the society where "he who does not obey shall also eat" because the so-called "human rights," as mentioned above, are the necessary, bottom-line minimum rights for a person to survive and develop as long as he is a member of the human society and is a human being. Therefore, in a society where human rights are enjoyed, anyone, as long as he does not violate the human rights of others and is a member of a society, is entitled to human rights and the right to basic material needs, regardless of how much he works, how much he contributes, and whether he is accustomed to obeying or not obeying the will of others, the will of the people, and the will of leadership. Thus, the humanistic principle is that "he who obeys eats, and he who does not obey shall also eat." On the contrary, if in a society "he who obeys eats, but he who does not obey, neither shall he eat," then this society violates the human rights principle that "as long as a member of human society, he should enjoy the right to basic material needs," and it therefore is a society without human rights.

To sum up, only when people live in a society where they enjoy human rights can they abandon the fear of being "he who does not obey, neither shall he eat," only then can they dare disobey and avoid social alienation. On the contrary, if we live in a society without human rights, we will dare not disobey for fear that "he who does not obey, neither shall he eat," and we will thus be bound to suffer from social alienation. Therefore, the rule of law and democracy alone cannot eliminate social alienation; to eliminate social alienation, we must also have human rights. Then, can we say that as long as a person lives in a society ruled by law, democracy, and enjoys human rights, will not suffer social alienation?

No. The realization of governing by the rule of law, democracy, and enjoyment of human rights is only the objective condition for eliminating social alienation. To avoid social alienation, a person must have the subjective condition, which means that he must have a passion for pursuing self-realization and therefore love liberty. In a society ruled by law, democracy, and human rights, even though an individual still survives despite his disobedience, such disobedience makes him to lose a lot of benefits which can be gained with his obedience. In this sense, if a person does not have the passionate pursuit of self-realization, why will he refuse to obey the leadership and the masses to get greater benefits? Obviously, only when he pursues self-realization passionately and, therefore, loves liberty dearly can he tolerate the loss of not following his own way but that of the crowd to avoid social alienation. Therefore, Lukacs says, "Alienation is ultimately a social phenomenon, so only through social channels can we overcome this social phenomenon."[207] However, "within the scope of inevitable sociality, people's life process is

*Humanity and liberty* 85

ultimately their own thing; whether people want to live materially and alienated, or want to realize their real personality through their own behavior, depends on people themselves."[208]

It can be concluded that a person's passionate pursuit of self-realization is a necessary condition for him to avoid social alienation. The important role of this condition in eliminating social alienation can be seen from the fact that there exist people with no social alienation in any society. The difference lies only in that in a society ruled by law, democracy, and human rights, if individuals want to avoid social alienation, there is no need for their resistance and sacrifice, so everyone can avoid social alienation if they want to. On the contrary, in a society without the rule of law, democracy, and human rights, if people want to avoid social alienation, they must resist tenaciously and suffer tremendous sacrifices. As a result, only very few people can avoid social alienation. These people are praised by Nietzsche and Chuang Tzu as the transcendent hermits, by Heidegger and Sartre as the mundane loners, and by Marx as the solitary travelers, who "go their own way and let others talk."

To sum up, social alienation is different from economic alienation and political alienation. The causes of economic alienation and political alienation are social and objective, not individual and subjective: economic alienation is caused by power—power monopoly and imbalance of economic power and political power; political alienation is mainly due to the monopoly of political power in non-democratic states, like under despotic rule. Therefore, the way to eliminate them is to transform society rather than individuals, which means to realize constitutional democracy and eliminate monopoly and imbalance of economic power and political power. On the contrary, the causes of social alienation are not only social and objective, but also personal and subjective. The objective cause of social alienation is the lack of rule of law, democracy, and human rights in the society, and the subjective cause of social alienation is the lack of passionate pursuit of self-realization in individuals. Therefore, the way to eliminate social alienation is double-fold: the objective condition and route to eliminate social alienation is to realize a society ruled by law, democracy, and human rights, and the subjective condition and route to eliminate social alienation is to cultivate individuals who passionately pursue self-realization.

Nevertheless, the ways to eliminate social alienation, economic alienation, and political alienation ultimately coincide in an approach represented by "constitutional democracy." On the one hand, as mentioned above, the rule of law belongs to the first principle of liberty, that is, "the principle of rule of law of liberty"; human rights belong to the principle of equality, that is, "the principle of complete equality of human rights." Therefore, the so-called society governed by rule of law, human rights, and democracy are democratic societies that follow the value standards of state institutions, such as "equality" and "liberty," and are thus constitutional democratic societies. On the other hand, whether the vast majority of people can pursue self-realization and love liberty without social alienation or not depends

86  *Humanity and liberty*

entirely on the society in which they live—whether they live in a society ruled by law, democracy, and human rights, or whether they live in a society of constitutional democracy. Only when people live in such a constitutional democratic society will they achieve liberty without resistance or sacrifice; thus in this society, most people are bound to pursue self-realization and love liberty to avoid social alienation. Constitutional democracy is, indeed, the only ideal state institution.

### Religious alienation

#### The concept of religion

Religious alienation is undoubtedly a very complex concept. To understand this concept, we must start from the very beginning and ask the question, what is religion? In Western languages, the word religion comes from the Latin word *"religare"* or *"religio"*: the former means "connection," referring to the connection between man and God; the latter means "respect," referring to man's respect for God. In Chinese, *zong* ("宗") means to worship ancestral gods: "*Zong* means worship of temples."[209] Religion (*zong-jiao*; 宗教) in Chinese refers to using gods to civilize people: "Saints are guided by gods to lead the world!"[210]

It can be seen from the Chinese and Western etymologies that all religions are activities of worshipping gods. Can religion, then, be defined as the activity of worshipping gods? The answer is, yes: the definition of religion is exactly the same as its etymology. Having faith in the existence of gods, as Max Müller says, is the fundamental characteristic that distinguishes religion from other human activities: "One of the basic elements of all religions is the recognition of the existence of gods."[211] This recognition, on the one hand, is subjectively manifested as the belief and emotional experience of worshipping gods; on the other hand, it is objectively manifested as behaviors, organizations, and systems that worship gods. Therefore, the definition of religion can be condensed into the activities of worshipping a deity. But what is a deity?

The so-called deity is a general term for all forms of supernatural beings, such as gods, demons, ghosts, spirits, souls, and so on. As Taylor says, gods, devils, spirits, and souls are essentially the same: "Soul, devil and angel have different names, but their essence is the same."[212] So what is that essence in these supernatural beings which is same? It is a spiritual entity: gods and spirits are spiritual entities. The so-called entity, as we all know, is something that can exist independently. The spiritual entity includes not only the non-material, pure spiritual entity (cognition, emotion, will) but also the material entity that has spirit and spirituality (intangible, illusory, and subtle, etc.). An example of the former is the God of the Christian Trinity, and an example of the latter is the contemporary European peasants who regard the soul as objects that are "as intangible as fog."[213]

In this way, the deity, like the spirit, has cognition, emotion, and will, is the dominator and master of all the activities of the body in which it resides, can enter and leave matters of all forms—human body, animal body, and even an object—and still exist independently. In this sense, the deity is defined as an independent spiritual entity that can control, enter, and leave all forms of matter and has knowledge, emotion, and will. From the point of view that a deity has properties of cognition, emotion, and will, the deity has been personified, which means that the nature of deity is the alienation of the nature of humans; from the point of view that a deity is a spiritual entity that can enter and leave all forms of matter and exist independently, an illusory and unreal supernatural being. In a word, a deity is a personalized supernatural being.

Any supernatural being, whether soul or spirit or god or devil, is a spiritual entity and a personified supernatural being. Their difference lies only in the place, form, and function of their existence: the supernatural beings existing in humans and other forms of animals are mostly called souls; the supernatural beings existing in objects are mostly called spirits, and the supernatural beings that exist in the vast space dominating the souls and spirits are mostly called gods or demons. After careful examination of the many gods believed by the nations across the world, Edward Burnett Taylor concludes:

> Just as the soul is considered to be the cause of man's ordinary life and activities, spirits, something similar to the soul of man, are considered to be the cause of all the events that bring bliss and disasters to the human world as well as of all of the various physical phenomena of the outside world.[214]
>
> The position of the supreme gods among the lower-level spirits is the same as that of the officials and the emperor among the masses. Gods are different from souls and spirits, but this difference is more the difference in their degree than the difference in their essence. They are individual spirits that dominate other individual spirits.[215]

It is clear that there is no essential difference among beliefs in gods, beliefs in spirits, and beliefs in souls. They are all beliefs in spiritual entities, beliefs in the existence of personified supernatural beings, and beliefs in a deity. Therefore, they all belong to the category of religion, which can be defined as follows: religion is the activity of worshipping supernatural beings, which is the surface definition of religion; religion is the activity of worshipping personified supernatural beings, which is the deep definition of religion. Given this, there can be no religion without a deity, but religion can exist without gods. From this, we can see that there are two main religions without gods. One is the religion believing in fairies, such as the "mana" worship by the Polynesian people. The other, as Edward Burnett Taylor says, is the religion that believes in the soul: "Respect for the ghost of the dead constitutes one of the broad branches of human religion."[216]

88  *Humanity and liberty*

*Concepts of religious alienation*

Once the concept of religion is clarified, it is not difficult to understand what religious alienation is. Religious alienation is the alienation by the deity as the enslaver, whereas the alienation by humans as the enslaver is secular alienation, namely, economic alienation, political alienation, and social alienation. The concept of religious alienation seems simple, but it is rather complicated. Due to its duality, religious alienation is actually not a single concept but contains two concepts. This duality is determined by the duality of the concept of alienation. As mentioned before, alienation as a scientific term is divided into two parts: one is alienation as a general scientific term, referring to the transformation and change of things into alien things; the other is alienation as a basic concept of humanism, referring to behaviors that individuals do, which are alien to them and doesn't belong to their selves.

Accordingly, religious alienation as a scientific term is also divided into two parts. One is the religious alienation as a general scientific term, which means that deities and religions are nothing but the alienated and transformed forms of the nature of humans: "The personality of God itself is nothing but the alienated and objectified personality of human beings."[217] The other is religious alienation as a humanistic concept, which refers to people's behavior according to the will of a deity rather than according to their own will; what they do does not belong to themselves, but belongs to the deity. Of course, what we study here is the religious alienation as a humanistic concept.

In terms of its inherent nature, this kind of "religious alienation" obviously belongs to "voluntary alienation"; it is the alienation of religious believers who voluntarily give up their own will and submit to the will of the deity. However, why do religious believers abandon their will voluntarily and yield to the will of the deity? Because believers think that their blessings and misfortunes are all determined by the deity. Religious believers voluntarily abandon their will and obey the will of the deity in order to get rid of sufferings and are thus alienated, just like workers who voluntarily abandon their will for wages and obey the will of capitalists, and are thus alienated. The reason why both kinds of people are alienated is that both are coerced. Economic alienation occurs when capitalists hold capital, which is a kind of coercion; religious alienation occurs when the deity holds the determining power of blessings and misfortunes. Is this determining power of blessings and misfortunes not stronger coercion? The nature of the believers' coercion, enslavement, and non-freedom in submitting to the will of the deity finds its embodiment in a passage by God in *The Book of Deuteronomy* in The Bible:

> But if you will not obey the voice of the Lord your God or be careful to do all his commandments and his statutes that I command you today, then all these curses shall come upon you and overtake you. Cursed

shall you be in the city, and cursed shall you be in the field. Cursed shall be your basket and your kneading bowl. Cursed shall be the fruit of your womb and the fruit of your ground, the increase of your herds and the young of your flock. Cursed shall you be when you come in, and cursed shall you be when you go out. The Lord will send on you curses, confusion, and frustration in all that you undertake to do, until you are destroyed and perish quickly on account of the evil of your deeds, because you have forsaken me. The Lord will make the pestilence stick to you until he has consumed you off the land that you are entering to take possession of it. The Lord will strike you with wasting disease and with fever, inflammation and fiery heat, and with drought and with blight and with mildew. They shall pursue you until you perish. And the heavens over your head shall be bronze, and the earth under you shall be iron. The Lord will make the rain of your land powder. From heaven dust shall come down on you until you are destroyed.

It becomes clear that religious alienation of believers who give up their will and obey the will of the deity is essentially a behavior of coercion, enslavement, and non-freedom, which is forced by the power of the deity, who holds blessings and bad fortunes. However, this kind of coercion is a kind of voluntary coercion. It is a behavior where believers voluntarily regard abandoning their will and obeying the will of the deity as means of gaining happiness and avoiding misfortune, and voluntarily regard being controlled, enslaved, and forced by the deity as means of gaining happiness and avoiding misfortune. Therefore, this behavior belongs to voluntary alienation. In terms of coercion, this behavior is alienation; in terms of voluntary coercion, this behavior is voluntary alienation. The nature of this voluntary coercion of religious alienation is clearly stated by Frederick J. Streng: "Believers and followers of religious traditions all limit or restrict their lives in accordance with this ultimate context.... Force yourself to live in a life that you are already conscious of."[218]

*The origins of religions and religious alienation*

Why on earth do people believe in a deity, an intangible, illusory, and supernatural thing? There are two reasons: rational superstition and emotional craving. What is superstition? In ancient times, people engaged in religious activities to worship deities because they thought that deities really exist, and the reason why they thought that deities really exist is because they thought that the soul really exists. According to Edward Burnett Taylor's textual research, all the concepts of supernatural beings originate from the concept of the soul.

> We have actually pointed out that the concepts of the soul, the devil, the god and other spiritual beings are essentially similar concepts, among

which the concept of the soul is only a primitive part of this chain of concepts. Obviously, once the concept of the human soul appears in people's minds, it becomes a template or archetype, based on which not only other concepts about other lower souls but also concepts about ordinary spirits are formed; they range from Alf (god of nature) of Germanic people playing on the tall grass to the Great Spirit of the North American Indians as creator of heaven and the ruler of the world.[219]

However, why do people believe that there is a soul? There are many reasons, but the main reason is the misunderstanding of dreams and death. This misunderstanding is generally manifested in two aspects: on the one hand, the images of people appearing in dreams are considered as the souls of people; on the other hand, because these images can be separated from the body and act independently, people conceive the soul as the spiritual entity that integrates with the human body when the human is alive but detaches from the human body upon the death of the human to live independent of the body.[220] This persisting superstition goes back to those ancient times of mankind and still remains indomitable today: "The belief of the soul is deeply rooted in the lower level of culture of the ignorant, goes through the barbaric period without much interruption, and is completely preserved and deeply entrenched in the modern civilization."[221]

However, in the modern society, science has been able to fully explain dreams, death, destiny and various physical phenomena in the outside world and thus prove that the existence of souls and gods is utter nonsense. Why do so many people, especially those scientists, still believe in the existence of the soul and a deity? This is because people believe in deities not only because of their cognitive errors about dreams, death, and fate, but also because of their emotional yearning for deities, which drives these believers of rational superstition to believe in the existence of deities even though they know deities do not exist. On this point, Max Müeller quotes Homer, saying, "Everyone has a yearning for God."[222] Then, one may wonder, why is that?

The reason is that the purpose and meaning of life is to pursue happiness and pleasure and avoid misfortune and suffering. However, our life is destined to go through endless sufferings and misfortunes. These sufferings and misfortunes, as Freud says, come not only from the physical pain and death of each individual, from external natural disasters, but also from social oppression from interpersonal relationships.

Suffering comes from three quarters: from our own body, which is destined to decay and dissolution, and cannot even dispense with anxiety and pain as danger-signals; from the outer world, which can rage against us with the most powerful and pitiless forces of destruction; and finally, from our relations with other men. The unhappiness from this last origin we find perhaps more painful than any other.[223]

There is no doubt that there are differences in the degree of individuals' sufferings, such as fear of death, natural disasters, and social oppression, as well as in the degree of the subjective feelings of these sufferings. Those who are more unfortunate or more sensitive to misfortunes may believe that it is impossible to get rid of misfortunes and miseries and seek happiness and pleasure in the real, human world; therefore, they feel that life is meaningless and unworthy of living it. As a result, they believe that if they can't live well in the real world they can only resort to the illusory world of the deity. Therefore, they yearn emotionally for—and then rationalize their blind faith in—the existence of and salvation by the deity, to invest their hope in the eternal future and the afterlife. In the end, they would give up their will and obey the will of the deity for happiness promised in the future and the afterlife. In this way, religions and religious alienation allow them to see the meaning of life so that they can endure the misfortune and suffering of the real world and continue to live. From this rationalizing process, we can see that religions and religious alienation are both a means for people to eradicate the sufferings that they feel they cannot get rid of in the real world, and a symbolic complement to and alternative compensation for people's unfulfilled happiness in the real world. In this sense, Paul Willem Pruyser says, "Religion is like a rescue job.... Religion was born when someone shouted 'help'."[224]

It can be seen that the origin of religion and religious alienation is twofold. On the one hand, it originates from the "emotional yearning" for religion and religious alienation which is caused by worldly sufferings (fear of death, natural disasters, and social oppression). In this case, religion and religious alienation are the means to get rid of the suffering that people believe they cannot get rid of in the real world. This is the purpose cause of the origin of religion and religious alienation. On the other hand, it originates from "rational superstition": people's belief in the existence of deity is the result of their misunderstanding of dreams, death, and destiny. This is the non-purpose cause of the origin of religion and religious alienation. In more specific terms, there are four causes of religion and religious alienation: the first is rational superstition, the second is the fear of death, the third is the fear of natural disasters, and the final one, also the most important one, is social oppression.

### Ways to eliminate religion and religious alienation

As the above analysis of the origin of religion and religious alienation shows, religion and religious alienation can effectively offer desperate and hopeless people the hope for living on, and therefore holds very important significance and value for life. Liang Shuming has made interesting comments on this kind of significance and value of religion and religious alienation.

> In terms of providing solace to people's miserable feelings and emotions, it is the only thing they are capable of doing regardless of how different they are. Take the very naive and inferior worship of snakes, weasels, and even the worship of the gods of fire, river, and plagues as an example. Neither the existence of these supernatural beings can be

proven nor can we know if this worship will produce the anticipated after-effect. But one thing can be sure: after he worships, he feels that there is peace and comfort in his heart, and that he can live on with hope.... In the beginning, it seemed that there was no way out for him, that he could not move on with life, and that he had nothing to live for. But now, it (worship) seems to open a new way out for him. Ultimately, what all religions share in common is to maintain people's life without break-down, thereby which religions came into being, and thus occupy a very important position in human culture. This explains why religion is necessary in human life.[225]

Nonetheless, such significance and value of religion and religious alienation are, at their best, non-fundamental, local, and temporary. From a fundamental, global, and long-term perspective, religion and religious alienation have only a negative value. Generally speaking, there are two fundamentally different ways of getting rid of suffering to achieve happiness, to make a meaningful life. One is to face up to reality, develop science, transform society, change the real world full of sufferings, to fulfill individuals' own will and obtain real happiness. This is an act that is not religious or religious alienation, and a fundamental and genuine way to eliminate miseries to attain happiness; thus, fundamentally speaking, it is the only correct, ought-to-be, and positive way. On the contrary, the other way is to escape reality with a belief in the existence of and salvation by the deity, give up one's own will, and submit to the will of the deity to attain illusory hope and happiness. This way is the mode of behavior for religion and religious alienation.

Religion and religious alienation can make believers feel that life is meaningful and offer them some comfort. However, this meaning and comfort is not realized through the realization of tangible hope and attainable happiness, but through their belief in the illusion of the world of deity. The problem with religion and religious alienation is that they trap people into deceptive, illusory, and impossible hope and happiness in the afterlife, so that people can tolerate miseries in real life and abandon their will to change the world of sufferings. So, as Marx, Freud, and other sages have said, religion is actually a narcotic drug for the human spirit, while religious alienation is a kind of drug addiction; their positive value is obviously non-fundamental, local, temporary, while their negative value is fundamental, global, and long-term. Therefore, religion and religious alienation must be abolished.

Given these four main causes, in order to eliminate religion and religious alienation, we ought to follow four principles accordingly. The first principle is to develop science and eliminate rational superstition which leads to the belief of a deity. Second, to treat death correctly and avoid the fear of death which leads to the belief of the said deity. Third, to improve productivity and eliminate the sufferings caused by natural disasters which lead to the belief in a deity. The last and most important principle is to transform society and get rid of the social oppression and suffering, which leads to the belief in a deity. The first three principles are very simple and need no further explanation, but the last one is rather complicated and paradoxical. This last principle is developed to eliminate the social root of religion and religious alienation, but the fact is that religion and religious alienation is a means for people to get rid of social oppression and social suffering that they cannot get rid of in the real world.

Then, what exactly is the social oppression and social misery that people suffer from? It is undoubtedly "oppression from economic power and economic alienation thereof," "oppression from political power and political alienation thereof," and "oppression from social power and social alienation thereof." Therefore, the main sources of religious alienation are, ultimately, economic alienation, political alienation, and social alienation. Religious alienation is, in fact, the means to get rid of economic alienation, political alienation, and social alienation that people cannot get rid of in the real world. Apparently, the principal way to eliminate religious alienation is to eliminate economic alienation, political alienation, and social alienation. The ways to eliminate economic, political alienation, and social alienation, as mentioned above, depend ultimately on the realization of constitutional democracy. Therefore, we can conclude that the principal way to eliminate religious alienation is, ultimately, the realization of constitutional democracy and that constitutional democracy is actually the only ideal state institution for eliminating alienation of all forms!

However, no matter how desperately we try to eliminate religious alienation, it is likely that religion and religious alienation will tend to decline gradually, but it is unlikely that they disappear and die completely. Religion and religious alienation are likely to show the tendency to decline because the sources of religion are likely to show a tendency to decline. First of all, with the development of science and improvement of productivity, the causes of religion and religious alienation, namely rational superstition and pains and sufferings from natural disasters, are likely to disappear and die. Second, with the development of society, the main causes of religion and religious alienation—economic alienation, political alienation, and social alienation—are likely to cease to exist because of the realization of constitutional democracy.

Religion and religious alienation will never disappear completely; it is mainly because of fear of death, the third major cause of religious sentiment that it is bound to last forever. The awareness that one will die one day is the inevitable pain and misfortune of human life. Thus, in any case, there will always be some people who wonder, if there is no afterlife, would there be any meaning to our life which is as ephemeral as the morning dew? The mortality of human beings is undoubtedly the eternal source of people's desire for the immortality of their soul and the existence of a deity; it is, ultimately, the eternal source of religion and religious alienation. Thus, Feuerbach says, "If people are immortal, if people live forever, then there will be no such thing as death in the world, then there will be no religion."[226]

## Notes

1 Sima Qian, "Treatise on Rites (Chap. 1)," *Records of the Grand Historian*, Volume 23.
2 Shen Hengyan and Yan Hongyuan, eds., *Scholars Abroad on Humans and Humanism*, Volume 3 (Beijing: Social Sciences Academic Press, 1991), 745.
3 *International Philosophy Today* 6 (1991): 20.
4 Zhou Fucheng, ed., *Selected Works of Western Ethics*, Volume 3 (Beijing: Commercial Press, 1987), 89.
5 Luo Guojie, ed., *A Collection of Thoughts on Humanism* (Beijing: Huaxia Publishing House, 1993), 449.
6 Immanuel Kant, *Foundations of Metaphysics of Morals* (Shanghai: Shanghai People's Publishing House, 1986), 87.
7 *Selected Works of Philosophy by Feuerbach* (Beijing: SDX Joint Publishing Company, 1984), 315.
8 Xin Ru, "Is Humanism Revisionism?" In *Collected Discussions on Issues Concerning Human Nature and Humanism* (Beijing: People's Publishing House, 1983), 21.
9 David Gorjkoch et al., *Humanistic Issues* (Beijing: Oriental Publishing Company, 1997), 392.
10 Paul Kurtz, *Defending Secular Humanitarianism* (Beijing: Oriental Publishing Company, 1996), 74.
11 *Selected Works of Bourgeois Writers and Artists on Human Nature from Humanistic Perspectives from Renaissance to the 19th Century* (Beijing: Commercial Press, 1973), 156.
12 Guojie, ed., *A Collection of Thoughts on Humanism*, 509.
13 Fucheng, ed., *Selected Works of Western Ethics*, 33–34.
14 *International Philosophy Today* 6 (1991): 22.
15 Alexis de Tocqueville, *Democracy in America*, Volume 2 (Beijing: Commercial Press, 1996), 551.
16 Hengyan and Hongyuan, eds. *Scholars Abroad on Humans and Humanism*, 745.
17 Guojie, ed., *A Collection of Thoughts on Humanism*, 448.
18 Alan Bullock, *The Humanist Tradition in the West* (New York: W.W. Norton, 1985), 45.
19 David Gorjkoch et al., *Humanitarian Issues*, 2–3.
20 Guojie, ed., *A Collection of Thoughts on Humanism*, 447.
21 Hengyan and Hongyuan, eds., *Scholars Abroad on Humans and Humanism*, 735.
22 Guojie, ed., *A Collection of Thoughts on Humanism*, 449.
23 Hengyan and Hongyuan, eds. *Scholars Abroad on Humans and Humanism*, 37.
24 Ibid., 745.
25 Hu Ming, *Collected Works of Hushi*, Volume 14 (Beijing: Guangming Daily Press, 2000), 68.
26 John Dalberg-Acton, *Freedom and Power* (Beijing: Commercial Press, 2001), 14.
27 Giovanni Sartori, *The Theory of Democracy Revisited* (Chatham: Chatham House Publisher Inc., 1987), 298.
28 David Miller, *Blackwell Encyclopedia of Political Thought* (Beijing: China University Politics and Law Press, 1992), 271.
29 Isaiah Berlin, *Four Essays on Liberty* (Oxford: Oxford University Press, 1969), 121.
30 Friedrich A. Hayek, *The Constitution of Liberty* (Chicago, IL: The University of Chicago Press, 1978), 11.
31 John Locke, *On Human Understanding* (Beijing: Commercial Press, 1958), 208
32 Joel Feinberg, *Freedom, Rights and Social Justice* (Guiyang: Guizhou People's Publishing House, 1998), 3.
33 Berlin, *Four Essays on Liberty*, liv.

34 John Rawls, *A Theory of Justice*, Revised ed. (Cambridge, MA: The Belknap Press of Harvard University Press, 2000), 32.
35 Berlin, *Four Essays on Liberty*, liii.
36 Ibid., 122.
37 Ibid., liv.
38 Thomas Hobbes, *Leviathan* (New York: Simon & Schuster Inc, 1997), 159.
39 Baruch Spinoza, *Ethics* (Beijing: Commercial Press, 1962), 205.
40 Ibid., 154.
41 Berlin, *Four Essays on Liberty*, 134.
42 Ibid., 146.
43 Ibid., lix.
44 Pavlov, *Collected Lectures on Conditioned Reflexes* (Beijing: People's Health Publishing House), 3.
45 Ibid., 224.
46 Abraham Maslow et al., *Potential and Value of Man* (Beijing: Huaxia Publishing House, 1987), 176.
47 Berlin, *Four Essays on Liberty*, 124.
48 Edgar Bodenheimer, *Jurisprudence: The Philosophy and Method of the Law* (Cambridge, MA: Harvard University Press, 1967), 201–202.
49 Ibid., 272.
50 Aristotle, *Nicomachean Ethics* (Beijing: China Social Sciences Press, 1990), 8.
51 Ibid.
52 Hayek, *The Constitution of Liberty*, 71.
53 Ibid., 9.
54 John Locke, *On Government*, Volume 2 (Beijing: Commercial Press, 1993), 13.
55 Hoy, *Liberal Political Philosophy* (Beijing: SDX Joint Publishing House, 1992), 40.
56 Abraham H. Maslow, *Motivation and Personality*, 2nd edition (New York: Harper & Row, Publishers, 1970), 46.
57 Ibid., 172.
58 Robert Maynard Hutchins, *Great Books of The Western World*, Volume 43, On Liberty, by John Stuart Mill (Encyclopedia Britannica, Inc., 1980), 299.
59 Ibid., 297.
60 Ibid., 159.
61 Martin Heidegger, *Being and Time* (Beijing: SDX Joint Publishing House, 1987), 288.
62 Wilhelm von Humboldt, *The Sphere and Duties of Government* (Beijing: China Social Science Press, 1998), 30.
63 Hutchins, *Great Books of The Western World*, Vol. 43, On Liberty, by John Stuart Mill, 162.
64 Ibid., 171.
65 Ibid., 174.
66 Ibid., 277.
67 Berlin, *Four Essays on Liberty*, 128.
68 Zhang Pinxing, ed., *Treasures of Philosophy of Life* (Beijing: China Radio and Television Publishing House, 1992), 237.
69 Hutchins, *Great Books of The Western World*, Volume 43, On Liberty, by John Stuart Mill, 300.
70 Kurtz, *Defending Secular Humanitarianism*, 8.
71 Ibid., 78.
72 Ibid., 17.
73 Ibid., 254.
74 Zhou Fucheng, *Selected Comments of Bourgeois Philosophers and Political Thinkers on Human Nature from the Perspective of Humanism from Renaissance to the 19th Century* (Beijing: Commercial Press, 1954), 104.
75 Ibid., 19.

76 Dalberg-Acton, *Freedom and Power*, 307.
77 Ibid., 49.
78 F.A. Hayek, *Law, Legislation and Liberty*, Volume 1 (Beijing: China Social Sciences Publishing House, Chengcheng Books Ltd., 1999), 94.
79 Jean-Jacques Rousseau, *Social Contracts* (Beijing: Commercial Press, 1994), 24.
80 Friedrich A. Hayek, *Road to Serfdom* (Beijing: China Social Sciences Press, 1997), 73.
81 Hayek, *The Constitution of Liberty*, 174.
82 L.T. Hobhouse, *Liberalism* (Beijing: Commercial Press, 1996), 10.
83 Friedrich A. Hayek, *Fatal Conceit* (Beijing: *China* Social Sciences Press, 2000), 5.
84 Ibid., 85.
85 Hobbes, *Leviathan*, 170.
86 Rawls, *A Theory of Justice*, Revised ed., 266.
87 Hayek, *The Constitution of Liberty*, 11.
88 von Humboldt, *The Sphere and Duties of Government*, 54.
89 Hutchins, *Great Books of The Western World*, Volume 43, On Liberty, by John Stuart Mill, 271.
90 Rousseau, *Discourse On the Origin and Basis of Human Inequality* (Beijing: Commercial Press, 1962), 146.
91 Carl Cohen, *On Democracy* (Beijing: Commercial Press, 1988), 6.
92 *Selected Speeches of Bourgeois Politicians on Human Rights, Freedom, Equality and Fraternity* (Beijing: World Knowledge Publishing House, 1963), 210.
93 Giovanni Sartori, *The Theory Democracy Revisited*, 298.
94 Adam Smith, *An Inquiry into The Nature And Causes of The Wealth of Nations*, Volume 2 (Oxford: Clarendon Press, 1979), 687.
95 Milton Friedman, *Capitalism and Freedom* (Chicago, IL: The University of Chicago Press, 1962), 15.
96 Paul A. Samuelson and William D. Nordhaus, *Microeconomics*, 16th edition (Boston: The McGraw-Hill Companies, Inc. 1998), 140.
97 Paul A. Samuelson, *Economics*, Volume 2 (Beijing: Commercial Press, 1986), 192–193.
98 Smith, *An Inquiry into the Nature and Causes of the Wealth of Nations*, 582.
99 J.B. Bury, *A History of Freedom of Thought* (Changchun: Jilin People's Publishing House, 1999), 1.
100 Ibid., 1.
101 Dalberg-Acton, *Freedom and Power*, 309.
102 Bury, *A History of Freedom of Thought*, 1.
103 Cohen, *On Democracy*, 141.
104 Ibid., 149.
105 *Selected Speeches of Bourgeois Politicians on Human Rights, Freedom, Equality and Fraternity*, 105.
106 Ibid., 53.
107 Hutchins, *Great Books of The Western World*, Volume 43, On Liberty, by John Stuart Mill, 292.
108 Bury, *A History of Freedom of Thought*, 129.
109 Milton, *On Freedom of Publication* (Beijing: Commercial Press, 1996), 44.
110 Hutchins, *Great Books of The Western World*, Volume 43, On Liberty, by John Stuart Mill, 275.
111 R.T. Nolan, *Ethics and Real Life* (Beijing: Huaxia Publishing House, 1988), 365.
112 Tocqueville, *On American Democracy*, Volume 2, 203–207.
113 James Bryce, *Modern Democracies*, Volume 2 (Changchun: Jilin People's Publishing House, 2001), 1027.

114 Nolan, *Ethics and Real Life*, 379.
115 *Selected Speeches of Bourgeois Politicians on Human Rights, Freedom, Equality and Fraternity*, 52.
116 Dalberg-Acton, *Freedom and Power*, 364.
117 Li Qiang, *Liberalism* (Beijing: China Social Sciences Publishing House, 1998), 14.
118 Ibid., 19.
119 *Collections of Hushi's Masterpieces: Liberalism*, 68.
120 Gu Su, *Basic Concepts of Liberalism* (Beijing: China Central Translation Publishing House, 2003), 3.
121 Berlin, *Four Essays on Liberty*, 128.
122 Dalberg-Acton, *Freedom and Power*, 307.
123 Ibid., 307.
124 Hayek, *The Constitution of Liberty*, 54.
125 Ibid., 68.
126 Dalberg-Acton, *Freedom and Power*, 309.
127 Ibid.
128 Hobhouse, *Liberalism* (Beijing: Commercial Press, 1996), 9.
129 Hayek, *The Constitution of Liberty*, 153.
130 Ibid., 154.
131 Ibid., 85.
132 Karl Popper, *Conjectures and Refutations* (Shanghai: Shanghai Translation Publishing House, 1968), 78.
133 *Selected Speeches of Bourgeois Politicians on Human Rights, Freedom, Equality and Fraternity*, 210.
134 Dalberg-Acton, *Freedom and Power*, 398.
135 Smith, *An Inquiry into The Nature And Causes of The Wealth of Nations*, 687.
136 *Selected Speeches of Bourgeois Politicians on Human Rights, Freedom, Equality and Fraternity*, 53.
137 Ibid., 283.
138 Dalberg-Acton, *Freedom and Power*, 310, 316.
139 Hayek, *Law, Legislation and Liberty*, 5.
140 Tocqueville, *On American Democracy*, 288.
141 Ibid., 289.
142 Liu Jun, ed., *Democracy and Democratization* (Beijing: Commercial Press, 1999), 73.
143 Kurtz, *Defending Secular Humanitarianism*, 75.
144 Miller, *Blackwell Encyclopedia of Political Thought*, 417.
145 Berlin, *Four Essays on Liberty*, 15, 17.
146 Guido De Ruggiero, *History of European Liberalism* (Changchun: Jilin People's Publishing House, 2001), 334.
147 Giovanni Sartori, *The Theory Democracy Revisited*, 380.
148 De Ruggiero, *History of European Liberalism*, 1.
149 Karl Popper, *Open Society and Its Enemies* (Shanxi: University Joint Press, 1992), 185.
150 *Japanese Modern Marxist-Leninist Dictionary*, s.v. "alienation."
151 *Selected Works of Philosophy by Feuerbach*, 267.
152 Wu Haoyuan, ed., *Biological Dictionary* (Beijing: Scientific and Technical Documentation Press, 1984), 287.
153 Karl Marx, *Das Capital*, Volume 1 (Beijing: People's Publishing House, 1975), 626.
154 *Britannica Encyclopedia*, s.v. "alienation."
155 Ibid.
156 Ibid.

157 *Scholars Abroad on Humanity and Humanism*, 739.
158 Ibid., 226.
159 Marx, *Economic and Philosophic Manuscripts in 1844* (Beijing: People's Publishing House, 1985), 54.
160 Berlin, *Four Essays on Liberty*, xxxix.
161 Ibid., xxxix.
162 Lukacs, *Ontology of Social Being*, Volume II (Chongqing: Chongqing Publishing House, 1993), 644.
163 Ibid., 676.
164 Marx, *Engels, Lenin and Stalin on Human Nature, Alienation and Humanitarianism* (Beijing: Tsinghua University Press, 1983), 224.
165 Marx, *Economic and Philosophic Manuscripts of 1844*, 49.
166 Ibid., 47.
167 Ibid., 50.
168 Ibid., 51.
169 Paul Anthony Samuelson, *Economics*, 192–193.
170 Ibid., 171.
171 Ibid., 232 (endnote).
172 John E. Roemer, *Free to Lose* (Cambridge, MA: Harvard University Press, 1988), 106.
173 Samuelson, *Economics*, 232–233.
174 Ma Yongjun, "On the Historical Forms of Exploitation," in *Papers of the 2006 Annual Sociology Conference in Fujian Province China National Knowledge Infrastructure*, 352.
175 Ibid., 352.
176 James D. Wright, *The Persistence of Classes in Post-industrial Societies* (Dalian: Liaoning Educational Publishing House, 2004), 36.
177 Yongjun, "On the Historical Forms of Exploitation," 352.
178 Liu Junning, *20 Lectures on Democracy* (Beijing: China Youth Publishing House, 2008), 41.
179 Zhang Shipeng et al., *Capitalism in the Age of Globalization* (Beijing: China Central Compilation and Publishing House, 1998), 79.
180 Ibid.
181 Gao Feng et al., *A Study of Contemporary Capitalist Economies* (Beijing: Renmin University Press, 2012), 365–366.
182 Kelso & Adler, *The Capitalist Manifesto* (Shanghai: Shanghai People's Publishing House, 1963), 3.
183 Ibid., 104.
184 Frederick Hayek, *The Fatal Conceit* (Chicago, IL: Chicago University Press, 2011), 87.
185 *Collected Works of Karl Marx and Frederick Engels*, Volume 1 (Beijing: People's Publishing House, 1971), 283.
186 Ibid.
187 Dalberg-Acton, *Freedom and Power*, 342.
188 Chen Jiagang, ed., *Consultative Democracy and Political Development* (Beijing: Social Sciences Academic Publishing House, 2011), 54.
189 Ibid., 84.
190 Lukacs, *Ontology of Social Being*, 232.
191 Rousseau, *Discourse on the Origin and Basis of Inequality among Men*, 148.
192 Nietzsche, *Thus Spoke Zarathustra: Before Sunrise*, Section 491.
193 Heidegger, *Being and Time*, 155.
194 Sartre, *Nausea and Other Works* (Shanghai: Translation Publishing House, 1987), 6.
195 Confucius, "On Virtues," *The Analects*.

196 Friedrich Nietzsche, *Beyond Good and Evil*, Chap.12.
197 Heidegger, *Being and Time*, 156.
198 Jean-Paul Sartre, *Being and Nothingness* (Beijing: SDX Joint Publishing House, 1987), 528.
199 Ibid., 390.
200 Ming Liu, ed., *Research on Sartre* (Beijing: China Social Science Press, 1981), 303.
201 Nietzsche, *The Gay Science*, Section 338 (Beijing: China Peace Press, 1987), 6.
202 Sartre, *Nausea and Other Works*, 6.
203 Heidegger, *Being and Time*, 354.
204 Hayek, *The Constitution of Liberty*, 205.
205 Cohen, *On Democracy*, 274.
206 Harold Joseph Raskey, *The Right to Freedom in Modern Countries* (Beijing: Commercial Press, 1959), 156.
207 Lukacs, *Ontology of Social Being*, 231.
208 Ibid., 180.
209 See He Guanghu, *Diversified Views of God* (Guiyang: Guizhou People's Publishing House, 1991), 1.
210 Ibid., 8.
211 Max Mueller, *Origin and Development of Religion* (Shanghai: Shanghai People's Publishing House, 1989), 16.
212 Edward Taylor, *Primitive Culture* (Shanghai: Shanghai Culture Publishing House, 1992), 575.
213 Ibid., 443.
214 Ibid., 574.
215 Ibid., 688.
216 Ibid., 577.
217 *Selected Works of Philosophy by Feuerbach*, 534.
218 Frederick J. Streng, *Man and God: Understanding Religious Life* (Shanghai: Shanghai People's Publishing House, 1991), 3.
219 Taylor, *Primitive Culture*, 575.
220 Ibid., 416.
221 Ibid., 505.
222 Mueller, *Origin and Development of Religion*, 22.
223 Sigmund Freud, *Civilization and Its Discontents* (Hefei: Anhui Literature and Art Publishing House, 1987), 16.
224 Mary Jo Meadow and Richard D Kahoe, *Religious Psychology* (Sichuan: People's Publishing House, 1990), 5.
225 *Religious Thoughts in China in the Past Decade* (Beijing: Jinghua Printing Bureau, 1927), 113–114.
226 Ludwig Andreas Feuerbach, *Selected Works of Philosophy by Feuerbach* (Beijing: Commercial Press, 1984) 534.

# 2 Justice, humanity, and increasing or reducing the quantum of interests of everyone—the system of value standards of state institutions

**26 value standards: the system of value standards for measuring state institutions**

*Justice, humanity, and an increasing or decreasing the quantum of interests of everyone*

Given previous discussions, the value standards of measuring state institutions and state governance can be summarized into 26 articles.

- "Increasing/decreasing the quantum of interests of everyone" is the ultimate value standard of state institutions and state governance that ought to be followed under any circumstances.
- "Increasing the quantum of interests without negatively affecting anyone" is the ultimate value standard of state institutions and state governance under the condition that the interests are not in conflict or that the conflicts can be compromised.
- "The maximum net balance of interests" is the ultimate value sub-standard of state institutions and state governance under the condition that interests are in conflict and incompatible with each other.
- "The greatest interests for the greatest number" is the ultimate value sub-standard of state institutions and state governance under the condition that there is a conflict of interests between the majority and the minority.

The above four value standards belong to the ultimate value standards of state institutions and state governance and are also the ultimate standards of morality, law, and politics.

The following eight value standards belong to the fundamental value standards of state institutions and state governance: justice and equality.

- The general principle of justice: equal exchange of benefits and losses.
- The fundamental principle of justice: equality in rights and duties.
- The "contribution principle" of social fundamental justice: contribution is the source and basis of rights; in other words, society ought to

*Value standards of state institutions* 101

distribute rights according to contributions, and duties according to rights; ultimately, the rights distributed by society to each individual ought to be directly proportional to his contributions and be equal to his duties.
- The "principle of virtue and talent" of social fundamental justice: "virtue" and "talent" are the potential source and basis of rights such as positions; in other words, society ought to appoint people on their merits and assign rights, such as positions, according to their "virtue" and "talent"; society ultimately ought to "employ people the way we utilize utensils" and distribute rights such as positions according to the nature of their virtue and talent.

If these principles of social justice, especially the principle of contribution, are applied to solve the problem of distributing basic and non-basic rights to each individual, then from these principles we can easily deduce the following four sub-principles of social fundamental justice, namely, the four principles of equality:

- The general principle of equality: on the one hand, everyone is equal in their basic contribution—everyone is equal as a shareholder in the formation and construction of a society—and thus ought to equally enjoy basic rights and equally enjoy human rights (the principle of full equality of basic rights); on the other hand, as a result of their unequal contributions, everyone ought to enjoy unequal non-basic rights accordingly; that is to say, the proportion of inequality of the non-basic rights everyone enjoys is fully equal with the proportion of inequality of their contribution (the principle of full proportional equality of non-basic rights).
- Principle of political equality: on the one hand, everyone, regardless of his specific political contribution, ought to enjoy political liberty completely and equally; this means that he ought to share in full equality the supreme state power and thus enjoy full equality in determining the political destiny of the country; on the other hand, everyone, according to his unequal political contribution (political talent and official morality), ought to be appointed unequal political positions correspondingly, to make the proportion of inequality of their political positions fully equal with the proportion of inequality of their specific political contribution (political talent and official morality).
- Principle of economic equality: on the one hand, in any society, no matter how much work and contribution each person makes, basic economic rights ought to be fully and equally distributed to him, according to the basic material needs of humans, (the principle of distribution on demand); on the other hand, non-basic economic rights of equivalent exchange value ought to be distributed to every individual, according to the marginal product value of the production factors provided by him,

102  *Value standards of state institutions*

  to make the proportion of inequality of the non-basic economic rights enjoyed by each individual fully equal with the proportion of inequality of the marginal product value of the factors of production provided by himself (distribution according to production factors—distribution according to work, and distribution according to capital).
- Principle of equal opportunities: the opportunity provided by society—mainly various management organizations such as the government—for non-basic rights, such as developing potentials, making contribution, and competing for titles and positions as well as power and wealth, is the basic right of everyone in the whole society, and the human right of everyone in the whole society, and thus ought to be equally enjoyed by everyone. On the contrary, the opportunities not provided by society, such as opportunities provided by family, talents, and fortune, are the personal rights of the fortunate people; no matter how unequal these opportunities are, no one else has the right to interfere with them. Nevertheless, the extra rights obtained by the fortunate people who take more advantage of common resources for social cooperation ought to be compensated to those who have fewer opportunities, correspondingly.

The above eight principles of justice and equality constitute the system of fundamental value standards of state institutions and state governance.

The following 14 principles of humanity, liberty, and alienation constitute the system of supreme value standards of state institutions and state governance:

- General principle of humanity in a broad sense: treating humans as humans (the behavior of treating humans as supreme value and thus treating everyone human with kindness).
- General principle of humanity in a narrow sense: making humans become humans (the behavior of treating the creative potential of humans as the highest value to allow humans to realize their creative potential and become the worthiest people possible).
- The positive fundamental principle of humanity: "making humans free." The principle is embodied specifically in the following five principles.
- The rule-of-law principle of liberty: any coercion of a country ought to conform to the law and morality of that country; all laws and morals of that country ought to be agreed on by all members directly or indirectly.
- The equality principle of liberty: everyone ought to enjoy liberty equally: everyone ought to be equal before liberty; everyone ought to obey coercion equally: everyone ought to be equal before the law.
- The limit principle of liberty: the coercion of a country ought to be kept to the minimum necessary for its existence; the liberty of that country ought to be extended to the maximum allowable by its existence.
- Principle of political liberty: the politics of a country ought to be agreed on with full equality by every citizen, ought to be carried out with full

equality according to the will of each citizen, that is, ultimately, ought to be carried out according to the will of the ruled.
- Principle of economic freedom: economic activities ought to be regulated by market mechanism than by the government, and government management ought to be limited to stipulating economic rules and guaranteeing their implementation. Within the scope of these economic rules, everyone ought to enjoy the freedom to conduct economic activities in full accordance with their own will, such as production, distribution, exchange, consumption, etc.
- Principle of freedom of thought: every member of society ought to have the freedom to think and communicate any thought. In other words, every member of society ought not to be prohibited from thinking and communicating any thought. Ultimately, speech and press ought to be completely free and ought not to be subject to any restrictions.
- The negative fundamental principle of humanity: "eliminating alienation." The principle is embodied in the following four principles.
- Principle of eliminating economic alienation: economic alienation originates from monopoly and imbalance of power—economic power and political power; the principle of eliminating economic alienation is to realize "democracy of universal suffrage by sortation," "economic democracy of co-determination," "welfare state system," "shareholder capitalism," and, ultimately, to realize "constitutional democracy": constitutional democracy refers to the democracy that regards the value standards of state institutions such as liberty as the guiding principle of the constitution and is subject to its restriction.
- Principle of eliminating political alienation: political alienation originates from a monopoly of political power in non-democratic systems such as despotism. The principle of eliminating political alienation is to realize universal suffrage democracy, deliberative democracy, and constitutional democracy. Deliberative democracy and constitutional democracy of universal suffrage are necessary and sufficient for every citizen to enjoy political liberty and avoid political alienation.
- Principle of eliminating social alienation: social alienation originates both from the society's lack of rule of law, democracy, and human rights and from the individual's lack of passionate pursuit of self-realization, so the principle of eliminating social alienation is to create a society ruled by law, democracy, human rights, and cultivate individuals who pursue self-realization with passion.
- Principle of eliminating religious alienation: religious alienation is mainly a means to get rid of economic alienation, political alienation, and social alienation which cannot be eliminated in the real world. Therefore, the principle of eliminating religious alienation is mainly to eliminate economic alienation, political alienation, and social alienation, and ultimately to realize constitutional democracy.

## System of value standards for state institutions

As these 26 value standards for state institutions demonstrate, they share a very important common feature: they are not only the moral principles of how each person ought to treat the other with goodness, but, more importantly, they are the moral principles of how the rulers of society and the state ought to govern, and the value standards of state governance and state institutions. Admittedly, the ruled also have the problem of how to treat others with justice and humanity, and the problem of how to use the ultimate standards of morality when moral norms are in conflict. However, mainly, they are the value standards for restraining the morality of the ruler rather than that of the ruled and the value standards for measuring state governance and state institutions.

The ultimate standards of morality are mainly "increasing or decreasing the quantum of interests of everyone," "the greatest interests for the greatest number," and "increasing the quantum of social interests without negatively affecting anyone"; therefore, aren't these mainly the value standards of regulating social governance and state institutions? The main principle of justice is social justice, which is the justice of society's distribution of each person's rights and duties. So, aren't the ruler and administrators of the state and the state institutions those who can distribute each person's rights and duties? The whole principle of equality is nothing but the deduction of the principle of social justice, nothing but the justice of the society's distribution of the more specific rights (basic rights, non-basic rights, political rights, economic rights, opportunity rights) of everyone: aren't the ruler and administrators of the state and the state institutions those who can distribute these rights, too? The main principle of humanity is about how one ought to and tries to make everyone realize the creative potential of the self, make humans free, and eliminate alienation: aren't these also the value standards for regulating social governance and state institutions?

It can be thus concluded that the principles of increasing or decreasing the quantum of interests of everyone, of justice, quality, humanity, and liberty seem to be arranged arbitrarily, but they actually belong to an organic whole; together, they constitute a system of value standards for how the ruler ought to govern the state and for measuring state institutions. The principle of increasing or decreasing the quantum of interests of everyone (especially the principle of the greatest interests for the greatest number and increasing the quantum of interests without negatively affecting anyone) is the ultimate value standard of state governance and state institutions; the principles of justice (especially the principle of equality) are the fundamental value standards of state governance and state institutions; and the principles of humanity (mainly the principles of making humans free and eliminating alienation) are the highest value standards of state governance and state institutions.

## Trade-off principles for conflicts among value standards of state institutions

Thus, Four standards, such as "increasing or decreasing the quantum of interests of everyone," eight standards of justice and equality, and fourteen standards, such as humanity and liberty, are combined to form the system of value standards of state governance and state institutions. However, as Berlin says, these values sometimes may be in conflict and incompatible with each other: "Not all kinds of good are compatible with each other, and it is even more difficult for all human ideals to be fully compatible."[1] So how should we choose in such a situation?

Ultimately, we need to resort to the ultimate value standard of state institutions, especially the net balance of maximum interests. According to this standard, we ought to preserve and follow the value standard of greater value, while sacrificing and violating the value standard of smaller value to maximize the net balance of value. Justice and equality are the fundamental value standards of state institutions; humanity and liberty are the highest value standards of state institutions. Then, which one has a greater value? The value of most fundamental things is undoubtedly the greatest and the most important: the value of "justice and equality" is greater and more important than the value of "humanity and liberty." Therefore, Aristotle writes: "in all kinds of virtues, people think that justice is the most important thing."[2] Smith elaborates on it:

> Beneficence, therefore, is less essential to the existence of society than justice. The society may subsist, though not in the most comfortable state, without beneficence, but the prevalence of injustice must destroy it. . . . [Beneficence] is the ornament that embellishes, not the foundation which supports the building, and which it was, therefore, sufficient to recommend, but by no means necessary to impose. Justice, on the contrary, is the main pillar that upholds the whole edifice. If it is removed, the great, the immense fabric of human society . . . must in moment crumble into atoms.[3]

It is clear that the value of justice and equality is greater than the value of humanity and liberty, so when these two values are in conflict with each other, and the conflict cannot be compromised, justice and equality should be preserved at the expense of humanity and liberty, that is, the principles of justice and equality should be followed in violation to the principles of humanity and liberty. Justice and equality have absolute, sacred, and inviolable priority over humanity and liberty.

### *Justice takes precedence over humanity and liberty*

First of all, let's examine the conflict between justice and humanity, with the principle of distribution according to need as an example. In fact,

106  *Value standards of state institutions*

distribution according to need ought to be implemented only in a society with love as its basic connection, not in a society with self-interest as its basic connection. If a society, such as a family, whose members are basically connected with each other by love rather than by their own interests, then all the members of the society will not care about their gains and losses, but will be willing to distribute according to the other's need. Thus, according to the principle of justice, those who contribute more ought to get more, and those who contribute less ought to get less, but within the family the distribution that those who contribute more and need less have fewer rights while those who contribute less need more and should have more rights, is not unjust and does not violate the principle of justice. Within the family, those who contribute more but need less are those who need more love for less contribution and are ready to distribute according to need voluntarily. That is to say, they voluntarily transfer their due rights according to the principle of justice to those who contribute less and need more. Therefore, if distribution according to need is implemented in a society based on love, it is not just, but it is not unjust, either. This is because it follows the principles of benevolence and humanity, which are higher than the principle of justice and therefore transcend it. Therefore, the distribution within a family is not so much a matter of justice and injustice. The rationale for arguing that the principle of humanity of distribution according to need ought to be applied only in a society with love as its basic connection is as follows: this principle does not violate the principle of justice.

However, if a society, such as a factory, is formed with interests, rather than with mutual love, as the basic connection among all its members, then the members of the society will dispute over their gains and losses. Therefore, those who contribute more and need less will not voluntarily transfer and gift their extra due rights, in accordance with the principle of justice, to those who contribute less and need more. Therefore, if we distribute according to need, we will deprive forcibly those who contribute more but need less of their due rights according to the principle of justice. This distribution violates the principle of justice and is thus unjust. In this way, the humanity principle of distribution according to need conflicts with the principle of justice. What ought to be done under such circumstances? Obviously, we ought to violate the principle of humanity and abandon the principle of distribution according to need, and follow the principle of contribution in accordance with the principle of justice. The rationale for arguing that the humanity principle of distribution according to need should not be applied in a society with self-interest as its basic connection is as follows: it violates the principle of justice and is unjust.

As we can see, following the principle of humanity is not conditioned on a violation of the principle of justice: only when it does not violate the principle of justice ought the principle of humanity to be followed; when it violates the principle of justice, the principle of justice ought to be followed at the expense of the principle of humanity. That is to say, when there is a conflict of interests between humanity and justice and the conflict cannot be compromised, we ought to follow the principle of justice in violation of the principle of humanity. The sacred and inviolable priority of the principle of justice becomes even more obvious when the principle of justice conflicts with the principle of liberty, namely, the most fundamental principle of humanity. Clearly, the principle of justice is a principle of pure good, so behaviors conforming to the principle of justice must be, ought-to-be, benevolent, good, and are thus bound to have a positive value. The same is true of the principle of equality. Of course, equality is not necessarily good, just, or ought to be. However, the principle of equality is fundamentally different from equality: the principle of equality is the most important principle of justice. The principle of equality is also a principle of pure good: behaviors conforming to the principle of equality must be good, and ought-to-be, and are thus bound to have a positive value.

On the contrary, the principle of liberty is not a principle of pure good, but the principle of either good or bad with a net balance of extremely great good. Behaviors of liberty or behaviors conforming to the principle of liberty are not necessarily ought-to-be and are not necessarily of positive value. Quite opposite to it, there is no doubt that numerous crimes such as murder, arson, rape, adultery, robbery, and so on are likely to be the results of liberty. Therefore, Mrs Roland exclaimed, "freedom, freedom, and how many evils are committed under your name!" This is because the so-called liberty means behaviors carried out when there is no external obstacle and one can thus act according to one's own will. Undoubtedly, behaviors carried out according to one's own will or behaviors of liberty may possibly conform to the principle of good and thus be good and ought-to-be; they could also possibly violate the principle of good and thus be bad and ought-not-to-be. However, the crimes or negative moral values caused by behaviors of liberty or by behaviors conforming to the principle of liberty, no matter how serious and numerous they are, are only local, temporary, and non-fundamental, but their positive moral values are fundamental, long-term, and global. Because liberty is the most fundamental necessary condition for the realization of everyone's creative potential and social prosperity and progress, it has the highest value. Thus, the net balance of behaviors of liberty or behaviors conforming to the principle of liberty is essentially great good. This is why liberty has been established as the highest value standard of state institutions.

However, can it be concluded that liberty is not limited by any other value standard, but only by greater liberty? Acton's answer to this question is affirmative: "Freedom is the supreme law. It is restricted only by greater freedom."[4] Regarding this question, Acton is wrong this time. Because the liberty advocated by the principle of liberty is undoubtedly the liberty that is harmless to others and conforms to the principle of good, and is the liberty that is good and ought-to-be; it is neither the liberty that harms others and violates the principle of good nor the liberty that is bad and ought-not-to-be.

108  *Value standards of state institutions*

In this way, only those behaviors which conform to the principle of good can be allowed liberty, but those which violate the principle of good should not be allowed liberty. In a word, the so-called principle of liberty is to give people only the liberty of behavior to act without harm to other people and in accordance with the principle of good.

Therefore, the principle of liberty as the highest value standard of state institutions is premised fully on accepting the restriction by such value standards as good and just, and on conforming to these value standards. As long as liberty or the principle of liberty is subject to the restriction of other value standards, especially the principles of good and justice, and accords with the value standards of good and justice, then liberty or the principle of liberty is pure good. Such a truth is so obvious that even the liberalist master, Benjamin Constant, also acknowledges that the principle of public will, people's sovereignty or political liberty must be restricted by the principle of justice: "People's sovereignty is not unlimited; quite opposite, it should be restricted within the limits of justice and individual rights. Even the will of all the people must not turn injustice into justice."[5] In this way, when the principle of liberty is incompatible with the principle of justice or with the principle of equality, it is obvious that the principle of justice or the standard of equality should be followed in violation of the principle of liberty. In this sense, the principle of justice and equality has absolute priority over the principle of liberty. The following is an example.

According to the principle of liberty, any coercion of society, especially the distribution of everyone's rights and duties, must be directly or indirectly agreed by all members. According to the principle of justice, society should appoint people of virtue and distribute their corresponding rights according to their virtues and talents. Generally speaking, these two principles, of course, agree with each other. However, what is agreed by all members is not necessarily just, and public will might be unjust sometimes. Let's imagine a situation in which all members of a society agree upon the rule that the appointment and removal of all officials is determined by the amount of their property. If we act in accordance with this principle, it undoubtedly conforms to the principle of liberty, but it violates the principle of justice of "appointing only people with virtue." In this case, the principle of liberty conflicts with the principle of justice. What should we do under such circumstances? Obviously, people ought not to be appointed only according to property; they ought to contravene the principle of liberty and follow the principle of justice. The principle of justice has absolute priority over the principle of liberty.

### *Equality takes precedence over liberty*

Equality is the most important principle of justice. Therefore, the principle of justice has absolute priority over the principle of liberty. Let's take the conflict between the principle of economic equality and economic freedom as an example.

## Value standards of state institutions 109

According to the principle of economic equality, on the one hand, in any society, no matter how much work and contribution each individual makes, basic economic rights according to the basic material needs of humans ought to be fully and equally distributed to them (distribution according to need). On the other hand, each individual ought to be distributed, according to the marginal product value of the factors of production provided by each individual, non-basic economic rights of equivalent exchange value, to make the proportion of inequality of non-basic economic rights enjoyed by each individual fully equal to the proportion of inequality of the marginal product value of the factors of production contributed by him(distribution according to production factors—distribution according to work, and distribution according to capital).

According to the principle of economic freedom, economic activities ought to be regulated by the market mechanism, not by the government, and government management ought to be limited to stipulating economic rules and guaranteeing their implementation. Within the scope of these economic rules, everyone ought to enjoy the freedom to conduct economic activities in full accordance with their own will. The freedom of economic activities such as production, distribution, exchange, and consumption will be carried out in accordance with their own will.

Generally speaking, these two principles are, of course, consistent. However, if the economic freedom of the strong deprives the economic human rights of the weak, this deprivation, though conforming to the principle of economic freedom, violates the principle of economic equality—the principle of economic freedom conflicts with the principle of economic equality. What ought to be done under such circumstances? Obviously, the principle of economic equality ought to be preserved at the expense of the principle of economic freedom. That is to say, the government ought to restrict the economic freedom of the strong—the activities of establishing and guaranteeing economic rules belong to the domain of government management—and, through individual income tax, take part of the income of the strong to compensate the weak, to follow the principle of economic equality so that everyone can fully and equally share basic economic rights. The principle of equality takes precedence over the principle of liberty.

However, the best, yet the most puzzling, demonstration of the priority of the principle of equality over the principle of liberty is the so-called Popper's "paradox of freedom." This paradox, according to Popper, was first used by Plato to successfully oppose the principles of freedom and democracy:

> In his criticism of democracy, and in his story of the rise of the tyrant, Plato raises implicitly the following question: What if it is the will of the people that they should not rule, but a tyrant instead? Plato suggests, 'The free man may exercise his absolute freedom, first by defying the laws and ultimately by defying freedom itself and by clamoring for a tyrant. This is not a far-fetched possibility; it has happened a number

of times; and every time it has happened, it has put in a hopeless intellectual position all those democrats who adopt, as the ultimate basis of their political creed, the principle of the majority rule or a similar form of the principle of sovereignty.'[6]

Did this paradox of freedom by Plato, exactly as Popper says, succeed in negating the principle of democracy, namely, the principle of political liberty? Of course, it did not. The paradox of freedom only shows that when the principle of political liberty conflicts with the principle of political equality, we ought to negate the principle of political liberty and follow the principle of political equality. If, as Plato says, the so-called paradox of freedom occurs, that is, the will of the people of a country is to elect a tyrant and entrust him with the right to rule with despotism, then the tyrant's autocratic rule according to the will of the people, though conforming with the principle of political liberty, violates the principle of political equality. Thus, the principle of political liberty conflicts with the principle of political equality. What ought we to do under such circumstances? Obviously, the principle of political equality ought to be preserved at the expense of the principle of political liberty. That is to say, the principle of political equality ought to be followed and the tyrant ought to be abolished in violation of the will of the people so that everyone can fully and equally hold the supreme power of the state. The principle of political equality has priority over the principle of political liberty.

It can be concluded that justice and equality are not only the most important value standards of state institutions and state governance, but also the principle of pure good. On the contrary, although humanity and liberty are the highest value standards of the state institutions and governance, they are not the fundamental and most important value standards. Moreover, the principle of liberty is the principle of both good and bad with a net balance of good, and the principle of liberty is the principle of pure good only when it is premised on conformation to the value standards of justice and equality. Therefore, when the principles of justice and equality and the principles of liberty and humanity conflict with each other and the conflicts cannot be compromised, we ought to contravene the principles of humanity and liberty and follow the principles of justice and equality. The principles of justice and equality have absolute priority over the principles of liberty and humanity. So, liberalist, Rawls writes:

> Justice is the primary virtue of a social system, just as truth is the primary virtue of the thought system. A theory, no matter how noble and concise, must be rejected or amended as long as it is not true. Similarly, some laws and systems, no matter how efficient and appropriate, must be reformed or abolished as long as they are unjust. Everyone should enjoy the inviolable justice, which cannot be surpassed even for the well-being of the whole society.[7]

## *The ultimate value standards of state institutions take precedence over all other value standards including justice*

The last sentence of Rawls, "Everyone enjoys an inviolable justice, which can't be surpassed even for the well-being of the whole society" is untenable. As it is hardly realized, justice does not have absolute priority over all value standards. The value standards with absolute priority over any value standard can only be the ultimate general value standard of state institutions, "increasing or decreasing the quantum of interests of everyone," which is exactly what Rawls calls "the well-being of the whole society," as well as the ultimate standards for conflict of interests, namely, "the net balance of maximum interests" and "the greatest interests for the greatest number."

What makes the ultimate value standard of state institutions as the ultimate standard is that it is the absolute standard that ought to be observed under any conditions. This means that if any standard conflicts with the ultimate standard, it ought to be sacrificed to follow the ultimate value standard of state institutions. Therefore, when the principle of justice and other principles conflict with the ultimate value standard of state institutions, "the well-being of the whole society," and this conflict cannot be compromised, we ought to sacrifice the principle of justice and follow the ultimate value standard of state institutions: the ultimate value standard of state institutions is the ultimate trade-off principle to resolve any conflict among value standards of state institutions. Take the famous ideal experiment of "punishing the innocent" as an example.

The judge is fully aware that a person is innocent, but if he follows the principle of justice and thus does not punish the innocent by sentencing him the death penalty, there is bound to be a city-wide riot in which hundreds of people will die. If he violates the principle of justice and does not sentence this innocent person to death, the city-wide riot can be avoided. What ought the judge to do? Obviously, he ought to punish this innocent person. Punishing this innocent person is unjust, but it can avoid the greater injustice of deaths of hundreds of innocent people; thus, it accords with the ultimate value standards of state institutions of "the net balance of maximum interests" and "the greatest interests for the greatest number." Therefore, this punishment ought-to-be and is good. The ultimate value standards of state institutions take precedence over justice and all other value standards.

## Despotism: a state institution and a theoretical system that is extremely inhumane, unfree, unjust, unequal, and harmful to the interests of the largest majority

Humanitarianism, liberalism, egalitarianism, and utilitarianism as mentioned above, are state institutions and thought systems that regard "humanity," "liberty," "equality," "justice," and "increasing the quantum of interests of everyone" as the value standards of state institutions. So, is there a contrary state institution and a thought system defending this contrary state institution? Are there, ultimately, state institutions of "inequality," "non-freedom," "injustice," "inhumanity" and "harming the interests of the largest majority" and a thought system defending this system? The answer is absolutely yes: it is despotism.

## The concept of despotism

Despotism (it is despotism in English, *despotisme* in French, and *despotie* in German) originated from the Greek *despotes* and was originally intended as a parent and a master of slaves. Later, its meaning gradually evolved into a monarch who ruled his slave-like subjects, that is, a monarch who held the supreme power of the state. So when S. E. Finner defines "despotism," he writes, "A kind of relationship between the ruler and the ruled is a form of domination of master-slave relationship. . . . It is almost impossible to separate despotism from dictatorship conceptually."[8]

The Chinese word *zhuan-zhi* (专制) for despotism has been in use for a long time. *Zhuan* (专) has such meanings as "alone, monopoly, exclusive use, autocracy, arbitrary," and so on. *Zhi* (制) means "assertion, decision, supervision, ruling," and so on. The meaning of *zhuan-zhi* is "monopoly or autocracy," which is the same as that of *zhuan* used alone. In the chapter "Treatise on the Omens of the Destruction" of *Han Feizi*, Han writes: "If the commander-in-chief on dispatch is granted too much power, if the officer stationed in the frontier enjoys too much prestige and power, if they monopolize the power and make decisions without authorization, the state is likely to perish." Therefore, when referred to as a regime, the word despotism means a regime in which a person holds supreme power without the restriction of others or their organizations. Therefore, Yan Fu stresses repeatedly, "Despotism is a regime governed by a ruler who does everything according to his own will"; "a despot is a ruler who has unlimited power, does whatever he wants, and tolerates no disobedience."[9]

Therefore, given its etymological origins both in China and in the West, the so-called despotism refers to an autocratic regime, a regime in which one individual alone holds the state power. Is this the definition of despotism? The answer is, yes. As mentioned earlier, "despotism," "monarchy," "unlimited monarchy," and "complete monarchy" are all the same concepts: they are all a regime in which a person holds and exercises the supreme power of the state without the restriction of others or their organizations.

Therefore, the so-called despotism is a state institution and a theoretical system in which one individual holds the supreme power of the state; it's a theoretical system defending such a state institution. This corresponds to the definition of "despotism" in the *Encyclopedia Britannica*: "Despotism is a kind of political theory and practice, referring to unrestricted centralization and autocratic rule."

This definition could explain why in everyday life as well as in academic writings, especially in some historical writings, despotism, just as it's English definition, as a term means autocratic rule, "despotic rule," "despotic system," and "despotic regime"; for example, the Roman imperial despotism, the Egyptian autocratic rule of Pharaoh, and the Western Zhou despotic regime, and so on. However, generally speaking, autocratic rule mainly falls under the category of a political regime while despotism belongs to the category of political theory. To be more exact, despotism mainly refers to the theory of autocratic rule, namely, the theory defending the value of autocratic rule—one individual holds the supreme power of the state: "Despotism, when referred to as a value and behavioral orientation, is a theory of autocratic rule."[10]

Thus, despotism, as a theory justifying autocratic rule, means the following: it's a theory subscribing to the value that autocratic rule is ought-to-be, of positive value, benevolent, and good. Such is actually the case. Aquinas, Hobbes, and Jean Bodin are well-known proponents of despotism. They all believe that monarchy or the autocratic rule by one person holding the supreme state power is ought-to-be, of positive value, and good and is the best form of government. Aquinas says: "The best form of government in human society is the regime ruled by one person."[11] Hobbes believes that "the most absolute monarchy is the best form of government."[12] Bodin echoes this by saying that "The state ruled by monarchy is the best state."[13] Nevertheless, does not the autocratic rule by one person holding the supreme state power without restriction violates, in an extreme way, the principles of equality and liberty that "everyone ought to hold the supreme state power on an equal footing to enjoy political liberty on an equal footing"? Is not the autocratic rule an extreme violation of the principles of justice and humanity (equality as the most important justice and liberty as the most fundamental humanity)? Is not the autocratic rule extremely harmful to the interests of the overwhelming majority and in extreme violation of the value standard of "the greatest interests for the greatest number"? Ultimately, is not the so-called despotism a state institution and a theoretical system that is extremely unequal, unfree, inhumane, and harmful to the interests of the largest majority?

*Classification of despotism: hegemonic despotism and kingly despotism*

From discussions above, it becomes evident that the difficulty to understand the concept of despotism is less a difficulty in defining it than difficulty in classifying it, especially in making a scientific classification of diverse variations of despotism. Classifying and analyzing the Chinese despotism poses an extra challenge as thinkers of almost all schools in China since ancient times to the Qing Dynasty, such as Confucianism, Mohism, Legalism and Taoism, are advocates of despotism.

The most important representative of China's despotism is undoubtedly Confucianism. The theory of Confucian despotism can be summed up and deduced from "despotism of ruling the state as one's family," Confucius's well-quoted reply to Qi Jing gong's inquiry about governance: "Let the lord be lordly, the retainer loyal, the father fatherly, and the son sonly." This means that the monarch should behave like a monarch. But how can the monarch behave like a monarch? First of all, he should hold the supreme state power alone because that's what makes a monarch a monarch, and monarchy is a regime governed by a monarch who holds supreme state power alone. Thus, the primary sense of Confucius's claim "let the lord be lordly" is that the monarch himself should hold the supreme state power alone.

> When there is *Tao* in the state, then it is the Son of Heaven who decides on important matters such as establishing rituals, making music, issuing military orders, and dispatching troops; when there is no *Tao* in the state, then it is the princes and the lords who decide on important matters such as establishing rituals, making music, issuing military orders, and dispatching troops. . . . Therefore, when there is *Tao* in the state, the state will not fall into the hands of scholar officials; when there is *Tao* in the state, ordinary people will not bother themselves with the state affairs.[14]

Ultimately, what Confucius implies by saying "let the lord be lordly" is that the monarch should monopolize the supreme state power, that is, the monarch should rule by despotism, and that the autocratic rule is ought-to-be. Confucius's saying of "Let the lord be lordly, the retainer loyal, the father fatherly, and the son sonly" is actually a theory of despotism on the value standards of state governance and state institutions. On this point, Li Dazhao makes an incisive statement,

> Confucius has been the guardian of the kingly despotism in the past dynasties. . . His philosophy has, indeed, represented the morality of an autocratic society and has been usurped by autocratic rulers of past dynasties to shield their despotism.[15]

Confucius's despotism of ruling the state as one's own family, as well articulated by Dong Zhongshu, a great Confucian scholar in the Western Han Dynasty, can be summed up as "Three Cardinal Guides": "Let the lord be the guide of the retainers; let the father be the guide of the son; let the husband be the guide of the wife."[16] It is true that the term "Three Cardinal Guides" was not found until later in *Hermeneutics of Classics in the Spring and Autumn Period* and *Hermeneutics of Classics at the White Tiger*, but as far as its core concept is concerned, it is undoubtedly the proper meaning of Confucius's saying "Let the lord be lordly, the retainer loyal, the father fatherly, and the son sonly." As despotism means extreme inequality, does not

Confucius's advocating of autocratic rule by the monarch himself with the supreme state power mean that he believes the extreme inequality between the monarch and the officials is ought-to-be? Does not it mean that the monarch is superior and the officials are inferior, and the monarch is the guide to the officials? Therefore, it is safe to say that though Confucius does not use the term "Three Cardinal Guides," it is a logical deduction from Confucius's saying; it is a despotism justifying the Confucianism's sophisticated and systematized theory on the autocratic rule of the state as one's own family. This can be summarized in Chen Duxiu's comment, "The founder of the trinity of Chinese rituals, which prescribes the superiority of the monarch over the officials, father over sons, and men over women, is Confucius."[17]

Although Confucianism, Mohism, Taoism, Legalism, and Yin-Yang School are all proponents of despotism of ruling the state as one's own family, there are still tremendous disparities among the despotic thoughts they advocate. These differences can be classified into two categories: the hegemonic despotism represented by Han Fei and the Legalists, and the kingly despotism represented by Confucius and Confucians. So, what is kingly despotism, and what is hegemonic despotism? Fung Yulan offers us a very incisive answer:

> According to Mencius and later Confucians, there are two ways of governing. One is the royal way, and the other is the hegemonic way. They are completely different kinds of governing. The saint king rules through moral instruction and education; the hegemon rules through violence and coercion. Therefore, the kingly rule promotes virtues while the hegemony resorts to force.[18]

Therefore, the so-called hegemonic despotism is a barbaric and evil form of despotism, as well as a theory that justifies the autocratic rule as ought-to-be even when such rule is barbaric, evil, and immoral. The most complete and perfect manifestation of hegemonic despotism is the despotism advocated by Han Fei's theory of despotism through "law, schemes, and power." According to this theory, a wise monarch rules only through laws, schemes, and power regardless of whether they are moral or not, resorts to all means when necessary, and treats his officials with little moral obligation by sticking to the principle of "kill or reward":

> What a wise monarch relies on to rule his officials is nothing but two kinds of power: the power of penalty and the power of morality. What does the power of penalty and morality mean? It means killing as manifestation of the power of penalty and rewarding as a manifestation of the power of morality. As officials are all afraid of penalty and hungry after reward, the monarch who is in charge of the power of penalty and the power of morality earns deference from the officials, who are desperate for his reward.[19]

116  *Value standards of state institutions*

The representative figures of the barbaric and evil hegemonic despotism in the West are Bodin, Philma, Hobbes, and Machiavelli. Machiavelli defends despotism in this way: "The monarch must be cautious enough to know how to avoid the evils that will bring him down; on the contrary, if these evils may protect his throne, he should keep them."[20] Hobbes even declares, "The toleration of a professed hatred of tyranny is a toleration of hatred to Commonwealth in general"[21]

The so-called kingly despotism is an enlightened and benevolent form of despotism, as well as a theory justifying the autocratic rule as ought-to-be only on the premise that the rule conforms to morality. The complete and perfect form of this theory is the despotism in the form of "benevolent government" and "rule by the saint king" advocated by Confucianism. According to this theory, the wise king must rule the state in conformity with morality. Given this theory, only on the premise that his rule conforms to morality can the rule of the king be justified as ought-to-be, ought he to be a king, ought his officials and subjects submit to him. Otherwise, if his rule violates morality, then his rule is ought-not-to-be, he ought not to be a king, his officials and subjects ought not to submit to him. As Mencius says,

> The monarch who rules against benevolence is called an evil while the monarch who rules against morality is called a brute. A monarch who is both an evil and a brute is called a tyrant. I have heard of King Zhou Wuwang killing a tyrant, but not of King Zhou's regicide of a monarch.[22]

Plato, Aquinas, and Dante are the representatives of the enlightened form of kingly despotism. Plato says, "Just as politics under a king is the best form of governance, politics under a tyrant is the worst form of governance."[23]

The highest state of the benevolent kingly despotism is definitely the "people-centered" theory by Confucianism. What "people-centered" means is that "people are the foundation of the state," that "the state regards the people as its foundation," that "governance is orientated toward the people," or that "the monarch takes the people as the foundation." In summary, it means that the monarch should rule treating his subjects as the foundation of the state. "The government should take the people as its foundation, as a solid foundation will guarantee a unified state." This Confucian theory of "people-centered" rule can be summarized as the theory that "the people are more precious over the king," the theory that "the king should submit to the will and wishes of the people," the theory that "the king is ordained to serve the people," or the theory that "a king should win the heart of the people."

Then, what does "the people are more precious over the king" mean? According to Mencius,

> The people are the most precious, the state is the second, and the monarch is the last. Thus, he who wins the heart of the people can be the Son of Heaven, he who wins the heart of the Son of Heaven can only be a lord, he who wins the heart of the lord can only be a scholar official.[24]

*Value standards of state institutions* 117

Then, what does the theory of "the king is ordained to serve the people" mean? Dong Zhongshu answers,

> Heaven begets the people not for the sake of the king, but ordains the king to serve the people. Thus, if he has virtues enough to comfort the people, then Heaven will allow him to be the king; if he has evils enough to hurt the people, then Heaven will depose him.[25]

Then, what does the theory that "a king should win the heart of the people" mean? Mencius says,

> What caused Jie and Zhou to lose their kingdoms is that they failed their people. Failing the people means failing to win the heart of the people. Thus, the way to win the world is to win the heart of the people, only through which can the world be conquered.[26]

Finally, how to understand the theory that "the king should submit to the will and wishes of the people"? Mencius says it well, "According to 'King Qin Mugong's Oath' in *Shangshu*, 'Heaven sees what the people see and hears what the people hear; this is the truth.'"[27]

Clearly, the people-centered theory is a theory of governance that the monarch ought to rule the country with the people as the foundation and can be called the people-based despotism, which is a form of enlightened despotism. Though far superior to barbaric hegemonic despotism, people-based, enlightened despotism still advocates that the supreme power of the state ought to be controlled by the Son of Heaven alone and all other people ought to be deprived of their due right to the supreme power of the state and of other kinds of rights such as equality, liberty, and human rights. In this way, it also advocates that the Son of Heaven is the Master and the Lord, and all people are slaves, cattle, sheep, pigs, dogs, and livestock; it thus makes everyone live in a hierarchical—extremely unequal, unjust, human-right-less, and inhumane—society suffering from complete slavery and total alienation, and consequently allows no one to be a human being.

Therefore, the difference between the people-based despotism and the barbaric, hegemonic despotism is that the barbaric hegemonic despotism knows nothing about how to cherish the slaves, cattle, sheep, and livestock and instead abuses them at will, thus forcing the slaves, cattle, sheep, and livestock to rebel against it; but, the people-based, enlightened despotism knows how to cherish and be kind to the slaves, cattle, sheep, and livestock, thus deceiving them into abandoning their desire for rebellion. This is the ultimate purpose of those autocrats and proponents of people-based despotism in advocating the governance by "loving the people" and by "treating the people as the foundation of state."

Admittedly, it is possible that the autocrats and proponents of people-based despotism harbor sincere love for the people when they advocate "loving the people" and "treating the people as the foundation of the state."

However, the crux of the problem is not how sincere the owner of the hog farm is when he advocates "loving the pigs" and "treating the pigs as the foundation of the farm"; the problem is rather how tearfully grateful those "pigs" are of the benevolent words of the owner of the hog farm when he advocates "loving the pigs" and "treating the pigs as the foundation of the farm," and how excitedly they run and tell each other, "Our owner has said that he regards us as the foundation of the farm, and we will become the masters!" It is pathetic that similar to these silly pigs, some scholars have regarded the people-based benevolent Confucian despotism as an equivalent to the democratic theory; what is worse is that such an equation has been repeated and reinforced for nearly a 100 years.

This equation is absolutely wrong. Clearly, the people-based theory does not repudiate the monarch or claim that the monarch should not exist; on the contrary, it is premised entirely on the recognition and affirmation of the monarch and makes a complete affirmation and justification that the monarch ought to exist. It repudiates only the hegemonic, evil, and immoral monarchs and claims that only hegemonic, evil, and immoral monarchs ought not to exist. Fully affirming that the kingly, moral, and benevolent monarchs ought to exist, this theory advocates that the monarchs ought to abide by the moral way of governing the people, namely, following the so-called "people-based" morality. Given this, the people-based theory is a theory of governance. Such being the case, isn't it abundantly clear that it is an enlightened despotism? How could it possibly be a theory of democracy? Does a theory of democracy that affirms the existence of the monarch exist? Could it be possible for a theory of democracy to advocate benevolent despotism? Is not equating people-based theory as theory of democracy the same as affirming the existence of "round square" and "wood iron?"

Reviewing these concepts of despotism, we can say that despotism, though diverse and complex, is, in a nutshell, nothing more than a theory justifying that autocratic rule is ought-to-be, or a theory claiming that autocratic rule (the enlightened despotism) can be justified only on the premise that it is in conformity with morality, or a theory defending autocratic rule (barbaric hegemonic despotism) even when it is evil and immoral. Therefore, it seems that whether despotism is a justifiable truth or not depends entirely on whether an autocratic rule ought-to-be or not. The key to solving this problem is undoubtedly to understand these questions. How was despotism born and how did it come into being? Are its birth and existence necessary or accidental? These are questions concerning the "what-is" of despotism. Only when we understand the "what-is" of despotism can we deduce whether despotism is "what-ought-to-be" or not.

Just imagine this: if the holder of the supreme power of the state, as Confucius and Aquinas have said, can only be one person, and, just as there is only one sun in the sky, it is necessary, inevitable, and not freely chosen, so it follows that despotism is natural. Or we can say that despotism per se cannot be talked about in terms of good and bad, but only despotism of a particular kind of free choice—enlightened despotism and barbaric despotism—can be talked about in terms of good and bad. On the contrary, if the holder of the supreme power of the state can be one individual, a number of people, or the majority, if the holder can be so accidental, arbitrary, and freely chosen, then despotism, in violation of the value standards of state institutions, such as those of equality and liberty, is not ought-to-be. In this sense, is not despotism a fallacy? Therefore, the key to proving whether despotism is an ought-to-be or not is to unveil the "what-is" of despotism, namely, to disclose the origin and nature of despotism. So, the first question to ask is, was the birth and existence of despotism necessary or accidental?

## The origin and nature of despotism: the fundamental problem of despotism

### The universal origins of despotism: the nature of humans and the nature of the social structure

As far as human nature is concerned, everyone pursues personal interests, especially personal rights. As humans are social animals, all the interests of any individual human are ultimately given by the society and others; his most fundamental and important interests are the interests that the society and others must and ought to give him, and the interests guaranteed by power and laws, namely, his rights: rights are the interests guaranteed by power. Given this, isn't power itself the greatest interest? Because of this, people all thirst for power, that is to say, people all seek high power and avoid low status; even Confucius and Mencius, the representative figures of the doctrine of morality who think that morality and interests are dichotomies, have to admit that "the desire to be a noble person is shared by all."[28] "To be noble and rich is what everyone desires."[29]

Apparently, the degree of people's effort to pursue a noble position or power is directly proportionate to the level and size of the power or the position: the greater the power is, the more effort they exert in pursuing the power. This could explain why people's pursuit of the supreme power of society or state can reach a frenzied state as insane and reckless as the bloody battle between father and son. The crux of the problem is that the size of power, as Ma Qihua says, is inversely proportionate to the number of holders of the power.

> In terms of the number of people exercising the same power, the smaller the number, the greater the power of each person will be; the bigger the number, the smaller the power of each person will be. So the power of the head in the sole- head system is greater than that of the head in the committee system.[30]

Therefore, if possible, everyone is bound to desperately pursue or thirst for the supreme power of society or state by himself. This human nature is the root of the behavior of military commanders or chiefs in primitive societies—they are most likely to hold the supreme power of the tribe by themselves—who dared to usurp and monopolize the supreme power in bold violation of the democratic clan society of that time. This human nature is the root of the emergence of despotism in primitive societies. This is the human-nature root of the birth and existence of despotism.

From the point of view of the nature of the social structure, political leaders or supreme political leaders of any society or country—primitive societies are no exceptions—are generally a single person, such as a chieftain, a military commander-in-chief, a governor, or a president of a country. Even the supreme leader of a democracy, the president, is also just a single person. On this point, Kautsky offers a very penetrating exposition:

> Every social structure, like every animal organism, must have a head to unify its aspirations and actions. In animal or human societies, the role of such a head can only be played by one single individual of their kind. A social will is only an abstraction. Only a single animal or a single person can have a wish. It is neither possible for any animal kingdom to survive without a head animal nor possible for any human society to survive without a leader. Even the most loosely organized bowling club needs a chairman. Sometimes it is not an individual but a group or a committee that serves as the head of a social organization, but it must elect a chairman to negotiate and perform its functions.[31]

The supreme leader must be a single person, but of course, this does not mean that the holder of the supreme power is one single individual, as these two are fundamentally different. In a democratic country, although the supreme leader or president is an individual with the greatest power in the country, he does not hold the supreme power; in terms of the supreme power, he has the same as any citizen, as well illustrated in the saying "one for one, but not one for two." That is to say, the president and every citizen hold the supreme power of the state equally; otherwise, it will not be a democratic country. However, as far as human nature is concerned, the supreme leader is bound to strive for the supreme power of the society or the state, and may easily turn the situation that "the supreme leader is a single individual" into the situation that "the holder of the supreme power is one single individual," thus, easily becoming an autocratic monarch. This is the root of the emergence and existence of despotism from the perspective of the social structure. Due to this root of despotism, societies as early the Iroquois clan society, where democratic traditions were deeply rooted, elected two supreme leaders in violation of the nature of social structure:

> Electing two, instead of one, military chiefs, and granting them equal power demonstrates a shrewd and deliberate policy of preventing

one-man monopoly can be applied even in military affairs. They have no precedent to follow, but they have done something no different from the Romans, who set up two instead of one governor after the abolition of Rex.[32]

In summary, it is true that the supreme leader of any society is generally one single individual and the supreme leader of any society is also a single individual human, who is endowed with the human nature of craving for holding the supreme power alone. Therefore, in a nutshell, the nature of the social structure that "the supreme leader is a single individual" and the human nature that "the supreme leader is bound to pursue desperately monopoly of the supreme power" are not only the root of the emergence of autocratic regimes in China, Russia, and India, but also the root of the emergence of autocratic regimes in Western countries such as Europe and the United States. Both are the universal roots of the emergence of despotism in all societies and the universal roots of despotism.

However, the nature of the social structure that "the supreme leader is one single individual" and the human nature that "the supreme leader is bound to pursue the supreme power desperately" are only the abstract and general roots of the emergence of despotism in all societies, not the specific and special root of its emergence. As a result, these general roots cannot explain why China and other Eastern countries have been autocratic regimes for 5,000 years since the Era of the Five Emperors—the transitional period from primitive society to classed society; on the contrary, non-autocratic regimes such as democracy have dominated Western countries such as Europe and America. This phenomenon can only be explained by the specific causes of the emergence and existence of despotism. The specific causes of the emergence and existence of despotism vary from society to society, from time to time. The most important and realistic cause is the so-called "Asiatic mode of production," which has existed since the transition from primitive society to classed society; it has been considered as the primary cause of despotism in China and other Eastern countries for 5,000 years, and the fundamental cause for the differences between Eastern political systems and Western political systems.

*The official ownership of means of production and economic power: the fundamental characteristics of the Asiatic mode of production*

In Marx's view, the Asiatic mode of production was born at the end of the primitive society, that is, at the point of transformation and transition to classed society. It is actually the "Chiefdom," which was not known even to Morgen but discovered later by anthropologists today. As widely known, the fundamental characteristics of chiefdom are that they produced specialized, formal, independent, permanent bureaucracy and political organizations. Harveland and Ember call this society "chiefdom" or "chieftain territory." Such a formal and permanent bureaucracy has undoubtedly greatly enhanced the power and status of the chief, and may even make him an absolute monarch with the supreme power.[33]

The claim that Marx believed that the Asiatic mode of production was born in chiefdom is based on Marx's ideas on "all Asiatic Modes of production" stressed in his works such as *Pre-Capitalist Economic Formations*. According to Marx, the so-called Asiatic mode of production was, on the one hand, a closed, isolated, decentralized, natural mode of production that combined agriculture and family handicraft industry under the patriarchal clan system. On the other hand, more importantly, the form of ownership in the Asiatic mode of production—the decisive factor of the Asiatic mode of production—is autocratic monarchical land ownership, which is characterized by the "public ownership" of tribes or communes. Doesn't the word "tribes" mean primitive society? Doesn't "autocratic monarch" mean classed society? In a word, does this not mean that the chiefdom is in the transitional period from primitive society to classed society? To quote Marx:

> This form of social commune per se, which is based on the same basic relationship [i.e. public ownership of property], can be realized in many different ways. For example, a basic variant of this form present in most Asiatic societies, which not incongruent with this form, is an aggregate commune above all the smaller communes, which is ruled by a superior owner or a sole owner of property. In this way, the commune is nothing but a hereditary possessor of property. As this commune is the actual possessor of property and the real premise of public property, the commune itself can possess something special that is beyond the many actual separate communes. In this way, each individual within the commune has in reality lost ownership of property; or property, the natural condition of labor and reproduction which is considered as his condition, as an objective condition, as subjective body he discovered in the organic nature, becomes indirect property to this individual, because this property is granted to him through separate communes from the aggregate commune ruled by the despotic monarch. Thus, the surplus goods (which in fact is defined by the law as products possessed through labor) will belong to the highest aggregate commune without doubt.[34]

It can be seen that the so-called Asiatic mode of production, on the one hand, in terms of the ownership of means of production such as land, is the "land ownership by the autocratic monarch," which takes "public ownership" of tribes or communes as its phenomenon, and is ultimately kingly ownership. On the other hand, in terms of its economic form, it is an isolated and decentralized natural economy that combines agricultural economy with family handicraft industry. In a word, it can be called a natural economy of kingly ownership. So when Marx summed up the ownership of Asia, he quoted Bernie as saying, "The king is the sole owner of all the land in the state."[35]

Richard Jones once commented, "We know China, and we know that the monarch there is the sole owner of the land, as in other parts of Asia."[36]

However, Marx also points out that the real owner of the land is actually the person who can represent the commune, that is, the head of the commune: "The land owner may be an individual representing the commune, as in Asia, Egypt, etc."[37] Doesn't this mean that this form of ownership in Asia is actually the ownership of the monarch and the official class who represent the state and the government? Ultimately, can't we call it "official ownership"? In fact, James Muller discovered a long time ago the crucial truth that "the form of land ownership in Asia is official ownership":

> Based on all the facts we have investigated, we can only draw this conclusion, that is, the land ownership in India belongs to the rulers.[38]

So, does the Asiatic mode of production exist only in the transition from primitive society to classed society? Marx's answer was no:

> The Asiatic mode is bound to remain the most stubborn and lasting mode. This depends on the premise of the Asiatic mode: that individual people are not independent of communes, that the scope of production is limited to self-sufficiency, to a combination of agriculture and so on.[39]

Therefore, as Marx pointed out again and again, in India the Asiatic mode of production had been dominant and unchanged for 5,000 years, right from the remote ancient times until India became a British colony. "From ancient times to the first decade of the nineteenth century, no matter how much political change India had made in the past, its social situation remained unchanged."[40]

Though the typical examples of the Asiatic society that Marx and his predecessors mentioned are India, Russia, and China, in fact, as Melotti says, it refers actually to China. The title of Chapter 17 of his far-reaching masterpiece *Marx and the Third World* is "China—the most typical example of the Asiatic society in Marxian Terms." He says:

> This chapter does so with reference to the history of China, which for centuries best epitomised the 'Asiatic society' as defined by Marx, even though he himself, for reasons enjoined on him by his work as a scholar and revolutionary, took India, the historical object of British imperialism, as the chief source of his analysis. China can be called the most classic and significant example of a society based on the Asiatic mode of production, in that it achieved the fullest social development of any society so based. Moreover, it did so without having any contacts with the rest of the world, not even those important periodic relations with the West experienced by India and the Middle East back to Hellenic times at least.[41]

The reason why China is the most typical example of the Asiatic society in Marxian terms is that, since the Era of the Five Emperors, especially from Xia, Shang, Zhou, to Qing Dynasties, the means of production and its economic power throughout the country—land and property rights, industry and commerce, and industrial and commercial economic power—have always been under official ownership and mainly owned by the official class. On the one hand, in the Era of the Five Emperors, especially in Xia, Shang, and Zhou Dynasties, "all the land under the heaven belongs to the king; all people living on the land are the king's subjects"; kingly land ownership and official land ownership were implemented. This means not only that the king is the sole "official" who enjoys ownership of the land of the whole state; it also means that the property right and economic power of the land—the economic power to control land and labors to build cities and collect rents—are entirely owned by the king and his officials. The landowners are the king and his officials, but there are no common people landowners. In this sense, it can be called "an extreme official ownership of land and property right." From the Spring and Autumn Period to Qing Dynasty, with the abolition of king's ownership of national land, there emerged landowners among the common people, but the ownership of national land still mainly belongs to the officials, which means the national land ownership and national property rights—the economic power to control land and labor to build cities and collect rents—mainly belong to the official landowners. The dominant form of land ownership is still official ownership, so it may also be called "common official ownership of land and property rights" because the land ownership and property rights, as well as the economic power of the land, are shared by the official landowners and the common-people landowners.

On the other hand, in the Era of the Five Emperors, especially in Xia, Shang, and Zhou Dynasties, the craftsmen and businessmen sponger official system—in which craftsmen and official businessmen worked for the local officials, who in turn provided them with food, clothing, housing, and other expenses—was practiced. The system allowed the king and his official class to monopolize all industry and commerce as well as all industrial and commercial economic power; thus, it can be called "extreme official ownership of industry and commerce and industrial and commercial economic power." From the Spring and Autumn Period to the Qing Dynasty, the official ownership which allowed "the handicraftmen and businessmen as sponger officials" to monopolize all industry and commerce, as well as all industrial and commercial economic power in Xia, Shang, and Zhou Dynasties, was gradually abolished; however, the king and his official class still granted, through unrestricted totalitarian government control, various privileges (including the privilege to monopolize) to official-owned industry and commerce—public industry and commerce owned by the officials and those owned by the officials; these privileges allowed them to restrain and suppress the industry and commerce by the common people, thus allowing the official-owned industry and commerce of low efficiency remain dominant. In this way, the king and his official class not only monopolized main industry and commerce, but also monopolized almost all the economic power of industry and commerce; they even owned the economic power to plunder the private property of civil industrialists and business people, deprived civil industrialists and business people of any economic power over the government and the officials, and eventually drove them to seek protection from the government and the officials. Therefore, the official ownership of industry and commerce, as well as its economic power, has remained dominant from the Spring and Autumn Period to the Qing Dynasty. In this sense, it can be called "universal official ownership of industry and commerce and economic power of industry and commerce."

*Civil ownership of means of production and economic power: the fundamental characteristic of the production mode in Europe and the United States*

In Western countries land and other means of production and their economic power have always been mainly owned by the common people (class or stratum), so the dominant mode is the civil ownership of the means of production and their economic power. In the first stage, the earlier classed society in ancient Greece and Rome—the Greek Archaic Age and the early and middle period of the Roman Republican Age—was the feudal society with civil ownership of means of production and their economic power. Later the society developed into a slave capitalist society (i.e., a capitalist society in which the main workers were slaves), with slaveowners owning the overwhelming majority of land, industry, commerce, and other means of production and their economic power, so the society was a civil slaveowner capitalist ownership.

In the second stage, medieval Europe mainly belonged to the serfdom feudal society, with land and other means of production and their economic power owned by the lords at all levels; this was a kind of aristocratic land ownership that monopolized both economic power and political power. Meanwhile, the city was a free civil commercial capitalist society, in which the majority of property owners or capitalists—workshop handicraft capitalists and commercial capitalists—are common people, not officials, so the mode was civil ownership of the means of production and their economic power, namely, a common people capitalist ownership.

Finally, in the modern capitalist era of Europe and America, before the realization of democracy of universal suffrage in the 20th century, the means of production and their economic power were mainly owned by common people capitalists, so the mode was bourgeois civil ownership. Since the realization of universal suffrage democracy, everyone was able to fully and equally hold the supreme power of the state, and the monopoly of political power was eliminated; moreover, through establishing a series of systems such as "welfare state system," "economic democracy of co-determination," "employee shareholder system," everyone was able to own more or less of means of production as well as capital and assets and became capital owners, property owners, or capitalists. In this way, the monopoly of the means of production and economic power was on the way to being eliminated to realize universal ownership of capital and economic power by all the people.

Therefore, when Marx talked about the social revolution caused by Britain in India, he pointed out that, contrary to the Asiatic official ownership of the means of production, the fundamental feature of the Western society was that the means of production belonged to the people; it was universal ownership by all the people; to liberate Asian people, it was necessary to lay the material foundation for the introduction of western society in Asia, and make means of production owned by the people and realize universal ownership of means of production by all the people.

> Britain has a dual mission in India: one is to destroy the old Asian society; the other is to rebuild it, that is, to lay a material foundation for introducing Western society in Asia... All that the British bourgeoisie was forced to do in India would neither liberate the people nor fundamentally improve their social conditions, both of which depend not only on the development of productive forces, but also on whether the productive forces belong to the people. But one thing they can do is to create material premises for both.[42]

*Geographical environment: the ultimate reasons for the oriental official ownership and the western civil ownership of means of production and their economic power*

The difference between official ownership of means of production and their economic power and the civil ownership of means of production and their economic power is the fundamental difference between the Chinese and the Western economic systems. What causes this ultimate difference is the geographical environment. With a vast geographical environment of huge river basins, such as the Yellow River and the Yangtze River, which are suitable for farming, China is a "hydraulic society" that must build large-scale flood control systems and artificial irrigation facilities. As the autocratic ruler and his government were the only builders capable of undertaking these large-scale flood control systems and artificial irrigation facilities, the ownership of the national land and other means of production and their economic power inevitably fell into the hands of the king and his official class, who represent the state and its government.

On the contrary, in the West, there is no such vast geographical environment of huge river basins suitable for farming. "As river basins are mostly concentrated in the Oriental societies,"[43] the west is not a "hydraulic society" and doesn't need to build large flood control projects and artificial irrigation facilities that only the government could undertake, like in the

*Value standards of state institutions* 127

East. Most of the Western flood control projects and irrigation facilities can be built by the farmers and common people themselves without the help of the government and its officials; thus most of the ownership of means of production (including the land) and their economic power falls into the hands of the common people, not the king and his officials.

First of all, ancient Greece was a "non- hydraulic society" with no big rivers, less of land, and more of mountains. Second, there were no large-scale flood control projects and artificial irrigation facilities that only the government could undertake in ancient Rome. Third, the geographical environment of the ancient Germanic people was mainly forested and abundant in land, which allowed the Germanic people to rely on dairy and livestock instead of farming and commit little effort to irrigation; eventually, even if there were any water treatment projects and irrigation facilities, they would be rather small in scale and fairly insignificant and could be undertaken by the farmers and common people themselves, not by the government and its officials. Finally, the Western European world, such as Britain, France, and Germany, developed by the ancient Germanic people, had very few flood control projects and artificial irrigation facilities.

> The biggest difference between agriculture in Western Europe and that in the East in ancient times was that there was no artificial irrigation. Of course, artificial irrigation is not universal in the East, but it is always more than that in Western Europe. Topographically, Western Europe is a large plain, with the exception of the Alps and Apenningshan, most of which belong to plains and hilly areas. It has an altitude as low as about 150 meters below, is surrounded by the ocean, and enjoys a warm and humid climate. Moreover, it has a rather small annual temperature difference and enjoys abundant annual rainfall of more than 750 millimeters, which is suitable for the growth of crops. So unlike many cold and dry plateaus in Asia, there is no need for artificial irrigation. The Europeans learned about some irrigation facilities from the Arabs in the Middle Ages and only occasionally used them later in vegetable gardens and orchards, leaving large areas of farmland maintained by rainfall.[44]

The same is true of the United States. Faulkner says,

> Rainfall also has a fundamental impact on people's happiness. For example, grain wheat, most important food for the people, cannot be planted and grown when the annual rainfall is less than ten or more than forty-five inches. The annual rainfall in the United States is 26.6 inches, ranging from five inches in southern Utah to sixty inches in the Western Valley of Northern California, Washington, Oregon and Gulf Stream coasts. The humid and Pacific coastal climate of island becomes drier in mountainous areas and hardly humid in vast dry plateaus. However, the annual rainfall increases near the Gulf of Mexico and the Pacific, and

the average annual rainfall to the east of the Appalachian Mountains is 30 to 50 inches. Because agricultural production must have rainfall of twenty inches, and because the rainfall for keeping the ideal soil temperature is 30 to 35 inches, this area is most conducive to agricultural production. Although the temperature and rainfall in the United States fluctuates more greatly than that in Europe, it is basically the same as the climate in Europe, as far as the whole country is concerned.[45]

Moreover, as Luo Rongqu says, "The United States is essentially a nation composed of immigrants."[46] Generally speaking, the principle of land distribution of these migrants who crossed the sea to a new place is undoubtedly the most thorough democratic system of equal distribution, as in the colonies of the ancient Greek city-state era. "In terms of land distribution, whether it is the Great Colonial Movement in the early period of the archaic era or the later colonial activities of the Greeks, the general practice is to distribute land equally among the original colonists."[47]

The United States is a free country composed of immigrants. Marx calls it a free colony:

> The essence of a free colony, on the contrary, consists in this—that the bulk of the soil is still public property, and every settler on it therefore can turn part of it into his private property and individual means of production, without hindering the later settlers in the same operation.[48]

Luo Rongqu calls it "free land + free immigration,"[49] which caused the prevailing preemptive occupation of land. In particular, in the 19th-century-immigration wave in the United States, as many as two-thirds of the land occupied by individuals at will was created by self-farming family farms without employees.[50] Therefore, the colonial era of the United States can be regarded as the thorough-est, extrem-est, and maximum civil ownership of land and other means of production in human history.

*The results of official ownership of means of production and their economic power: totalitarian despotism of full monopoly by the official class*

Whether in China or the West, despotism has existed since the chiefdom era of the primitive society; the nature of the Chinese despotism is, however, fundamentally different from that of the Western despotism. Chinese despotism is based on the official ownership—kingly ownership, the most extreme official ownership—of the means of production and their economic power. The autocrats and their official class monopolize not only all the political power, but also the main means of production and their economic power of the whole country, and consequently monopolize even social power, such as assembly and association, as well as cultural power, such as speech and publication. In this sense, it is a kind of despotism of "he who does not obey, neither shall he eat," a totalitarian despotism that the autocrat and his official class fully monopolize all the political power, economic power, social power, and cultural power. On the contrary, the Western despotism is based on civil ownership of means of production and their economic power, which makes it possible for the autocrat and his official class to monopolize only political power, but impossible for them to monopolize economic power; as a result, it is rather difficult for them to monopolize social power, such as assembly and association, and cultural power, such as speech and publication. In this sense, it is a despotism that "he who does not obey shall also eat," a non-totalitarian despotism without the full monopoly of political, economic, social, and cultural power.

In this way, the most enslaving system in the West, the monarchical despotism, seems a paradise of liberty and equality, compared with the monarchical despotism of full monopoly of the Asiatic mode of production. The story of "German King William and the old mill" quoted by Yang Changji, a professor at Peking University, well illustrates this point. King William was very pleased with and proud of the reunification of Germany. When he saw an old mill in front of his villa, which hindered his view of the landscape, he wanted to have it demolished. However, the minister informed him that the mill was the private property of its owner, who did not agree to have it demolished. So, King William offered to pay the owner a large sum of money. But the minister returned with the news that the mill was the ancestral heritage of the mill owner, who would not sell it for any amount of money. William got furious and ordered to have the mill demolished with force. The mill owner sued the king at the Supreme Court, where the three judges unanimously adjudicated that King William should build a new mill at the original site for the mill owner.

Ancient Chinese, on hearing such an end to the story, would be tremendously amazed by the mill owner and the judges at their spirit of pursuing liberty and equality, for the ancient Chinese officials and people were so submissive that they would be willing to submit anything—be it a mill, a treasure, or their beloved—to the emperor for his enjoyment. Even if when the emperor believed in scandalous talks and ordered to have them beheaded, they would kneel on the ground and kowtow to the emperor and thank the emperor for his grace and for his issuing the order of beheading them. This contrast reveals the degree of enslavement in the full monopoly in the Asiatic mode of production. Yan Zi says, if tangerines grow in Huainan (the South of Huai River), they are still tangerines, but they will become trifoliate oranges when they grow in Huaibei (the north of Huai River). If Montesquieu, who despised the servility of the Chinese people extremely, and the three judges who announced the verdict of William's defeat, had been unfortunately born in ancient China, they would have surely been so servile!

Since the Era of the Five Emperors in China, the autocrat and his official class have always fully monopolized and possessed mighty power while the common people have been fully deprived of their power and left powerless and vulnerable. For 5,000 years, the common people have been too feeble to defend the rights and interests of their own class, to pursue the interests of their own class, to create a new state institution that safeguards the rights and interests of their own class. Instead, they have only attempted to seek shelter in a new government of a wise monarch and righteous officials.

> They can't represent themselves; they must be represented by others. Their representatives must be their masters at the same time, the authorities high above them, and the government of unrestricted power.[51]

That is why thousands of peasant uprisings have taken place in China on a massive scale unprecedented in world history since the Era of the Five Emperors, especially from the Spring and Autumn Period and the Warring States Period to the Opium War in the Qing Dynasty; yet, each uprising resulted in the same disaster: civilizations were reduced to ashes, the social economy was demolished, one-third of the population died. The truth is that the uprisings of the common people or peasants in the past dynasties were not actually class struggles between the common people class (the peasant class) and the official class (the landlord class), but the struggle between the "new official stratum" represented by the leaders of the peasant uprisings and the "old official stratum" of the imperial court that the uprisings wanted to overthrow. The uprisings were essentially the struggle between the old and the new official strata within the official class system, where every member only wants to be a bigger official, or at best, a more righteous official or a wise monarch. The common people class is incapable of defending their own rights and interests, so they never pursue the rights and interests of their own class and the new state institution that could safeguard their own rights and interests; instead, they concentrate solely on their individual interests: the elite among the common people class only want to get a toehold into the official class while the majority of common people only wish for a wise emperor and righteous officials.

That is why the wars in the past 5,000 years have brought about the same result: old dynasties are replaced by new dynasties, and the old kings and their officials are replaced by new kings and their officials; in other words, the old kings and their officials stepped down while new kings and their officials ascended the throne. They did not change the state institution at all; they didn't change the slavery and oppression by the official class with the full monopoly, which later ignited the peasant uprisings (the monopoly of power is the root of slavery and oppression; the degree of slavery and oppression was in proportion to the degree of monopoly of power). They did not change the state institution that led to the totalitarian despotism by the official class with full monopoly of power, which resulted in extremely cruel exploitation and oppression. Ultimately, they have not changed the official ownership of the means of production and their economic power.

*Value standards of state institutions* 131

It becomes evident that the official ownership of the means of production and their economic power is the fundamental cause of totalitarian despotism of full monopoly by the official class, and ultimately, the fundamental cause of Eastern despotism. In this sense, Engels says, "The basis of the despotism in the East is based on public ownership."[52] When Marx talks about the causes of Eastern despotism, that is, Asian theocracy, he also quotes Jones as saying that the reason and basis of Asian theocracy lies in the monopoly of economic powers, such as "the sole domination of the surplus means of livelihood" by the political leaders of such theocracy, and further points out that "this power of Asiatic and Egyptian kings or Etruscan theocrats, etc., has in modern society been transferred to the capitalist."[53]

*The result of the civil ownership of means of production and their economic power: a democratic society or a society that is moving toward or bound for democracy*

Western civil ownership of the means of production and their economic power puts its state institution into the mode of constant change, development, and improvement. Because the civil ownership of land and other means of production and their economic power means that the means of production and their economic power are mainly owned by the common people, the common people have thus had enough power and strength to fight against the monarch and his officials; in this class struggle, the common people class is able to be aggressive and defeat the official class. As a result, democracy and capitalism have been realized and continuously improved.

In the early stage, on the one hand, the despotic monarchy of the Aegean civilization in ancient Greece was replaced by the limited monarchy of Homer's era; and at the turn of Homer's era and the Archaic era, the limited monarchy was gradually replaced by the aristocratic oligarchy; finally, the constitutional democracy of Athens was established through Solon's reform. On the other hand, it made the transition from the primitive society of the Homer era to the classed society, and advanced into the feudal society of self-farming and tenant farming in the Archaic era, and then leaped into the capitalist society of slavery in the classical times.

> At the second stage, since the kingly monarchy of ancient Rome, as in the Homer era of Ancient Greece, the main struggle in society has been the class struggle of the common people class and the civilian class against the noble class and the official class. The result of the struggle is that the continuous victory by the common people class. Meanwhile, the state institution has been transformed from kingly monarchy to aristocratic republic, and even a series of democratic systems have been established, such as the common people congress, whose decision is the law that all people must abide by. The struggle has also led to the

development of the feudal society in the early and middle periods of the Roman Republic into a slave capitalist society in the late Republican and Empire Era.

At the third stage, although the Roman Empire in the later period regressed to a feudal society, it created an amazing and most beautiful feudal society in the Middle Ages: the feudal system of Western Europe is a state institution that allows the least power to the ruling class—the lords or the aristocrats—and promoted free contract for the first time in human history; it is a state institution with the smallest degree of monopoly and concentration of power; it is a political system with the smallest degree of power to act independently and autonomously; it is a state institution that is almost anarchic and official-less yet orderly. Meanwhile, it created a glorious, great, free city, a free capitalist society of civil ownership, thus transforming the feudal society in the vast rural area into a free feudal society of civil ownership.

Further on, around the 16th century, the West has evolved into a modern capitalist society. Although it has regressed to a capitalist society of monarchy and slavery for more than a 100 years, yet, with the continuous development of capitalism and the increasing growth of the means of production and economic power owned by the bourgeoisie, a bourgeois political revolution had been carried out. The despotic monarchy was replaced by the representative democracy of exclusive political rule by the capitalists. Later, with the industrial revolution of the 18th century, the slavery capitalist society has evolved into a free capitalist society of civil ownership.

The final, and also the most glorious, the greatest, and the most enviable stage is the time since the beginning of the 20th century. As the struggle of the working class and other common people for political and economic power continued to grow, the democracy of limited suffrage had been abolished and replaced by the universal suffrage democracy; everyone was in charge of the supreme power of the state on an equal footing and monopoly of political power was completely abolished. At the same time, through the construction of a series of systems, such as high decentralization of stocks, popularization of capital, employee stock ownership, economic democracy of co-determination, and welfare state system, everyone could have more or less means of production and become property owners, capital owners, and capitalists of differing values; the monopoly of the means of production and economic power is on the way to being eliminated to realize the universal civil ownership of capital and economic power by all the people. In short, the European and American joint-stock capitalist countries since the beginning of the 20th century are democratic capitalist countries with the most thorough, extreme, and complete civil ownership of the means of production and their economic power by all people in human history—the civil ownership by all people, and with universal suffrage.

*Absolute contingency: the nature of the emergence and existence of despotism*

A review of the root causes of despotism reveals that the emergence and existence of despotism can be summarized into three aspects. The first root cause is the "Asiatic mode of production" which is characterized by the "official ownership of the means of production and their economic power." On the one hand, it leads to the "totalitarian despotism of full monopoly of power by the official class." On the other hand, it originates from the geographical environment in the East, which is different from that in the West, for example, "China and India, as well as Egypt and Persia, have large river basins suitable for farming"; "Russia has a vast territory with an open central plain in Eastern Europe." In addition, the nature of the social structure that "the supreme leader is one single individual" and the human nature that "the supreme leader is bound to desperately pursue the supreme power" are also the root causes.

Are these three fundamental causes the only causes of the emergence and existence of despotism? No! First of all, it is obvious that despotism also stems from the political condition, that is, some domestic and international political situation and political needs, such as revolution, war, division, disorder, military conquest, and fierce class struggle, etc., which demanded unity, centralization, and dictatorship. Second, despotism also stems from the lack of social connections among the members of the common people class, who are isolated and separated from each other like potatoes. Even though there are hundreds of millions of them, they are as powerless as a bunch of people, who not only are too feeble to resist despotism but also are bound to seek refuge in a wise emperor or a benevolent government. Finally, despotism also stems from the servility of the people, traditional habits, the master-slave culture of advocating royal power and savior, the king-subject culture, and the emergence of despotic theories of some thinkers and great leaders. However, it is obvious that these causes are non-fundamental causes, and are thus not the root causes of despotism.

Clearly, these non-fundamental causes of despotism are not necessarily and intrinsically related to despotism, but the human-nature root as well as the social-structure-nature root of despotism is necessarily and intrinsically related to the emergence and existence of despotism. Imagine this: if contrary to human nature, the supreme leader of the state does not seek to be the sole owner of the supreme state power, if contrary to the nature of the social structure, the supreme leader of the state is not a single person but a number of people, then will an autocratic regime of one single individual holding the supreme power of the state ever emerge in such a state?

Obviously, it will not. Therefore, the universal origin of despotism, that is, the nature of the social structure that "the supreme leader is one single individual" and the human nature that "the supreme leader is bound to desperately pursue the supreme power" are the most essential conditions for the emergence and existence of despotism and have a necessary and intrinsic relation with the emergence and existence of despotism.

## 134  *Value standards of state institutions*

However, these roots, though intrinsic, do not necessarily lead to the emergence and existence of despotism, for such roots undoubtedly exist universally in all societies; the supreme leader is also a human being, who follows the nature of a human being to crave the supreme state power. However, as it is known, not all societies are autocratic regimes. Therefore, although the universal roots of despotism, that is, the human nature and the nature of the social structure, are inevitably and intrinsically related to the emergence and existence of despotism, these roots do not necessarily lead to the emergence and existence of despotism, they are only necessary conditions, but not sufficient conditions for its emergence and existence.

Only in terms of the special origin of despotism, that is, the Asiatic mode of production, it seems that the emergence and existence of autocracy is historically inevitable: despotism is the inevitable product of the Asiatic mode of production. The fact seems to prove this supposition: every country that practices the Asiatic mode of production is a despotic country; also the major countries that practice the Asiatic mode of production—China and India—have been despotic countries for 5,000 years. For this reason, most people believe that despotism is the inevitable product of economic development at a certain historical stage and that the emergence and existence of despotism has historical inevitability. Kautsky writes as follows:

> The reason why the Eastern countries so far have not gone beyond the form of despotism; the reason why this form seems to be manifested as the final and highest form of a country lies in the economic conditions on which the countries depend have not allowed a superior mode of production to emerge from these conditions.[54]

However, such a claim is untenable. Although Marx and other thinkers have proved that Eastern despotism originated from the Asiatic mode of production, they point out that the Asiatic mode of production does not necessarily lead to despotism. Whether it leads to despotism depends entirely on whether the representative of the unity or community of the Asiatic mode of production—tribes or countries—is a single person (a household head) or several people (the union of household heads). "The community is represented by the head of a household in the tribe or joined by the association of household heads. Correspondingly, the form of this community is either more authoritarian or more democratic."[55] Even Karl A. Wittfogel, the widely reputed author of *Oriental Despotism*, has to admit that the economic structure of the hydraulic agricultural society in Asia does not necessarily lead to despotism, but is only an opportunity for despotism to come into being.

> Primitive man has known water-deficient regions since time immemorial; but while he depended on gathering, hunting, and fishing, he had little need for planned water control. Only after he learned the reproductive process of plant life did he begin to appreciate the agricultural

possibilities of dry areas, which contained sources of water supply other than on-the-spot rainfall. Only then did he begin to manipulate the newly-discovered qualities of the old setting through small-scale irrigation farming (hydro-agriculture) and/or large-scale and government-directed farming (hydraulic agriculture). Only then did the opportunity arise for despotic patterns of government and society. The opportunity, not the necessity.[56]

Ultimately speaking, even if all the origins and causes of despotism are combined, they can only make the emergence and existence of despotism close to inevitable but still not absolutely inevitable. For the political regime is fundamentally different from the economic form and economic system. What kind of economic form and system a country implements, as Marx says, is not freely chosen by its people, but determined by the productivity and economic development of the country at a certain historical stage. It thus acquires a historical inevitability that is not independent of people's will: "People make some definite and inevitable relationships independent of their will in the society in which they live, relationships of production compatible with the material productivity at a certain developmental stage."[57]

How great these words sound! However, the economic form is determined by the development of the productive forces, so it has the historical inevitability independent of human will. For example, the primitive Communist economic form or economic system is determined not by people's free choice, but by extremely low productivity. Similarly, capitalist economic form or economic system is not freely chosen by people, but determined by productive forces, for capitalism is an economic form in which commodity economy dominates the whole society. During the transition from primitive society to classed society, no matter how great the leaders and masses that have emerged, no matter how hard they have struggled to realize capitalism, it was impossible for the commodity economy to dominate the whole society and realize capitalism at that time.

On the contrary, what kind of regime a state implements, whether it implements democracy or monarchy and other non-democratic state institutions, depends entirely on the number of people holding the supreme state power; whether the number of people holding the supreme state power is a single person (monarchy), or a minority (oligarchy), or the majority (democracy), is totally accidental and of free choice, without historical inevitability; thus, a regime is not necessary, not selectable, or not inevitable. Indeed, how can it not be accidental that the number of people in charge of the supreme state power—whether it is a single person or a minority or a majority? World history has proven the following view:

On the one hand, almost all regimes—democratic republic and oligarchic republic, limited monarchy and monarchal despotism, and other regimes of hybrid forms—have emerged in any historical stage of productivity and economic development, in almost all of the past dynasties defined according to the nature of economic form, in almost all forms of society—in primitive, slavery, feudal, and capitalist society. This means that any political regime, whether autocratic or democratic, is not necessarily determined by the level of productive forces and economic development, and thus has no historical necessity. In this sense, it is beyond the economy, history, society, class, and historical age; it can be applied to any country, any historical age, and any level of productivity and economic development; it thus has both absolute contingency and universality.

On the other hand, the fact that the vast majority of feudal societies practiced monarchy and the vast majority of capitalist societies practiced democracy, especially the fact that human beings have lived in democratic societies for more than 99% of the time up to now—in the primitive age of two or three million years of teams, groups, and tribes, all have clearly indicated that the type of political regime is closely related to the level of economic development. This means that what political regime that a society practices depends largely on the level of productivity and economic development. However, in any case, the decisive role of productivity and economic development level on the type of political system is neither inevitable nor necessary; it does not necessarily lead to democracy or non-democracy.

This explains why the countries that have practiced the Asiatic mode of production for 5,000 years have always been, but not necessarily, autocratic. Despotism, under any condition, even when all the roots and causes of despotism exist in a given society, is directly determined by the specific and accidental circumstances of the struggle of the people who strive for supreme power. It is accidental, contingent, and of free choice. Despotism is absolutely accidental and absolutely with no historical necessity. This is the nature of the emergence and existence of despotism.

### *Value of despotism: the fallacies of despotism*

Bryce has a famous saying: "All systems are not perfect."[58] How true these words are! There can be no perfect state institution. With every advantage there comes some disadvantage. Any state institution, whether democratic or autocratic, must have something excellent, good, benevolent, or right in it as well as something vicious, bad, evil, or wrong in it; it can't have all the good and right things or all the bad and wrong things. This is why thinkers since Plato and Aristotle have always rejected democracy and supported the politics of sages or aristocracies. They deny democracy because it has many disadvantages and demerits; they support aristocratic politics because aristocratic politics has many advantages and merits. Of course, such a method is unscientific for measuring the value of various state institutions, for according to this method, we can claim that any state institution is good because it has many advantages and merits, or that any state institution is bad because it has many disadvantages and demerits.

Therefore, measuring whether a state institution has good value or bad value can be based only on its basic and core values—values that are decisive: if its basic and core values are excellent, then this state institution is excellent; if its basic and core values are bad, then this state system is bad. The three major value standards—the ultimate value standard, the fundamental value standard, and the supreme value standard—undoubtedly constitute the basic and core value standards of measuring a state institution, because what these three standards evaluate are exactly the basic and core values of a state institution. Thus, in any case, a state can be a good state as long as it conforms to these three value standards or a bad state as long as it violates these three value standards. The value standard system formed by these three value standards is the scientific standard for measuring whether a state institution is good or bad.

As long as it conforms to these value standards, a state institution, regardless of how many demerits and errors it has, is a positive, ought-to-be, good, and excellent state institution; as long as it violates these value standards, a state institution, regardless of how many merits, correctness, and goodness it has, is a negative, ought-not-to-be, bad, and inferior state institution.

Despotism is a regime in which one individual holds the supreme power of the state without restriction. This means that the autocratic monarch, no matter how liberal, wise, and benevolent he is, no matter how well he governs his country, is, after all, like the worst tyrant, holding the supreme power of the state alone. Therefore, the following is true of a despotic state, no matter how it is governed, whether by the enlightened despotic monarchs such Yao, Shun, and Yu, or by atrocious autocratic monarchs such as Xia, Jie, Shang, and Zhou.

It always protects, without exception, the interest of the autocrat that he must hold the supreme state power alone; in this way, it violates the principles of political equality, economic equality, and equality of opportunities, and thus deprives every one of their due rights to equality in various aspects, driving everyone to live in a classed society of extreme inequality and injustice. A despotic state violates, without exception, the principles of political liberty, economic freedom, and freedom of thought, and thus deprives everyone of their due rights to various freedoms, driving everyone to live in a fully enslaved, alienated, and unfree society without human rights, justice, and humanity, which robs them of their personality and prevents them from realizing their creative potentials. In a nutshell, isn't despotism harmful to the interests of the largest majority of people? Isn't despotism an extreme violation of the standard of "the greatest interests for the greatest number"? Doesn't despotism violate the standard of "increasing the quantum of interests of everyone"?

Despotism violates the value standards of state institutions, namely, the supreme value standard of "humanity and liberty," the fundamental value standard of "justice and equality," and the ultimate value standard of "increasing the quantum of interests of everyone"; therefore, it is an extremely immoral, ought-not-to-be, and evil state institution. Of course, a crucial question about despotism is, whether the emergence and existence of despotism necessary or accidental. If it is necessary, inevitable, and un-selectable, and has historical inevitability like slavery, isn't despotism, though an extreme bad, a necessary bad like slavery, and a progressive good thing?

However, as mentioned above, studies of the origin and nature of despotism show that under any condition, even under the condition when all the root causes of despotism exist, despotism is completely accidental, contingent, avoidable, and selectable, and has no historical necessity. In summary, in any society, in any era, and under any condition, despotism is extremely evil, extremely bad, extremely negative, extremely undesirable, and extremely immoral because it violates all the value standards of state institutions.

Despotism as an absolute extreme bad means clearly that the theory that despotism is ought-to-be is an absolute extreme fallacy. Despotism, in any society, in any historical period, and under any condition, is absolutely and unconditionally an extreme fallacy. Therefore, for any thought system, as long as its basic or core value is not despotism, the net balance of truths and fallacies and merits and demerits that it produces is likely to be truth and goodness, and thus may deserve to be called a thought system of "truth and goodness." On the contrary, no matter how great it is, how profound it is, how deep-rooted and long-standing it is, as long as its core or main value is despotism, its net balance must be an absolutely colossal fallacy with tremendous negative value, and, therefore, an absolute extreme fallacy and harmful thought system.

Socrates, Plato, and Aristotle are more or less proponents of despotism, but their thoughts on despotism are but a few words and insignificant in the thought system that they construct, therefore, they do not affect the value of their thought system. On the contrary, the thought system of Confucius and Confucians is different. The Confucius and Confucians' despotism theory of ruling the state as a family, following the so-called "theory of Three Cardinal Guides," undoubtedly occupies the central position in their thought system. On this point, Chen Duxiu makes some very penetrating comments: "What is the unique claim of Confucianism? Nothing but the rituals required of the three cardinal guides. Confucius is just an honest and studious gentleman. Why did people regard him as an exemplar of all ages?"[59] "The so-called doctrine that the monarch and the officials follow the three cardinal guides and rituals are only the main part of the Confucianism, not the whole of Confucian thought system."[60]

Given this, although the thought system of Confucius and Confucianism is deep-rooted and long-standing and contains inexhaustible truths and benevolence, the greatest law of human beings, such as "the different degrees of love," its foundation and core—despotism of ruling the state like a family—is an absolute and extreme fallacy and has an absolute negative value. Therefore, as far as the net balance of truths and fallacies, and virtues and evils, in the thought system of Confucius and Confucians is concerned, it is undoubtedly an extreme fallacy and has extreme negative value; therefore, as a whole, it is an absolutely and extremely wrong and harmful thought system. The fallacies, negative values, and evils of the thought system of Confucius and Confucians, as Wu Yu points out, have increased and expanded incomparably because of their domination and corruption of China for more than 2,000 years: "Its pernicious influence is definitely no less than that of the fierce beasts or floods." Therefore, Lu Xun, in his *Diary of a Madman*, through the words of the Madman, incisively and pertinently condenses the essence of the moral system of Confucius and Confucians as "cannibalism":

> I turned to a history book, which did not refer to a particular historical time, with every page filled up with the same crooked words, 'benevolence, righteousness, and morality.' I couldn't sleep at all, so I read carefully at the middle of the night until I could see the words between lines. I found that the whole book was written up with two words: 'eating man'!

How true these words are! The despotism of ruling the state as a family by Confucius and Confucianism was an absolute extreme fallacy to Confucius's time, to the societies in the next 2,000 years, and even to the modern society today; it will remain a fallacy forever. That's why Yuan Shikai, who wanted to be emperor, would regard Confucianism as the guiding ideology of state governance. That's why Li Dazhao found that the autocrats of past dynasties "offered sacrifices to Confucius and Confucianism, worshipped them as their forefathers and sages." That's why Chen Duxiu laments that "whenever the democratic movement fails, the reactionary trend will rise once, and Confucius will be elevated one more time!"[61]

## *The theoretical basis of despotism*

Despotism is a state institution and a theoretical system that is extremely "unequal, unfree, unjust, inhuman, and harmful to the interests of the largest majority." It is a kind of extremely absurd theory that regards "extreme inhumanity, extreme un-freedom, extreme injustice, extreme inequality, and extreme harm to the interests of the largest majority" as the value standard of the state institution. However, what is more absurd than this is that not only almost all Chinese thinkers— Confucianism, Mohism, Legalism, Taoism, *Yin-yang* School, etc.—but also all the greatest thinkers in the West, such as Socrates, Plato, and Aristotle, agree with despotism.

Indeed, liberalism, since its rise during the Renaissance, has defeated, after two or three hundred years of struggle, despotism in the 17th century and become the mainstream ideology of Western society. For 400 years, the academic community seems to have reached a consensus that autocratic

140  *Value standards of state institutions*

rule is ought-not-to-be, and thus despotism is fallacious. However, in closer examination, we find that, as Karl A. Wittfogel points out, "But by and large, what Bury said at the close of the period of liberalism is true: little effort was made to determine the peculiarities of absolutism through detailed comparative study."[62]

In particular, the claims and supports of despotism advocated by the masters of despotism, such as Plato, Aristotle, Aquinas, Hobbes, Dante, and Machiavelli in the West, and Confucius, Mozi, Mencius, Xunzi, Lao Zi, Zhuang Zi, and Han Fei in China, have not been systematically refuted; the fallacy of despotism has so far not been systematically and scientifically confirmed. In short, whether despotism is ought-to-be, whether despotism is a fallacy or not, is still a theoretical question that remains unresolved and unproven. The ultimate key to tackle this question is: what is the theoretical basis of despotism?

The theoretical basis of Chinese and Western despotism can be summed up as "the theory of the divine rights of kings," "the theory of rule by elites," "the theory of national unity," "the theory of no two suns in the sky," and "the theory of despotism as a historical necessity." The *Encyclopedia Britannica*'s entry of "despotism" concludes,

> The simplest argument to justify monarchy is that the power of the king comes from God, that is, 'divine rights of kings' . . . In addition to the theory of the divine rights of kings, some more practical arguments have been put forward to defend autocratic monarchy. Complete obedience to a single will is said to be necessary to maintain order and security in the country; otherwise, hostile or decentralized political power can lead to chaos.

The doctrine of "the divine rights of a monarch" was once profusely refuted by many thinkers such as Locke, but today it seems that the doctrine of divine rights of a monarch seems so nonsensical that it is not even worth refuting. On the contrary, "the theory of rule by elites," "the theory of national unity," "the theory of no two suns in the sky," and "Confucians' unique defense of hereditary despotism of ruling the state as a family" still need careful analysis and consideration.

*The theory of rule by elites*

The representative figures of "the theory of rule by elites" are mainly ancient Greek philosophers, Heraclitus, Democritus, Socrates, Plato, and Aristotle. Among them, Aristotle epitomizes "the theory of rule by elites" and discovers in it the theoretical weapon that seems to make despotism invincible: "The principle of distribution of political positions and rights is this: political positions and rights ought to be distributed according to each person's talent, virtue, or contribution." According to this principle, the person

*Value standards of state institutions* 141

holding the supreme power of the state ought to be the person with the best talent and virtue; obviously, the person with the best talent and virtue cannot be the common people and can only be very few people, or even just one person. Therefore, Aristotle reiterates, "The most excellent regime is one governed by the most excellent people. The ruler of this type of regime may be one person, one clan, or a number of persons."[63]

This theory seems to be sensible, but it is a one-sided fallacy. As we all know, political rights are divided into rights of political liberty and rights of political positions. Only the right of political positions ought to be distributed according to the contribution of talent and virtue so that the most excellent person ought to hold the highest political position. On the contrary, the right of political liberty ought to be enjoyed equally by everyone regardless of their talent, virtue, and contribution. Therefore, no matter the talent, virtue, or contribution, each person ought to hold in full equality the supreme power of the country and thus participate, in full equality, in deciding the political destiny of the country. Given this, democracy is an ought-to-be regime. The fallacy of "the theory of rule by elites" lies obviously in its one-sidedness: instead of promoting both principles of political rights, it promotes only the principle of distribution of rights in political positions and ignores the principle of distribution of rights of political liberty, thus mistakenly assuming that the highest power of the state, like the highest political positions, ought to be held by the most excellent person.

*The theory of national unity*

According to "the theory of national unity," the most fundamental condition for the existence and development of any society, regardless of its size or number of people, is unity, and only despotism can bring about unity and existence of a nation and avoid national division and collapse. Aquinas writes,

> . . .for 'whatever is, exists in so far as it is a unity.' So also we see that things avoid disintegration as far as possible, and that the dissolution of a thing comes about because of some defect in it. So the first object of whoever rules a multitude is unity, or peace: but the cause of unity must be that which is in itself one. It is in fact evident that a number of individuals could not unite and bring others to harmony unless they were themselves in some way united. But what is a natural unity can be more easily a cause of unity than that which is artificially united. So a multitude can be better ruled by one than by several. It follows, then, that the government of the universe, which is the best, is the work of one ruler. This is what the Philosopher said (XII, *Metaphysics*): 'Nature abhors disorder and there is no goodness in a multiplicity of rulers. So there is one Sovereign.'[64]

It is true that the most fundamental condition for the existence and development of any society, regardless of size or number of people, is undoubtedly unity and "integration into a whole unit." Only when society "forms a whole" like one person, that is to say, when it becomes a unity, a "public ego," and a "public personality" can it exist and develop; otherwise, it will be fragmented and chaotic and thus inevitably collapse and perish. The division, collapse, and disappearance of a society and a state is undoubtedly the greatest and unmatched bad. Because human beings are social animals, if society and state are divided, collapse, and no longer exist, noone can survive, human beings will perish. Is there a greater bad than this? Of course, not. Therefore, if, as Aquinas says, only despotism, rule by one individual with the supreme power of the state, can bring about the unity and existence of society and state and avoid the division and collapse of society and state, despotism, though an extreme bad because it extremely violates the value standards of state institutions, is also a necessary bad because it avoids greater bad— the collapse of society and the state; it is, therefore, ultimately good and ought-to-be, not bad or not ought-not-to-be.

However, Aquinas, Dante, and Mo Zi's views are not valid. For there is no doubt that any form of government—monarchy, constitutional monarchy, oligarchic republic, and democratic republic—can guarantee the unity and existence of society and avoid its division and collapse. One may wonder, is it possible that only autocracy, rule by one individual with supreme state power, can unite the state and society while democracy, where the supreme power of the state is shared by all citizens, cannot unify the society? Isn't the "public will" formed by democracy through a representative system and the principle of majority rule a unity? Is the democratic United States not a unified country? The only difference is just this: the unity created by autocracy is a unity of the will of one single individual and thus a unity of alienation, enslavement, and un-freedom while unity created by democracy is a unity of "public will," and thus a unity of non-enslavement, non-alienation, and liberty.

Democracy not only guarantees, through "the unity of liberty" it forms, the existence of society, but also promotes rapid development of society: liberty is the fundamental condition for realizing everyone's creative potential. On the contrary, autocracy can only guarantee the existence of society, but cannot promote social development through the "unity of un-freedom" it creates. Even worse, it is not just that autocracy cannot promote social development, but also that it hinders social development to a very great extent. The reason why the despotic society can still drag on is not due to autocracy itself, but, on the contrary, due to the liberty fighters' courageous resistance against autocracy. Therefore, although it can guarantee the unity and existence of society and avoid its split and collapse, autocracy hinders social development extremely and violates the value standards of state institutions. On the contrary, democracy can not only guarantee the existence of society, but also promote the rapid development of society, which fully conforms to the value standards of state institutions. Given this, if any country chooses

*Value standards of state institutions* 143

autocracy, it can protect the unity and existence of society and avoid its split and collapse, but compared with the choice of democracy, the net balance is of great negative value. Therefore, autocracy is not a necessary bad, but a pure bad.

*The theory of no two suns in the sky*

The premise for the above conclusion that despotism is pure bad is that despotism is not necessary, not un-selectable, but is totally accidental and selectable. If despotism were necessary, not of free choice, or independent of human will, then wouldn't despotism be natural and right? A close examination of the writings by proponents of despotism in China and the West reveals that the major support for their claim that despotism is ought-to-be is their belief that despotism is necessary and not of free choice. According to them, that the supreme power holder of society or state is only one person, that is, monarchy, is the nature of the social structure of a society or a state; it is as natural, necessary, independent of human will, and objective as the one sun in the sky, the one father in the family, the one heart in the human body, the one king among the bees, and the one God in the universe; therefore, it is naturally reasonable, naturally ought-to-be, and naturally good. This view may be called "the theory of no two suns in the sky."

Confucius called the monarch "the Son of Heaven" and compared the monarch to the heavenly sun. "Confucius said, 'There are no two suns in heaven, and there are no two kings among the people.'"[65] Given this, isn't monarchic despotism of the supreme power of the state held by one monarch just as natural and ought-to-be as there is only one sun in heaven? Guo Xiang resonates, "The subjugation of officials to the monarch and the hierarchical relationship among family members are as natural as the heaven and are nothing of human creation!"[66] He is echoed by Western thinkers supporting despotism, such as Aquinas:

> That is best which most nearly approaches a natural process, since nature always works in the best way. But in nature, government is always by one. Among members of the body there is one which moves all the rest, namely, the heart: in the soul there is one faculty which is pre-eminent, namely reason. The bees have one king, and in the whole universe there is one God, Creator and Lord of all. And this is quite according to reason: for all plurality derives from unity. So, since the product of art is but an imitation of the work of nature, and since a work of art is the better for being a faithful representation of its natural pattern, it follows of necessity that the best form of government in human society is that which is exercised by one person.[67]

If the supreme power of a society or a state can only be held by one person, as the proponents of despotism claim, just as there is only one sun in the

144  *Value standards of state institutions*

sky, only one heart in the human body, only one king among the bees, and only one God in the universe, and if, as they further claim, such is the necessary, inevitable, and not-of-free-choice nature of the structure of a society or state, then it will seem true that despotism is natural and ought-to-be, no matter how much it violates the value standards of state institutions, or rather that despotism per se has nothing to do with moral good and bad, but the choice of a certain type of despotism, say enlightened despotism, tyrannical despotism, kingly despotism, or hegemonic despotism, has something to do with moral good and bad.

However, this view—that the holder of the supreme power of the state can only be one person is the necessary nature of the state structure—is also untenable. It is true, as mentioned earlier, that, by the nature of social or state structure, the political head or supreme political leader of any society or state, in general, must be a person: a chieftain, a military commander-in-chief, a governor, a president of a country. Even the "president" or "prime minister" of a democratic country is just one person.

Nevertheless, the fact that the supreme leader is one person does not mean that the holder of supreme power is one single person. The two concepts are fundamentally different. In a democratic country, although the supreme leader or the president is the most powerful person in the country, he does not hold the supreme power alone. In terms of the supreme state power, he has exactly the same as any other citizen, which means "one for one, not one for two." That is to say, the president and every citizen hold the supreme power of the state on the same footing; otherwise, it will not be a democratic country. However, as far as human nature is concerned, the supreme leader is bound to strive for the supreme power of the society or the country, thus easily turning the democratic system that "the supreme leader is one person" into a despotic system that "the holder of the supreme power is one person." The problem with theorists of despotism in believing that despotism is the necessary nature of the state structure lies in their equating the concept that "the supreme leader is one single person" with "the holder of the supreme state power is one single person." As a result of their mistake, they deduce from a correct premise that "that the supreme leader is one single person is the inevitable nature of the state structure" a wrong conclusion that the holder of supreme state power is one single person—monarchic despotism—is the necessary nature of the state structure.

*Hereditary despotism of ruling the state as a family: the unique defense by Confucianism*

As Confucians' unique defense of despotism, "the theory of hereditary despotism of ruling the state as a family" not only rationalizes despotism in general, but also, in particular, rationalizes totalitarian despotism with full monopoly—of political power, economic power, social power such as assembling and association, and cultural power, such as speech and publication—the worst type of state institution that human beings are capable of creating. The theory has been very persuasive in making people believe that such an extremely evil system is a benevolent system beyond doubt, so much so that almost all Chinese thinkers (Confucianism, Mohism, Legalism, and Taoism) have been supporters of the hereditary despotism of ruling the state as a family since ancient times, even up to the Qing Dynasty.

Fundamentally speaking, despotism in China is different from that in the West. The major difference between China's despotism in the past 5,000 years, from the Era of the Five Emperors to the Opium War, and its western counterpart can be summarized as follows. China's despotism is "kingly and official ownership of land" and resulting in totalitarianism that "he who does not obey, neither shall he eat"; it is a totalitarian despotism of full monopoly that grants the king and the official class power to "monopolize not only political power and economic power but also social power and cultural power." The Western despotism is civil ownership of land and its resulting non-totalitarian despotism that "he who does not obey shall also eat"; it is a non-totalitarian despotism that allows the king and this official class "only the power to monopolize political power."

The root of this fundamental difference lies in the difference between Chinese society and Western society. As China is a so-called "hydraulic society" that must build large-scale flood control projects and artificial irrigation facilities, which could only be undertaken by the monarch and his government, and the owner of the national land resources is bound to be the king and his official class, who can represent the state and the government. On the contrary, as the West is not a "hydraulic society," and does not need to build large-scale flood control projects and artificial irrigation facilities that only the government can undertake. So the builders of flood control projects and artificial irrigation facilities are mainly farmers and common people themselves, not the government and its officials; as a result, the main owner of national land are the common people, not the king and his official class. This fundamental difference between Chinese despotism and Western despotism, as found by Marx's theory of the Asiatic mode of production, ultimately stems from the existence of a vast geographical environment of the large river basins suitable for farming in China, which does not exist in Western countries.

This characteristic of China's despotism that the monarch and his official class have full monopoly turns the whole country into a pseudo-family or a quasi-family. Family studies show that family has three major characteristics. First, the family is a society formed through sexual relationship and composed of parents and children and thus a parent-child society. This is the definition of the family and the fundamental non-statistical feature of the family: all societies with this feature are families in the true sense. The second feature is that the family is a society based on love rather than on interests. This is a statistical feature of the family, which is derived from the characteristic of the family's parent-child relationship: non-parent societies with this feature, such as some early Christian groups, are also societies based on love rather than on interests, and thus are pseudo families or quasi-families. Finally, the family is a totalitarian despotic society, in which parents have monopolized all power— political power, economic power, social power, and cultural power. This is also a statistical feature of the family, which is derived from the characteristic of the family's parent-child relationship; thus non-parent-child society with this feature is also a pseudo-family or quasi-family.

Given this, the King of China and his official class, because of their monopoly, are similar to parents, and the powerless common people class similar to family members, and thus the whole country is very much a family and can be called a quasi-family. This quasi-family state was further fabricated as a family by Confucians, where the parents of this quasi-family are the king and his officials monopolizing the full power of prefectures and counties at all levels and quasi-family members are the common people. In this way, their relationship is fabricated as a hierarchy in terms such as "monarch-father," "parent-official," and "child-subject." In this way, the totalitarian despotism of the king and his official class is reckoned as reasonable and ought-to-be, just as the totalitarian despotism of the patriarchal monopoly is reasonable and ought-to-be. This is the quintessence of the Confucian theory of "ruling the state with familial piety."

Confucian "despotism of ruling the state as a family" is not only different from Western despotism, but also despotism in other Eastern countries. It is the greatest characteristic of Chinese culture, and it has been recognized by scholars of various schools in China. The Mohist School says: "Failure to observe the rituals of monarch-official relationship, supervisor-subordinate relationship, the elder-younger relationship, father-son relationship, and sibling relationship is root of chaos in the state."[68] The Legalist school says, "The officials must submit to the monarch, sons to fathers, and wives to husbands; if three submissions are observed, then the state will be well-governed; failure to observe them will bring chaos to the state. This is the way to rule the state."[69] The Taoist school says,

> The monarch is the master to whom the officials must be subordinated; the father is the master to whom the son must be subordinated; the older brother is the master to whom the younger brother must be subordinated; the elder is the master to whom the younger must be subordinated; the men are the masters to whom women must be subordinated; the husband is the master to whom the wife must be subordinated. The hierarchy of masters and subordinates is like the hierarchy of heaven and earth, so ancient sages take this natural law and try to imitate it.[70]

This kind of despotism seems reasonable but is actually quite absurd and fallacious. In fact, parents' monopoly of all powers of the family—political power and economic power, social power and cultural power—means that the family is a totalitarian despotic society. In this sense, a family is therefore a society of extreme inequality and non-freedom, which violates the value standard of state institutions, that is, the supreme value standard of state institutions (humanity and liberty), the fundamental value standard (justice and equality), and the ultimate value standard (increasing or decreasing the quantum of interests of everyone), and undoubtedly an extreme bad. However, as a totalitarian despotic society with full power monopoly, the family is a necessary bad, for the following reasons.

On the one hand, most of the children in the family are under age, weak in reason, naive and ignorant, and totally need and rely on the nurture of parents. They lack the ability to hold the power of the family and the ability to grow up healthily on their own. If parents do not monopolize all powers and instead share family power equally with their children, as in a democratic society, isn't the family, though free, equal, and compliant with the value standards of state institutions, bound to collapse? Aren't human beings bound to perish? Given this, the family, though a bad due to its nature as totalitarian despotism with full monopoly, is a necessary bad because of its capability of avoiding a greater bad—such as the collapse of a family or the perishing of human beings, and can thus ultimately be considered as good and ought-to-be, instead of being bad and ought-not-to-be.

On the other hand, the relationship between family members is entirely based on love. Although parents monopolize all the powers in the whole family, their deep love for family members enables them to work in the interests of family members as they do for their own interests. Therefore, parents and their children and other family members are like one person: parents' decisions are generally the most rational and correct decisions for their children and other family members. The obedience of family members, such as children to the parents is in fact the obedience of their own desires to their own rationality, which means their own inferior, foolish, and wrong understanding submits to their own lofty, wise, and correct understanding. Therefore, generally speaking, family members such as children seem to have sacrificed equality and liberty because of the totalitarian dictatorship of their parents, but they have sacrificed, in fact, only the liberty to follow their wrong, irrational, and foolish desires, and gained the liberty to realize the right, rational, and wise desires, thus creating a net balance of great benefits, good, and positive values. Therefore, the totalitarian despotism of parents' monopoly, though an extreme bad in itself, results in great good, and a net balance of great good. In this sense, the family can be categorized as a necessary bad.

Therefore, totalitarian despotism with leaders' full monopoly can be categorized as a necessary bad under two preconditions: one is that the relationship between rulers and the ruled is based entirely on love rather than on interests; the other is that most of the ruled are young and ignorant, and totally dependent on the the ruler for their nurture. The only society with these two conditions is, without doubt, the family. Therefore,

148  *Value standards of state institutions*

only the totalitarian despotism with the family leader's full monopoly is a necessary bad and a good, while all other forms of totalitarian despotism are pure bad. The Confucian family-state despotism is based on the two correct premises of "the despotic family system of patriarchal monopoly is good" and "China-state belongs to the quasi-family category because of the monopoly by the king and his official class," but it mistakenly formulates this quasi-family state as a family and thus draws the wrong conclusion that the totalitarian despotic state institution with the king's full monopoly is good.

## Notes

1. Berlin, *Four Essays on Liberty*, 165.
2. *Complete Works of Aristotle*, Volume 8 (Beijing: China Renmin University Press, 1997), 96.
3. Adam Smith, *The Theory Of Moral Sentiments* (Beijing: China Sciences Publishing House, Chengcheng Books Ltd., 1979), 86.
4. Dalberg-Acton, *Freedom and Power*, 310.
5. Benjamin Constant, *Liberty of Ancients Compared with That of the Moderns* (Beijing: Commercial Press, 1999), 63.
6. Popper, *Open Society and Its Enemy*, 130.
7. Rawls, *A Theory of Justice*, Revised ed., 3.
8. Miller, *Blackwell Encyclopedia of Political Thought*, 194.
9. Liu Zehua et al., *Royal Power and Society* (Wuhan: Chongwen Book, 2005), 205.
10. Li Xiantang, *The Autocratic Spirit of Confucianism in Pre-Qin Dynasty* (Beijing: Renmin University Press, 2003), 33.
11. A.P. D'entreve, *Aquinas's Selected Political Writings* (Totowa, NJ: Barnes & Noble Books, 1981), 6–7.
12. Thomas Hobbes, *De Cive, or, The Citizen* (Westport, CT: Greenwood Press, 1982), 126.
13. Guo Huarong, *History of French Political Thought* (Beijing: People's Publishing House, 2010), 11.
14. *The Analects of Confucius*.
15. Li Dazhao, *Collected Works by Li Dazhao* (Beijing: People's Publishing House 1984), 264.
16. Ban Gu, *Bai Hu Tong*.
17. Wu Xiaoming, *Selected Works by Chen Duxiu* (Shanghai: Shanghai Far East Publishers, 1994), 370.
18. Fung Yulan, *A Short History of Chinese Philosophy* (Beijing: Peking University Press, 1985), 90.
19. *Han Feizi*.
20. Niccolo Machiavelli, *The Prince* (Danbury, CT: Grolier Enterprises Corp., 1981), 51.
21. Thomas Hobbes, *Leviathan*, A Touchstone Book Published by Simon & Schuster, 1962.
22. *Mencius*, "King Hui of Liang."
23. D'entreve, *Aquinas Selected Political Writings*, 8.
24. *Mencius*, "Jinxin."
25. Dong Zhongshu, *Luxuriant Dew in the Spring and Autumn Annals*.
26. *Mencius*, "Li Lou."
27. *Mencius*, "Wan Zhang."

28 Mencius, "King Hui of Liang."
29 *The Analects of Confucius*, "Liren."
30 Ma Qihua, *The Political Science*, Volume II (Taipei: Taiwan Commercial Press, 1977), 163.
31 Karl Kausky, *The Materialist Conception of History* (Shanghai: Shanghai People's Publishing House, 1964), 322.
32 Lewis H. Morgen, *Ancient Society* (Chicago, IL: Charles H. Kerr & Company, 1907), 151.
33 William A. Haviland, *Contemporary Anthropology* (Shanghai: Shanghai People's Publishing House, 1987), 476.
34 *Collected Works of Karl Marx and Frederick Engels*, Volume 46 (Beijing: People's Publishing House, 1979), 472–473.
35 *Collected Works of Karl Marx and Frederick Engels*, Volume 1 (Beijing: People's Publishing House, 1976), 79.
36 Richard Jones, *On the Distribution of Wealth and the Source of Taxation* (Beijing: Commercial Press, 2009), 96.
37 Karl Marx, *Capital*, Volume 3 (Beijing: People's Publishing House, 1973), 828.
38 Quoted in Zhu Jianjin, *Where Is the Oriental Society Going?* (Shanghai: Shanghai Academy of Social Sciences Press, 1996), 122.
39 *Collected Works of Karl Marx and Frederick Engels*, Volume 1, 850.
40 Ibid., 850.
41 Umberto Melotti, *Marx and the Third World* (Beijing: Commercial Press, 1981), 117.
42 *Collected Works of Karl Marx and Frederick Engels*, Volume 1, 857, 861.
43 Wu Ze, *On the History of Oriental Socio-economic Forms* (Shanghai: East China Normal University Press, 1991), 103.
44 Ma Keyao, *A Study of Feudal Economic Forms in Western Europe* (Beijing: People's Publishing House, 2001), 263–264.
45 Harold Underwood Faulkner, *American Economic History*, Volume 1 (Beijing: Commercial Press, 1965), 13–14.
46 Luo Rongqu, *General Introduction to American History* (Beijing: Commercial Press. 2009), 13.
47 Huang Yang, *Study on the Land System of Ancient Greece* (Shanghai: Fudan University Press, 1995), 68.
48 Marx, *Capital*, Volume 1 (Beijing: China Social Science Press 1983), 832.
49 Rongqu, *General Introduction to American History*, 105.
50 Ibid., 116.
51 *Collected Works of Karl Marx and Frederick Engels*, Volume 1, 678.
52 *Collected Works of Karl Marx and Frederick Engels*, Volume 20, 681.
53 *Collected Works of Karl Marx and Frederick Engels*, Volume 1, 387.
54 Kautsky, *Materialist Conception of History*, 336.
55 *Collected Works of Karl Marx and Frederick Engels*, Volume 46 (Beijing: People's Publishing House, 1979), 474.
56 Karl A. Wittfogel, *Oriental Despotism: A Comparative Study of Total Power* (New Haven, CT: Yale University Press, 1957), 12.
57 *Collected Works of Karl Marx and Frederick Engels*, Volume 2 (Beijing: People's Publishing House, 1995), 32.
58 James Bryce, *Modern Democracies*, Volume II (Changcun: Jilin People's Publishing House, 2001), 1027.
59 Ren Jianshu, *Selected Works of Chen Duxiu* (Shanghai: Shanghai People's Publishing House, 1993), 388.
60 Ibid., 388.
61 Ibid.
62 Wittfogel, *Oriental Despotism: A Comparative Study of Total Power*, 2.

63 Aristotle, *Political Science* (Beijing: Commercial Press. 1996), 173.
64 D'entreve, *Aquinas Selected Political Writings*, 54.
65 *Mencius*, "Wan Zhang."
66 Guo Xiang, *Collections of Commentaries on Zhuangzi.*
67 D'entreve, *Aquinas Selected Political Writings*, 7.
68 *Mozi.*, "Shang Tong Zhong."
69 *Han Feizi*, "Zhong Xiao."
70 *Chuang-tzu*, "Providence."

# 3 Happiness
## The moral principle of self-regarding

Almost every thinker from ancient times to the present, in China and the West, has discussed happiness. However, it is no exaggeration that every question about happiness has hitherto not been satisfactorily answered: happiness remains an eternally intriguing puzzle in ethics. Confronted with this difficult problem, Kant laments, "Unfortunately, the concept of happiness is so vague that although everyone wants it, no one can make clear and coherent what he decides to pursue or choose."[1] According to previous studies, this problem includes five aspects: the concept of happiness, the value of happiness, the nature of happiness, the law of happiness, and the principle of happiness.

## The concept of happiness

### *Definition of happiness: psychological experience of the realization of the great needs, desires, and purposes of life*

What is happiness? Mill answers, "Happiness is pleasure and the elimination of pain."[2] In fact, all happiness is pleasure, but not all pleasure is happiness. The difference between the two, as Elizabeth Telfer says, lies in their different meanings to life: "The definition of happiness, in my opinion, is a state of pleasure about one's life experiences, his whole life, and the sum of his life."[3] Ruut Veenhoven, among other Western scholars, also says, "'Happiness' refers to life as a whole."[4]

These words are very true! According to their significance to life, pain and pleasure can be divided into two kinds. One is the unimportant pain and pleasure, such as the pain of suffering hunger sometimes and the pleasure of enjoying an expensive and delicious meal once. Obviously, this kind of pain and pleasure is only just that, not misfortune and happiness. Who would say that suffering from hunger once is misfortune and enjoying some expensive and delicious meal once is happiness? On the contrary, the other kind is great or extreme pain and pleasure, such as suffering from hunger often and enjoying expensive and delicious meals often. This kind of pain and pleasure is misfortune and happiness, as the pleasure of enjoying expensive and delicious meals often is enjoyment of material happiness, and the pain of suffering from hunger often is that of material misfortune.

Thus, the difference between happiness and pleasure, between misfortune and pain lies in whether they hold any importance to the life of the person concerned. This kind of importance is specifically manifested first in its length of duration: happiness is a continuous and enduring pleasure. So Leibniz says, "Happiness is a kind of continuous pleasure... Happiness can be considered as a road passing through pleasure while pleasure can be said as a step up the ladder of happiness."[5] Then, it is also manifested in its amount: happiness is a great amount of pleasure. Leibniz continues, "Happiness, in its broadest sense, is the greatest pleasure we can have."[6] To sum up, happiness is the great and extreme pleasure of life, an enduring or immense pleasure; misfortune is the great pain of life, an enduring or immense pain.

Obviously, everyone's needs, desires, and purposes that are of great significance to his life, his enduring or great happiness are generally guided by his reason and achieved through his long-term striving to realize his ideal. That is why Leibniz says, "Rationality and will lead us to happiness, but feelings and desires only lead us to pleasure."[7] From this point of view, generally speaking, happiness is the psychological experience of realizing one's ideals, the pleasure derived from it; misfortune is the psychological experience of failing to realize ideals, the pain of failing to realize ideals. *Cihai*, the comprehensive Chinese dictionary, defines happiness in this way: "Happiness is the state of feeling satisfied when ideals are realized in the long struggle for the realization of these ideals."[8]

Their difference goes beyond this. The difference between happiness and pleasure is also that pleasure is not necessarily conducive to survival and development while happiness is necessarily conducive to survival and development. This is because pleasure can be divided into normal and healthy pleasure and abnormal and morbid pleasure: the psychological experience of satisfying normal and healthy needs and desires is normal and healthy pleasure; the psychological experience of satisfying morbid and abnormal needs and desires is a morbid and abnormal pleasure. For example, the pleasure of alcoholism, the pleasure of drug addiction, and the pleasure that a jealous mind experiences on the realization of his vicious purpose all directly or indirectly harm one's own survival and development, and are the so-called abnormal and morbid pleasures. Therefore, pleasure is not necessarily conducive to survival and development.

On the contrary, happiness cannot be similarly divided into normal and healthy happiness and abnormal and morbid happiness: happiness is definitely normal and healthy. Happiness is the psychological experience of the realization of the ideal of human life, the psychological experience of the realization of the needs, desires, and purposes that are of great significance to our lives, and the psychological experience of gaining interests of great significance to our life. Thus, it is only likely that there is the pleasure from alcoholism and drug abuse, but it is unlikely that there is happiness from alcoholism and drug abuse; it is only likely that there is the pleasure from fulfilling the vicious purpose of a jealous mind, but it is unlikely that there is happiness from fulfilling the purpose of a jealous mind. We would never regard the realization of the purpose of alcoholism, drug addiction, and jealousy, which is harmful both to ourselves and to others, as our ideals and major interests of life; we would never envy those who have achieved these purposes and experienced these pleasures and consider them as happy people. Therefore, there never exists happiness that is directly or indirectly harmful to one's own survival and development; there never exists happiness that is morbid and abnormal. Happiness, as Kant says, must be conducive to survival and development: "Happiness is the condition for rational being to exist in this world."[9]

Therefore, the difference between happiness and pleasure lies ultimately in whether survival and development is perfected or not. Happiness is a great pleasure of life and a pleasure that is necessarily conducive to survival and development. In this sense, happiness is some kind of perfection of survival and development; on the contrary, pleasure is not so. On the one hand, an abnormal and morbid pleasure just means a certain defect of survival and development; on the other hand, short-lived and insignificant pleasure, though conducive to survival and development, cannot achieve the perfection of survival and development. Who would say that the pleasure of a good meal can help attain the perfection of survival and development?

The pleasure a person feels upon receiving a letter of admission from a university and the pain a person feels when he/she fails the national college entrance examination is happiness and misfortune, respectively. This kind of pleasure and pain is significant to the perfection of his survival and development, so this kind of pain and pleasure is not only pleasure and pain but also happiness and misfortune. The great pleasure derived from the admission to college and the pain from the humiliating failure in the national college entrance examination is of great significance to one's life and the perfection of one's survival and development because admission to college provides an important platform for his survival and development which will lead to the perfection of his survival and development; the failure in national college entrance examination deprives him of that important platform which is essential for his survival and development and thus causes an imperfection in his survival and development.

Spinoza fails to see that the degree of perfection of survival and development is the fundamental difference between happiness and pleasure, and mistakes pleasure as perfection and pain as imperfection: "Pleasure is the transition from a smaller perfection to a larger perfection while pain is the transition from a larger perfection to a smaller one."[10] In this way, Spinoza, like Mill, equates pleasure and pain with happiness and misfortune.

Given this, happiness is profoundly complex with multiple concepts. Happiness is, in the literal sense, the great or extreme pleasure of life; in essential terms, happiness is the psychological experience of the realization of the great needs, desires, and goals of life. ultimately, happiness is the psychological experience of some perfection of survival and development. On the contrary, misfortune is, in the literal sense, the great or extreme pain of life; misfortune is, in essential terms, the psychological experience that the great needs and desires of life cannot be satisfied, the psychological experience of failing to realize major purposes of life; ultimately, misfortune is the psychological experience that one's survival and development have been seriously harmed.

## Structure of happiness: the subjective form of happiness, the objective standard of happiness, and the objective essence of happiness

Happiness is a great or extreme pleasure of life, a psychological experience of extreme pleasure from achieving the great needs, desires, and purposes of life, a psychological experience of extreme pleasure derived from the perfection of survival and development. This obviously means that happiness is composed of two factors: "the subjective form of psychological experience" and "the objective content of some perfection of survival and development when great needs and desires in life are satisfied." So, Richard Kraut says, "The concept of happiness seems to have two dimensions: happiness refers to the feeling of happiness sometimes and to the happy life at other times."[11] Kex also writes:

> Through superficial description, we can distinguish the two aspects of happiness. One is happiness as an attitude, and the other is a collection of events that contribute to this attitude. These events are satisfactory and come from all that one does and has.[12]

Nevertheless, these views under closer scrutiny might be puzzling. Apparently, psychological experience is subjective while achieving some perfection of survival and development is objective. Does it, however, mean that the satisfaction of great needs and desires in life is objective? Isn't desire subjective? Of course, desire is subjective, but the fulfillment and realization of desire are objective and independent of human will. Imagine this: a person has an appetite, which belongs to the category of desire and emotion and is therefore subjective, but whether his appetite is satisfied or not isn't subjective, and not dependent on his own will. His appetite can be satisfied only by eating and drinking; if he does not eat or drink, then, no matter how he imagines that he is satisfied, his appetite will not be satisfied. In this sense, whether his appetite is satisfied or not is objective and independent of his will.

However, there are differences between "the fulfillment or realization of great needs, desires, and purposes of life" and "the perfection of survival and development": the former is the objective standard of happiness while the latter is the objective essence of happiness. The satisfaction or realization of needs and desires is undoubtedly the fundamental means of survival and development; the whole meaning of a behavior lies in satisfying desires and needs, to make survival and development reach a certain degree of perfection. Therefore, the perfection of survival and development is the primary drive for everyone to pursue the realization of great needs, desires, and purposes of life, and is therefore the most profound objective content of happiness and the objective essence of happiness. Then, the question is, why is it that the realization of great needs, desires, and purposes of life is the objective standard of happiness?

Though it is true that one is happy as long as he feels happy, whether he feels happy is, in fact, independent of his own will, but is necessarily dependent on whether his major needs, desires, and purposes of life can be realized or not. In this sense, whether the major needs, desires, and purposes of life can be realized or not is the objective standard of the psychological experience of happiness. Richard Kraut has elucidated on this point:

> The objectivists, like us, admit that a happy person must have a certain emotional attitude towards himself; he must be satisfied with the life he has lived and must see that his plan is being realized. In other words, like the objectivists, we believe that a happy life does not consist only in having a high affirmative attitude towards one's own life; moreover, we agree that to enjoy a happy life, one must actually meet certain criteria.[13]

Meanwhile, the perfection of survival and development is a relative and unstable concept. A billionaire is fundamentally different from a poor man in terms of perfection of material life and development. A poor man can achieve, with tens of thousands of yuan, the perfection of material life and development; a billionaire may feel that with only one million yuan, his material life and development is extremely far from perfection. Therefore, the perfection of survival and development is a relative and unstable concept. So, to what is the perfection of survival and development relative?

Obviously, it is relative to everyone's great needs, desires, and purposes. If a person's great needs, desires, and purposes of life are satisfied or realized, his survival and development will reach a certain degree of perfection, otherwise, it will be imperfect. Each person's major needs, desires, and purposes of life are different, so their standards of perfection of survival and development will be different. In this sense, the satisfaction or realization of great needs, desires, and purposes of life is the objective standard of perfection of survival and development. This is the double meaning of realization of great needs, desires, and purposes of life as the objective standard of happiness: it is both the objective standard of whether the psychological experience of happiness can be produced or not and the objective standard of whether the survival and development is perfected or not.

It can be concluded that the psychological experience of extreme pleasure is the subjective form of happiness; the perfection of survival and development is the objective essence of happiness; between the subjective form and the objective essence is the satisfaction or realization of the great needs, desires, and purposes of life as the objective standard of happiness. This is the structure of happiness.

## Types of happiness

### Material happiness, social happiness, and spiritual happiness

The most important types of happiness are undoubtedly material happiness, social happiness, and spiritual happiness. The so-called material happiness, or happiness of material life, is the happiness achieved by realizing material needs, desires, and purposes, that is, the happiness achieved by satisfying physiological needs and physical desires. The main part of material happiness is happiness achieved by satisfying appetite and sexual desire, and its highest manifestation is a well-to-do life and a healthy body. Social happiness refers to the happiness of social life. It is the happiness of realizing a human's social needs, desires, and purposes. It mainly includes the happiness achieved when one's liberty needs, belonging and love needs, and power and esteem needs are satisfied. The highest manifestation of social happiness is probably dignity from high social status and a perfect romantic love relationship. Spiritual happiness refers to the happiness of spiritual life. It is the happiness of the realization of human spiritual needs, desires, and purposes. It mainly includes the happiness of the realization of cognitive needs and the happiness of the satisfaction of aesthetic needs. The highest manifestation of spiritual happiness is undoubtedly self-realization and the realization of one's creative potential, especially the realization of creative potential in the spiritual field, that is, the so-called "writing and publishing," creating and establishing one's own unique thoughts or theories. Then, what is exactly the relationship among these three kinds of happiness in terms of the level of their value?

Their relationship can be described as follows: material happiness is the low-level happiness, social happiness is the middle-level happiness, and spiritual happiness is the high-level happiness. Indeed, in life, what happiness can be higher than the spiritual happiness of realizing one's creative potential? Isn't the most fascinating and supreme happiness the happiness of becoming a Newton, an Einstein, a Tolstoy, or a Cao Xueqin? It is true that being a Napoleon, a Peter the Great, and an Emperor Taizong of the Tang Dynasty can be equally the highest level of happiness. However, becoming a Napoleon can be the highest level of happiness inone's life, not because he became a monarch and thus achieved the highest social happiness, but because he became a great epoch-making monarch and thus achieved the spiritual happiness of realizing his creative potential to become a great monarch.

Otherwise, to be a good-for-nothing Ah Dou can also be called the highest happiness of life, because both he and Napoleon are monarchs and enjoy the highest social happiness. Although the value of social happiness such as being an official and having power and reputation is not as high as the value of spiritual happiness, it is undoubtedly higher than the value of material happiness such as eating, drinking, and satisfying one's appetite. Material happiness, such as eating, drinking, and so on, is shared by all human beings and all animals with psychological activities and is undoubtedly the lowest state of happiness. However, why is spiritual happiness the highest-level happiness, material happiness the lowest-level happiness, and social happiness between the two kinds and, thus, the middle-level happiness?

The truth is that happiness is just the satisfaction of a need. Happiness has the low, middle, and high levels, because needs, as Maslow says, have corresponding levels: material needs are low-level needs, social needs are middle-level needs, and spiritual needs are high-level needs.[14] James also writes,

> The whole social self is higher than the whole material self. We value more about our fames, friends, promises, and trust than about our physical pleasure and personal wealth. The spiritual self is even more noble and precious than gold and money. A man should not lose it even if it means he must abandon his friends, despise and disregard his own reputations, lose his property, or even sacrifice his own life.[15]

However, why exactly are material needs, social needs and spiritual needs placed in the categories of low-level, middle-level, and high-level needs, respectively? This might be because, both in terms of phylogenetic evolution and in terms of ontogenetic development, spirituality and spiritual needs are the products of the latest and highest stages; material and material needs are the products of the earliest and lowest stages, and society and social needs lie between these two stages. Maslow makes a very penetrating exposition of this:

> The higher-level need is a later phyletic or evolutionary development. We share the need for food with all living things, the need for love with (perhaps) the higher apes, the need for self-actualization with nobody. The higher the need the more specifically human it is. Higher needs are later ontogenetic developments. Any individual at birth shows physical needs, and probably also, in a very inchoate form, needs safety, e.g., it can probably be frightened or startled, and probably thrives between when its world shows enough regularity and orderliness so that it can be counted on. It is only after months of life that an infant shows the first signs of interpersonal ties and selective affection. Still later we may see fairly definitely the urges to autonomy, independence, achievement, and for respect and praise over and above safety and parent love.[16]

## Creative happiness and non-creative happiness

Happiness, be it spiritual, social, or material, can be creative as well as non-creative. Happiness can be divided, according to its level of creativity, into two types of happiness: creative happiness and non-creative happiness. Creative happiness means the happiness of a creative life, that is, a life with creativity and creative achievements. On the contrary, non-creative happiness is the happiness of a non-creative life, life without any creativity, and no creative achievements; it is, in the terminology of Ignacio L.Gotz, consumer happiness: it may consume and use the creative achievements of others or consume material wealth and spiritual wealth of others.[17]

If a person devotes ten years to write his book and finally gets this original work published, the happiness he achieves is creative happiness. In contrast, if a person has no desire to write books and does not engage himself in book-writing, but is fortunate enough to have the leisure to entertain himself with traveling and reading all his life, the kind of happiness he achieves is non-creative or consumer happiness. The happiness that Picasso achieved from his success at painting, that Tolstoy achieved when his book *War and Peace* was published, and that Newton felt when he discovered the law of universal gravitation are all examples of creative happiness. On the contrary, the happiness that those mediocre scholars, painters, novelists, and scientists achieve when they create some success and sensation by following some trend is non-creative happiness or consumer happiness.

Evidently, creative happiness is at a much higher level than consumer happiness. While the latter dies away with consumption and cannot stay, the former is immortal. This kind of immortality finds its expression mainly in three major aspects, which are the three immortality ideals promoted by the ancients in China: establishing original thoughts, cultivating virtues, and making contributions to society. Establishing original thoughts is creative happiness in the academic aspect, such as the happiness of becoming artists, scientists, philosophers, and thinkers, etc. This happiness belongs to creative spiritual happiness. Making contributions to society is creative happiness in the field of career, such as the happiness of becoming politicians, military strategists, entrepreneurs, artisans, and so on. This kind of happiness belongs to creative social happiness, or creative material happiness, or both. Cultivating virtues is creative happiness in the field of moral character, such as the happiness of perfecting moral character and becoming a sage or a saint. This kind of happiness belongs to creative social happiness. Without doubt, these three kinds of happiness are the greatest happiness of life; as long as an individual achieves one of them, his life can be considered as a successful life. Therefore, Fung Yulan lists these three kinds of happiness together and calls them the success of life.

> There are only three kinds of success. The first kind is success in learning, the success of inventions and creative works, such as the success as

great writers, artists, scientists, etc. The second kind is career success, such as the success as great politicians, great militarists, and great entrepreneurs, etc. The third kind is moral success, the success of becoming a person of perfect morality, such as the success of becoming what ancients would call saints and sages. The three aspects listed above are, in the terms of ancient times, the three kinds of immortality ideals, namely, establishing original thoughts, cultivating virtues, and making contributions to society. Success in learning corresponds to establishing original thoughts; success in career, to making contributions to society; success in morality, to cultivating moral character. There are no other successes but these three.[18]

*Process happiness and result happiness*

Happiness, whether creative or non-creative, whether material, spiritual, or social, is a psychological experience of achieving some desired result, so happiness seems to exist only in the result, not in the process—it would appear that there is nothing happy or unhappy about the process, happiness is all about the result. In fact, this is not the case. Although happiness is a psychological experience of achieving certain results, the process of striving for happiness, on closer inspection, consists of a number of smaller purposes or expected results. In the process of pursuing happiness, every time a person achieves some of these smaller purposes or expected results, he experiences pleasure once. When these pleasures are seen in isolation, there is no doubt that they are simple pleasures, rather than happiness; however, when seen together, they are a kind of continuous pleasure, a pleasure of great significance, and therefore happiness. This kind of happiness is the so-called "process happiness."

Given this, happiness can be divided into process happiness and result happiness: the former is the sum total of the pleasures that a person experiences during the process of pursuing a certain kind of happiness, when smaller purposes and smaller expected results are achieved; the latter is the experience of the pleasure of achieving great purposes and expected results after a certain process of effort. For example, the happiness that a student experiences when admitted to a university is the result of three years of struggle in high school; thus, it is a "result happiness." During his three years of struggle, he worked hard almost every day, every week, every month, and every semester to achieve smaller purposes, such as finishing numerous exercises, memorizing numerous words, completing numerous compositions, and so on. Whenever these smaller purposes were achieved, he experiences small pleasures; the sum of these smaller pleasures is process happiness.

Obviously, result happiness and process happiness have their own advantages and disadvantages, merits and demerits. On the one hand, result happiness is stronger and greater than process happiness, yet it is a one-time experience, and therefore, momentary; on the other hand, process happiness is weaker and smaller than result happiness, but it is multiple and successive, and thus prolonged. The process of happiness is mostly tortuous and full of ordeals; during the process there are mostly successes and happiness, but it is not without failures and misfortunes. Therefore, process happiness is a kind of impure happiness mingled with pain and failure. However, each process happiness is followed by an experience of greater fulfillment and stronger motivation because each process happiness is getting closer to the intense and immense result happiness; each process happiness is followed by a call for new happiness. On the contrary, result happiness is pure happiness, but result happiness is often followed by an experience of emptiness and boredom. Because, as Schopenhauer says, "Possession of one thing makes it lose its excitement."[19] Once a person achieves result happiness, he will lose the need, desire, and purpose that he has so passionately pursued and consequently loses motivation. In summary, result happiness is strong and great but short and momentary, pure yet empty, and process happiness is weak and small but prolonged, impure yet fulfilling. As their advantages and disadvantages complement each other, these two kinds of happiness, both opposing and complementary to each other, become the two wings of a life of happiness that needs to be well balanced with each other.

Result happiness and process happiness are not just complementary to each other; they are also necessary conditions for each other. On the one hand, result happiness is often the condition for process happiness; without result happiness, more often than not there will be no process happiness. Because process happiness is a kind of impure happiness mingled with pain and failure, the condition that makes process happiness what it is must be that during the process the pleasures of success are more than, greater than, and bigger than the pains from failure, and consequently, its net balance is pleasures of success. Otherwise, wouldn't it be process misfortune rather than process happiness? Obviously, in general, only when the result is success and pleasure is it possible that the success and pleasure in the process are more than, greater than, and bigger than failure and pain. Otherwise, if the result is failure and pain, then the failure and pain in the process must be more than, greater than, and bigger than success and pleasure. Therefore, what makes the process of struggle happy is that in this process, there is more success and pleasure than failure and pain and that ultimately the expected results will be achieved and the result happiness thus obtained. Therefore, result happiness is the condition for the existence of process happiness.

On the other hand, process happiness is equally often the condition for the existence of result happiness. Without process happiness, there will be no result happiness. Because process happiness means that success and pleasure in the process is more than, greater than, and bigger than pain and failure, its net balance is success and pleasure; otherwise, it would be result misfortune rather than result happiness. The key is exactly that if success and pleasure in the process is more than, greater than, and bigger than failure and pain, then, generally speaking, the result must be success and happiness. Therefore, in general, process happiness is bound to lead to result happiness.

In summary, the interdependence between process happiness and result happiness is the rule, and their separation from each other is the exception to the rule. So, even if a person only wants to enjoy process happiness but has no intention to use the struggle of his whole life in exchange for the result happiness of having a happy old age, he is still bound to strive for result happiness and success. Otherwise, if the result is failure and misfortune, then, generally speaking, the net balance of his pursuit of happiness must be pain and failure; thus, no matter how much he cares only about cultivation and how little he cares about the harvest, he will by no means achieve process happiness. On the contrary, if a person only wants to achieve result happiness, but does not care whether the process is happy or not, he must still work honestly and advance gradually to achieve happiness in the process. Otherwise, if failure and pain in the process is more than success and pleasure, and its net balance must be failure and misfortune; thus, in general, the result will by no means be happiness and success.

## *Two concepts of happiness: the pleasure theory and the perfection theory*

There have been ongoing debates from ancient times to the present about the concept of happiness. These debates, as it is well known, can be divided into two groups: the pleasure theory represented mainly by Mill, Hume, and Hobbes, and the perfection theory represented mainly by Aristotle, Plato, Aquinas, and Paulsen. The differences between these two groups derive mainly from the structure and type of happiness. The pleasure theory neglects the objective factor of happiness, namely, "the realization of great needs, desires, purposes and the perfection of survival and development," and only heeds the subjective factor of happiness, namely, "the psychological experience of pleasure"; hence its claim that happiness is pleasure; "happiness refers to pleasure and elimination of pain."[20] As it is known, happiness is the great or extreme pleasure of life, so defining happiness as pleasure commits the fallacy of too broad a definition.

The perfection theory is more complicated. On the one hand, the perfection theory holds that happiness is the perfection of survival and development. Paulsen says, "Happiness refers to the perfection of our existence and the perfect movement of our life."[21] On the other hand, "the perfection theory" can also be called as "self-realization theory," because it further equates perfection of survival and development with self-realization. Aristotle repeatedly says, "We must discuss what virtue is, since its realization is happiness. Generally speaking, virtue is the best quality."[22]

> All virtues, as long as something regards them as virtues, must not only make something in good condition, but also give something excellent functions. For example, the virtue of the eye not only makes the eye bright, but also makes it function well.[23]

It can be seen that what Aristotle means by happiness is the realization of virtue, the realization of "excellence and excellent quality" of self, self-realization, and ultimately, the realization of the creative potential of self, for "self-realization must at least rely on creativity."[24]

Apparently, these definitions by the perfection theory are not tenable. On the one hand, they equate "perfection of survival and development of self" with "self-realization." This equation is one-sided because "self-realization" is the realization of the creative potential of self. On the contrary, "perfection of survival and development of self" are much broader—it can be creative happiness; it can also be consumer happiness. For example, in my whole life, I have accomplished nothing, but I have been prosperous and enjoyed a high position and great wealth. I have failed to realize my creative potential, and thus failed to accomplish self-realization; however, I have been enjoying material happiness and attained perfection of material survival and development. In this case, the perfection theory equates "perfection of survival and development of self" with "self-realization," further equates "happiness" with "happiness of self-realization," and thus commits the fallacy of taking a part for the whole.

On the other hand, even without making such equations, the perfection theory is still one-sided when defining happiness as the perfection of survival and development. A tree, whether it thrives because its need for sunshine, rain, and dew are satisfied and realizes the perfection of survival and development of the self, or it withers due to drought or is cruelly crushed, thus failing to achieve the perfection of its own survival and development, has no happiness or misfortune. The reason is that although trees, like human beings, can have a perfection of survival and development, trees do not have the psychological experience of perfection of survival and development that human beings have: happiness is a psychological experience of survival and development. The one-sidedness of the theory of happiness as the perfection of survival and development lies just in that it sees only the objective and substantive factors of happiness as "perfection of survival and development," but ignores the subjective form of "psychological experience of pleasure."

## The value of happiness

As mentioned earlier, happiness is, in terms of its form, a psychological experience of extreme pleasure; it is, in terms of its content, the satisfaction of great needs and perfection of survival and development. Happiness is of great value to everyone: happiness is the ultimate good. This is self-evident. However, why have thinkers been debating endlessly about the value of the ultimate good of happiness for 2,000 years? If happiness is the ultimate good, then it follows that pleasure is good. If pleasure is good, happiness is the ultimate good, then it follows that pain is bad and misfortune is the ultimate bad. The reason why people have been always debating over the value of happiness as the ultimate good is that the claim that pleasure is good and pain is bad is obviously controversial. Therefore, settling on the value of pleasure as good and the value of pain as bad is the premise for settling on the value of happiness as the ultimate good and the value of misfortune as the ultimate bad.

## *Pleasure: good*

The value of pleasure as good and pain as bad is manifested in the belief that all pleasures are good and all pains are bad. This assertion is almost an axiom because both hedonism and its opponents acknowledge it. For example, Epicurus, the master of hedonism, says, "Every kind of happiness is good… just as every kind of pain is bad."[25] Aristotle opposes hedonism, but he also believes that "pain is bad… So what is against it is good. So happiness is a kind of good."[26]

But, why exactly is it that all pleasures are good and all pains are bad? Ultimately, it is evidently because everyone has the need, desire, and purpose to seek pleasure and avoid pain. Just imagine, why do we like to play games from our childhood, to adulthood, and right upto old age? Isn't it because we all seek pleasure? Why is it difficult for drug addicts and alcoholics to get rid of their horrible weaknesses? Isn't it because they can bring them great pleasure? In fact, all animals with psychological activities of pain and pleasure—of course, human beings are among animals with psychological activities of pain and pleasure—have extremely strong needs, desires, and purposes of pursuing pleasure. This has been scientifically confirmed by the discovery of the "pleasure center" in the brain in modern physiology.

In the 1950s, James Olds found that the hypothalamus and some midbrain nuclei of animals were the "pleasure center." He implanted an electrode in these parts of the rat's brain, and connected it to a lever inside the rat cage. Every time the rat pushed the lever with its paws, this part of the rat's brain was stimulated electrically, which produced a psychological experience of pleasure. As a result, the hungry rat often ignored the food, ran up to the lever, and pressed the lever for the pleasure of electric self-stimulation. It kept pressing the lever as fast as 2,000 times an hour and as long as 24 hours in a row![27]

This discovery reveals that the pursuit of pleasure itself is not only a need, desire, and purpose of human beings and animals, but also an extremely strong and high-priority need, desire, and purpose. Sometimes it is even stronger and has higher priority than appetite—appetite is undoubtedly the strongest and the highest-priority desire of human beings and animals. Since the pursuit of pleasure is an extremely strong and high-priority need, desire, and purpose of humans and animals, it becomes clear that all pleasures can satisfy humans' need, desire, and purpose of pursuing pleasure and are thus good while all pains can hinder humans' need, desire, and purpose of pursuing pleasure and are thus bad.

164  *Happiness*

However, more often than not people believe that not all pleasures are good and not all pains are bad. Some pleasures, such as the pleasure from drug abuse, the pleasure from gambling, the pleasure from alcohol drinking, the pleasure from smoking cigarettes, etc. are not good, but bad. Some pains, such as the pain from enduring hardships, such as sleeping on the brushwood and tasting the gall, in order to nurse vengeance and accomplish some ambition, the pain from studying assiduously, etc., are not all bad but good.

Indeed, the pleasures derived from drug abuse, gambling, alcohol, and cigarettes are all bad. But on what basis do we say that these pleasures are bad? Obviously, it is based on the fact that these pleasures are not pure pleasures, but a mixture of pleasures and pains. These pleasures per se are intoxicating, relaxing, and fascinating pleasures, but their results are pains, such as the pain of ruining the family, dissipating fortunes, harming one's health, heading for death, and so on. As the pains are far greater than the pleasures, their net balance is pains. Therefore, pleasures such as drug abuse are bad, not because they are pleasures, but because their results are pains, and their net balance is pains. If their results are not pains, then these pleasures are not bad but good: if the results were not such pains as ruining the family, dissipating fortunes, harming one's health, heading for death, who would say that the intoxicating, relaxing, and fascinating pleasures of drug abuse are bad? In this sense, the claim that some pleasures are bad does not deny that all pleasures are good. This insight has been revealed a long time ago by Epicurus, who says "There is no pleasure that is bad in itself. But some things that can produce pleasure may be able to produce troubles greater than pleasures."[28]

Indeed, pains of enduring hardships, such as sleeping on the brushwood and tasting the bitter gall in order to nurse vengeance and accomplish some ambition, and studying assiduously sitting by the cold window, are good. But, on what basis do we say that these pains are bad? Obviously, these pains are not pure pains, but a mixture of pains and pleasures—these pains per se, the pain of enduring hardships are bad; their results are, however, pleasures, such as restoring the motherland, regaining the throne, success, and fame. Meanwhile, the pleasures are far greater than pains, so their net balance is pleasures. If the results of these pains are not pleasures, then these pleasures are definitely not good but bad. So, the claim that some pains are good does not deny that all pains are bad. The reason behind this insight has already been explained by Epicurus: "If enduring temporary pain can make us gain greater pleasure, we will often think that pains are superior to pleasures."[29]

Then, it follows that the claim that all pleasures are good and all pains are bad is an eternal truth full of dialectics. So, can we venture further and say that happiness is all the good and the sole good while pain is all the bad and the sole bad? This is a more profound question concerning the nature of pleasure and pain as good and bad. Pleasure, as Sidgwick and Moore say, is not all the good and the sole good. This is because, on the one hand, the so-called good is undoubtedly the same concept as benefit, both of which are what people need and pursue, on the other hand, what people need and pursue is not limited to pleasure; they still need and pursue many other things such as success, fame, self-realization, and so on. So, Sidgwick insists, "The claim I insist on is that people seek not only pleasures of the moment but also other things to a considerable extent."[30] In this way, pleasures can satisfy people's need to pursue pleasure and are thus good or beneficial, but success, fame, and self-realization can equally satisfy people's need to pursue it. Therefore, pleasure is not all that is good, not the sole good or benefit.

Pleasure is not all the good and the sole good, but pleasure is the psychological experience of the realization of needs and desires. Therefore, pleasure is not only a pure benefit or good, but also a signal and representative of all benefit and all good: pleasure means that the organism gains benefit or goodness, obtains things that can bring it pleasure, and thus realizes its needs and desires to survive and develop. On the contrary, pain is a psychological experience of non-satisfaction of needs and desires, and therefore it is not only a pure harm or bad, but also a signal and representative of all harm and all bad: pain means that the organism loses its benefit or good, suffers something that can bring it pain, fails to realize desires and satisfy needs, and thus cannot survive and develop. Therefore, pleasure is the signal and representative of all the good and the sole good and exemplifies that the organism obtains something that can satisfy needs and bring pleasure. What can satisfy needs and bring pleasure is all good and the sole good. Pain is the signal and representative of all the bad and exemplifies that the organism suffers something that can bring pain: what brings pain is all bad and the sole bad.

## *Happiness: the ultimate good*

Pleasure is good, which means that happiness is the ultimate good. As Epicurus says, the so-called ultimate good is the good that is ultimate and final, that is, the absolute good as an end, the intrinsic good; it is the good that can never be a means but only an end: "Thus we are enquiring what the final and ultimate good is, which, in the opinion of all philosophers ought to be such that everything must be referred to it, but it itself referred no further."[31] In this way, the ultimate good is happiness; they are actually the same concept. Because happiness is the psychological experience of extreme pleasure that "the great needs, desires, and purposes of life have been realized" to "achieve some perfection of survival and development," the psychological experience of extreme pleasure is the subjective form of happiness while the realization of great needs, desires, and purposes of life to achieve some perfection of survival and development is the objective content of happiness. Isn't the psychological experience of extreme pleasure the most perfect state of mind? Who would use it as a means to acquire other mental states, namely, less happy mental states? Isn't the perfection of survival and development the most perfect realm of life? Who would use it as a means to achieve imperfection of survival and development? Isn't the realization of great needs, desires, and purposes of life the most worthwhile outcome to choose? Who would use it in exchange for the realization of insignificant needs, desires, and purposes of life?

Therefore, as the Stoics say, happiness can only be the end people pursue, but cannot be the means to achieve any end: "One's aim, they say is being happy, for the sake of which everything is done, while it is not done for the sake of anything further." Julia Annas further explains: "Now a final end is that for the sake of which everything is done or considered, while it is not itself done or considered for the sake of anything else."[32] Ultimately, except happiness, any pleasure or any good can be the means to obtain other pleasures or other good; only happiness cannot be used as the means to achieve other pleasures or other good. Hence, happiness is the absolute good as an end, the intrinsic good, and the ultimate good.

Just try to imagine, why a person studies so hard? If he says that he studies hard to pursue happiness, then we can't ask him why he pursues happiness. For example, does he pursue happiness in order to be an official? In order to win love? In order to glorify his ancestors? Obviously, this is nonsense. But, if he says that he studies hard for the sake of studying, then, as he loves studying, he studies for the sake of studying, and studying, in this situation, is the end. The pleasure he experiences in studying is a kind of pleasure with intrinsic good and good as an end. So, obviously in this situation, we can ask further, what was the purpose of his studying in the beginning? Did he start out studying for the sake of studying? We can ask even further, does he study any book at any time for the sake of studying?

Obviously, in the beginning, he did not study for the sake of studying but he does not study for the sake of studying at any time. There are always times when he uses studying as a means to achieve other purposes, such as being an official because excellent learning in China always promises good official positions. In this case, his pleasure of studying is just a pleasure of extrinsic good and instrumental good, while the pleasure he experiences as an official is a kind of pleasure of intrinsic good and good as an end. However, being an official can make an ugly man realize his desire of marrying a beautiful wife and thus becomes a means to get a beautiful wife. Therefore, his pleasure of being an official can also be a kind of pleasure of extrinsic good and instrumental good while the pleasure he experiences when he sits at the bridal candles with his beautiful bride is a kind of pleasure of intrinsic good and good as an end.

If we press it further, we may continue to ask questions like these, which can all be answered only by the phrase "for the sake of happiness." We pursue happiness not for anything else, but because happiness is the absolute good as an end, intrinsic good, the ultimate good, the highest good, and the supreme good. Being the ultimate good is the nature of happiness.

Therefore, Plato says, "It is unnecessary to ask a person why he wants happiness, because the desire for happiness is the ultimate answer."[33] Aristotle moves further,

> The thing that we say that what we pursue for its own sake comes later than the thing we pursue for the sake of other things. It then seems that only happiness deserves to be called the absolute final. We choose it for its own sake, not for the sake of anything else.[34]

Happiness is the ultimate good, which clearly means that misfortune is the ultimate bad. As misfortune is the psychological experience of extreme pain and causes "serious harm to survival and development" as a result of the non-realization of "great needs, desires, and purposes of life," the psychological experience of extreme pain is the subjective form of misfortune, while "the non-realization of great needs, desires, and purposes of life" and its result, "serious harm to survival and development," is the objective content of misfortune. Isn't the psychological experience of extreme pain the worst and most evil state of mind? Isn't serious harm to survival and development the worst and most evil realm of life? Isn't the non-realization of great needs, desires, and purposes of life the worst and most evil result? Therefore, misfortune is the worst bad and the worst thing; thus, in any case it is bad, the absolute bad, and the ultimate bad. Being the ultimate bad is the nature of misfortune.

In this way, the ultimate bad nature of misfortune and the ultimate good nature of happiness have one thing in common: both can never and ought not to be used as a means. Except for happiness, any pleasure and any good can be a means to achieve greater pleasure and greater good; only happiness cannot and ought not to be used as means to achieve other pleasures or other good. Happiness is the absolute good as an end and the ultimate good. Similarly, except for misfortune, any pain and any bad can and ought to be the means to avoid any greater pain and any greater bad; only misfortune cannot and ought not to be used as a means to avoid any other pain and any other bad. If a man chooses a kind of misfortune, he must have chosen it to avoid a greater misfortune. Therefore, people's avoidance of misfortune is absolute and ultimate. There is no worse bad than misfortune: misfortune is the ultimate bad.

## *Purpose of life*

Within the good nature of pleasure and happiness there imbeds a more profound and important nature: pleasure and happiness constitute the purpose, meaning, and value of life. This is perhaps the deepest and therefore the most obscure nature of pleasure and happiness, over which people have been debating for 2,000 years. The first question for the debate is: what is the purpose of life?

The so-called life (*sheng-huo*; 生活), just as its name in Chinese suggests, is the life of people, is the total sum of the process of human life. However, as we move further to explore the purpose of life, this problem gets very complicated. First of all, humans' life can be understood with the literal meaning of *sheng-huo* in Chinese: *sheng* means life, and *huo* means activity or behavior, so what *sheng-huo* means is life, activity, and behavior. Therefore, life, or human life, actually consists of two aspects: one is human life; the other is human behavior. Therefore, on closer scrutiny, the so-called life is the total sum of human life and human behaviors. On this point, Fung Yulan makes a clear claim. He has repeatedly said that life, on the one hand, refers to human life and the birth of humans, as in "the birth of human life is nothing we can do about, so there is nothing we can do about life";[35] on the other hand, life refers to the activities and behaviors of human beings, as in "activities and behaviors of a human consist of life."[36]

However, the purpose of life clearly refers only to the purpose of human behavior. The human life belongs to the "the natural sphere" and is something beyond the control of consciousness. Its properties and activities that serve some purpose, such as heartbeat, blood circulation, gastrointestinal digestion, are unconscious and not controlled by consciousness. Therefore, they exist only to satisfy a purpose, but they do not have a purpose and are thus non-teleological. On the contrary, human behavior belongs to the "man-made sphere" and is something controlled by consciousness. Its properties and activities that serve some purpose, such as striving for fame in the royal court and for the best interests on the market, are conscious and controlled by consciousness, so they have a purpose and are thus teleological.

Therefore, the so-called purpose of life refers to the purpose of all human behaviors. However, each person's lifetime behavior is extremely diverse and numerous; therefore, the purpose of these behaviors must also be diverse and numerous. For example, the purpose of going to the market one day is to buy clothes, the purpose of going to the library is to borrow books, the purpose of going to the Summer Palace is to swim, and so on. Obviously, the purpose of life is not the purpose of this kind of behavior, which contains only some behaviors but not others. It is not such an accidental, arbitrary, and varied purpose. The purpose of life is undoubtedly the purpose that runs through people's lifetime behaviors, the purpose that all human behaviors pursue in their lifetime, and the universal, necessary, and independent-of-human-will purpose that all human behaviors possess. The so-called ultimate purpose of life is the ultimate purpose of all human behaviors.

The so-called ultimate purpose, according to great thinkers such as Aristotle, Epicurus, the Stoics, and so on, is one such purpose: all human behaviors are for it, but it is not for anything. As Julia Annas points out, in summarizing the concepts of the ultimate purpose by Aristotle, Epicurus, and the Stoics, what makes a purpose the ultimate purpose of life must have two conditions:

> (1) completeness and (2) self-sufficiency. Completeness here implies a final end. If I pursue A for the sake of B, but I pursue B for the sake of B, then B is complete, but A is not... Self-sufficiency here means comprehensiveness: an ultimate purpose must include all the behaviors of an agent.[37]

Therefore, the purpose of life is the same concept as the ultimate purpose: on the one hand, it is absolute, that is, it is absolutely the purpose rather than the purpose as means; on the other hand, it is universal, and it is the purpose pursued by all behaviors. Therefore, in explaining the moral philosophy of ancient Greece, John M. Cooper equates the ultimate purpose with the purpose of life: "Obviously, the Stoics followed Aristotle and believed that the purpose of our life was one of the purposes: 'Everything we do is for it, but we don't get it for anything else.'"[38]

There still remains the question, is it possible that such a purpose exists? Yes, it does exist. As is known to all, all behaviors are triggered by needs and desires: needs produce desires that can satisfy these needs, and desires then produce purposes for behaviors that can satisfy them. Therefore, the purpose of all behaviors is the satisfaction of certain needs and desires; the purpose of life is the satisfaction of needs and desires. The thing that can satisfy needs and desires is called benefit or good: good or benefit is what can satisfy needs and desires, is what is needed and desired, namely, the object of needs and desires. In this sense, the purpose of every person's behavior is to obtain some kind of good and benefit to satisfy his needs and desires; the purpose of life is thus to pursue some kind of good or benefit to satisfy his needs and desires.

This might be the first principle of life, so *Nicomachean Ethics* begins in this way: "Every art and every *inquiry*, and similarly, every *action* and every intention is thought to aim at some good."[39] All the good and the sole good, as discussed above, is pleasure and a thing that can bring pleasures; on the contrary, pain and the thing that can bring pain are all the bad and the only bad. Therefore, the purpose of all human behaviors is, in a positive sense, to pursue pleasure and things that can bring pleasure, and, in a negative sense, to avoid pain and things that can bring pain. Hence, to pursue pleasure and things that can bring pleasure—to avoid pain and things that can bring pain—is the purpose of all behaviors and thus the purpose of life.

Apparently, the purpose of each behavior of an individual may vary: the purpose of some behavior is eating; for some it's drinking; for some it's romantic love; for some it's making a dedication. However, these are the direct, special, and superficial purposes of behavior. Behind these purposes, there is no doubt an indirect, fundamental, and common purpose, which is to pursue some kind of good or benefit to meet our needs and desires, that is, to pursue pleasure and things that can bring pleasure while avoiding pain and things that can bring pain; it is ultimately to seek pleasure and avoid pain, to seek good and avoid bad. Therefore, seeking pleasure and avoiding pain, seeking good and avoiding bad is the purpose of life. The person who has shed light on this important truth most accurately is still Epicurus: "All our choices depart from pleasure, and our ultimate destination is to obtain happiness."[40]

The purpose of life is bound to seek pleasure and avoid pain. So, ought the purpose of life to be to seek pleasure and avoid pain? The answer is yes: everyone ought to seek pleasure and avoid pain in all his behaviors. Because all pleasure is good and all pain is bad, good things ought to be pursued and bad things ought not to be pursued. On the one hand, when various pleasures conflict with each other and cannot be all satisfied, we ought to abandon the small pleasures and pursue the great pleasures; ultimately, we ought to abandon pleasures and pursue happiness; contrarily, when pains are inevitable, we ought to endure the small pains and avoid the great pains; ultimately, we ought to endure pains to avoid misfortune.

On the other hand, when various pleasures are not in conflict with each other, we ought to seek all pleasures. In this situation, the pursuit of any pleasure is the increase, promotion, and accumulation of pleasures; it is to make pleasure change from less to more, from small to big, from short-lived to long-lived. It is, thus, also the approaching and pursuit of happiness. Contrarily, when suffering some pains cannot avoid greater pains or bring greater pleasures, we ought to avoid all pains. In this situation, the avoidance of any pain is the reduction of pain; it is to make pain change from more to less, from big to small. It is, thus, the avoidance of misfortune.

In summary, the so-called purpose of life, in terms of what "it is," is to seek pleasure and avoid pain; but in terms of what "it ought to be," it is to pursue happiness and avoid misfortune. It is only necessary that we pursue pleasure and avoid pain, but it is not necessary—but only ought to be—that we pursue happiness and avoid misfortune. Therefore, it is unlikely that all behaviors of an individual do not seek pleasure to avoid pain: seeking pleasure and avoiding pain is the common ultimate purpose of all human behaviors and the inevitable objective law independent of human will. However, it is not necessary that all the behaviors of individuals seek happiness and avoid misfortune. Pursuing happiness and avoiding misfortune is the common ultimate purpose that all human behaviors ought to follow—it is an ought-to-be human rule, rather than an inevitable objective law independent of human will. In a word, the purpose of life is all about pursuing pleasure and happiness and avoiding pain and misfortune: on the one hand, it is necessary that the purpose of life is to seek pleasure and avoid pain; on the other hand, the purpose of life is that one ought to pursue happiness and avoid misfortune.

## *The value of life and the meaning of life*

The purpose of life gives meaning to life, exactly as Annas says: "The ultimate purpose gives our life meaning."[41] The meaning of life and the value of life are the same concepts, and both refer to the effect "life" has on "the purpose of life." As the purpose of life is to pursue pleasure and happiness and avoid pain and misfortune, it follows that the value and meaning of life is the effect of "life" on "pursuing pleasure and happiness and avoiding pain and misfortune." What, then, is the effect?

Evidently, the life of each individual is not only the ultimate source of his pleasure and happiness, but also of his pain and misfortune. Obviously, it is only through his life and activities can the individual obtain pleasure and happiness and suffer pain and misfortune; if he did not have life and activities, how would he have pain and pleasure, happiness and misfortune? However, does life bring more pleasure and happiness than pain and misfortune, or vice versa? Everyone's life consists of their activities and behaviors. Therefore, the pain and pleasure, the happiness and misfortune brought about in each person's life is ultimately the pain and pleasure, the happiness and misfortune, which is the result of his own life and behaviors. So, the question actually is, do each person's life and behaviors give him more pleasure and happiness or more pain and misfortune?

This question can be approached first from the perspective of behavior. The purpose of an individual's behaviors is to meet certain needs and satisfy certain desires. If he succeeds in satisfying his needs, fulfilling his desires, and achieving his purposes, he will be happy; if it's the contrary, he will suffer pains. Let's look at a person's daily behavior. He gets up in the morning and has a desire to jog. If he jogs, he will satisfy his desire and achieve his goal, and then he will be happy; otherwise, he will suffer pain. After coming back from his morning jog, he has the desire to take a shower. If he takes a shower, he will realize his desire and be happy, otherwise he will suffer pain. After breakfast, he has the desire to read the newspaper. If he reads it, he will realize his desire and be happy; otherwise, he will suffer pain. After reading newspapers, he has the desire to write. If he writes, he will realize his desire and be happy; otherwise, he will suffer pain. Admittedly, these are small daily pleasures and pains. However, this kind of small pains and pleasures undoubtedly occupies the majority of the total amount of pains and pleasures in everyone's life. Therefore, no matter how often he fails, in the total sum of a person's behaviors, there must be more success than failure, more behaviors that achieve his purposes than the behaviors that fail to achieve his purposes, more needs and desires that can be satisfied than needs and desires that cannot be satisfied. Otherwise, he would not be able to survive. So, as far as the sum of each person's behaviors is concerned, his own behaviors will give him more pleasure than pain. Therefore, in terms of the sum of his behaviors, the net balance of every person's life is pleasure. Although this kind of pleasure is a small pleasure, the sum of these small pleasures is not a small pleasure, but happiness. The so-called happiness, on the one hand, is a great pleasure; on the other hand, it is a continuous and enduring accumulation of small pleasures. So, Franklin says, "Human happiness does not come entirely from good luck, but more from the small gains of everyday life."[42] Therefore, in terms of his behaviors, the net balance of each person's life is pleasure and happiness.

The question can also be approached from the perspective of life. In the long run, natural selection undoubtedly produces in humans and animals the desire and need to survive, which is the most fundamental, the most important, and the greatest desire and need in human beings and all animals; other desires and needs are smaller, less important, and non-fundamental desires and needs. Therefore, as long as a person can survive and live, as long as his desire for survival is satisfied, his greatest needs and desires will be realized in the long run, and he will get the greatest pleasure and the most fundamental happiness. Therefore, Feuerbach says, "Life itself is happiness." "Life is the sum of all happiness and benefits."[43] Zhuang Zi says it more tersely: "To live is the supreme happiness."[44] Therefore, as long as a person can survive, as long as his desire for life is satisfied, even if his other desires are not realized, he will, in the long run, get more pleasure and happiness because his desire for life is satisfied than suffer pain and misfortune because his other desires are frustrated. Therefore, as long as a person can live, as long as his desire to live is realized, then, in the terms of the total sum of his life, his own life gives him more pleasure and happiness than all his pain and misfortune. Therefore, no matter how hard and difficult the life of people is, how unlucky and unfortunate they are, they still feel that it is better to live miserably than die happily. Even the disabled who have been bedridden all their lives are unwilling to die because they can enjoy the greatest pleasure and happiness after all, which is the pleasure and happiness of life.

Based on the above discussions, we can see that everyone's life, whether in terms of his life or his behavior, must bring more pleasure and happiness than pain and misfortune. Of course, the life mentioned here refers to a life that is normal, general, and conforming to human nature, rather than to life that is abnormal, exceptional, and deviating from human nature. Some people suffer, since the first day of birth, from some serious illness every day, some people suffer from life imprisonment and torture, and so on. These people do have more pain and misfortune in their life than pleasure and happiness. But these are obviously anomalies and exceptions to life, not the general rule of life. Therefore, the net balance of normal and ordinary life must be pleasure and happiness; if the net balance of life is pain and misfortune, then it must be an abnormal and exceptional life.

In this way, the purpose of life, the value of life, and the meaning of life all lie in pleasure and happiness. The purpose of life is to pursue pleasure and happiness and avoid pain and misfortune; the value and meaning of life lie in that the pleasure and happiness that life can bring are always more than the pain and misfortune that it causes, and its net balance is pleasure and happiness. Therefore, if a person's life brings more pleasure and happiness than pain and misfortune, and its net balance is pleasure and happiness, then his life is a valuable and meaningful life, a life worth living, and a life that is normal, common, and conforms to the nature of life. On the contrary, if a person's life brings more pain and misfortune than pleasure and happiness, then his life is worthless and meaningless, not worth living, a life that is abnormal, exceptional, and deviates from the nature of life.

Try to imagine the reason why we love life and keep busy all day: Isn't it because we feel that life is meaningful and worth living? Ultimately, isn't it because we enjoy more pleasure and happiness than pain and misfortune? Otherwise, if we have more pain and misfortune than pleasure and happiness, will we still feel that life is meaningful and worth living? If, for example, I was sentenced to life imprisonment and often flogged, would I still find it meaningful and be willing to live on? Therefore, whether a person's net balance of life is pleasure and happiness or not is the ultimate reason why he feels that his life is meaningful and, thus, be willing to live on or not: if the net balance is pleasure and happiness, he will feel that life is meaningful and thus be willing to live on; if the net balance is pain and misfortune, he will feel that life is meaningless and will be unwilling to live on.

Admittedly, it is likely that people's subjective perception of their life's pain and pleasure, misfortune and happiness, and their objective reality of life's misfortune and happiness will be consistent with each other, and it is also likely that they are not consistent with each other. A typical example of this kind of inconsistency is what psychiatrist Frankl calls "the void of existence." The void of existence, as Frankl sees it, is a common phenomenon in the 20th century. The characteristic of this phenomenon is that people live in happiness without being aware of happiness. People are in good economic condition, have made great progress in their work, and have good interpersonal relationships, however, they feel no pleasure and happiness but endless boredom and unspeakable misery. Therefore, they feel that their life is meaningless and not worth living: "Not a few cases of suicide can be traced back to this existential vacuum."[45]

The key to the problem is that as long as a person subjectively feels that his life is more pain and misfortune than pleasure and happiness, and therefore thinks that his life has no value and significance, then no matter what the objective reality of his life is, he will still feel that life is not worth living. There is undoubtedly only one scientific way to enable him to live, which is to help him understand and find the pleasure and happiness of his life, the value and significance of his life. Therefore, Frankl regards "knowing and finding the meaning of life" as his motto of psychotherapy.

> Man's pursuit of meaning and value may cause internal tension rather than internal balance. However, this tension is an indispensable prerequisite for mental health. I would venture to say that there is nothing in the world that can help a person survive in the worst case unless the

human body recognizes that his life is meaningful. As Nietzsche says with wisdom: "See through the why, then you can meet anything." I think this sentence can serve as a motto for any psychotherapy.[46]

## *Hedonism*

For 2,000 years, people have been arguing about the good nature of pleasure and happiness and about whether the purpose of the resulting behavior lies entirely in pleasure and happiness. This kind of debate revolves around hedonism. There are many hedonists; their representatives are the Cyrenaic School, Epicurus, Democritus, Spinoza, Locke, Hume, Bentham, Mill, Spencer, Sidgwick, and Bain. So, what is hedonism? Moore answers, "We can give a precise definition of hedonism: nothing is good but pleasure";[47] "hedonism believes that pleasure is the object of all desires and that pleasure is the universal purpose of all human activities."[48] To be more precise, hedonism is the doctrine that the sole good is that which brings pleasure or can bring pleasure, while the sole bad is that which brings pain or can bring pain; thus, the ultimate purpose of all behaviors is to seek pleasure and avoid pain. The belief that happiness is the sole good and pain is the sole bad, and, thus, the purpose (whether ultimate or direct) of all behaviors is to seek pleasure and avoid pain is extreme hedonism; the belief that happiness and what can bring happiness is the sole good—pain and what can cause pain is the sole bad—and, thus, the ultimate purpose of all behaviors is to seek pleasure and avoid pain is moderate hedonism.

Bentham is the representative of extreme hedonism. He believes that pleasure is the sole good and pain is the sole bad: "Pleasure is in itself a good, even setting aside immunity from pain, the only good: pain is in itself an evil; and, indeed, without exception, the only evil."[49] He believes that the purpose of all behaviors is to seek pleasure and avoid pain:

> Nature has placed mankind under the governance of two sovereign masters, pain and pleasure. It is for them alone to point out what we ought to do, as well as to determine what we shall do. On the one hand the standard of right and wrong, on the other the chain of causes and effects, are fastened to their throne.[50]

Locke and Epicurus are the representatives of moderate hedonism. On the one hand, they think that pleasure and what can bring pleasure is the sole good, pain and what can cause pain is the sole bad: "Good and evil are nothing but pleasure and pain, or what causes and promotes pleasure and pain in us."[51] On the other hand, they think that seeking pleasure and avoiding pain is the ultimate purpose of all behaviors: "Pleasure is the ultimate purpose."[52]

Moderate hedonism is undoubtedly the truth. It correctly reveals that pleasure and what can bring pleasure is the sole good, and pain and what can cause pain is the sole bad, and the ultimate purpose of all behaviors is to only seek pleasure and avoid pain. On the contrary, extreme hedonism commits the fallacy of overgeneralization. First of all, extreme hedonism fails to see that pleasure is fundamentally different from things that can bring pleasure, and thus, equates things that can bring pleasure with pleasure, thereby obliterating what can bring pleasure as good, and asserting that pleasure is the sole good. Moreover, extreme hedonism equates the purpose of behavior with the ultimate purpose of behavior, and thus draws, from the correct claim that the ultimate purpose of all behaviors is to seek pleasure and avoid pain, the wrong conclusion that the purpose of all behaviors is to seek pleasure and avoid pain.

Hedonism has been refuted by many sages such as Socrates, Plato, Aristotle, Kant, Darwin, James, Tilley, Paulsen, Moore, and so on. The refutation of hedonism by Moore synthesizes and epitomizes all refutations and makes a very systematic and profound counterargument against hedonism. He synthesizes the refutation of the sages, especially Sidgwick, on the claim that pleasure is the only object of human desires, and concludes that:

> I assume it to be perfectly obvious that the idea of the object of desire is not always and only the idea of a pleasure. In the first place, plainly, we are not always conscious of expecting pleasure, when we desire a thing. We may be only conscious of the thing which we desire, and may be impelled to make for it at once, without any calculation as to whether it will bring us pleasure or pain. And, in the second place, even when we do expect pleasure, it can certainly be very rarely pleasure only which we desire. For instance, granted that, when I desire my glass of port wine, I have also an idea of the pleasure I expect from it, plaining that pleasure cannot be the only object of my desire; the port wine must be included in my object, else I might be led by my desires to take wormwood instead of wine. If the desire were directed solely towards the pleasure, it could not lead me to take the wine; if it is to take a definite direction, it is absolutely necessary that the idea of the object, from which the pleasure is expected, should also be present and should control my activity. The theory then that what is desired is always and only pleasure must break down.[53]

Let's analyze these two arguments by Moore. The first obviously boils down to one sentence: the purpose of some of our behaviors is not pleasure. Indeed, sometimes what we want and desire is not pleasure but something else. However, this can only show that the direct purpose of these behaviors is not pleasure, but something else; it cannot show that the ultimate purpose of these behaviors is not pleasure. We may ask further: why do we have to crave for something that is not pleasure? Isn't it ultimately because obtaining it can bring pleasure while failing to get it can bring pain? Therefore, the ultimate purpose of these behaviors is still to seek pleasure and avoid pain.

Moore's second argument against hedonism can also be summed up in the following sentence: even if the purpose of a behavior is pleasure, it's not just for pleasure. Indeed, what we want and desire is not only pleasure, but also other things, such as red wine. However, this can only show that the direct purpose of our behaviors is often not just pleasure, but "pleasure + other things"; it cannot prove that the ultimate purpose of these behaviors is not pleasure only. We can ask further, why do we have to crave these "other things"? Isn't it ultimately just because getting these things can bring pleasure while failing to get them can bring us pain? Therefore, the ultimate purpose of these behaviors must only be seeking pleasure and avoiding pain.

As shown, although Moore and other "opponents of hedonism" hold claims opposite to "extreme hedonism," they commit the same error, which is rooted in their failure to distinguish the "direct purpose" from the "ultimate purpose" of behavior. Opponents of hedonism such as Moore, draw, from the correct premise that "the direct purpose of all behaviors is not just to seek pleasure and avoid pain," the wrong conclusion that "the (ultimate) purpose of all behaviors is not just to seek pleasure and avoid pain." Extreme hedonism draws, from the correct premise that "the ultimate purpose of all behaviors is to seek pleasure and avoid pain," the wrong conclusion that "all purposes (ultimate purpose and direct purpose) of all behaviors are to seek pleasure and avoid pain."

## The nature of happiness

### *Subjectivity and objectivity of happiness*

The conceptual analysis of happiness shows that the psychological experience of happiness is the subjective form of happiness, while the objective content of happiness is the realization of great needs, desires, and purposes of life to achieve a certain degree of perfection of survival and development. In this way, happiness has both subjectivity and objectivity and is a unity of subjectivity and objectivity.

The subjectivity of happiness obviously lies in that happiness per se is a psychological experience of pleasure, namely, an emotion, which belongs to the category of subjective consciousness. Happiness itself is subjective, so it is completely dependent on subjective feelings, as long as a person feels happy, he is indeed happy, as long as he feels unfortunate, he is indeed unfortunate. A farmer in northern China will feel very happy as long as he has "three *mu's* of land, two cows, a warm home with children and a wife." Does he really get happiness? Yes, because "three *mu's* of land, two cows, a warm home with children and a wife" is the most important need, desire, and purpose of his life and because this is realized, the farmer will have the psychological experience of extreme pleasure and consider himself very happy. If he feels happy, then he is indeed happy.

On the contrary, a greedy millionaire, despite his millions-worth of wealth, will still suffer because he is far from achieving the goal of a billionaire, and will never feel happy. Does he really fail to get happiness? Yes, because the goal of this millionaire is to be a billionaire; becoming a billionaire is his great need, desire, and purpose. If he does not become a billionaire, his great need, desire, and purpose will not be realized, and he will feel the psychological experience of pain and, thus, feel very unhappy. If he feels unhappy, he is indeed unhappy.

Therefore, both happiness and misfortune are subjective and dependent on the subjective feelings of persons concerned themselves; as long as a person feels happy, then, no matter how unfortunate he is in the eyes of others, he is indeed happy. On the contrary, as long as a person feels unfortunate, then, no matter how happy he seems to others, he is indeed unfortunate. So, Ignatius L. Gotz says, "It's not wrong to conclude that 'I'm happy,' just as it's not wrong to conclude that 'I'm thinking' or that 'I have a headache.'"[54] So, can we conclude that happiness and misfortune are totally subjective and not objective? No!

The analysis of the concept of happiness shows that happiness is a kind of psychological experience of achieving a certain degree of perfection of their survival and development when their great needs, desires, and purposes are realized. Therefore, it is only in terms of happiness itself and the form of happiness that happiness is a kind of psychological experience, a kind of emotion, which belongs to the category of subjective consciousness. In terms of its content and essence, happiness is totally an objective thing, which is the realization of major needs, desires, and purposes, and the perfection of survival and development. Thus, just as all forms of subjective consciousness are determined by the objective content it reflects, everyone's happiness is also determined by the objective content it reflects, which is the realization of great needs, desires, and purposes, and the perfection of survival and development. This kind of determination is mainly manifested in the following two aspects:

On the one hand, the happiness of each person depends on whether his great needs, desires, and purposes are realized or not and on whether his survival and development are perfected or not. That is to say, although a person is happy as long as he feels happy, whether he feels happy or not does not depend on his own will, but depends on whether his major needs, desires, and purposes of life are realized and whether his survival and development has reached a certain degree of perfection. If his major needs, desires, and purposes are realized and his survival and development have achieved a certain degree of perfection, he must feel happy. If his major needs, desires, and purposes are not realized, and his survival and development have not achieved a certain degree of perfection, he will by no means feel happy. Consider a miser who thinks he is happy. He is really happy. But why does the miser feel happy? Isn't it because of his great purpose, the pursuit of large amounts of money, that has been realized so that he has achieved some perfection in his survival and development as a miser? If he doesn't procure and hoard a lot of money, then no matter how much he wants to feel pleasure and happiness, he will not feel it.

On the other hand, although a person is happy as long as he feels happy, what kind of happiness he attains and the nature of the happiness he enjoys depends on the objective nature of the needs he meets, on the objective nature of his survival and development, but never on his subjective experience. For example, an illiterate millionaire who is able to indulge all desires feels that he enjoys the fullest and highest happiness. So, the question is, is he happy? Yes, he is indeed happy. But, is his happiness the most perfect and supreme as he feels it is? No. On the contrary, he enjoys the lowest level of happiness, namely, material happiness. As material happiness is the lowest level of happiness, it has nothing to do with the subjective feeling of the happiness he enjoys, but completely depends on the objective nature of human needs: material needs are the lowest level of human needs, while spiritual needs, self-realization needs, and creative needs are the highest level of human needs.

It can be concluded that on the surface happiness is indeed subjective, psychological experience of extreme pleasure, and therefore a subjective thing of what one feels; however, in essence, it is not subjective or arbitrary, but necessarily determined by the satisfaction of human needs and the perfection of the objective condition of survival and development, and therefore, an objective thing. The psychological experience of extreme pleasure is the subjective form of happiness and the subjective nature of happiness; the satisfaction of human needs and the perfection of survival and development are the objective content of happiness and the objective nature of happiness. According to the dual nature of subjectivity and objectivity of happiness, happiness can be divided into subjective happiness and objective happiness. Subjective happiness has the subjectivity of happiness, which is the psychological experience of extreme pleasure; objective happiness has the objective nature of happiness, which is the satisfaction of great needs and the perfection of survival and development.

It becomes clear that in the unity of subjectivity and objectivity of happiness, subjectivity or subjective happiness is passive, determined, and secondary, while objectivity or objective happiness is active, determining, and primary. This relationship is especially manifested in the fact that if a person enjoys objective happiness and thus his great needs are met and his survival and development is perfected, he will be extremely happy and thus enjoy subjective happiness; this means that the satisfaction of great needs and the perfection of his survival and development are the sufficient conditions for happiness. On the contrary, if he enjoys subjective happiness and therefore feels extreme pleasure, he may not necessarily have his major needs met and his survival and development perfected, and thus he may not enjoy objective happiness; this means the psychological experience of extreme pleasure is a necessary condition for happiness. As the subjective form of happiness he enjoys may not have the corresponding objective content or objective happiness, what he enjoys is illusory happiness rather than real happiness; this means that the psychological experience of extreme pleasure is a sufficient condition only for illusory happiness. So, what is illusory happiness and what is real happiness?

## *The authenticity and illusion of happiness*

Since happiness is both subjective and objective, and is the unity of the subjective form and the objective content, happiness, just like all subjective forms and subjective things, may or may not be consistent with its objective content. However, the question of whether the subjective form of happiness is consistent with the objective content is extremely complicated and puzzling. Pojman seems to be the first person to systematically address this question. He writes:

> Let's take a closer look at how we judge whether some people are happy or not. The following examples will help to show our thoughts. Suppose a person is asked what his idea of happiness is, he replies: 'Be loved, praised, or at least respected by my friends. But I hate my friends when they are just pretending to love and respect me... Suppose the something that this person abhors does happen. His so-called friends cleverly deceived him, giving him ample reason to believe that they loved and admired him, although that was not the case. In this way, he fell into the illusion of happiness. So is it a happy life? Is he a happy man?"[55]

Pojman's answer is very subtle:

> We do admit to some extent that the deceived person is happy, but at the same time, we do not want to admit that... We don't totally deny that this person is happy with his life. However, we do not admit that his life is a happy one at all.[56]

Why does this answer seem so vague and misleading? It is just because the deceived person's happiness is so vague and illusory. If we say that he is unhappy, but he has the subjective form of happiness, that is, the psychological experience of happiness from being admired by friends. If we say that he is happy, but he does not live the objective life of happiness because his friends do not admire him in fact. In a word, the subjective form of his happiness and the objective content of his happiness are not consistent with each other. So, ultimately, is he happy or unhappy? As Kex points out, he is indeed happy, although his happiness is illusory happiness rather than real happiness: "Just as baseless fear is still fear, baseless happiness is still happiness."[57]

In fact, whether a person feels happiness and extreme pleasure depends on whether his great needs, desires, and purposes are realized, and whether his survival and development reach a certain degree of perfection. However, there are two possibilities for the realization of each person's major needs, desires, and purposes and the perfection of survival and development: one is the real realization and the real perfection; the other is the illusory realization and the illusory perfection. If a person feels happiness and extreme pleasure, because his great needs, desires, and purposes have been really realized, because his survival and development has really reached some perfection, then the happiness he gets is real happiness. On the contrary, if a person feels happiness and extreme pleasure because of the illusory realization of his great needs, desires, and purposes, and an illusory perfection of his survival and development, then his happiness is illusory. Let's take Pojman's example to illustrate it.

My great needs, desires, and purposes, and the perfection of my survival and development are to be loved, praised, and respected by my friends. If my friends sincerely admire me and think that my work is an original and enduring work, then my great needs, desires, and purposes will be truly realized, my scholarly career will reach some real perfection, and the happiness I get will be real happiness. On the contrary, if my friends think that my work is not original, but they just want to please or pity me, so they lie to me that my work is an original and enduring work, then the realization of my great needs, desires, and purposes will be illusory, my academic career will reach some sort of illusory perfection, and the happiness I get will be illusory.

Apparently, the so-called illusory happiness is the happiness whose objective content is not consistent with its subjective form, which means this happiness has only subjective form but no corresponding objective content. It is the happiness that has only real psychological experience of happiness but no real realization of needs. Ultimately, it is the happiness that has only real psychological experience of pleasure but no real perfection of survival and development. The happiness with only the happy psychological experience is purely subjective; the illusion of happiness is the nature of pure subjective happiness. On the contrary, the so-called real happiness is the happiness whose objective content is consistent with its subjective form. Ultimately, this happiness has both the subjective form and the corresponding objective content; this happiness has both the real psychological experience of extreme pleasure and the real realization of needs; this happiness has both the real psychological experience of extreme pleasure and the happiness from real perfection of survival and development. In this case, happiness is the unity of subjectivity and objectivity; the true authenticity of happiness is the nature of the unity of its subjectivity and objectivity.

In conclusion, all real happiness may be objective happiness or subjective happiness based on objective happiness; all objective happiness is real happiness. Meanwhile, all illusory happiness is subjective happiness, but not all subjective happiness is necessarily illusory happiness. If the subjective happiness has corresponding objective content, is based on objective happiness, and is the psychological experience of real realization of great needs, then this subjective happiness is not illusory happiness but belongs to the category of real happiness. If the subjective happiness has no corresponding objective content and is divorced from objective happiness, and is the psychological experience of illusory realization of great needs, then this subjective happiness is illusory happiness.

However, is illusory happiness harmful and real happiness beneficial? We can't generalize about them. For a man, there is some happiness he can attain, and some misfortune he can avoid; however, there is also some kinds of happiness that are impossible for him to attain, and some other types of misfortune that are impossible for him to avoid. Therefore, when a person gets some illusory happiness but cannot get real happiness, then this kind of illusory happiness is beneficial to him and harmless; thus, he ought not to give up this kind of illusory happiness.

The truth is that if he abandons this illusory happiness, he cannot get real happiness, either; after all, illusory happiness is also a kind of happiness and a psychological experience of extreme pleasure. The psychological experience of pleasure is a very important positive psychological experience; it may even lead to the real happiness of a different kind: health and longevity. As Liu Mo says, "The human nature is to seek feeling of pleasure, which is good both for the body and for the spirit, thus conducive to longevity; it can not only cure disease but also extend life."[58] Therefore, illusory happiness, though not as good as real happiness, is much better than no happiness at all. This is the positive meaning of drawing cakes to ease hunger: if it is impossible to get real cakes, you may as well draw a picture of cakes to ease hunger; the drawing of a cake is better than no cake at all. However, if a person can get real happiness, then obviously he ought to abandon this illusory happiness and pursue real happiness—real cakes are undoubtedly much better than cakes in a drawing. From this discussion, we may better understand the question of whether we ought to believe in religion or not, which is an eternal controversy at all times and all over the world: people who cannot get real happiness ought to believe in religion and get illusory happiness, but people who may get real happiness ought to abandon religion and pursue real happiness.

### *Relativity and absoluteness of happiness*

Since happiness itself is a psychological experience, a feeling, a subjective thing that is dependent on one's subjective feelings, it will inevitably vary from person to person. What is happiness for one person may not be happiness, or may even be a misfortune, for another. This is the relativity of happiness. The relativity of happiness, on careful examination, manifests itself in both quality and quantity.

The qualitative relativity of happiness suggests that the happiness of different people or the happiness of the same person at different periods differs fundamentally in quality. Let's suppose that a person, all his life, does nothing more than eating, drinking, having fun, and living the life without worrying about the basic needs of clothing and food; for an ordinary person in utter poverty this is real happiness, but it's undoubtedly a misfortune for a Napoleon, a Beethoven, or a Marx. To occupy oneself with thinking, writing books, formulating new ideas, or devoting many hard years to writing a book are sources of great happiness for Cao Xueqin, Marx, and Hegel; but for a miser, an illiterate peasant, or a vegetable seller, aren't these unbearable sufferings? Building sophisticated relationships with people, understanding worldly affairs, handling all kinds of things resourcefully, and bustling around are sources of real happiness to a man with empleomania, but a huge pain for a loner, a hermit, a thinker like Yang Zhu, or Zhuangzi who would shun it. Happiness varies not only from person to person, but also varies to the same person at different times. Showing a tender heart to lovely girls, licking rouge from the cheeks of his maids, and fooling around with girls all day long are sources of happiness for Jia Baoyu in *A Dream of the Red Mansion*, but will these things still be so to Jia Baoyu after he leaves home and becomes a monk?

The so-called quantitative relativity of happiness shows that the happiness of different people or happiness of the same person in different time differs fundamentally in quantity. As the so-called "great needs, desires, and purposes" and "the perfection of survival and development" are relative and unstable concepts, a billionaire differs greatly from a poor man in terms of "material needs, desires, and purposes." For a poor man, the desire for tens of thousands of yuan is the great need of his life. If he gets tens of thousands of yuan and meets his great needs, he will feel extreme pleasure and material happiness. However, for a billionaire, the need for tens of thousands of yuan is obviously not great need. Whether he gets or loses tens of thousands of yuan is of course far from being extreme pleasure or pain, and therefore far from being happiness or misfortune. The material life and growth of a billionaire are fundamentally different from that of a poor man. With tens of thousands of yuan, the poor man can achieve the perfection of material life and development; and if a billionaire has only one million yuan, his material life and development may still be extremely imperfect for him. Therefore, when Jia Zhen in *A Dream of the Red Mansion* saw his tenant, Mr. Wu, delivering to his mansion an assortment of goods for his mansion to use for the Chinese New Year, which was worth about 2,500 *liangs* of silver, Jia frowned, "How is it enough to celebrate the New Year with this much?"

It can be concluded that happiness varies not only qualitatively but also quantitatively with different subjects: what is happiness for one subject may not be happiness, or may even be a misfortune for another. So, happiness is relative. Then, can we conclude that happiness is only relative but not absolute? Allen Parducci's answer is yes: "Happiness is entirely relative."[59] This view is, however, untenable. In fact, happiness has both relativity and absoluteness; there is not only relative happiness but also absolute happiness. Relative happiness, as mentioned above, varies according to the subject; on the contrary, absolute happiness is the happiness that does not vary, it's the happiness that is not dependent upon the subject, and is happiness for any subject.

Imagine this: obtaining tens of thousands of yuan is happiness for a poor man, but is not happiness for a billionaire. Therefore, the happiness of getting tens of thousands of yuan is relative happiness. On the contrary, material happiness is a kind of happiness not only for the poor, but also for the billionaires, why, for all people. So, material happiness is absolute happiness. Being able to read newspapers and write is happiness for an illiterate person, but not for famous writers like Jiang Yan and Cao Xueqin. Therefore, the happiness of reading newspapers and writing is relative happiness. Contrarily, spiritual happiness is also a kind of happiness for not just illiterates, writers but for all the people. So, spiritual happiness is absolute happiness. Marrying a rich man is happiness for a gold digger, but not necessarily happiness for a woman pursuing the love of a talented man. Therefore, the happiness of winning a rich man's love is relative happiness. Contrarily, the happiness of love is a kind of happiness for those who love money, for those who pursue talented people, and thus, for all people. Therefore, the happiness of love is absolute happiness.

The truth is that like other things, human needs (as well as desires and purposes) have different types, some are universal needs while some are particular needs. The so-called particular human needs are needs that only some people have but others do not. The so-called universal human needs are the common needs of all people. For example, people who are illiterate need to read newspapers, write etc. while others, such as writers and scholars, also need to read newspapers and write; people like writers need to write for an educated public and enjoy public speaking, which the illiterate people do not need. Therefore, reading newspapers and writing books are important needs that only some people have but others don't, so they are the particular needs of some people. These people—illiterates, writers, and so on— may have different needs, but they all share the same spiritual needs: spiritual needs are the common needs of all people shared by everyone; therefore, spiritual needs are the universal needs of people.

The happiness from satisfying the particular human needs such as the need to read and write is called particular happiness; in other words, particular happiness is when people's particular needs are realized; it is the happiness that only some people pursue, the happiness that only some people want to experience. Therefore, particular happiness varies from person to person: what is happiness to some people may not be happiness to others. Therefore, particular happiness and relative happiness are one and the same concept: the relativity lies in the nature of the particular happiness. On the contrary, happiness when people's general needs, such as spiritual needs, are realized is universal happiness, therefore, it's the happiness that all people pursue. Therefore, general happiness does not vary according to the people; in other words, general happiness is independent of the people; general happiness is happiness for everybody. Therefore, universal happiness and absolute happiness are the same concepts: absoluteness is the nature of universal happiness.

Apparently, any kind of universal, absolute happiness exists in all kinds of particular, relative happiness, and any particular, relative happiness contains universal, absolute happiness. Try to imagine this: if "happiness of love" is universal and absolute happiness, can it exist independently without the particular, relative happiness of love, such as the happiness of love by "marrying a rich person" or the happiness of love by "winning the heart of a talented person"? It obviously cannot, just as "fruit" cannot exist independent of kinds of fruit like an "apple," "pear," "banana," and so on. Therefore, at the time when we achieve particular, relative happiness, we also achieve universal absolute happiness; and vice versa.

In choosing among various kinds of happiness, it is impossible to choose between "particular, relative happiness" and "universal, absolute happiness" (such as "happiness of love" and "happiness of love from marrying a rich man"); the choice is made only among "various relative, particular happiness" (such as "happiness of love from marrying a rich man" and "happiness of love from marrying a talented man"), or among various kinds of universal, absolute happiness (such as between "happiness of love" and "happiness of career").

### *Two theories on the nature of happiness: subjectivism and objectivism*

The analysis of the nature of happiness reveals that all natures of happiness, such as objectivity and subjectivity, authenticity and illusion, absoluteness and relativity, universality and particularity, can ultimately be attributed to objectivity and subjectivity, which means that objectivity and subjectivity are the most fundamental natures of happiness. This is why all the controversies about the nature of happiness can ultimately be attributed to the two schools: subjectivism (the subjectivist happiness theory) and objectivism (the objectivist happiness theory). The subjectivist happiness theory, mainly represented by Mill, Hume, and Hobbes, holds that the nature of happiness is not an objective necessity, but a subjective arbitrariness. According to this view, as long as a person feels happy, he is happy; the subjective psychological experience of extreme pleasure is sufficient condition for happiness. On the contrary, the objectivist theory of happiness, mainly represented by Aristotle, Plato, and Aquinas, holds that the nature of happiness is not subjective arbitrariness but an objective necessity. Therefore, in its view, the happiness one feels is not necessarily happiness; subjective psychological experience of extreme pleasure is a necessary condition for happiness. In this regard, Kex says clearly:

> According to subjectivism, if people sincerely feel that they are happy, then they have reached the necessary and sufficient conditions for happiness, and they have undoubtedly achieved happiness. According to the objectivist point of view, people's sincere feeling of happiness is a necessary condition rather than a sufficient condition for their true happiness. This debate between subjectivists and objectivists is one of the greatest controversies in ethics. Plato, Aristotle, Thomas Aquinas and so on believe that there is a kind of life suitable for human beings; if a person thinks that he is happy, then unless he is living such a life, it will be wrong. Hobbes, Hume, and Mill, in addition to many sentimentalists, existentialists, and egoists, think that our lives are made by ourselves. If a person sincerely feels that he is happy, then he is happy.[60]

However, why is the subjectivist theory of the nature of happiness, like the pleasure theory of happiness, still represented mainly by Mill, Hume, and Hobbes? In fact, the premise for the subjectivist theory of the nature of happiness is the pleasure theory of happiness, which holds that happiness is pleasure. As happiness is the psychological experience of needs being realized, the theory of happiness as pleasure means that happiness is a subjective psychological experience of pleasure. Thus, the subjectivist theory of happiness holds that a person is happy as long as he feels happy subjectively, regardless of his objective reality: the subjective experience of happiness is a necessary and sufficient condition for happiness; this is the basic feature of the subjectivist theory of happiness. In this way, happiness does not have any objective nature, but is an entirely subjective thing: "Happiness is only a state of mind, and nothing else."[61] Is the subjectivist theory of the nature of happiness as narrow and wrong as its premise, the theory of happiness as pleasure? The answer is, yes.

Indeed, as long as a person feels happy, he is happy. However, whether he feels illusory happiness or real happiness is not subjective and arbitrary; it depends entirely on whether the realization of his great needs is illusory or real: if his needs are truly realized, the happiness he feels is real happiness; if the realization of his needs is illusory, the happiness he feels is illusory happiness. If a person who pursues the happiness of a faithful love thinks that his lover is faithful to him, he is happy regardless of the fact whether his lover is faithful or not, and he is indeed happy. But if the fact is that his lover is not faithful, the happiness he feels is illusory happiness; if the fact is that his lover is truly faithful, the happiness he feels is real happiness. Therefore, a person's feeling of happiness is only a necessary condition rather than a sufficient condition for real happiness; a person's feeling of happiness is a necessary and sufficient condition only for illusory happiness, not for real happiness. To conclude, a person's feeling of happiness is not a necessary and sufficient condition for all happiness; thus, it is not a necessary and sufficient condition for happiness. The error of the subjectivist theory of happiness lies in that it exaggerates the necessary and sufficient condition of illusory happiness as the necessary and sufficient condition of real happiness, equates illusory happiness with real happiness, and eventually confines happiness only to a subjective psychological state.

If the subjectivist theory of happiness is one-sided and wrong, can we then say that objectivist happiness theory is true? Let's first look at the history of the objectivist theory of happiness. The objectivist theory of the nature of happiness, like the perfection theory of happiness, is mainly represented by Aristotle, Plato, and Aquinas. Obviously, the premise of the objectivist theory of happiness is the perfection theory of happiness: happiness is the perfection of survival and development, which ultimately means self-improvement, self-realization, self-achievement, and the full realization of the potential of the self. Whether a person lives and develops perfectly and whether he has realized his potential to achieve self-realization is objective and not dependent on whether he has the psychological experience of pleasure or happiness. If his life purpose of survival, development, and self-fulfillment has been realized, he is bound to have the psychological experience of extreme pleasure and feel happiness; however, no matter how much happiness and extreme pleasure he feels, it is absolutely possible that he may have not fully realized his needs and reached the perfection of survival and development. Therefore, based on the theory of happiness as full self-realization and perfection of survival and development, the objectivist theory of happiness naturally holds that the nature of happiness is entirely objective, inevitable, and independent of human will; the psychological experience of extreme pleasure is only the necessary subjective manifestation and accompaniment of the objective nature of happiness. In short, the subjective psychological experience of happiness is only a necessary condition for happiness, not a sufficient condition.

Richard Kraut makes it very clear that "the complete realization of desire is only a necessary condition for happiness, not a sufficient condition for happiness because according to Aristotle's theory, these desires must be directed to valuable goals... Otherwise, no matter how satisfied a person feels, he is not a happy person."[62] The so-called "valuable goals" here undoubtedly refer to self-realization and perfection of survival and development. So Kraut goes on to say,

> We can define objectivism as the view that people cannot be considered happy unless they are approaching appropriately the best life they can achieve. According to objectivism, everyone has certain talents and gifts that can be fully developed under ideal conditions.[63]

Apparently, the mistake of the objectivist theory of happiness lies in its failure to acknowledge that if a person feels happy and has a very happy psychological experience, then he is indeed happy even though he may experience only subjective illusory happiness, rather than objective real happiness; even if the realization of his great needs is illusory rather than real—and the perfection of his survival and development is illusory rather than real—he will still feel happy and have a very happy psychological experience. Imagine if a person is confident that he has written innovative books, then, even if his books are not actually original, does he not feel happy and have the psychological experience of extreme pleasure? Nevertheless, what he gets is illusory, subjective happiness of self-realization, not real, objective happiness of self-realization.

Therefore, the feeling of happiness is a sufficient condition only for illusory subjective happiness, not for real and objective happiness. So, is the psychological experience of happiness or extreme pleasure a necessary condition for real and objective happiness? Yes. If the realization of a person's great needs is real—and the perfection of survival and development is real—and he thus enjoys objective and real happiness, then he is bound to feel happy and have the psychological experience of extreme pleasure; thus, the feeling of happiness is a necessary condition for real and objective happiness. The mistake of the objectivist theory of happiness lies in that it denies "subjective, illusory happiness," equates "happiness" with "real, objective happiness," confines happiness only to objective, real happiness of "self-realization," and consequently elevates "feeling of happiness" as "the necessary condition for real and objective happiness" to "feeling of happiness" as "the necessary condition for happiness." Because of this mistake, this theory deduces wrongly that what one feels as happiness is not necessarily happiness, because the nature of happiness is totally objective and independent of human will.

In this way, the objectivist theory not only makes no sense in theory, but also perhaps declares that in practice it is impossible for ordinary people to achieve happiness. According to the objectivist theory, ordinary people who struggle with making a living and do not have the objective conditions for self-realization are doomed to be unhappy no matter how happy they feel. Therefore, Richard Kraut accuses the objectivist theory of happiness of "doing something inhumane":

> The objectivist theory sets the value goal of happiness too high; this drives us to feel unsatisfied with our life that cannot reach the standard of objective happiness. If a person is permanently mentally retarded, then, even though he is far from the ideal life he ought to have, we have no reason to convince him that his life is doomed for misfortune. If, instead, its objectivist standard took into account of the abilities and circumstances of individuals that are independent of their will, the objectivist theory would be a more humane theory.[64]

## Laws of happiness

### Laws of the fact of happiness

#### Law of the intensity of happiness

The intensity of different kinds of pleasure and happiness varies. Happiness and pleasure of love are intoxicating and fascinating, and thus extremely intense. On the contrary, the pleasures of reading, thinking, and aesthetic appreciation are as extremely quiet as flowing clouds and running water. So, what does the intensity of happiness and pleasure depend on? Obviously, it depends on the intensity of needs and desires: the stronger the needs and desires, the stronger the psychological experience of their realization; the weaker the needs and desires, the more apathetic the psychological experience of their realization. Why is the pleasure and happiness of sex so strong? Isn't it because sexual desire is the strongest desire? Why is the pleasure of reading and learning less intense? Isn't it because the desire for reading and learning is less intense? Then, what determines the intensity of needs and desires?

Maslow found that the intensity of needs and desires depends on their level: the lower the level of the needs and desires, the more intense the needs and desires; the higher the level of the needs and desires, the less intense the needs and desires. In this way, "physiological needs are more intense than security needs, security needs are more intense than love needs, love needs are more intense than esteem needs, and esteem needs are more intense than self-realization needs."[65] This means that the lower the level of happiness and pleasure, the more intense it feels, and the higher the level of happiness and pleasure, the less intense it feels. Indeed, this is a common experience for everyone. What is the most intense happiness and pleasure we have experienced? Of course, it is the happiness and pleasure of food and sex (material happiness). What happiness and pleasure are the least intense? Of course, it is the happiness of "learning and gaining knowledge" (spiritual happiness). The intensity of happiness of fame and power (social happiness) lies between the intensity of the material happiness and the intensity of spiritual happiness. Therefore, the intensity of happiness and pleasure is inversely proportional to its level: the higher the level of happiness and pleasure, the less intense and urgent it feels; the lower the level of happiness and pleasure, the more intense and urgent it feels. This is the law of intensity of happiness and pleasure. But why is it this way?

The so-called needs, as we all know, are actually the dependence that things have on something in order to survive and develop; human needs are the dependence that people have on something in order to survive and develop. That is to say, as all human needs originate from survival and development, they can be classified into two major needs, survival needs and development needs: our needs can be survival needs, or development needs, or both. Material needs or physiological needs, such as appetite, sexual desire, survival desire, health needs, sleep needs, safety needs, and so on, are obviously survival needs; spiritual needs, such as self-realization needs, creative needs, curiosity, inquiry needs, game needs, aesthetic needs, etc., are obviously development needs; social needs, such as the desire for power, sense of honor, conscience, self-respect, sense of fairness, desire for revenge, and so on, are mostly both survival needs and development needs. To put it simply, the lower the level of the needs, the closer they are to survival needs.

The lowest needs, such as food and sex, are purely survival needs. The higher the level of the needs, the closer they are to the development needs. The highest needs, such as self-realization, are purely development needs.

Therefore, the nature of low-level needs is survival, so they are survival needs; the nature of high-level needs is development, so they are development needs. There is no doubt that survival needs are more intense than development needs, while the development needs are more moderate than survival needs. Anyone, no matter how indifferent he is toward survival and how passionate he is toward development, must first survive and then develop. If he cannot survive, how is development possible? The lower the level of the need, the stronger it is; the higher the level of the need, the weaker the need. Isn't this because the low-level needs are survival needs, and the high-level needs are development needs? Isn't this because survival needs are intense and development needs are moderate? This is also the reason why the lower the level of happiness and pleasure, the more intense it feels: the nature of the low-level pleasure and happiness is the realization of survival needs while the nature of high-level happiness and pleasure is the realization of development needs.

*The law of duration of happiness*

Intense psychological experience cannot be lasting, and lasting psychological experience is bound to be moderate. The same applies to the psychological experience of happiness and pleasure. The lower the level of the happiness, the more intense it feels, and thus the shorter it lasts; the higher the level of happiness, the more moderate it feels, and thus the longer it lasts. The happiness and pleasure of good wine and delicious food is low-level, and the psychological experience of them is intense but extremely short: after a full meal of delicious food and good wine, the experience is totally gone. On the contrary, the happiness of writing books is high-level happiness, and the psychological experience of this happiness is much more moderate than that of eating and drinking, but this psychological experience lasts much longer, right through one's life. Sexual intercourse is the lowest level of happiness; sexual intercourse of human beings is no different from the mating of animals. The psychological experience of sexual pleasure and happiness is also the most intense, and its psychological experience is soul-stirring, wonderful, unparalleled, and beyond language. But the psychological experience of this pleasure and happiness is undoubtedly the shortest. In ancient Chinese fiction, sex is often described as transient: "in an instant, clouds gather and rain disperse." Some animals are even more miserable, as this blissful moment of sex is the end of their lives.

Conversely, the realization of the creative potential of self is the highest level of happiness and pleasure; it is the most significant difference between human beings and other animals. The psychological experience of happiness and pleasure of self-fulfillment is also the most moderate: this psychological experience is as tranquil as if it is non-existent; it is so vague and illusive that the feeling is sometimes present and sometimes absent; it feels nothing like pleasure and happiness. But this kind of pleasure and happiness lasts the longest; it lasts forever and becomes a kind of eternal enjoyment for life. Therefore, Mill even believes that the superiority of high-level happiness lies in the permanence of its psychological experience: "Mental happiness is superior to physical happiness, mainly because the latter is more permanent."[66] Scheler then regards duration as the criterion of the value of happiness: "That which has the higher value lasts longer."[67]

Then, why do happiness and pleasure last longer when it is higher level and shorter when it is lower level? The answer to this question may also lie in the fact that the nature of low-level happiness and pleasure is the realization of survival needs and the nature of high-level happiness and pleasure is the realization of development needs. The process of realizing survival needs is rather short. Take the process of satisfying the appetite of a person as an example, generally speaking, it takes only half an hour; half an hour later, his stomach is full and he doesn't have to eat anymore; his survival needs are realized. When he is hungry again, he will eat for another half an hour, and then enjoy the pleasure of the realization of his appetite for that time. Regardless of who he is, no matter how he gluttonous he is, the fact is that he can't eat all day long. If he eats all day long, as he reads books all day, he will be stuffed to death. The process of fulfilling sexual desire is even more short-lived, needless to say.

On the contrary, the process of realizing development needs lasts longer. Take a look at the most fundamental development need, thirst for knowledge. The process of fulfilling this need is obviously ongoing, gradual, and continuous. A person who is never tired of learning can always keep a book in his hands all day long and year after year. If a person reads and writes like he eats a meal—three times a day, half an hour at a time, then he must be a person who lacks thirst for knowledge or a person who is too busy to satisfy his thirst for knowledge. Needless to say, the process of satisfying the need of self-realization lasts even longer. The process of fulfilling the survival need is short, so the psychological experience (i.e. low-level happiness and pleasure) of realizing the survival needs is short; the process of realizing development needs lasts longer, so the psychological experience (i.e. high-level happiness and pleasure) of realizing development needs is long-lasting.

Obviously, the duration of happiness and pleasure is directly proportional to its level: the lower the level of happiness and pleasure, the shorter its psychological experience lasts; the higher the level of happiness and pleasure, the longer its psychological experience lasts. This is the law of duration of the psychological experience of happiness and pleasure. Putting the law of duration of happiness and the law of intensity of happiness together, we can see that the level of happiness is inversely proportional to its intensity but directly proportional to its duration: the lower the level of happiness and pleasure, the more intense and the more transient its psychological experience is; the higher the level of happiness and pleasure, the more moderate and the more lasting is its psychological experience. This is the law of psychological experience of happiness and pleasure. With this law, we may conclude: in terms of intensity of the psychological experience, low-level happiness and pleasure seem to take precedence over high-level happiness and pleasure, but in terms of duration of the psychological experience, high-level happiness and pleasure appear to take precedence over low-level happiness and pleasure. Then, we may wonder, which kind of happiness is the ultimate priority?

*The law of succession of happiness*

Perhaps the greatest achievement of Maslow's psychology is to reveal the law of intensity, as well as priority, of needs at different levels: the lower the level of the need, the more intense the need and, therefore, the higher the priority; the higher the level of the need, the more moderate is the intensity of the need, and therefore the more delayed is its gratification. This is because the higher-level need is the result of the relative satisfaction of the lower-level needs. Maslow attaches great importance to this discovery and calls it "the Principles of Human Motivation":

> We have seen that the chief, principle of organization in human motivational life is the arrangement of basic needs in a hierarchy of less or greater priority or potency. The chief dynamic principle animating this organization is the emergence in the healthy person of less potent needs upon gratification of the more potent ones. The physiological needs, when unsatisfied, dominate the organism, pressing all capacities into their service and organizing these capacities so that they may be most efficient in this service. Relative gratification submerges them and allows the next higher set of needs in the hierarchy to emerge, dominate, and organize the personality, so that instead of being, e.g., hunger obsessed, it now becomes safety obsessed. The principle is the same for the other sets of needs in the hierarchy, i.e., love, esteem, and self-actualization.[68]

Indeed, the lower the level of the need, the higher the level of its priority. Imagine this: everyone needs food, sex, security, fame, self-esteem, morality, self-fulfillment, and so on; however, if he is hungry and his appetite is not satisfied, his need for fame and other desires will retreat or disappear, and all he wants is to satisfy is his appetite. Only when his appetite is satisfied will other desires arise and he will want to satisfy them. This is a universal law, no matter who he is, no matter how noble and great he is, or how contemptuous he is of material pleasure when he is hungry, he cannot help but stop pursuit of some noble ideal and attempt to satisfy his appetite. Marx's favorite words are: "The enjoyment of thought is the highest enjoyment." These words sound rather lofty, but if Marx doesn't eat food or drink water

192  *Happiness*

and thus stays hungry and thirsty all the time, can he still conceive *The Capital*? At the time when he is hungry and thirsty, his great mind must be filled with ideas of bread, beef, and red wine. Only when his appetite is satisfied can the ideas of "value" and "surplus value" come back to dominate his mind and help him conceive *The Capital*. In short, low-level needs take precedence over high-level needs; high-level needs are the result of the realization of low-level needs. However, Maslow further points out:

> This statement might give a false impression: a need must be met 100% before the next need emerges. In actual fact, most members of our society who are normal are partially satisfied in all their basic needs and partially unsatisfied in all their basic needs at the same time. A more realistic description of the hierarchy would be in terms of decreasing percentages of satisfaction as we go up the hierarchy of prepotency. For instance, if I may assign arbitrary figures for the sake of illustration, it is as if the average citizen is satisfied perhaps 85 percent in his physiological needs, 70 percent in his safety needs, 50 percent in his love needs, 40 percent in his self-esteem needs, and 10 percent in his self-actualization needs.[69]

That is to say, the satisfaction degree of the low-level needs that leads to the high-level needs is relative and dependent on individuals and society However, no matter what the society, no matter who the individual is, one thing is absolute: only when his low-level needs are met at least to the smallest extent is it likely that his high-level needs will emerge and be met, and finally his high-level happiness and pleasure be achieved. Then, from this statement can we deduce that the lower the level of happiness, the higher the priority of the happiness, the higher the level of happiness, the more delayed the happiness, and the higher-level happiness is the result of the realization of the lower-level happiness?

The conclusion seems sensible. However, does this not mean that only those who get low-level happiness can get high-level happiness or those who do not get low-level happiness must not get high-level happiness? If so, Bao Zhao in ancient China would not have sighed that "all saints and sages have been poor and humble since ancient times." In fact, although what Bao Zhao said may seem rather absolute, many thinkers, artists, theorists, writers, and philosophers—such as Socrates, Spinoza, Cao Xueqin, Lu Xun, Chernyshevsky, Lermontov, and so on—who enjoy high-level happiness at all times and all over the world, do not get material happiness; they suffer from poverty, or die young, or endure many ordeals and hardships. So, what goes wrong here?

The truth is that the so-called happiness is the psychological experience of realizing some great needs of life, that is, the psychological experience of realizing some ideals of life. Therefore, low-level happiness is the psychological experience of the realization of some great low-level needs of life, and the realization of some low-level ideals of life; high-level happiness is the psychological experience of the realization of some great high-level needs of life, and the realization of some high-level ideals of life. Therefore, the necessary condition for a person to enjoy high-level happiness is that he must have high-level needs.

However, high-level needs are only the result of the relative and minimum realization of low-level needs; they are neither the result of the realization of low-level ideals, nor the result of the realization of low-level happiness. Therefore, the relative and minimum realization of low-level needs must take precedence over high-level happiness, because without the relative and minimum satisfaction of low-level needs, people will never have high-level needs, and will not pursue or enjoy high-level happiness. If thinkers, such as Socrates, Spinoza, Marx, Cao Xueqin, Lu Xun, Chernyshevsky, Lermontov, and so on, are not clothed or fed, their material needs not met at the lowest level, and they have to struggle for survival all the time, then they will never have attained the high-level needs and, ultimately, high-level happiness of writing books and self-realization.

Nonetheless, people without low-level happiness can also have the relative and minimum realization of low-level needs, so they can also have high-level needs, which they can pursue and, ultimately, enjoy high-level happiness. Therefore, although low-level happiness is more intense than high-level happiness, it does not take precedence over higher-level happiness, because higher-level happiness takes the minimum realization of low-level needs as the necessary condition, but does not take low-level happiness as the necessary condition; in other words, high-level happiness and low-level happiness are relatively independent of each other. Therefore, Maslow repeatedly says: "The higher develops only on the basis of the lower, but eventually, when well established, may become relatively independent of the lower"[70] The objective reason why the ancient sages were able to settle down in poverty is this: high-level happiness does not have to be based on low-level happiness as a necessary condition, and can exist independently.

In conclusion, the priority of needs is inversely proportional to their level in the hierarchy: the lower-level the need, the higher its priority, the higher-level the need, the more it is postponed, because high-level needs are the result of the minimum realization of low-level needs. However, low-level happiness does not take precedence over high-level happiness. High-level happiness is the result of relative and minimum realization of low-level needs, not the result of the realization of low-level ideals, not the result of realization of low-level happiness. High-level happiness is placed after the minimum realization of low-level needs, but not after the minimum realization of low-level ideals because high-level happiness and low-level happiness are relatively independent of each other. This is the law of succession or priority of happiness.

The law of succession of happiness, the law of duration of happiness, and the law of intensity of happiness are, in short, all about the "is," "fact," or "what is" of happiness; thus, they may be considered as "laws of fact" and be called "three laws of fact" of happiness. But "what is creates what ought to be."[71] With these three laws of the fact of happiness put together, people may be easily confused about "how we ought to choose happiness." The value of low-level happiness seems to be greater than that of high-level happiness in terms of the intensity of its psychological experience; the value of low-level happiness seems to be less than that of high-level happiness in terms of the duration of psychological experience; in terms of succession and priority, high-level happiness and low-level happiness are relatively independent and can be chosen freely. So, what kind of happiness ought we to choose when there is a conflict between high-level happiness and low-level happiness? Which kind of happiness has more value? These questions can be further addressed by the laws of the value of happiness.

## Laws of the value of happiness

Mill once made a wise choice about the values of happiness of different levels in a condensed statement: "It is better to be a human being dissatisfied than a pig satisfied; better to be Socrates dissatisfied than a fool satisfied."[72] Why is it better to be an unsatisfied person than a satisfied pig? It is obvious because it is likely that those who are not satisfied may enjoy spiritual happiness, while those who are satisfied can only enjoy material happiness. The truth is that the value of spiritual happiness is greater than that of material happiness. Why is it better to be an unsatisfied Socrates than a satisfied fool? Obviously, Socrates, though unsatisfied and with no material happiness, enjoys spiritual happiness while the fool, though satisfied, has only material happiness, but no share of spiritual happiness. In other words, the value of spiritual happiness is greater than that of material happiness.

In this sense, Mill's view can be boiled down to one critical question: if a person can choose at will, then ought he to choose to be a fool who enjoys material happiness or a thinker who does not have material happiness? Mill answers that the latter ought to be chosen. Fools have material happiness but no spiritual happiness; thinkers have spiritual happiness though they have no material happiness: the value of spiritual happiness is greater than that of material happiness, and the value of high-level happiness and pleasure is greater than that of low-level happiness and pleasure. Maslow reaches the same conclusion through his research on high-level needs and low-level needs.

> A greater value is usually placed upon the higher need than upon the lower by those who have been gratified in both. Such people will sacrifice more for the higher satisfaction, and furthermore will more readily be able to withstand lower deprivation. For example, they will find it easier to live ascetic lives, to withstand danger for the sake of principle, to give up money and prestige for the sake of self-actualization. Those

who have known both universally regard self-respect as a higher, more valuable subjective experience than a filled belly."[73]

That is to say, high-level happiness has greater value than low-level happiness: the value of spiritual happiness is greater than that of social happiness, and the value of social happiness is greater than that of material happiness. Roughly speaking, what Maslow and Mill said is quite accurate. But can we say that the satisfaction of esteem needs is more valuable than satisfying the appetite of a person who has no food or clothing? Spiritual needs are the highest level needs, but does the realization of spiritual needs really have the greatest value for all people? For a poor peasant who budgets all day on how to support his family, isn't the value of the realization of material needs and material happiness far greater than that of the realization of spiritual needs and spiritual happiness? So, what goes wrong exactly?

Happiness and pleasure are, in terms of its objective content, the realization of needs. Needs are the dependence of things on something for the sake of their existence and development; human needs are the dependence of human beings on something for the sake of their existence and development. Therefore, the value of all kinds of happiness and pleasure is ultimately the value of the realization of various needs for human survival and development; this is the starting point for us to examine the value of all kinds of happiness and pleasure. From this point, it then follows that the realization of needs of different levels has fundamentally different values for the survival and development: the lower-level the need, the greater the value of its realization for survival and the smaller the value of its realization for development; the higher-level the need, the smaller the value of its realization for survival and the greater the value of its realization for development.

Material and physiological needs, such as appetite and sexual desire, are at the lowest level. Their realization has undoubtedly the greatest value for survival: only when one's appetite is satisfied can he survive; only when one's sexual desire is satisfied can he reproduce and survive. However, the satisfaction of appetite and sexual desire is of the least value to a person's development: if he has only basic needs such as appetite and sexual desire to satisfy, then he will be no different from a pig or a dog; in this case, how can he develop himself?

On the contrary, though the need for self-realization and realization of one's creative potential is the highest level, its satisfaction is of the least value to a person's survival, because he can survive whether he is self-actualized or not. Maslow also saw this, saying, "The higher the need the less imperative it is for sheer survival."[74] However, the higher level the need, the greater value its realization has for development: the realization of self-realization needs is the greatest value for a person's development. Because self-realization is the realization of a person's creative potential, isn't the realization of creative potential a person's greatest development? Is it not the highest state of development?

Consumer needs are low-level needs while creative needs are high-level needs. For a person's survival, the realization of consumer needs has obviously more value than creative needs, because whether a person's creative needs are satisfied or not, he will survive all the same; but if his consumptive needs are not met, he will not survive. On the contrary, for a person's development, the realization of creative needs has more value than consumptive needs. The reason is that if a person only consumes and does not create, then he only exists but does not develop, as human development mainly lies in the realization of creative needs.

Spiritual needs are at a higher level than social needs; social needs are at a higher level than material needs. Therefore, for a person's survival, the value of the realization of material needs (such as food and sex) is the greatest; the value of the realization of social needs (such as fame, status, and power) is the second; and the value of the satisfaction of spiritual needs (such as curiosity and aesthetic needs and self-realization needs) is the last priority. On the contrary, for a person's development, the value of realizing spiritual needs is the greatest, the value of realizing social needs is the second, and the value of realizing material needs is the least.

In short, for a person's survival, the value of the realization of needs is inversely proportional to the level of needs; for a person's development, the value of the realization of needs is directly proportional to the level of needs: the higher level the need, the smaller value its realization holds for survival and the greater value its realization holds for development; the lower level the need, the greater value its realization holds for survival, the smaller value its realization holds for development. As the psychological experience of the realization of needs is happiness and pleasure, we can draw the following conclusions:

The value that happiness and pleasure holds for survival is inversely proportional to the level of happiness and pleasure; the value that happiness and pleasure holds for development is directly proportional to the level of happiness and pleasure: the higher the level of happiness and pleasure, the smaller the value it holds for survival, the greater the value it has for development, and, thus, the more moderate and more lasting its psychological experience; the lower the level of happiness and pleasure, the greater the value it holds for survival, the lesser the value it holds for development, and the more intense and shorter its psychological experience.

This is the law of the value of happiness: the value of happiness varies according to the nature and the level of happiness. This law shows that it is one-sided for Mill and Maslow to think that "the value of high-level happiness and pleasure" is greater than "the value of low-level happiness and pleasure." Their view is surely true only for development needs, but the opposite is true for survival needs. Imagine for a hungry person who has no food or clothing, or for a busy person who works hard and struggles to make both ends meet, the value of low-level material needs is undoubtedly greater than that of high-level spiritual needs. Therefore, for him, the value of low-level, material happiness and pleasure is greater than that of high-level, spiritual happiness and pleasure; when the two levels of happiness and pleasure conflict, he would choose low-level material happiness and pleasure, rather than the other. On the contrary, for a person who has no problem of survival but the desire to develop his self, the value of high-level spiritual needs is indeed greater than that of low-level material needs. Therefore, for him, the value of high-level spiritual happiness and pleasure is indeed greater than that of low-level material happiness and pleasure; when the two levels of happiness conflict, he would choose high-level spiritual happiness and pleasure, rather than the opposite.

Mill's view only sees "development" needs but ignores "survival" needs, so the choice of whether to be a painful Socrates or to be a happy fool is a development-based and not a survival-based one. Both the painful Socrates and the happy fool have solved the problem of survival, and they face only the problem of development. Therefore, from the point of view of this choice, higher-level happiness and pleasure indeed have greater value; this means that the value of the painful Socrates is greater than that of the happy fool, and thus one ought to choose to be the painful Socrates rather than the happy fool.

However, this is only a development-based choice. It ought to be supplemented by a survival-based choice—to be a living fool or to be a dead Socrates? To be a living rat or a dead emperor? This is a survival-based choice, not a development-based one. For this choice, there is no doubt that low-level happiness and pleasure is of great value: the value of the living mice is greater than that of the dead emperor. Therefore, in this case, we ought to choose to be a living rat rather than a dead emperor. As the Taoists believe, the value of life is the greatest: "the dead emperor would rather be the living rat"; the dead emperor is not as good as the living rat!

## Laws of the realization of happiness

In our life, how can we realize our dream of happiness and avoid suffering and pain? This enigmatic problem has given birth to many theories and has been hitherto unsettled. Around this enigmatic problem, the theory of asceticism and abstinence holds that desires ought to be reduced to the minimum; on the contrary, the theory of hedonism advocates that desire ought to be satisfied at will without restraint while the theory of disciplining and channeling desires advocates that desires ought to be restrained to make desires conform to reason. Which theory can make people achieve happiness and avoid misfortune?

### Desire: the negative correlation with the realization of happiness

As mentioned above, the so-called desire is one's consciousness and awareness of the need, the need that one is conscious of, and the reflection of this need in the brain. It includes wishes, ideals, or aspirations: desires which are about to be realized or will be realized are wishes; wishes that are broad and must be realized through great effort are ideals or aspirations. How to deal with desire is, indeed, the most fundamental issue in the realization of happiness, for happiness is the psychological experience of the realization of great needs, desires, and purposes, while misfortune is the psychological experience of the non-realization of great needs, desires, and purposes. That is to say, the reason why happiness and misfortune exist is because there are needs, desires, and purposes; if there were no needs, desires, and purposes, where is the question of their realization? Where do happiness and misfortune come from? Therefore, needs, desires, and purposes are the common roots of happiness and misfortune; thus, they are also the motivation for people to pursue happiness and to realize happiness.

But, then, why do the theory of asceticism, the theory of hedonism, and the theory of abstinence emphasize desires rather than needs and purposes? The truth is that the most representative, typical, and pure root of and motivation for happiness and misfortune is desire rather than need and purpose. As mentioned earlier, needs cannot directly trigger behaviors, so it is impossible for needs to directly trigger the behavior of pursuing happiness; only when needs are perceived and then transformed into desires can they trigger people's behaviors of pursuing happiness: needs can produce only desires to meet these needs; only desires can then produce behavioral purposes of realizing desires, and behavioral purposes then produce the means to realize purposes. Therefore, only desire is the real root of and motivation for behaviors, the real source of happiness and misfortune, and the real motivation for the realization of happiness. As Russell says, "Our impulses and desires are the elements which create our happiness."[75]

Therefore, it is true that without desire, there will be no misfortune, but there will be no happiness, either. Without sexual desire, there would be no love, there would be no misfortune of failed love, but there would be no happiness of fortunate love, either. The lesser, the smaller, and lower-level the desire one has, the lesser, the smaller, and lower-level the pain and misfortune one may suffer, but the lesser, the smaller, and lower-level happiness one may enjoy, too. The more, the greater, and the higher-level the desire one has, the more, the greater, and the higher-level the misfortune one may suffer, but the more, the greater, and the higher-level the happiness one may enjoy, too. People often escape into religions, such as Buddhism, in order to escape pain and misfortune. If their hearts are numb and their six desires are eliminated, then they will no longer feel any pain and misfortune, but they will not enjoy any happiness and pleasure, either. People who may suffer tremendous pain and misfortune are indeed those with strong and lofty desires, those with lofty aspirations, such as Chernyshevsky, Marx, Bronquil, Spinoza, Socrates, and Confucius. These people are undoubtedly the ones who may enjoy great and high-level happiness.

It can be concluded that desire is the root of and motivation for happiness and misfortune and is directly proportional to the likelihood of happiness and misfortune: the more desire one has, the more happiness and misfortune one is likely to get; the less desire one has, the less happiness and misfortune one is likely to get. However, the more and the higher-level one's desire is, the harder it is to achieve happiness, and the easier it is for misfortune to befall him; the less and the lower-level the desire is, the easier it is to achieve happiness, and the harder it is for misfortune to befall him. If a person's desire is at a very low-level and he only wants to live a life of mediocrity, then it is obviously easy for him to achieve happiness. As it is easy for him to achieve ordinary happiness and pleasure that he pursues, so is it also easy for him to avoid pain and misfortune. On the contrary, if he desires to rise above others, to be famous, to be an authority, and to live a spectacular life, then it will be very difficult for him to realize his desires; it is, thus, difficult for him to achieve the extraordinary happiness and pleasure he pursues, and it is also difficult for him to avoid pain and misfortune. In a word, desire is inversely proportional to the realization of happiness and directly proportional to the occurrence of misfortune. As Ignacio L. Gotz says, "The nature of happiness can be summed up as an equation":[76]

$$\text{happiness} = \frac{\text{realization}}{\text{desire}}$$

In summary, desire is the motivation of happiness and misfortune. Desire is directly proportional to the likelihood of happiness and misfortune, inversely proportional to the realization of happiness. To put it simply, desire is in negative correlation with the realization of happiness and positive correlation with the likelihood of happiness; it is directly proportional to the likelihood of happiness and inversely proportional to the realization of happiness. This is the negative correlation motivation law of the realization of happiness. People can often get confused easily with this law. It seems that in terms of the likelihood of happiness, desire ought to be increased. In this sense, Zhuge Liang says, "We ought to harbor lofty ambitions." However, in terms of the realization of happiness, it seems that desire ought to be reduced. In this sense, the ancients said, "A contented mind is a perpetual feast." So, ought the desire to be high and lofty or low and realistic? To what extent must it be to be appropriate? This extent is determined by other factors that contribute to the realization of everyone's happiness, such as talent, effort, destiny, and virtue.

*Talent: the first positive correlation with the realization of happiness*

Talent, effort, and destiny are actually the three elements that contribute to the success of life that Fung Yulan has talked about with delight. The so-called talent refers to a person's natural gift: "A person's natural gift, as we call it, is talent."[77] Natural gift, as is generally known, is the innate and potential talent, which is mainly the inborn and potential creativity, or the so-called "intelligence." The research of modern humanistic psychology shows that, on the one hand, there is no such person who has no talent or creativity of any kind at all; on the other hand, there is no such person who has all the talents and all the creativity: every normal person is endowed with talent, intelligence, and creativity in one aspect or another. Therefore, Fung Yulan says, "We humans are born stupid or smart; as long as a person is not born an idiot, he will be quite smart in some aspect."[78]

Talent and intelligence vary from person to person, just like their facial features. This difference, though various and complicated, can be summarized in two aspects. On the one hand, there are differences in kinds and types of talent and intelligence. For example, some people have a talent for drawing, some for intellectual thinking, some have a talent for music, and some for long-distance running, and so on. On the other hand, there are differences in the degree of talent and intelligence; people with the same kind of talent vary in degrees—quantity, size, and level—of such talent. Both Marx and Engels have the same talent for logical thinking, but the talent of logical thinking in Marx is undoubtedly higher than that in Engels. Those who are literarily skilled have the talent of writing essays, poetry, or fiction; however, the talent of Tolstoy, Cao Xueqin, Pushkin, and Li Bai is obviously much higher than that of many people. The difference between genius and mediocrity lies in the degree of their talent but not in the type of talent. Mediocrity can do what genius does: what makes them different is just that the talent in a genius is of a higher degree and quantity than that in ordinary people. Therefore, Fung Yulan says,

> The talent of a genius is only marginally higher or greater than that of the average people. Though the difference is not much, such difference matters greatly. A tall man is usually only a few inches taller than the average person, but these inches can make him 'rise above others'.[79]

So, what is the relationship between one's talent, intelligence, wisdom, and one's happiness? They seem to be in inverse proportion, the more intelligent one is, the more pains one will have—there is the so-called "pain of wisdom." Qoheleth even claims, "Intelligence and knowledge are just madness and stupidity; they are as crazy and stupid as catching the wind: the more intelligence one has, the more distress he gets, and the more knowledge one gets, the more pain he gets."[80] Indeed, talent, intelligence, and knowledge often bring forth pain; the higher one's talent and intelligence, the more the knowledge one has, the more pain one will feel; this is because he will a higher level of desire and, thus, his pain and misfortune will correspondingly be of a higher level, but contrarily, the more and the higher-level the happiness and pleasure he will get as well. As desire is the motivation of happiness and misfortune and is directly proportional to the likelihood of happiness and misfortune, it is one-sided to say that the more talent and intelligence one has, the more pain he will suffer. In a comprehensive sense, talent and intelligence is the common root of pain and pleasure, happiness and misfortune.

However, intelligence as the common root of happiness and misfortune is only one of the many links between talent and intelligence, and happiness and misfortune. There are other links between talent and intelligence, and pain and pleasure, happiness and misfortune, especially the link between talent and intelligence, and the realization of happiness: talent and intelligence are a necessary condition for the realization of happiness. It is self-evident that the kind of happiness a person can achieve depends on the kind of talent he has; if he lacks certain kind of talent, it is impossible for him to achieve that kind of happiness: a certain kind of talent is the necessary condition and factor for achieving a certain kind of happiness. As we may have seen, some people are bent on becoming novelists, and for many long, hard years they continue to write, unable to quit it. But, strangely enough, they tend to write the beginning and then come to a standstill. In the end, they have just begun several novels one after another; or they have produced totally unreadable novels. Why? It is apparently because they don't have the talent for writing novels. If a person does not have the talent of writing, it is impossible for him to achieve the happiness of becoming a novelist in any case. If he wants to become a novelist, he must have the talent of writing: the talent of a novelist is a necessary condition for realizing the happiness of a novelist.

As a necessary condition for the realization of happiness, talent varies not only in type but also in level. The level of a person's talent in a field determines his level of achievement in that field, as well as the level of happiness he is likely to attain; in other words, the level of happiness he is likely to achieve is determined by the level of his talent. A person with a talent for poetry can become a poet and realize the happiness of being a poet. However, whether he can become a great poet and realize the happiness of becoming a great poet depends on the level of his talent for poetry. If he is extremely talented, a genius in poetry, then he is likely to become a great poet. If his talent for poetry is just mediocre, then he is unlikely to become a great poet. From ancient times to the present, both in China and in the West, there are a great number of people, like Jia Dao, who write poems painstakingly. But, why are there only one Li Bai and one Pushkin? There are so many novelists today, but why are there no Cao Xueqin and Tolstoy anymore? I'm afraid it's because they don't have the peerless genius of Li Bai, Pushkin, Cao Xueqin, or Tolstoy. Without that peerless genius, it is impossible to write a masterpiece.

Ultimately, the level of happiness a person is likely to achieve is directly proportional to the level of his talent: the lower the talent he has, the smaller his achievement, and the smaller the happiness he is likely to achieve; the higher the talent he has, the greater his achievement and the greater happiness he is likely to achieve. So, if the happiness people pursue is set, or if the happiness people pursue is the same, then the likelihood of realizing happiness is obviously directly proportional to the level of talent: the higher the talent, the more likely it is to realize happiness; the lower the talent, the less likely it is to realize happiness. The happiness pursued by those hard-working Chinese high school students is the same: to get admitted to

Peking University. The likelihood of realizing this happiness is undoubtedly in direct proportion to the talent of those high school students: the higher their talent, the greater the likelihood of getting admitted to Peking University; the lower their talent, the lesser the likelihood of getting the admission.

Thus, we may conclude that only when we have a talent of a certain kind can we achieve happiness of that kind, and talent is thus the necessary condition and necessary factor for the realization of happiness; they are in direct proportion to each other. In terms of the size of the happiness realized, the lower one's talent is, the smaller the happiness he is likely to achieve; the higher one's talent is, the greater will be the happiness. In terms of the difficulty of realizing happiness, the lower one's talent is, the more difficult it is for him to achieve the happiness he pursues; the higher one's talent is, the easier it is for him to achieve the happiness. This is the intrinsic connection between intelligence and talent and the realization of happiness, and this is the law of talent for the realization of happiness.

*Effort: The second positive correlation with the realization of happiness*

The so-called effort means making effort: "The effort one makes is what we call 'effort'."[81] A man without a talent for poetry cannot be a poet, but a talent for poetry alone cannot make him a poet, either. This point can be illustrated in the article, "Sorrows to Zhongrong," by Wang Anshi of the Song Dynasty. Zhongyong was so gifted that he could write good poems at the age of three. However, in the next ten years or so, he did not study hard or write poems but was paraded around by his father as a money-spinner. As a result, when he met Wang Anshi again around the age of 17 years, his poems were just mediocre: "All of his talents are so gone that he is just as ordinary as everybody else." Therefore, a talent for poetry alone cannot make the person achieve the happiness of being a poet. In order to achieve the happiness of becoming a poet, we must also make the effort: effort is another necessary condition and factor for the realization of happiness.

This could explain why, at all times and in all countries, people who have made great achievements are not only highly talented, but also extremely hard-working. Cao Xueqin wrote *A Dream of Red Mansions*; this is how he reflected on his effort: "Over ten years, I have been poring over the book, revising and editing it for five times"; it took six years for Tolstoy to finish writing *War and Peace*; Leonardo Da Vinci spent five years painting "Mona Lisa"; Darwin conceived *On the Origin of Species* for more than 20 years; Marx spent 40 years writing *The Capital*. Goethe spent 60 years writing *Faust*. Therefore, Fung Yulan says,

> In the history of the world, all those who have made great achievements in some areas are those who have made special efforts in these areas. The ancient saying is, 'excellence comes from diligence'. No one can

excel in a profession without diligence. A great poet can be lazy in his clothes and appearances, but he can't be lazy in composing poems. If he is too lazy to write poetry, he will by no means become a great poet.[82]

Then, why is it that without effort we can't achieve success and happiness despite our extremely high talent? This is because the so-called talent or gift is only a potential ability. The transformation of talent from potential ability to real ability is totally accomplished by effort, as illustrated by this equation: ability = talent × effort. Without effort, talents, no matter how high they are, are only potential talents, and are thus, in fact, equal to zero. This means he is just a person without talent, and a person without talent, of course, will not achieve success and happiness. In this sense, a person with higher talent and less effort, and a person with lower talent and greater effort, can achieve the same success and happiness. The ability of a person with higher talent and less effort may be equal to that of a person with lower talent and greater effort. Suppose that the talent of the former is 100 of talent, but he makes only 50% of effort, while the talent of the latter is only 50, but he makes 100% of his effort. In the end, only 50% of the talent of the person with higher talent is realized, and the ability of this person is 50, while 100% of the talent of the person with lower talent is realized through his effort and his ability is also 50. Hence the truth is that diligence can make up for lack of talents.

Nevertheless, we can only say that ability depends on diligence, or partly on diligence and partly on talent, to be more exact. We can neither say that genius depends on diligence, nor can we say that effort can create abilities. Genius, that is, a talent of higher level, belongs to the category of natural gift and talent, so it is inherent and has nothing to do with effort and diligence after birth. Diligence after birth can only fully develop the talent and realize talent as an ability, but diligence cannot make anybody's talent greater. Therefore, we can only say that the realization of talent depends on diligence, not that talent depends on diligence. Effort cannot create ability, it can only realize talents; ability is the realization of talent. Effort is the medium, through which talents are transformed into abilities. Therefore, although ability is the result of talent multiplying effort, the limit of one's ability is determined only by the limit of one's talent and has nothing to do with effort. So, Fung Yulan says:

> One's talent is given by nature, and natural talent must be developed and realized through human effort. In this regard, realization of talent depends on human effort, but human effort can only develop and realize human talent, but cannot increase or enhance human talent. In this sense, the effort one can make is limited by one's talent. If a person makes effort to the ultimate limit that his talent allows him, then he will be considered as having made the best of his talent. Beyond the ultimate limit of his talent, he makes no further progress despite his effort, and then he will be considered as having exhausted his talent.[83]

Therefore, as the Chinese sayings go, the fragrance of plum blossom comes from the bitter coldness; there is no sweet without sweat. The more effort one makes, the fuller the transformation of his potential ability to real ability is, the more easily he will achieve success and happiness, the more likely he will achieve greater success, the more likely he will achieve greater happiness: the difficulty and magnitude of happiness he can achieve determines the intensity of his efforts. However, we cannot move further to say that as long as one makes effort, one can achieve success and happiness as great as one desires. There is a limit to one's abilities; the limit of one's abilities is determined by the limit of one's talents, not by one's effort. Therefore, there is a limit to the success and happiness one is likely to achieve. This limit depends directly on his abilities, and ultimately on his talents. Li Bai became a poet because he had the talent, ability, and made the effort to become a great poet. However, he became a great poet and one of the best poets because he had the natural talents and abilities of a great poet, not because he made the effort. A person with second-class talent in poetry, no matter how much effort he makes, can only become a second-class poet, and will never become a first-class poet. As Fung Yulan says:

> The ultimate limit of one's talent in certain area is the limit of the function of his effort. Beyond this limit, the work he can do in that area can only be increased in quantity, but not in quality. A poet can become a master poet or simply a famous poet; a painter's painting can be a masterpiece or simply a piece of artwork of some kind of talent. All of these are determined by his talent. If the talent of a poet can only allow him to be a famous poet, and then, no matter how much effort he makes to write poems, no matter how countless poems he has produced, he will only be a famous poet, not a master poet. If the talent of a painter can only allow him to produce good artwork of some achievements, then, no matter how much effort he makes in painting, no matter how many paintings he produces, he will only be a painter of good paintings, not a painter of masterpieces.[84]

It can be concluded that success and happiness can be achieved only through effort. Effort is the necessary condition and necessary factor for the realization of happiness, and the two are in direct proportion with each other. In terms of the magnitude of happiness achieved, within the limit of one's talent, the more efforts he makes, the more likely it is for him to achieve greater success, the more likely it is for him to achieve greater happiness. In terms of the difficulty of achieving happiness, the more effort one makes, the easier it is for him to achieve the happiness he pursues. This is the intrinsic link between effort and making effort, and the realization of happiness. This is the law of effort for the realization of happiness.

*Destiny: the third positive correlation factor of the realization of happiness*

The so-called destiny, that is, fate, as Zhuang Zi said, is the vicissitudes a person experiences in his life: "Life and death, survival and tragedy, poverty and wealth, virtue and disgrace, hunger, thirst, cold, and heat, etc. are changes in life and functions of destiny."[85] However, if we reverse this statement, regard all the changes in one's life as destiny, and claim that all the fortunes or misfortunes of a person are destined, we will then be following so-called fatalism. Fatalism is wrong, for although the changes that a person encounters in his life is destiny, not all changes are destined. A man who became the head of the Red Guard in the "Cultural Revolution" is a kind of change he encountered in his life, but it cannot be said that this change was his destiny. The reason is that this kind of change is dependent on his own will and can be changed by himself: he can choose to be or not to be the head of the Red Guard. However, the historical period of the "Cultural Revolution" he encountered is his destiny, because the "Cultural Revolution" was independent of his will, and it was impossible for him to change it. It can be seen that fate and destiny are the events that a person encounters in his life, but cannot be changed by the person himself. Therefore, Zhuang Zi also said, "Know what you can't do and be at peace with your fate."[86]

The events that a person encounters may be his activities and the results of his activities, such as the tragic death of Lord Xiang Yu at Gaixia, or may be the external environment, circumstances, chances, and opportunities, such as the troubled times in which Xiang Yu was born and his encounter with Liu Bang and Han Xin. Undoubtedly, one's own activities and the results thereof can be changed by oneself. Therefore, the so-called "destiny"—the events that a person encounters that he himself cannot do anything to change—is ultimately the environment, circumstances, chances, and opportunities that a person encounters that he cannot change by his efforts. Therefore, Fung Yulan says, "Destiny does not refer to the fate in a superstitious sense; it rather refers to chances and opportunities, or environment."[87] "Destiny refers to the events in the world that an individual encounters in his lifetime and which are beyond the control of the individual."[88]

It becomes evident that destiny or opportunity is a necessary condition and stage for a person to achieve success and happiness; if a person has only talent and effort but no opportunity, he cannot make a successful career, just like a hero with no stage to demonstrate his talents. For example, if a man grows up in a peaceful age, no matter how talented he is in military affairs or how much effort he makes, he cannot become a battle-wise general. If it had not been for the early death of Emperor Qin Shihuang and the uprising of Chen Sheng and Wu Guang, which provided opportunities for the lords to compete for the thrones and territories, then Xiang Yu would never have become the overlord of the Western Chu Dynasty and Liu Bang would never have become the first king of the Han Dynasty. Without the French

Revolution, no matter how talented Robespierre, Saint-Just, and Danton were, nor how much effort they made, they would never have accomplished such a magnificent feat. If the old system in France lasted for another 75 years, as Plekhanov said, Napoleon would be just a general, while the military geniuses gathering around him would still be actors, type-setters, barbers, dyers, lawyers, and peddlers. Therefore, what kind of destiny or opportunity a person has determines the kind of happiness he may achieve; if he does not have a certain destiny or opportunity, he cannot achieve a certain kind of happiness: opportunity is the necessary condition and factor for the realization of a certain kind of happiness. Therefore, Aristotle says, "Happiness needs to be supplemented by external luck; thus, some equate good luck with happiness."[89] Ignacio L. Gotz even says, "Happiness is not so much a result of one's own efforts as of luck, or more precisely, as of opportunity."[90] The same is true for the etymology of happiness: the root of the English word happiness is "hap," which means chance, good luck, and fortune; the Chinese words *xing* (幸) for luck and *xing-fu* (幸福) for happiness both include the meaning of good luck.

As the necessary condition for the realization of happiness, opportunity matters, not only in terms of whether the opportunity is present or not, whether a particular type of opportunity is present or not, but also in terms of whether the opportunity, within the same type of opportunity, is favorable or not: opportunities conducive to the development of talents, the exertion of efforts, and the realization of happiness are the so-called favorable circumstances and good fortunes; opportunities that are not conducive to the development of talents, the exertion of efforts, and the realization of happiness are the so-called adverse circumstances and misfortunes. Feng Tang in Han Dynasty did not have a good fortune in pursuing a career as an official. When Feng Tang was young, Emperor Wen liked to appoint old adults as officials, so Feng could not be promoted when young. By the time Emperor Wu came to the throne, Feng Tang had aged, but Emperor Wu preferred to appoint promising young people as officials. As a result, Feng could not be promoted. This example illustrates whether one's destiny is favorable or not makes a huge impact on a person's success and happiness. The worse a man's destiny is, the harder it is for him to achieve success and happiness, the harder it is for him to attain greater achievements, and the harder it is for him to achieve greater happiness. On the contrary, the better his destiny is, the easier it is for him to achieve his success and happiness, and the more likely he is to achieve greater achievements, the more likely he is to achieve greater happiness: The difficulty and magnitude of happiness he can achieve is determined by the degree of how favorable or unfavorable his destiny is.

Nonetheless, adversity and misfortune have not blocked the road to the realization of success and happiness. On the contrary, suffering misfortune in adversity may, under certain conditions, facilitate the achievement of greater success and happiness. The so-called conditions are mainly two kinds of conditions: exerting greater efforts and switching to different goals.

A person in adversity is often unable to achieve his original goal and, thus, gets stuck in depression and misfortune. However, adversity may also pave the way for the realization of his other ideals, and give him an incentive to temper himself and to strive harder, to realize these new ideals and achieve perhaps even greater achievements. Feng Tang's fortune for becoming an official did not go well, but "he turned to a literary career, endured poverty, and then succeeded." His bad fortune of being an official may make him realize the hopelessness of his career as an official, and drive him to devote himself to learning, writing books, and making a great success in that field instead. The Chinese historian, Sima Qian, said,

> Emperor Wen composed *The Book of Changes* when he was imprisoned; Confucius wrote *Spring and Autumn* when he suffered from poverty; Qu Yuan was banished and wrote his masterpiece poetry *Lisao* when in exile; Zuoqiu Ming got visually impaired, and then wrote *Guoyu*; the three hundred poems in *The Book of Poetry* were mostly written by sages to express their frustrations.[91]

Given this, Zhang Zai wrote: "Wealth, noble birth, and prosperity endow me a prosperous life; poverty, humble birth, and adversity refine me into a person as valuable as jade."[92] This means that wealth, noble birth, and good fortune are favorable conditions and good fortune; poverty, humble birth, and adversity are unfavorable conditions and misfortune, but poverty and adversity may inspire people to make greater efforts and attain a different kind of achievement that is probably even greater: the realization of the creative potential of the self. This is exactly the meaning of the so-called maxim "out of adversity come success." Obviously, success in adversity does not negate the theorem that good fortune facilitates success because success in adversity is premised on much greater efforts than in favorable circumstances.

Synthesizing above discussions on talent, effort, and destiny, we can see that only with certain kind of talent, effort, and opportunity can we achieve a certain kind of happiness; talent, effort, and opportunity are all necessary conditions and necessary factors for the realization of happiness, and they are positively correlated to the realization of happiness: the higher-level the talent one has, the greater effort one makes, the better the opportunity one has, the easier it will be for him to achieve success and happiness, the greater his achievements, the greater the happiness he is likely to realize. The lower-level the talent one has, the less effort he makes, the worse the opportunities he has, the more difficult it will be for him to achieve his success and happiness, the more difficult will it be for him to attain greater achievements, the more difficult it will be for him to achieve greater happiness. So, are all of the three elements, talent, effort and opportunity, all necessary for the realization of happiness and the success of life? To this question, Fung Yulan's answer is affirmative: "In the process of achieving success in life, three factors are necessary and ought to be combined so as to achieve success."[93] As we all know, in fact, these three factors are only non-statistical positive correlative factors of success and happiness in life, and the realization of success and happiness in life must also have a statistical positive correlative factor, which is virtue.

*Virtue: the statistical positive correlation with the realization of happiness*

The so-called virtue is a person's morality and moral character. Suppose that there is such a person who has talents, makes effort, and encounters good opportunities; if he has a corrupt moral character and is cursed by everyone, he will inevitably encounter obstacles everywhere he goes and will meet difficulties in everything he does; he will thus find it impossible to achieve success and happiness. Humans are social animals, so the survival, happiness, and everything of an individual are ultimately given by society and others. So, how exactly can an individual obtain happiness from society and others? Bentham asked the same question and answered it himself:

> How can one obtain happiness? Isn't it only through winning the friendship and love of those people on whom his happiness depends? But, how can he win the friendship and love of those people? Wouldn't it be only by convincing them that he would return them with the same thing?[94]

Therefore, whether a person can obtain happiness from society and others requires that he has not only talent, effort, and destiny, but also moral character: if his moral character is good enough to benefit society and others, then he will be praised and honored by society and others and thus rewarded with happiness; if his moral character is bad and thus harms society and others, then he will be condemned by society and others and thus be deprived of the chance to obtain happiness. Hence, moral character is a necessary condition and factor for happiness and it is positively correlated with happiness: the more virtue one has, the more fortune he will have, and the more fortune one has, the more virtue he will have; virtue and fortune are bound to be consistent with each other.

Therefore, Mencius says, "Benevolence is the noblest title in the world and the most comfortable place to reside in. It is unwise not to choose to reside in the place of benevolence when not prevented to do so."[95] Epicurus makes similar comments repeatedly,

> It is impossible to live happily without prudence, respectability, and fairness; likewise, it is impossible to live prudently, respectably and fairly without feeling happy. The reason why a man is unable to live a happy life is that his life is not prudent, respectable, and fair; it is impossible for a man living a life without virtue to have a life with happiness.[96]

However, virtue is, after all, different from talent, effort, and destiny: talent, effort, and destiny are non-statistical positive correlative factors of happiness, so they are completely consistent with happiness; virtue is the statistical positive correlative element of happiness, and is only "generally" consistent with happiness. That is to say, whether in terms of one behavior or in terms of the total sum of one's behaviors, talent, effort, and destiny are positive correlative factors of happiness and are completely consistent with happiness. On the contrary, only in terms of the sum of one's behaviors can we say that the more virtue a person has, the more happiness he will obtain; that virtue and happiness are consistent with each other; and that virtue is positively correlated with happiness. In terms of one or some of his behaviors, it is also likely that the more virtue he has, the less fortune he will have, and, consequently, virtue deviates from happiness and is negatively correlated with happiness. In this regard, Paulsen made excellent comments:

> The undeniable fact is that virtuous people don't always seem to be doing well. A man may get sick even if he lives a temperate and wise life; contrarily, a man who ignores his body may still be strong and full of energy. A competent and honest man may still fail despite his great efforts, while a scoundrel may accumulate tremendous wealth through unfair means. Our honest words are often frowned upon by people of powerful positions, while flattery gets their favor. Nonetheless, the fact that these phenomena have been able to attract so much attention and arouse so much fury seems to just demonstrate that these phenomena are not the rule, but the exceptions... In this case, the exceptions prove the rule once again. If these events were not against the nature of things, they would not cause such excitement. Here is the rule: honest labor is a more reliable way to achieve economic benefits than fraud and dishonesty. Sincerity and frankness bring trust, while lies and deception are bad ways to find friends.[97]

It can be then concluded that virtue is a statistical positive correlation factor and a necessary condition for happiness; it is a statistical law that virtue is consistent with happiness and is generally positively correlated with happiness. That is to say, in terms of the sum of one's behaviors, the number of times that a person's virtue is consistent with his happiness and is positively correlated with his happiness is more than the number of times that a person's virtue deviates from his happiness and is negatively correlated with his happiness. In other words, the consistency of virtue with happiness is the rule while the deviation of virtue from happiness is the exception: virtue and happiness must be generally consistent. This is the law of consistency of virtue and happiness.

However, Kant denies the conclusion that virtue is a necessary condition for happiness and holds that virtue is not necessarily related to happiness: "But the moral law of itself does not promise any happiness, for according to our conceptions of an order of nature in general, this is not necessarily connected with obedience to the law."[98] Kant's view is obviously based on facts in practice. In fact, as Julia Annas points out, "We see a grossly immoral person flourishing and a moral person in circumstances reduced by injustice or bad luck."[99] We often see that many people lack virtue but are happy their whole life while many people have virtue but are unhappy their whole life. This fact seems to confirm Kant's view: virtue is not a necessary condition for happiness, and there is no necessary connection between virtue and happiness. In fact, it does not. Virtue is not the only factor determining the happiness or misfortune of an individual, but only one of the factors; besides virtue, there are three other factors determining the happiness or misfortune in the life of an individual: talent, effort, and destiny. Given this, a person's lack of virtue should generally bring ruin to his happiness, but his high-level talent, great effort, and good opportunities, and so on can bring him more blessings than the misfortune that is caused by his lack of virtue, thus allowing him to live a happy life despite his lack of virtue. On the contrary, a person with virtue is generally blessed, but his inferior talents, his inadequate effort, and his poor opportunities can bring him more misfortune than the blessings given him by his virtue, thus allowing him to live an unhappy life.

Therefore, the life-time happiness of the virtue-less is not the result of his lack of virtue, but the result of his talent, destiny, and other non-moral conditions; conversely, the life-time misfortune of a virtuous person is not the result of his virtue, but the result of his talent, destiny, and other non-moral conditions. If two people differ only in virtue while other conditions are exactly the same, then the one who lacks virtue is bound to be miserable all his life and the one with virtue is bound to be happy all his life. Therefore, a life of happiness for those without virtue or a life of misfortune for those with virtue indicates only that other conditions of those without virtue are good and other conditions of those with virtue are poor. It by no means indicates that their virtue and happiness generally deviate from each other, nor does it mean that virtue and happiness have no necessary connection with each other. Kant's mistake lies obviously in that he sees only the necessary connection between happiness and conditions such as talent, effort, and destiny, which are determined by what he calls the "law of nature" and "physical capability," but fails to see the connection between happiness and the condition, such as virtue, which is governed by what he calls "the law of freedom" and "the law of ought," thus denying virtue as a necessary condition for happiness.[100]

On the contrary, the Stoic school holds that with virtue comes happiness and virtue is a sufficient condition of happiness: "Virtue itself suffices to guarantee happiness."[101] "A life of happiness needs only virtue itself."[102] In a word, "that virtue is sufficient to make people happy is a famous claim of Stoic ethics."[103] The Stoic view, as Annas points out, is absolutely absurd: "But it seems absurd to talk of happiness when someone meets great misfortunes and is virtuous, but dying on the wheel."[104] So, on what basis does the Stoic school argue that virtue is a sufficient condition for happiness?

The truth beneath the Stoic view is this: on the one hand, the Stoics believe that virtue itself is happiness, "Happiness is in morality."[105] Zeno even says, "Happy life exists in virtue alone."[106] Virtue itself indeed can be happiness. However, this kind of happiness is undoubtedly only one kind of happiness: moral happiness. It is the kind of happiness that a person's moral need to be a good person, a moral person, and a noble person is realized. In this sense, a person's moral happiness and his virtue are just one thing: where there is virtue, there is happiness, and where there is happiness there is virtue; virtue is happiness, and happiness is virtue. In this sense, virtue is undoubtedly a sufficient condition for moral happiness. Nonetheless, virtue is not a sufficient condition for non-moral happiness. Non-moral happiness is happiness that considers things other than virtue—such as money, beauty, fame, wealth, status, and so on—as the purpose, so non-moral happiness is not the same thing as virtue: virtue is not happiness and happiness is not virtue; though happiness needs virtue, virtue is not necessarily bound to lead to happiness. Virtue, like talent, effort, and destiny, is only one of the necessary conditions for non-moral happiness. The mistakes of the Stoic school are obviously that they only see the moral happiness but ignore the non-moral happiness; they obliterate talent, effort, and destiny as the necessary conditions for happiness, thus elevating "virtue as the necessary condition for moral happiness" into "virtue as the sufficient condition for happiness." Meanwhile, the Stoic school also bases their view of virtue as the sufficient condition for happiness on the exaggerated role of virtue:

> Virtue is the good because it can guide us to the right life; it is desirable because it is praised without hesitation; it is greatly valuable because its value cannot be surpassed by anything; it is excellent because it deserves our greatest concern; it is worshipped because it is wise to worship it. It's wonderful because everyone who gets it thinks so; it's worthy because it can make life happy; it's useful, because it can meet our needs; it's chosen because facts show that it is reasonable to choose it; it's necessary, because it brings benefits and without it there would be no benefits; it is beneficial because it offers benefits far greater than the effort required to obtain them; it is self-sufficient because it can adequately satisfy its owners; it can satisfy various needs because it will free its owners from all shortages; it is sufficient because it can adequately and extensively satisfy all the needs of life.[107]

Apparently, from the perspective of the Stoics, with virtue we can obtain everything, and, of course, we can obtain happiness; this means that virtue is sufficient condition for happiness. Therefore, with regard to the connection between virtue and happiness, the Stoics' view and Kant's theory are the two poles of the same error: Kant obliterates the necessary link between virtue and happiness, thus denying that virtue is a necessary condition for happiness; the Stoics exaggerate the necessary link between virtue and happiness, thus claiming that virtue is sufficient condition for happiness. The truth, as Carneades puts it, is that virtue is the necessary condition for happiness: "No matter how philosophers argue about the ultimate purpose, virtue is always a necessary condition for a life of happiness."[108] Only when combined with talent, effort, destiny, and desire can virtue become the sufficient condition for happiness, or to be more precise, the sufficient and necessary condition for happiness.

*Desire, talent, effort, destiny, and virtue: the sufficient and necessary conditions for realization of happiness*

The claim that talent, effort, destiny, and virtue are the four elements for the realization of happiness means that no matter what kind of happiness, its realization needs the cooperation of these four elements. But different types of happiness need different proportions of these four elements. Cultivating virtues is creative happiness in the aspect of moral character, such as the happiness of perfecting moral character and becoming a sage or a saint.

The most important type of happiness is undoubtedly the so-called "three immortality ideals" promoted the ancients in China: establishing original thoughts, cultivating virtues, and making contributions to society. Establishing original thoughts is creative happiness in the academic aspect, such as the happiness of becoming artists, scientists, philosophers, and thinkers, etc. Generally speaking, for the realization of this kind of happiness, the role of talent is the greatest, that of effort is the second, that of virtue is the third, and that of opportunity is the smallest. Making meritorious contributions gives creative happiness to politicians, military strategists, entrepreneurs, and so on. Generally speaking, for the realization of this kind of happiness, the role of opportunity is the greatest, that of virtue is the second, that of talent is the third, and that of effort is the least. Cultivating virtue is the creative happiness of moral character, such as the happiness of perfecting moral character and becoming saints and sages. Generally speaking, for the realization of this kind of happiness, the role of effort is the greatest, that of talent is the next, and that of opportunity is the least. Zeng Guofan says:

> What makes famous sages and scholars since the ancient times so outstanding in the world is nothing but their literary achievements and meritorious contributions. For literary achievements, natural talent accounts for 70% of their realization and effort only for 30% of their realization. For meritorious contributions, opportunity accounts for 70% of their realization and effort for only 30% of their realization.

For nurturing and developing virtues, which means taking the best advantage of what is given by nature, effort plays a dominant role and accounts for to 70% of their realization.[109]

To extend Zeng's view, we can say that the higher-level the happiness is, the greater the proportion of natural talent, and the smaller the proportion of opportunity; the lower-level the happiness is, the greater the proportion of circumstances and the smaller the proportion of natural talent. The proportion of effort and the proportion of virtue are not necessarily related to the level and type of happiness.

No matter what kind of happiness, its realization requires the cooperation of talent, effort, destiny, and virtue. So, if these four elements are combined, will happiness be realized? Not necessarily. The realization of happiness requires not only the cooperation of talent, effort, destiny, and virtue, but also the cooperation of these four elements with desire. Desire is a negative correlative element of happiness: the greater the desire, the harder it is to achieve happiness. On the contrary, talent, effort, destiny, and virtue are the positive correlative factors of the realization of happiness: the higher level the talent, the greater the effort, the better the opportunity, and the greater the virtue, the easier it is to realize happiness. In this way, even if a person is talented, hard-working, fortunate, and virtuous, it is still likely that he cannot satisfy his desire and obtain happiness if his desire is too high. On the contrary, even if a person has average talent, make average effort, have average fortune and virtue, he can achieve his desire and obtain happiness if his desire is very low.

It becomes apparent that whether happiness can be realized or not depends entirely on the relationship between positive factors such as talent, effort, destiny, virtue, and the negative factor—desire. If one's desire exceeds one's talent, effort, destiny, and virtue, his desired happiness, though great and high-level, will not be realized and will rather keep him trapped in great misfortune; if one's desire is below one's talent, effort, destiny, and virtue, his happiness will be realized, but the realized happiness will be rather small and low-level, too. Only when desire is consistent with talent, effort, destiny, and virtue can happiness be perfectly realized. That desire is consistent with talent, effort, destiny, and virtue is the sufficient and necessary condition for the realization of happiness. As Rousseau writes:

> Where is the path to wisdom or true happiness? It does not lie in the reduction of our desires, because if our desires are less than our abilities, then part of our abilities will be idle and cannot be tapped, we cannot fully enjoy our existence. Nor does it lie in the expansion of our abilities, because if our desires increase proportionally with the expansion of our abilities, we will only suffer more. Therefore, the key to this question is to reduce the desires that exceed our abilities, and to achieve a full balance between ability and desire.[110]

214  *Happiness*

The "theory of asceticism" and "theory of abstinence" fail to understand that "if our desire is lower than talent, effort, destiny, and virtue, happiness will be realized, but the realized happiness will be rather small, less, and low-level, too," so they advocate a reduction of the human desire to the minimum, which can definitely reduce his misfortune and pain to the minimum, but will also reduce happiness and pleasure to the minimum. "When man reduces desire to the minimum, life will lose its varieties and become extremely dull and even life itself will also lose its original glory."[111] On the contrary, the "theory of hedonism" fails to see that "if one's desires exceed talent, effort, destiny, and virtue, then he will only be trapped in great misfortune," so it advocates that desire should be carried out at will and without restraint. As a result, we simply exchange "temporary happiness" for "permanent misfortune," "minor happiness" for "great pain." Only the "the theory of tempered desire "and "the theory of guided desire" that keep a balance between the above two extremes is reasonable, because desire must, indeed, be moderated and guided to prevent it from being too high or too low. Unfortunately, they fail to find this criterion for balancing abstinence and indulgence: desire is consistent with talent, effort, destiny, and virtue.

In summary, desire, talent, effort, destiny, and virtue are the five sufficient and necessary factors for the realization of happiness. Desire provides the motive factor and negative correlation factor of the realization of happiness: the greater the desire, the more difficult it is to realize happiness. Talent, effort, destiny, and virtue are the non-motive factors and positive correlation factors of the realization of happiness: the higher the talent, the greater the effort, the better the destiny, and the greater the virtue, the easier it is to realize happiness. When desire is consistent with talent, effort, destiny, and virtue, happiness will be perfectly realized. This is the realization law of happiness. This realization law of happiness can be summed up into an equation:

$$\text{realization of happiness} = \frac{\text{talent effort destiny virtue}}{\text{desire}}$$

## Principles of happiness

The definition, structure, and type of happiness, the value of happiness, the nature of happiness, and the laws of happiness have all demonstrated that the needs and desires in everyone's life are all extremely diverse and complex; if a person wants to meet these needs and desires to achieve happiness, he must comply with the objective nature of happiness and follow a series of norms. The norms that enable us to realize happiness are mainly "the principles of happiness" that everyone ought to follow regardless of the type of happiness he pursues.

Apparently, to achieve happiness, everyone, no matter what type of happiness he pursues and what kind of success he wants to achieve, must go through three stages: cognition, choice, and action. The principles that ought to be followed during these three stages can be summarized, according to the objective nature of happiness, into three principles: (1) having correct cognition: The subjective cognition of happiness must be consistent with the objective nature of happiness. This is the "principle of cognition" for pursuing happiness. (2) making proper choices: One's desire for and choice of happiness must be consistent with one's talent, effort, destiny, and virtue. This is the "principle of choice" for pursuing happiness. (3) working hard and cultivating moral character: This is the "principle of action" for pursuing happiness.

*The principle of cognition: make one's cognition of happiness consistent with the objective nature of happiness*

It is self-evident that a person's subjective cognition of happiness may be or may not be consistent with the objective nature of happiness. If it is not, then, under its direction, something will go wrong with his choice and pursuit of happiness, and he is unlikely to obtain happiness or unlikely to obtain the most valuable happiness he can possibly get; only when it is consistent, will his choice and pursuit of happiness will go in the right direction, and he is likely to obtain happiness or likely to obtain the most valuable happiness he can possibly get. For example:

As far as the objective nature of happiness is concerned, the higher-level the need is, the smaller the value of its realization for survival and the greater the value of its realization for development; the lower-level the need is, the greater the value of its realization for survival and the smaller the value of its realization for development. Only when a person's subjective cognition is consistent with this objective nature can he make the right choice when the realization of his higher-level needs and realization of his lower-level needs conflict: when his problem of survival has not been solved, he ought to choose to satisfy his lower-level needs; when his problem of survival has been solved, he ought to choose to satisfy his higher-level needs. If one's subjective cognition is not consistent with this objective nature, there will be two opposite scenarios.

One scenario is that he believes that the value of low-level needs is always greater than that of high-level needs. For example, to a materialistically obsessed and greedy person, the value of happiness from wealth and sensual pleasures is greater than that of everything else, so he is more likely to pursue and enjoy only the happiness of making money and seeking pleasure, and unlikely to pursue and enjoy the happiness of a higher level and greater value, namely, the spiritual happiness of realization of the creative potential of the self. Contrarily, thinkers such as Mill and Maslow have made the opposite mistake: They believe that the value of satisfying high-level needs is always greater than that of satisfying low-level needs. According to their view, even when a person struggles with the problem of survival, he still ought to give up the satisfaction of low-level material needs and instead pursue the satisfaction of high-level and spiritual needs. Perhaps being guided by this misconception many of the world's greatest geniuses, such as Cao Xueqin, Spinoza, Belinsky, Dubroliv, and so on, were destitute in their life and died when they were in their 30s and 40s.

In terms of the objective nature of happiness, the value and significance of life lies in that life—if it is a normal and ordinary life rather than a life of abnormality and exception—which always brings more pleasure and happiness than the pain and misfortune it causes, so its net balance is pleasure and happiness. However, each person's subjective cognition of his life's pain and pleasure, misfortune and happiness may or may not be consistent with the objective nature of his life's pain and pleasure, misfortune and happiness. If he makes an error in his subjective cognition and believes that his life brings him more pain and misfortune than pleasure and happiness, and thus feels that his life is worthless and meaningless, then he will feel that it is not worth living any longer, let alone pursue happiness. There is undoubtedly only one scientific way to enable him to live on and achieve happiness: to help him correctly understand or find pleasure and happiness of his life, as well as the value and significance of his life.

In terms of the objective nature of happiness, when it is likely that a person may get real happiness, the pursuit of real happiness is ought-to-be, good, and right for him, while indulging in illusory happiness is ought-not-to-be, bad, and wrong for him. However, when it is unlikely that a person may get real happiness, the pursuit of illusory happiness is ought-to-be, good, and right for him while the pursuit of real happiness for him is ought-not-to-be, bad, and wrong. Only when a person's subjective cognition is consistent with the objective nature can he make a correct choice between real happiness and illusory happiness: when it is unlikely that he may get any real happiness, he chooses illusory happiness, like drawing pictures of a cake to satisfy hunger because cakes in the drawings are better than no cakes at all; when it is likely that he may get some real happiness, he gives up illusory happiness and chooses real happiness, because real cakes are undoubtedly much better than cakes in the drawing. When one's subjective cognition is not consistent with this objective nature, it will make him think that illusory happiness is always bad. As a result, when it is unlikely that he may get any real happiness, he will refuse even illusory happiness, and thus pitifully miss the opportunity to enjoy the psychological experience of pleasure that could at least keep him healthy.

In terms of the objective nature of happiness, the process happiness is weak yet long, and the result happiness is strong but short, and the lack of either will result in an unhappy life. Only when one's subjective cognition is consistent with this can one pursue both result happiness and process happiness, thus enjoying overall happiness. Otherwise, if he thinks that only result happiness is the goal, he will then ignore process happiness and miss the opportunity to enjoy it; as a result, it is more likely that he will experience the misery of a life-long painful pursuit just for the sake of happiness in his old age.

It can be concluded that if a person wants to obtain happiness or the most valuable happiness he may possibly get, he must make his subjective cognition of happiness consistent with the objective nature of happiness. This is the first principle of how everyone ought to pursue happiness, which may be called "the principle of cognition."

### *The principle of choice: make choice of happiness consistent with one's talent, effort, destiny, and virtue*

If a person has a correct cognition of happiness that is consistent with the objective nature of happiness, can he achieve happiness? Not yet. If he wants to obtain happiness, he must also make the right choice of happiness, that is, his choice of happiness must be consistent with his talent, effort, destiny, and virtue: if a person's choice of happiness is consistent with his talent, effort, destiny, and virtue, then his choice is correct; if his choice is inconsistent with his talent, effort, destiny, and virtue, then his choice is wrong. As the laws of the realization of happiness tell us that desire, talent, effort, destiny, and virtue are the five necessary and sufficient factors of happiness, so only when a person's desire for and choice of happiness are consistent with and suitable for his talent, effort, destiny, and virtue can he obtain the happiness he desires and chooses and that too the most valuable happiness he can possibly get. If a person's desire for and choice of happiness is not consistent with or suitable for his talent, effort, destiny, and virtue, then, even if he has a correct cognition of the nature of happiness, it is unlikely that he will obtain the happiness he desires and chooses, let alone the most valuable happiness he may possibly obtain.

First of all, one's desire for happiness must be consistent with one's "talent." For example, whether a person ought to choose to pursue the happiness of becoming a painter depends on whether he has the talent of a painter. If he has no talent as a painter, it is unlikely that he will become a great one. Then, his choice of becoming a painter is inconsistent with his "talent," and therefore wrong. On the contrary, if he has the talent for painting, he will likely become a painter, so his choice to be a painter is consistent with his "talent."

Second, one's desire for happiness must be consistent with one's "destiny." For example, whether a person ought to choose the happiness of becoming a courageous and battle-wise general depends on whether he has the opportunity to fight in a war. If he was born in a peaceful and prosperous age, it is unlikely that he will become a battle-wise general; then his choice of becoming a courageous and battle-wise general is not consistent with his "destiny," and his choice is wrong. On the contrary, if he was born in troubled times when various parties competed for the throne, he may likely become a battle-wise general; then, his choice of becoming a courageous and battle-wise general is consistent with his "destiny," and his choice is correct in terms of "destiny."

Third, one's desire for happiness must be consistent with one's own "effort." For example, whether a person ought to choose to obtain great happiness of great achievements depends on whether he possesses great perseverance and stamina and makes the effort to persevere and strive for it all his life. If he makes such an effort, he will likely get great achievements, then, his choice is consistent with his "effort," and his choice is correct in terms of "effort." On the contrary, if the person is lazy by nature and lacks perseverance and stamina, it is almost impossible that he will make such effort; thus, it is unlikely that he will achieve great heights. He will likely end up being "unable to do big things and unwilling to do small things" and achieving nothing all his life; then, his choice is inconsistent with his "effort," and his choice is wrong.

Finally, one's desire for happiness must be consistent with one's own "virtue." For example, whether a person ought to choose the happiness of pursuing the career of an official depends on whether he has the virtue of resourcefulness and sociability. If he has the virtue, he will likely be successful in his official career and take to it like a fish to water; his choice is consistent with his "virtue," and his choice of becoming an official is right in terms of "virtue." On the contrary, if he does not possess such a virtue, in other words, if he is unsociable, isolated, and hard to get along with, then it is very difficult for him to become an official, and his choice of becoming an official is wrong.

A person's desire for happiness must be consistent with his talent, effort, destiny, and virtue: desire must be consistent not only with the qualitative aspects of talent, effort, destiny, and virtue, but also with the quantitative aspects (level and magnitude) of talent, effort, destiny, and virtue. For example, if a person has the talent of a painter, his choice of happiness of becoming a painter is consistent with his talent, so in terms of talent, his choice is correct. However, his choice is consistent with his talent only in the qualitative aspect of his talent. A right choice of happiness must also be consistent with the quantitative aspect (level and magnitude) of talent. From the perspective of this kind of consistency, we still must ask further: does this person choose to be a great painter or an average painter?

If he chooses to become a great painter, then he must possess the talent of a great painter. If he has, his choice is consistent with his talent in terms of the level and magnitude of quantity, so his choice is correct both in terms of quality of talent and quantity of talent. Only in this way can we say that his choice is completely correct in terms of talent. On the contrary, if he has the talent of an average painter but lacks the talent of a great painter, then his choice of becoming a great painter is consistent with his talent only in terms of quality, but not in terms of quantity. Therefore, his choice is correct only in terms of quality, but wrong in terms of quantity. In this case, no matter how hard he tries he can only be an average painter, not a great painter. Therefore, his choice of wanting to become a great painter is ultimately wrong.

It becomes clear that only when a person's choice of happiness is consistent with his talent, effort, destiny, and virtue, not only in terms of quality but also in terms of quantity can he achieve happiness and the most valuable happiness he may possibly achieve; if there is inconsistency, it is impossible that he will obtain the most valuable happiness he can possibly experience. Therefore, choosing happiness in accordance with one's talent, effort, destiny, and virtue is the second principle in pursuit of happiness, which can be called "the principle of choice."

## *The principle of action: align the effort to pursue happiness with the cultivation of one's virtue*

Can a person obtain happiness if he has a correct cognition and choice of happiness? Not fully. If he wants to obtain happiness, he must also take the right action, that is, he must combine his effort of pursuing happiness with the cultivation of his virtue. As the laws of the realization of happiness show, to achieve the happiness of his desire and choice, one must—and only need to—possess the four factors of happiness, talent, effort, destiny, and virtue. Among them, talent and destiny are factors of non-action, which cannot be changed by actions; only effort and virtue are the factors of action, which can be changed by actions. While effort itself is action, virtue is the result of continuous and lasting actions. Therefore, the action needed to achieve happiness is making an effort and cultivating virtue, that is, combining the effort to strive for happiness with the cultivation of moral character.

So, can one's chosen happiness be achieved just by making an effort to achieve it without cultivating virtue? No. Take Gu Guangyao, a master's student at a university in China, as an example. Guangyao was a man who worked very hard and succeeded in transforming himself from a dung cleaner to a college student, and then to a graduate student. In pursuing his happiness, he did make a great effort. However, with the pursuit of his own happiness as his only goal, he did not cultivate virtue; his conscience was so lost that he killed his wife cruelly and was put to death; the result was that he failed in achieving happiness. From ancient times to the present, both in China and abroad, there exist many Gu Guangyaos! Therefore, if one makes effort to only pursue happiness without cultivating virtue, he cannot achieve the desired happiness, so this is the wrong action of pursuing happiness. On the contrary, can a person achieve desired happiness only by cultivating virtue without making effort to pursue happiness? He can't. If a person pursues happiness as a painter, how can he become a painter only by cultivating his moral character instead of making effort in painting? Obviously, the pursuit of happiness cannot be achieved only by cultivation of virtue without making the effort; this too is a wrong action of pursuing happiness. Therefore, only by combining effort with virtue can the desired happiness be achieved, and this balanced way is the right action of pursuing happiness. The combination of effort to pursue happiness with the cultivation of one's virtue is the "principle of correct action" of pursuing happiness.

220  *Happiness*

In summarizing the principles of happiness, it can be thus concluded. If one wants to pursue and obtain happiness, one ought to first make his cognition of happiness consistent with the objective nature of happiness, which is the "principle of correct cognition" in pursuit of happiness. Second, he ought to make his choice of happiness consistent with his talent, effort, destiny, and virtue, which is the "principle of correct choice" in pursuit of happiness; "combining the effort to pursue happiness with the cultivation of one's own virtue" should be the "principle of correct action" in pursuit of happiness. These are the three principles of pursuing happiness. These are the three steps on the way up to the paradise of happiness. Those who can accomplish this triad in order, climb these three steps in sequence, and follow these three principles carefully can achieve real happiness and will become real happy people.

**Notes**

1. Zhou Fucheng, *Selected Works of Western Ethics*, Volume 2 (Beijing: Commercial Press, 1987), 366.
2. Robert Maynard Hutchins, *Great Books of The Western World*, Volume 43, Utilitarianism, by John Stuart Mill, 448.
3. Elizabeth Telfer, *Happiness* (The Macmillan Press Ltd, 1980), 8.
4. Ruut Veenhoven, *Databook of Happiness* (Dordrecht: D. Reidel Publishing Company, 1984), 8.
5. Gottfried Wilhelm Leibniz, *A New Theory of Human Reason* (Beijing: Commercial Press, 1982), 188.
6. Ibid., 187.
7. Leibniz, *A New Theory of Human Reason*, 188.
8. *Cihai* (Shanghai: Shanghai Lexicographical Publishing House, 1980).
9. Victoria S. Wike, *Kant on Happiness in Ethics* (Albany: State University of New York Press, 1994), 2.
10. Spinoza, *Ethics*, 140.
11. Louis P. Pojman, *Ethical Theory: Classical and Contemporary Readings* (Belmont, CA: Wadsworth Publishing Company, 1995), 150.
12. Lawrence C. Becker, *Encyclopedia of Ethics*, Volume I (New York: Garland Publishing, Inc., 1992), 431.
13. Pojman, *Ethical Theory: Classical and Contemporary Readings*, 151.
14. Abraham H. Maslow, *Motivation and Personality*, 2nd ed. (New York: Harper & Row Publishers, 1970), xii, xiv.
15. W. James, *Compendium of Psychology* (Beijing: Commercial Press, 1993), 23.
16. Ignacio L.Gotz, *Conceptions of Happiness* (New York: University Press of America, Inc., 1995), 21.
17. Ibid.
18. Yulan Fung, *Complete Works of Sansongtang*, Volume 4 (Beijing: Peking University Press, 1986), 627.
19. Schopenhauer, *The World as Will and Representation* (Beijing: Commercial Press, 1982), 433.
20. Hutchins, *Great Books of The Western World*, Volume 43, Utilitarianism, by John Stuart Mill, 448.
21. Paulsen, *A System of Ethics* (Beijing: China Social Sciences Press, 1986), 191.
22. *The Complete Works of Aristotle*, Volume 8 (Beijing: China Renmin University Press, 1992), 310, 252, 34.
23. Ibid., 310, 252, 34.

24 Maslow, *Motivation and Personality*, 114.
25 Zhou Fucheng, ed., *Selected Works of Western Ethics*, Volume 1 (Beijing: Commercial Press, 1954), 104.
26 Ibid., 161.
27 R. F. Thompson, ed., *Physiological Psychology* (Beijing: Science Publishing House, 1981), 336–337.
28 Miao Litian, ed., *Ancient Greek Philosophy* (Beijing: Renmin University Press, 1990), 642.
29 Litian, ed., *Ancient Greek Philosophy*, 639.
30 Henry Sidgwick, *The Methods of Ethics* (Bristol: Thoemmes Press, 1996), 42.
31 Julia Annas, *The Morality of Happiness* (New York: Oxford University Press. 1993), 339.
32 Ibid., 388.
33 Gotz, *Conceptions of Happiness*, 118.
34 Aristotle, *Nicomachean Ethics*, 8.
35 Yulan, *Complete Works of Sansongtang*, Volume 4, 350.
36 Ibid., 350.
37 Annas, *The Morality of Happiness*, 40–41.
38 Stephen Engstrom, *Aristotle, Kant, and the Stoics* (Cambridge: Cambridge University Press, 1996), 261.
39 Translated by Hippocrates G. Apostle, *Aristotle's Nicomachean Ethics* (Iowa: The Peripatetic Press, 1992), 1.
40 Fucheng, ed., *Selected Works of Western Ethics*, volume 1, 103.
41 Annas, *The Morality of Happiness*, 43.
42 Feng Yihan, trans. *Collections of Wisdoms on Success* (Beijing: Peking University Press, 2000), 147.
43 *Selected Works of Philosophy by Feuerbach*, 545.
44 "The Biggest Happiness," *Zhuangzi*.
45 Viktor Frankl, *The Will to Meaning* (Beijing: SDX Joint Publishing Company, 1991), 90.
46 Frankl, *The Will to Meaning*, 69.
47 G.E. Moore, *Principia Ethica*, Revised ed. (New York: Cambridge University Press, 1993), 113.
48 Ibid., 120.
49 Jeremy Bentham, *The Principles of Morality and Legislation* (New York: Prometheus, 1948), 97.
50 Ibid., 210.
51 Henry Sidgwick, *Methods of Ethics* (Beijing: China Social Sciences Press, 1993), 225.
52 Fucheng, ed., *Selected Works of Western Ethics*, Volume 1, 103–104.
53 Moore, *Principia Ethica*, Revised ed., 122.
54 Gotz, *Conceptions of Happiness*, 7.
55 Pojman, *Ethical Theory: Classical and Contemporary Readings*, 150.
56 Ibid., 150.
57 Becker, *Encyclopedia of Ethics*, Volume I, 150.
58 Cai Jingfeng, *Wisdom on Preserving Health* (Beijing: China Youth Publishing House, 1995), 35.
59 Allen Parducci, *Happiness, Pleasure, and Judgment* (Mahwah, NJ: Lawrence Erlbaum Associates Publishers, 1995), vii.
60 Becker, *Encyclopedia of Ethics*, Volume I, 434.
61 Pojman, *Ethical Theory: Classical and Contemporary Readings*, 150.
62 Ibid., 149.
63 Ibid., 151.
64 Ibid., 156.
65 Maslow, *Motivation And Personality*, 2nd ed., 98.

66 Hutchins, *Great Books of The Western World*, 448.
67 Wolfgang Stegmueller, *Main Currents in Contemporary German, British, and American Philosophy*, Volume I (Beijing: Commercial Press, 1989), 69.
68 Maslow, *Motivation and Personality*, 34.
69 Ibid., 59.
70 Ibid., 34.
71 Ibid., 104.
72 Abraham H. Maslow, *Vision of Human Nature* (Kunming: Yunnan Publishing House, 1987), 122.
73 Ibid.
74 Hutchins, *Great Books of The Western World*, 449.
75 Maslow, *Motivation and Personality*, 98.
76 Ibid.
77 Bertrand Russel, *Why I am Not a Christian* (Beijing: Commercial Press. 1982), 14.
78 Gotz, *Conceptions of Happiness*, 6.
79 Yulan, *Complete Works of Sansongtang*, Volume 4, 665.
80 Fung Yulan, *Collections of Academic Essays of Sansongtang* (Beijing: Peking University Press, 1986), 625.
81 Fung Yulan, *Complete Works of Sansongtang*, Volume 4 (Zhengzhou: Henan People's Publishing House, 1986), 666.
82 Gotz, *Conceptions of Happiness*, 152.
83 Yulan, *Complete Works of Sansongtang*, 665.
84 Yulan, *Complete Works of Sansongtang*, 665
85 Ibid., 666.
86 Yulan, *Complete Works of Sansongtang*, 665.
87 *Chuang-tzu*,"De chongfu."
88 *Chuang-tzu*,"The World."
89 Yulan, *Collections of Academic Essays of Sansongtang*, 625.
90 Ibid., 626.
91 *The Complete Works of Aristotle*, Volume 8, 18.
92 Gotz, *Conceptions of Happiness*, 5
93 Qian Sima, *Reply to Ren An.*
94 Zhang Zai, *Xi Ming.*
95 Yulan, *Collections of Academic Essays of Sansongtang*, 625.
96 Gotz, *Conceptions of Happiness*, 286.
97 *Mencius*, "Gaozi."
98 Gotz, *Conceptions of Happiness*, 173.
99 Paulsen, *System of Ethics*, 341.
100 Immanuel Kant, *Critique of Practical Reason* (Beijing: China Social Sciences Publishing House, Chengcheng Books LTD., 1993), 135
101 Annas, *The Morality of Happiness*, 432.
102 Kant, *Criticism of Practical Reason* (Beijing: Commercial Press, 1960), 127, 117.
103 Litian, *Ancient Greek Philosophy*, 622.
104 Zhao Dunhau, *A Survey of Western Philosophy* (Beijing: Peking University Press, 1996), 288.
105 Annas, *The Morality of Happiness*, 388.
106 Ibid., 431.
107 Zhou Fucheng, ed., *Selected Works of Western Ethics,* Volume 1 (Beijing: Commercial Press, 1954), 216.
108 Annas, *The Morality of Happiness*, 434.
109 Yulan, *Complete Works of Sansongtang*, 681.
110 Jean-Jacques Rousseau, *Emile* (Beijing: Commercial Press, 1978), 74.
111 Sigmund Freud, *Totem and Taboo* (Beijing: Chinese Folk Literature and Art Publishing House, 1986), 10.

# 4  The system of moral rules

It is evident that the more common, the more general, and the more abstract moral norms are, the rarer they are; the more special, the more specific, and the more concrete they are, the more numerous they are. There are eight general moral principles, which are grouped in four categories: first, the ultimate standard of morality: "increasing or decreasing the quantum of interests of everyone"; second, the general moral principle of goodness; third, the moral principle of treating oneself with kindness, namely, the principle of "happiness"; finally, the five moral principles of treating others with kindness, mainly the principles of state governance and state institutions, including principles of justice, equality, humanity, liberty, and alienation.

On the contrary, there is a myriad of specific moral rules. However, as ethics is a philosophy of morality, its system of moral norms can and ought to, undoubtedly, accommodate only the more important moral rules, leaving others to common sense and intuition or applied ethics. These more important moral rules boil down to eight rules: honesty, cherishing-life, self-respect, modesty, wisdom, continence, courage, and the doctrine of the mean. It is evident that honesty is the most important among the eight moral rules: honesty is the basic bond that maintains interpersonal cooperation and ensures the existence and development of society. Therefore, honesty ranks first in the system of moral rules.

## Honesty

### *The concept of honesty*

Broadly speaking, honesty means telling the truth, and deception means telling lies: this is the popular definition of honesty and deception. However, in more exact terms, speech and language are not the only forms of honesty and deception. Isn't the ancient Chinese king's misuse of power in lighting the beacon tower—just to win a few laughs from the beautiful girl seeing the hurried arrival of his dukes and princes who responded to this emergency military alarm signal—a kind of deception? Isn't General Han Xin's building a trestle road to confuse his enemies to launch a secret attack upon them also a kind of deception? Obviously, all behaviors, such as keeping silent, nodding, gestures, and actions, can be honest or deceptive. Therefore, honesty or deception takes both the form of language and action and, thus, belongs to the category of behavior. Based on this view, the following could be said: honesty is the behavior of conveying true information and deception is the behavior of conveying false information. In fact, this is not entirely true. Imagine if the information is false, but John thinks it's true and conveys it as true information to others; he is conveying information that "is subjectively intended as true" but "false in objective reality." Is his behavior honesty or deception? Of course, it is honesty, not deception.

According to this point of view, whether a behavior is classified as honesty or deception does not depend on whether the information conveyed is true or false in objective reality, but on whether the information conveyed is true or false in the subjective intention of the communicator. Therefore, honesty is the behavior of having the intent to convey true information, the behavior of "making others believe what the communicator himself thinks is true is true," or the behavior of "making others believe what the communicator himself thinks is false is false." Deception is the behavior of having the intent to convey false information, the behavior of "making others believe what the communicator himself thinks is true is false," or the behavior of "making others believe what the communicator himself thinks is false is true." This is the precise definition of deception and honesty. However, this definition does not completely negate the previous popular definition. It is self-evident that language is, after all, the main form of information conveyed by honesty and deception. Therefore, honesty mainly refers to speaking the truth, or the behavior of conveying the truth while deception mainly refers to speaking untruth or the behavior of conveying the untruth.

Honesty can be divided into sincerity and faithfulness. The definition of "honesty as the behavior of having the intent to convey true information" means that the information conveyed by an honest person is true, not because it is consistent with objective facts, but because it is consistent with the "subjective thought" of the communicator and with his "own actual action" caused by the intention. The consistency of the information conveyed by one with one's subjective thought is called sincerity; the consistency of information conveyed by one with one's actual action is called faithfulness. On the contrary, the false information conveyed by deception is false information, not because it is inconsistent with objective facts, but because it is inconsistent with the communicator's "subjective thought" and with his "own actual action" caused by the intention. The inconsistency of information conveyed by one with one's own subjective thought is called lying; the inconsistency of information conveyed by one with one's actual action is called faithlessness.

To be more precise, sincerity and faithfulness are two types of honesty based on the nature of the source of true information. Sincerity is the behavior of conveying information consistent with one's thoughts, and its main manifestation is "agreement of heart and mouth." Faithfulness is the behavior of conveying information consistent with one's actual actions, and its main manifestation is "consistency of words and deeds." On the contrary, lying and faithlessness are two types of deception based on the nature of the source of false information. Lying is the behavior of conveying information inconsistent with one's own thoughts, and its main manifestation is "discrepancy between heart and mouth"; faithlessness is the behavior of conveying information inconsistent with one's actual actions, and its main manifestation is "discrepancy between words and deeds."

Deception can also be divided into malicious deception and goodwill deception according to the nature of its intent. Malicious deception is conventional deception; it is deception with the intent of harming others, such as rumor, slander, flattery, hypocrisy, and perjury. Goodwill deception is an exception to deception; it is a deception with no intent of harming others, a deception with the intent of benefiting others or self, such as deceiving murderers, comforting patients, joking, and polite words, and so on. Similarly, honesty can be divided into goodwill honesty and malicious honesty. Goodwill honesty is honesty with no intention of harming others; this kind of honesty is conventional honesty, which does not need much elaboration. On the contrary, malicious honesty is the exception to honesty; it is honesty with the intention of harming others, such as telling the truth to provoke conflicts. Malicious honesty is mostly intentional, but there are also forced ones; for example, a person is being chased by his would-be killer takes refuge in my house, and when questioned by the would-be killer, I am forced to tell the truth because I am afraid of being hurt by the murderer or because I want to be an honest person. This is malicious honesty, because this honesty, after all, has the intention of sacrificing and hurting the lives of others to avoid being hurt or to be shown as an honest person.

## *The moral value of honesty*

As mentioned above, the standard to measure the moral value of all behaviors is the ultimate goal of morality and the ultimate standard of morality: to guarantee the existence and development of society and promote the interests of everyone. Based on this point of view, the moral value of people's honesty and deception can be measured according to their effects on society, on others, and themselves. First, from the perspective of others who are deceived but treated honestly. Just think, who does not want to be treated honestly? Who wants to be deceived? Thus, being deceived, even with goodwill, is undoubtedly a kind of harm; being treated honestly, even with malicious honesty, is undoubtedly a kind of benefit.

Second, it can be measured from the perspective of deceivers and honest people themselves. Deception and dishonesty can indeed obtain temporary, local, or specific benefits; but from a long-term, global, and general point of view, deception is bound to harm the deceivers themselves, while honesty is bound to benefit those who are themselves honest. The overall value is

## 226  The system of moral rules

greater than the immediate value while the long-term value is greater than the temporary value. Therefore, for the deceivers and the honest people, the net balance of deception is harm while the net balance of honesty is benefit. As the Western motto goes, "honesty is the best policy." Ancient Chinese sages also make a similar point, "If a man is honest and faithful, he can save himself; if a monarch is honest and faithful, he can save a country."[1]

Finally, from the point of view of society: the so-called society, as Rawls said, is nothing but "a system of cooperation designed to advance the good of those taking part in it."[2] The reason why interpersonal cooperation can take place and why society can exist and develop is obviously that the basic interpersonal relationship is mutual trust rather than mutual deception; and that people have more honest behaviors with each other than deceptive behaviors. Otherwise, if the basic relationship among people is mutual deception rather than mutual trust, and people have more deceptive behaviors with each other than honest behaviors, then cooperation is bound to collapse as will the society. Therefore, honesty is the basic bond that sustains interpersonal cooperation and guarantees the existence and development of society.

Thus, all honest behaviors, no matter how different—whether they are based on goodwill or malice—they are, in terms of their common nature of honesty, beneficial to others, themselves, and the existence and development of society. Therefore, all honest behaviors conform to the ultimate goal of morality and the ultimate standard of morality; thus, they are all moral, good, and ought-to-be. On the contrary, all deceptive behaviors, no matter how different—whether they are based on goodwill or malice— they are, in terms of their common nature of deception, harmful to others, themselves and the existence and development of society. Therefore, all deceptive behaviors do not conform to the ultimate goal of morality and the ultimate standard of morality; thus, they are all immoral, ought-not-to-be, and bad. As Luther says:

> It seems to me that there is no more pernicious vice on earth than falsehood and faithlessness, which divide all human societies. For falsehood and faithlessness first divide hearts; when hearts are divided, hand also separate, and when hands separate, what can we do to accomplish?[3]

Nonetheless, although all deception is harmful to society, others, and self, and is thus bad, the degree of its damage to society, others, and self, or the degree of its bad is inversely proportional to its goodwill and directly proportional to its malice: the greater the goodwill of deception, the greater its benefit to the deceived, the more forgivable it will be; thus, the less harm it does to society, others, and self, the lesser its bad will be. The more malicious the deception is, the greater the harm it does to the deceived, the more unforgivable it will be; therefore, the greater the harm it does to society, others, and self, the greater its bad it will be. As Aquinas said:

If a person lies with the intent to harm others, then the evil of his lie is aggravated; this is a malicious lie. On the contrary, if a person lies to achieve some kind of good or happiness, the evil of his lie is alleviated.[4]

"Obviously, the greater the good will of a lie, the less serious its crime."[5]

In a similar vein, though all honesty is beneficial to society, others, and self, and is thus good, the degree of its benefits to society, others, and self or the degree of its good is directly proportional to its goodwill and inversely proportional to its malice. The greater the goodwill of honesty, the greater the benefit to the recipient, the more praiseworthy it is, the greater its benefit to the society, others, and self, and the greater its good will be. The greater the malice of honesty, the greater its damage to the recipient, the less praiseworthy it is, and the smaller its benefits to society, others, and self, the smaller its good will be.

In summary, all honesty, in any case, is itself moral, ought-to-be, and good, so it is the moral norm of what interpersonal behavior ought to be; all deception, in any case, is in itself immoral, ought-not-to-be, and bad, so it is the moral norm of what interpersonal behavior ought not to be.

## *Scope of application of honesty*

The moral value of honesty and deception shows that honesty is ought-to-be and deception is ought-not-be. So, ought people be honest and ought people not deceive others under any circumstances? Kant's answer to this question is affirmative: "To be truthful (honest) in all declarations is therefore a sacred command of reason prescribing unconditionally, one not to be restricted by any conveniences."[6] Kant gives an example; If an innocent person, being chased by a killer, were to take refuge in your house, and the murderer were to question you about it, you should tell him the truth honestly instead of lying to save a life. "In a non-negotiable statement, no matter how much a harm it may cause to oneself or others, honesty is everyone's Uncompromisable responsibility to others."[7] "For [a lie] always injures another; if not another individual, yet mankind generally, since it vitiates the source of justice."[8]

The mistake made by Kant is that he has been able to see honesty as good and deception as bad, but unable to see the ultimate moral standard of "the maximum net balance of interest" for "choosing the greater good when two goods are in conflict" and "choosing the smaller bad when two bads are in conflict." When the murderer asks about the innocent person who has taken shelter in your house, the good of honesty and the good of saving people are in conflict: if one chooses to be honest, then he cannot save the life of the innocent; if one chooses to save the life of the innocent, then he cannot be honest. If he does not want to deceive, he will have the innocent killed; if he does not want to have the innocent killed, he must deceive. Nonetheless, honesty is a lesser good and saving people is a greater good, so when the two goods are in conflict and cannot be compromised, he ought to choose the greater good, which is saving the life of the innocent; deception is a lesser bad and harm is a greater bad, so when the two bads are in conflict and cannot be compromised, he ought to choose the lesser bad, which is deception. Therefore, in this case, we ought not to be honest and hand over the innocent to his killer, but instead, we ought to deceive the murderer and save the life of the innocent. Mencius says, "A noble man does not need to keep every word he promises, or accomplish everything he starts, but he does need to conform to morality."[9] This is so true. Otherwise, isn't avoiding a lesser bad (deception) for the sake of a greater bad (having others killed), and getting lesser good (being honest) at the expense of greater good (saving others' life) the behavior of an average person? "Keeping every word one promises, insisting on finishing things one starts doing, and holding on to one's opinion without considering its morality is just what an average person does!"[10]

It can be concluded that in normal situations, when the good of honesty is not in conflict with other good, honesty, instead of deception, is the ought-to-be rule; in exceptional situations, when honesty is in conflict with a greater good and both goods cannot be achieved, deception is the ought-to-be rule to be followed to preserve the greater good as per the ultimate moral standard of "the maximum net balance of interests." Given this, honesty, no matter how significant it is, is not a moral principle, but a basic moral rule that is subordinate to and dominated and determined by the moral principles of goodness, love, and justice.

Thus, in the structure of each person's morality, honesty, and deception are subjective, determined, subordinate, and secondary factors, while kindness, malice, benevolence, justice, and so on are the controlling, determining, dominant, primary, and dominating factors. That is why the moral level of a benevolent but hypocritical person is higher than that of a vicious but honest person. Even a hypocrite is better than an honest wicked man, for the hypocrite knows shame while the honest wicked man is shameless; thus, shamelessness is undoubtedly the lowest level of morality. Therefore, Wang Chuanshan says, "The honesty of a wicked man is worse than the honesty of a hypocrite."[11]

> Honesty is an empty moral quality, but knowledge, benevolence, courage, and faithfulness can fill up its emptiness. Therefore, those who say that they are honest people must say that they are benevolently honest, wisely honest, or courageously honest, but they cannot just say that they are honest.[12]

The honesty of a person is far from being enough to make him a morally good person; to be morally good, a person needs more important virtues such as benevolence, kindness, justice, and so on.

Based on this understanding, the controversy between "the theory of moral decline" and "the theory of moral ascendency" in the academia in

China can be settled: the former is the truth, and the latter is a fallacy. In recent years, there has been a generally known ascendency of honesty in the moral character of Chinese nationals, but there has also been a decline of benevolence, selflessness, kindness, and justness; though deception has become less, selfishness, malice, unfairness, and shamelessness has increased. These changes indicate that the morality of the nationals shows no sign of ascendency, it has declined instead. The mistake of the theory of moral ascendency lies obviously in that it exaggerates the basic nature and importance of the virtue of honesty and regards it as the decisive factor of moral character.

As shown above, the essence of honesty is to treat others with goodness, thus honesty is the most important moral rule. So, what is the most important moral rule of treating oneself with goodness? It is cherishing-life. As people often say, the happiness a person enjoys, no matter how abundant or high-level it is, is always based on his own life: his own life is like the number "1," and those abundant and high-level happiness, such as wealth, official prosperity, perfect love, writing books, establishing learning, self-realization, and so on, are nothing but the numerous zeros ("0") after the number "1." If one loses his life, he will lose "1" and have only a large "0," which still amounts to a "0." As a Taoist saying goes, a dead king envies the life of a living rat. Therefore, after establishing honesty as the most important moral principle of treating others with kindness, honesty ought to be followed by "cherishing-life": cherishing-life is the most important moral rule of treating oneself with goodness.

## Cherishing-life

The most important problem for treating oneself with goodness is obviously how one treats his own life with goodness, and how he treats both his own life and things beyond his own life properly. The Taoist solution to this problem now seems to be a good one: the solution is cherishing-life; cherishing-life is the most important moral rule of treating oneself with goodness.

### *The concept of cherishing-life*

The so-called cherishing-life is cherishing life and devaluing things. This means that we divide what we own into life (our own life) and things (anything beyond our life) and then value our life more than things beyond our life, thus treating our life as most precious and valuable. On this point, the Taoist school says it very well:

> The life I have owned is my greatest interest. In terms of its nobility, even the title of a king cannot match the nobility of my own life; in terms of its importance, even all the wealth on earth cannot purchase my own life; in terms of its safety, once I lose my own life, I will never be able to recover it.[13]

Therefore, "The sages care deeply about the world and consider nothing more precious than life",[14] "the dead king is not as good as the living rat"; "the dead king envies the life of the living rat."[15]

Many people share these Taoist ideas. Even Mozi, the rival or opponent of Taoists, admitted:

> If someone asks you, 'if I buy you new clothes and shoes, and then cut off your hands and feet, do you want it?' Of course you will say no to it. Why? Because the whole world is not as precious as the life. If asked again, 'If I make you the king of the country, and then have you killed, do you want it?' Of course, you will not want it. Why? Because the world is not as precious as the life.[16]

Feuerbach has repeatedly said, "Life is man's greatest treasure."[17] "Man sacrifices his life to God, just because God's eyes, like man's, see life as the highest, the most valuable, and the most sacred treasure."[18]

It can be seen that the essence of cherishing-life is to regard one's own life not just as a precious thing but as the most precious thing; cherishing-life as a moral norm is the behavior that one ought to regard one's own life as the most precious and valuable thing. However, why is our life the most precious thing?

Analysis of the concept of value shows that if we say something is valuable and precious to us, we mean that something has a function that can satisfy our needs, desires, and purposes. In this sense, that our life is the most precious and valuable thing to us means that life can satisfy one's most important, most fundamental, and greatest need, desire, and purpose. What then is the most important, fundamental, and greatest need, desire, and purpose of men?

Without doubt, it is the desire to survive; it is the need, desire, and purpose of surviving. Feuerbach says:

> The desire of men, at least those whose desire is not confined by natural necessity, is first and foremost the desire to live an eternal life; yes, this desire is the last and the highest desire of men, the desire behind all desires.[19]

The exact reason why the life of a person is his most precious and valuable thing is that his life can satisfy his most important, most fundamental, and greatest need: the desire for survival. The psychological experience of satisfaction of desire is the so-called pleasure, and the psychological experience of satisfaction of great desire is the so-called happiness; thus, life itself or living itself, owing to its ability to satisfy his most important, most fundamental, and greatest desire, is one's most important, most fundamental, and greatest pleasure and happiness. Therefore, Feuerbach says, "Life itself is happiness." "Life is in fact the sum of all welfares."[20] Zhuang Zi says it even better: "The greatest happiness is life."[21]

*The system of moral rules* 231

Given this, life is the most precious thing of a person is literally because the pleasure of life is the most important, the most fundamental, and the greatest happiness of life, and fundamentally because life can satisfy the most important, the most fundamental, and the greatest desire of a person: the desire for survival.

### *The value of cherishing-life*

From the claim that life is most precious, we can deduce whether a person's behavior is most beneficial and harmful to himself: the behavior of cherishing-life is the most beneficial to oneself, because if a person values his life more than things, then even if he loses his things, he will still have the most precious and valuable thing: health and longevity; contrarily, the behavior of valuing things more than one's life is most harmful to oneself, because if a person values things more than his life, then even if he gets fame and success, he may lose his life. Isn't this the same as sacrificing one's body for the sake of new clothes or beheading oneself for the sake of a new hat?

Cherishing-life is most beneficial to one's self and thus the primary norm for treating oneself with goodness; valuing things more than life is most harmful to oneself and thus the primary norm for treating oneself bad. However, from ancient times to the present, numerous people have failed to appreciate this truth and vied to endanger and harm their life for the sake of fame and success. The consequence of their behaviors is just like what is said in *Master Lü's Spring and Autumn Annals*:

> Though on the outside, the king achieves fame and success, inside the body his life is already so depleted that his ears cannot hear music, his eyes cannot see beautiful colors, his mouth cannot eat delicacies, his mind is so deranged that he speaks nonsense, and on his deathbed his heart is filled with fear. Isn't consuming your life in vain a pitiful thing?[22]

Nevertheless, most people think that morality ought not to advocate cherishing-life for one's self-interest; instead, it ought to promote harming-life for the benefit of others. This view is untenable because whether cherishing life for one's self-interest and harming one's own life for the benefit of others is ought-to-be and has positive moral value or not depends entirely on their effect on the ultimate standard of morality—increasing the quantum of interests of everyone. From this point of view, cherishing-life for one's self-interest accords with the ultimate standard of morality, and thus has positive moral value; it is, thus, moral, ought-to-be, and good. Harming one's own life for the benefit of others violates the ultimate standard of morality and thus has negative moral value; it is, thus, immoral, ought-not-to-be, and bad.

However, both the positive moral value of cherishing-life for one's self-interest and the negative moral value of harming one's own life to benefit others are relative and conditional. It is self-evident that only in normal circumstances—when there is no conflict between one's own life and another person's life—it is moral, ought-to-be, and good to cherish one's life for self-interest, and it is immoral, ought-not-to-be, and bad to harm one's life. Under extraordinary circumstances (that is, when one's own life conflicts with another person's life and both the lives cannot be protected at the same time), one ought to make that supreme sacrifice and harm one's own life to benefit the lives of others; in this situation, cherishing-life for one's self interest is immoral, ought-not-to-be, and bad. The mistake of the popular view that we ought to harm our own life to benefit others—we ought not to cherish our own life for self-interest—lies in that it eliminates normal circumstances and instead exaggerates extraordinary circumstances. As a result, one the one hand, this view deduces from the right claim that it is moral to harm one's own life to benefit others under extraordinary circumstances, and then draws the wrong conclusion that it is also moral to harm one's own life to benefit others under normal circumstances. On the other hand, this view deduces from the right claim that it is immoral to cherish one's life for self-interest in extraordinary circumstances and then draws the wrong conclusion that it is immoral to cherish one's life for self-interest under normal circumstances.

Given this, just like honesty and courage, cherishing-life is relatively ought-to-be, relatively moral, and relatively good, and is a basic moral rule subordinated to "the ultimate standard of morality," to the moral principles of "goodness," "justice," etc. So, how exactly should we cherish life? The answer is being happy with our life, which is the foundation of cherishing-life. Human life is the most precious thing and can satisfy the greatest desire of the human; it is thus the most important pleasure and happiness of human beings. Doesn't this mean that satisfying the greatest desire and obtaining the most important pleasure and happiness is the most precious? Therefore, the so-called cherishing-life is ultimately valuing "satisfaction of desires and realization of pleasures"; thus, the behavior of cherishing-life is to live a happy life and satisfy one's desires and needs, rather than to have a miserable life and inhibit one's desires and needs. Hence, living a happy life is the foundation of cherishing-life.

Therefore, Taoists claim that "mistreating-life," in which six desires of a person are not fully satisfied, is not "cherishing-life" or "respecting-life." For "cherishing-life" or "respecting-life" is "fulfilling-life," in which all the six desires of a person are properly satisfied. However, it often happens that various kinds of happiness pursued by a person can conflict with each other and cannot be achieved at the same time. For example, indulging in sex may bring tremendous pleasure but may also harm your body, so this kind of pleasure often depletes your energy and ought not to last too long. Then, should we choose temporary pleasure or long-term pleasure? Of course, we ought to choose long-term pleasure. To achieve a long-term pleasure we must, as recommended by the Taoists, stay healthy and live a life of longevity:

> Ancient people who get the *Tao* knows the importance of healthy life, so they would be able to live a life of longevity, could hear what they want to hear, see what they want to see, and eat what they want to eat and enjoy these pleasures for a long time....[23]

In this way, behaviors benefiting one's own life is the premise for enjoying one's own life; therefore, cherishing-life is enjoying one's own life premised on benefiting one's own life. So, enjoying one's own life as promoted by cherishing-life is not the kind of enjoying one's own life indulgently, not the kind of enjoying life by indulging oneself in all desires and pleasures; rather it is the enjoying of life through continence, the behavior of satisfying only the desires beneficial to life, and pursuing only the pleasures beneficial to life. "This is how the ancient sages enjoy all kinds of pleasures: they choose pleasures beneficial to the nature of life and abandon pleasures harmful to the nature of life; this is the way of achieving full life."[24] Then, what can we do to make pleasures beneficial to life to enjoy our own life? The answer is preserving life, which the way of cherishing-life.

### The approaches to cherishing-life

What is preserving life? According to *Master Lü's Spring and Autumn Annals*, "Those who understand cherishing-life know what to do to avoid harming their life; this is called life preservation."[25] *Qian Jin Yao Fang* (*Essential Formulas Worth a Thousand in Gold to Prepare for Emergencies*) is more specific about life preservation:

> Among the creatures between the heaven and the earth, humans are the most precious; there is nothing more precious in human beings than their life. Among the endless absurd things and ordeals that will happen to our life, life is as short-lived as the instant flash of a lightening; upon realizing this, I suddenly lament that if passed life can never be recovered, why shouldn't we moderate our desires to preserve our own life?[26]

It can be seen that life-preserving is the only way to live a long and healthy life and thus also the basis of cherishing-life and enjoying-life. So, how exactly should we preserve life?

### Have a quiet spirit and an active body

Man's life is nothing more than the spirit and the body, and the spirit is the commander of the body. Life-preserving is all about preserving the spirit and preserving the body, and preserving the spirit is more important than preserving the body. "Preserving the spirit is of supreme importance, and preserving the body comes after it."[27]

The principle of preserving the spirit is "quiet." Because only when the spirit is quiet and stable can it run normally with the visceral functions coordinated and balanced, and the immunity strengthened, so that it can achieve health and longevity. Otherwise, if the spirit is restless, it will not function normally, the viscera will dysfunction, and the immunity will wane and become vulnerable to disease. Therefore, in *Huainanzi* (*Great Words from Huainan*) it says: "If a person is quiet, his spirit and body get stronger day by day while if a person is restless, his spirit and body wane day by day."[28] However, the spirit, as the master of all human life activities, is easy to move and difficult to be quiet. How can we be quiet but not restless? In other words, what are the specific ways to preserve the spirit?

First of all, we ought to "have a happy and relaxed mood." *The Yellow Emperor's Classic of Internal Medicine* says: "All illnesses arise from *qi*: anger brings *qi* up, joy slows *qi* down, sadness drains *qi* away, fear brings *qi* down, anxiety makes *qi* congested."[29] That is to say, any abnormality in the seven emotions (joy, anger, worry, anxiety, sadness, fear, fright) is an important factor that disturbs the spirit and causes disease. There are two cases of this so-called abnormality: the first case is that these emotions are too intense, such as ecstasy, rage, shock, horror; the second case is that these emotions last too long, such as brooding state and melancholy. So, how can we have a quiet spirit and bring normalcy to our seven emotions? The only way is to have a happy spirit and a relaxed mood. Liu Mo also wrote in *100 Questions on Syndromes and Treatments*:

> It is the human nature to be inclined to have a happy and relaxed mood, which is most conducive for rejuvenating the body and the spirit and leading to longevity; a happy and relaxed mood can not only cure our illnesses but also allow us to stay healthy forever.[30]

Then, how can we have a happy and relaxed mood? Chen Zhi, an expert on life-preserving in the Song Dynasty, summarized a set of methods called "Ten Pleasures":

> The master of Shuqi House says, read good books, practice calligraphy, sit and meditate, have relaxing chats with good friends, drink some wine, plant flowers and bamboos, listen to music and watch birds, burn incense and make tea, climb the city towers and enjoy mountain views, and play chess.[31]

Second, desire ought to be moderate. If one's desires are excessive, it will be difficult to realize one's desires, and as a result, his spirit will become restless with an all-consuming desire to realize the desire. Therefore, the experts on life-preserving remind us, "The less the desire, the more energetic and refreshing the spirit; the more the desire, the less the energy and blood."[32] In this sense, moderate desire and contentment are the basic methods of preserving the spirit. *Dao Yuan Ji Yao* (*The Collection of Taoist Academies*) summarizes this method as "eliminating six harms":

> Those who want to preserve life should first eliminate six harms: first, belittle fames and interests; second, refrain from indulgence in music and sex; third, devalue wealth and material things; fourth, have a light taste of food; fifth, block illusions and falsehood; sixth, stay away from jealousy. If we preserve these six harms, our health is bound to deteriorate and decline.[33]

Sun Simiao summarized this method as "Twelve Less": "Less thinking, less worry, less desire, less action, less speech, less laughter, less sadness, less pleasure, less joy, less anger, less predilection, less detestation. The principle of Twelve less is essential to health preservation."[34]

Finally, we ought to "cultivate moral character." Man is a social animal, so everyone's desires are realized with the help of society and others. Whether a person can get the help of society and others and thus have a happy and peaceful mind depends on whether he has virtue, that is, whether society and others think he has virtue; if yes, he will not only get honor and help from society and others, but also satisfy his conscience and feel rewarded, and consequently, achieve a happy and peaceful state of mind. On the contrary, if he lacks virtue, if society and others think that he lacks virtue, he will not only be condemned by public opinion and rejected by society and others, but also not have a clear conscience and suffer self-punishment; consequently, he will have a worried, restless, and anxious mind all day. Therefore, health preservers make this comment:

> In ancient times those who are good at preserving health not only take herbal medicines and take in energy from nature but also cultivate virtues in everything. With various virtues, they, without herbs, can live a rather long life. If their virtues are not adequate, even the elixir of immortality cannot make him live longer.[35]

*The Secrets of Longevity* even says, "A man good at preserving health ought to first cultivate virtues and then nurture his spirit and body."[36] Thus, cultivating moral character is actually the basic method of cultivating spirit and longevity.

### *The principle of preserving the body: kinetic movement*

The principle of preserving the body is "kinetic movement." Zhuangzi says,

> Adequate respiration helps us breathe out waste *qi* and breathe in fresh air; movements, such as climbing like bears and stretching the body like

birds, can allow us to keep fit. This method of preserving the body is preferred by the Immortal Peng Zu.[37]

Gao Lian says, "Preserving *qi* allows us to protect spirit, as clear *qi* refreshes spirit; moving the body cures illness, as movement enhances the circulation of blood and *qi*, which helps cure illness."[38] Sun Simiao says, "If a man works his body, he will be immune to all diseases."[39] But, how can kinetic energy preserve the body? Hua Tuo answers,

> The human body needs movement, but the movement ought not to be so excessive as to consume all the energy. When the body moves often, the food gets digested, the blood gets circulated, and the disease gets blocked. Don't you see the pivot of the door in a room? Although it is made of perishable wood, it opens in the morning and closes at night, and thus it, among all the parts of the door, perishes the last. In this way, the pivot has inspired the ancient immortals, Chisong and Peng Zu, for their ideas of longevity.[40]

So, how should we exercise our body?

First of all, there are many forms of kinetic movements, such as swimming, playing ball, boxing, running, walking, travelling, dance, massage, *qigong*, physical labor, and so on. Exactly what kind of kinetic movement ought to be carried out depends on the individual, on his time, and his local conditions. Second, after exercise, allow at least half an hour of rest before meals; before exercise, allow at least one and a half hours of rest after meals. Finally, exercise ought to be moderate; too little exercise cannot do much to keep us fit; too much exercise can harm the body. Therefore, Sun Simiao says, "The way to preserve one's body is to do light exercises often, but refrain from overworking one's body to a degree or level that is beyond the capability of the body."[41] Nowadays, heart rate is often used to determine the amount of exercise: the difference between 176 and one's age is considered as the moderate heart rate per minute. It is advisable to exercise once or twice a day for 20–40 minutes each time. If your appetite increases, your sleep is good, and your energy is abundant after exercise, it means that the amount of your exercise is appropriate; if your appetite decreases, your spirit is tired after exercise, it means that the amount of exercise is excessive.

### *Moderate Dieting*

Human life is nothing but the transformation of food into life. Therefore, "The foundation of body must be food; those who do not know proper dieting cannot survive."[42] As we all know, in preserving life, the principle for food is "moderate dieting." The so-called moderate dieting refers, on the one hand, to the appropriate quality of the diet, that is, a reasonable collocation of various foods and, on the other hand, to the moderate amount of diet, that is, diet on time with an appropriate amount of food.

How should food be collocated? *The Emperor's Classic of Internal Medicine* says,

> Five kinds of grain provide essential nourishment, five kinds of fruit provide auxiliary nourishment, five kinds of livestock provide beneficial nourishment, and five kinds of vegetable provide supplementary nourishment. When all these different kinds of food are well made with pleasant taste and taken into our body, they will increase essence and preserve *qi*.[43]

Since then, health preservation experts of later generations all agree that the principle of food collocation is "plant-based dieting with a good balance of meat food and vegetarian food": "Meat food means the meat (of five kinds of animals), and vegetarian food includes grains (five kinds of grains), vegetables (five kinds of vegetables), fruit (five kinds of fruits), and so on." As Sun Simiao recommends, "A person who wants to preserve health should always eat less meat and more grain": "they should often eat light food; for grains, they should eat both barleys and wheat and take more japonica rice."[44] Wan Quan explains, "If the food is light in the five tastes, it can nourish people and make people refreshing; if the food is heavy in the five tastes, it will harm the body when going through the viscera."[45] Modern health science shows that "plant-based dieting with balance of meat food and vegetarian food" is indeed one of the secrets of human health and longevity.

What does "dieting on time with an appropriate amount of food" mean? The so-called "on time" means around 7 o'clock for breakfast, 12 o'clock for lunch, and 6 o'clock for dinner. The interval between meals should be 5 to 6 hours because in general, food stays in the stomach for about 4 to 5 hours, and the digestive organs need to rest for a certain period to restore their functions. After each meal, massage your belly with your hands and walk slowly for a while. The so-called "appropriate amount" means that the distribution of the amount of food for three meals should have a certain proportion: 30–35% for breakfast, 40% for lunch and 25–30% for dinner. The basic spirit of "appropriate amount," as Confucius says, is that "there is no need to eat to one's full." In this regard, experts on preserving health in past dynasties have made abundant elaborations: "The way to eat is to keep fit without hunger";[46] "eat when hungry but do not eat to one's full; drink when thirsty but do not drink too much"; "exercise the body more often and keep the appetite small, but do not exercise to an extreme or stay in extreme hunger."[47] Some contemporary health preservation experts even infer that people can extend their life span by 40 years by relying on less food without hunger.

In short, "vegetable-based dieting with a good balance between meat and vegetarian food" and "dieting on time with appropriate amount of food"

238  *The system of moral rules*

are the two principles of preserving health through diet. From this point of view, scientific dietary methods, as stated in *The Secrets of Longevity*, can be extended to "Seven Ought-to":

> The way to eat is as follows: in general, we ought to eat more grains and less meat, vegetable, and other kinds of food; we ought to eat early than late; we ought to eat slowly than fast; we ought to eat to an almost full, but not to a complete full; we ought to eat light food instead of heavy food; we ought to eat warm food instead of cold food; we ought to eat well-cooked and soft food rather than hard food.[48]

*Have a regular daily routine*

Experts on preserving the health of past dynasties have consistently regarded "having a regular daily routine" as an important principle of health preservation and mentioned it on par with the principle of "moderate dieting." Guan Zhong says,

> Having a regular daily routine, keeping a moderate diet, and keeping the body comfortable in hot summer and cold winter is beneficial to health and life expectancy; when daily routine is not regular, the diet is not moderate, the body is not comfortable in cold winter and hot summer, then the body is tired and the life expectancy is shortened.[49]

The so-called regular daily routine means that we ought to arrange daily activities and rest by conforming to the objective law of nature and the human body and adjusting them to one's own specific conditions. Generally speaking, this principle is manifested in the following five aspects:

**Morning Routine**: Get up on time every morning. More specifically speaking, we ought to rest early and rise early in spring and autumn, rest late and rise early in summer, and rest early and rise late in winter. In a word, the best time to get up is around sunrise: "Get up in the morning, not as early as before cockcrow, not as late as after sunrise."[50] Generally speaking, it is advisable to get up at 5 or 6 a.m. and go to bed by 9 or 10 p.m. For morning exercise, while in bed, we can slap the chest gently with our hands, click our teeth, comb our hair with fingers, and wipe our face with hands, and so on. Then, we can get out of bed and go outside to do *Tai Chi* or go for a jog, and so on.

**Work Routine**: Morning and afternoon are working hours. There should be a proper time to rest and a good balance of work and leisure. Tao Hongjing says, "From morning till dusk, we often engage in some activities and keep on doing without stop; but when feeling tired, we should take a break from work and come back to it after rest."[51] The workload should not be too heavy: "If the spirit is overworked, then it will be exhausted; if the body is overworked, then we may die."[52]

**Rest in the Evening**: It is not advisable to work hard after dusk. In the evening, rest and recreation are the main ways to relax and prepare for sleep.

**Sleep at Night**: Sleep is no less important to living than a diet. People die in about 40 days without food, and in only half that time without sleep. Therefore, health preservation experts attach great importance to sleep and believe that "sleep and food are the most important things for health preservation." Wang Anshi says: "If I can meet the immortals of Huashan Mountian, I will ask them not for regimes for becoming immortals but for secrets to good sleep."[53] Generally speaking, adults should sleep eight hours a day and the elderly should sleep about nine hours a day. To avoid insomnia, we should first go to bed regularly every day to form a conditioned reflex and establish a fixed mode of sleep pattern. Second, we ought to "live in a quiet place and have a peaceful mind":

> Before sleep, abandon all worries and thoughts: once we start thinking about something, eliminate it immediately; the more worries get eliminated, the less is there to be worried about. Their gradual disappearance will bring us naturally to sleep. If we feel restless all day long with seven emotions agitated, then when we go to bed, we will toss and turn in bed. How can we relieve all worries in a short time?[54]

Finally, we ought to find a proper way to fall asleep:

> There are two ways of sleep manipulation: if the individual wants to control oneself, he can try manipulation like thinking from the top of his head, counting his nasal breath silently, and moving his breath back to *dantian* acupoint, and in this way he can make his spirit focus on something, instead of wandering restlessly, and then go to sleep easily. If the person wants to indulge himself, he may release all thoughts and worries and let his mind wander freely and eventually into a dreamlike state. What should be avoided the most is having a strong desire to sleep, which can make it even harder to sleep, for the mind has no control over the borderland between the waking state and the sleeping state. The only solution is abandoning the desire to sleep; only in this way, the mind, whether controlled or indulged, will be on the way to dreamland.[55]

**Fourteen Do's for Living and Fitness:** Do massage your face more often; do comb your hair more often; do move your eyes more often; do flick your ears more often; do click your teeth more often; do lick palate with your tongue more often; do swallow your saliva more often; do breathe out waste breath more often; do refrain from speaking when urinating and defecating; do massage your stomach more often; do inhale more often to lift anus; do massage the soles of your feet more often; do massage your skin more often; do shake your limbs more often.[56]

240   *The system of moral rules*

The methods of preserving life have been handed down from generation to generation; up untill now there has been a myriad of methods. However, if we trace their origin, they all originate from the three principles and ways of life-preserving, which are "keeping the spirit peaceful and the body active," "moderating the diet"; and "having a regular daily routine." Therefore, *The Emperor's Classic of Internal Medicine* says that if a person adheres to these three ways of preserving life, he will be expected to live a long life of 100 years; otherwise, his life will inevitably decline by the age of 50 years.

> Ancient people versed in ways of preserving life knew the law of *Yin* and *Yang*, followed the right way to preserve health, kept regular diet and daily routine, and avoided overworking themselves; therefore, they could preserve both their spirit and body and live their full life span of one hundred years before their natural death. Nowadays, people drink wine as water, take disorder as normality, have sex when drunken to exhaust their essence and their primordial *qi*, pursue things with no stop and contentment, often fill their mind with ambitions and desires out of accordance with seasons, have no regular daily routine, so they die at the age of 50 years old. The ancient sages often taught their people to cautiously avoid diseases and evil winds in the four seasons, keep their mind at ease and peace, and refrain from pursuing things beyond their abilities; in this way, the primordial *qi* in their body would run smooth, and their mind would be collected and free from temptations. In this case, how is it possible for diseases to invade them? Therefore, people at that time were able to keep a quiet, peaceful mind with fewer desires, feel settled and content with fewer worries and fears, work their bodies without feeling tired, keep their primordial *qi* harmonious and smooth; as a result, everyone felt their desires were satisfied, enjoyed their food, felt comfortable with their clothing, found comfort and pleasure with their living place and customs, and harbored no jealousy toward those who are superior. These people are indeed what we call simple and sincere people. To these simple and sincere people, desires cannot affect their body, evil ideas cannot corrupt their mind; with such a body and mind, everyone, whether wise or not, whether talented or not, is capable of keeping a peaceful mind free from worries and fears. What they do is in line with the way of preserving health; they could live to the age of 100 years with little sign of senility because they have mastered the way of preserving health and prevented their life from threats and dangers.[57]

Although cherishing-life is the most important moral rule to treat oneself with kindness, cherishing-life is not the highest moral rule to treat oneself with kindness. The highest moral rule to treat oneself with kindness is self-respect. A person's self is composed of his own life and his own personality. Cherishing-life is the expression of self-love of one's life, personal love of life, and a love of life per se. It triggers only a basic, low-level, egoistic behavior, namely, survival. On the contrary, self-respect is the expression of self-love of one's personality, personal love of one's own personality, and the love of personality per se; it triggers an egoistic act for a higher-level purpose: to live a productive, accomplished, and valuable life. Therefore, after cherishing-life, we should study self-respect.

## Self-respect

### *The concept of self-respect*

It is generally understood that self-respect is relative to respect for others. Respect for others is to respect others; it is the others who are respected. Self-respect is to respect oneself; it means that it is the self that is respected. Therefore, the so-called self-respect means the psychology and behavior of making oneself respected, and ultimately the psychology and behavior of making oneself respected by oneself and others. The psychology of making oneself respected by oneself and others is called the sense of self-respect; the behavior of making oneself respected by oneself and others is called self-respecting behavior.

Then, how can a person be respected by himself and others? Of course, there is only one way: produce something, make some achievements and contributions, and to have some value. "Those who degrade themselves to behave like chickens, dogs, birds, and beasts still want to be respected as humans; however, this would never happen."[58] Therefore, the so-called self-respect is, ultimately, the psychology and behavior of making oneself useful and valuable to win respect from oneself and others; self-confidence is the fundamental feature of self-respect. Therefore, Fung Yulan writes, "Mencius said, 'Who is Shun? Who am I? If I can do something important, then I will be respected like Shun.' Those who have such aspirations and motivations are people with a sense of self-respect."[59] Rawls said, "We can define self-respect in two ways: first, self-respect includes a person's perception of his own value... secondly, self-respect means self-confidence in one's abilities."[60]

Therefore, the opposite of self-respect is the sense of inferiority: a sense of inferiority refers to the psychology and behavior of believing oneself incapable of making oneself respected, and the psychology and behavior of thinking oneself incapable of accomplishing something and creating some value; diffidence is the basic feature of the sense of inferiority. Fung Yulan says: "People without self-respect think that they are not capable enough to do something important, so they feel inferior, which can also be called inferiority."[61] Therefore, what makes diffidence the basic characteristic of sense of inferiority is not just that the person believes himself to be inferior but that he believes that he does not have the capability to change his inferior status. So, Adler, after elaborating on the inferiority complex, says:

> Now, we ought to define the inferiority complex: when a person is faced with a problem he cannot adequately deal with, he shows that there is no way that he can solve this problem; this is when inferiority complex emerges.[62]

Given this, thinking oneself inferior alone is not inferiority. Thinking that oneself is inferior but is capable of changing this inferior state is self-confidence and self-respect. Thinking oneself as inferior and incapable of changing one's inferior state is inferiority: inferiority is the psychology and behavior of thinking oneself incapable of changing one's inferior state. This explains why people with birth defects are most likely to feel inferior, as birth defects are something that makes oneself feels incompetent and something that one is incapable of changing.

Apparently, according to the nature of the giver of respect, self-respect can be divided into two categories: one kind of self-respect is respecting your self, which is called internal self-respect; the other kind is getting the respect of others, which is called external self-respect. Maslow also wrote about these types of self-respect needs:

> These needs can be divided into two sub-series: the first is the desire to pursue strength, achievement, wealth, power and ability, self-confidence in everything, independence, and freedom; the second is the desire to seek fame or prestige, status, reputation and honor, superiority, recognition, attention, importance, dignity or appreciation.[63]

Obviously, internal self-respect and external self-respect are opposite and complementary. If a person only seeks external self-respect and pursues other people's respect for himself, but does not seek internal self-respect or respect from his self, his self-respect remains no longer that but is transformed into vanity. On the contrary, if he only seeks internal self-respect without seeking external self-respect or other people's respect for himself, his self-respect degenerates into self-arrogance. Therefore, this consistency between internal self-respect and external self-respect is the basic condition for self-respect.

Self-respect can also be divided into three categories according to the nature of self-achievement. First, material self-respect is the self-respect of the material self. It is the self-respect of making oneself capable of achieving something in material life—such as making a fortune and living a long and healthy life—to win respect. Second, social self-respect is the self-respect of the social self, which is to make oneself capable of achieving something in social life—such as having a noble moral character and becoming high-ranking officials—to win respect. Third, spiritual self-respect is the self-respect of the spiritual self, which is the self-respect of making oneself capable of achieving something in one's spiritual life—such as writing books, establishing a school of learning, and becoming an esteemed master—to win respect. The value of spiritual life is higher than that of material life, while the value of social life lies between them. Therefore, material self-respect is low-level self-respect, social self-respect is middle-level self-respect, and spiritual self-respect is high-level self-respect. James makes an excellent comment on this point:

> The whole social self is higher than the whole material self. We ought to care more about honors, friends, promises, faith, justice than about our physical pleasures and wealth. The spiritual self is even more noble and precious that it cannot be measured by quantity or calculated in monetary terms. A man would rather abandon his friends, despise his reputation, lose his property, or even sacrifice his life than lose it.[64]

### *Values of self-respect*

Modern psychology believes that self-respect is the basic need and basic desire of humans, which is shared by all; it is merely that this kind of need and desire is stronger in some people but weaker in some others: "Everyone in the society (except a few psychos) has the need or desire to pursue stability, reliability, and being often highly-appreciated, the need or desire to pursue self-respect, self-esteem, and respect by other people."[65] If this need or desire of a person is satisfied, then he will feel the pleasure of self-pride; thus, self-pride is a psychological response to his sense of self-respect being satisfied. Otherwise, if this need or desire is not satisfied, he will feel ashamed; thus, shame is the psychological response to his sense of self-respect being frustrated.

Then, what kind of behavior will people display to satisfy their sense of self-respect? To satisfy one's sense of self-respect, one must undoubtedly be respected by one's self and others, and for that, one must do something praiseworthy and achieve something: a person with self-respect must be a person of self-improvement and self-reliance. This is satisfaction in qualitative terms. Quantitatively speaking, the degree of respect which a person receives from himself and others, and then the degree of the satisfaction of his self-respect needs, is obviously proportional to the magnitude of his achievements: the more he achieves, the more respect he receives, the fuller the satisfaction of his self-respect needs, the more proud and happy he will feel; the less he achieves, the less respect he receives, the less the satisfaction of his self-respect needs is, and the more ashamed and pained he will feel.

It can be thus concluded that both quantitatively and qualitatively speaking, self-respect is the motivating factor that drives people to self-improvement and self-reliance, achieve great things, and create values. Therefore, Liang Qichao says, "What has driven people to make significant contributions, to drive history to move forward, and leave glorious names in history is the strong sense of never abasing themselves, never abandoning themselves."[66] Rawls says,

> It's evident why self-respect is a basic good. Without self-respect, it seems that nothing is worth doing, or even as if something is of value to us, we would lack the will to fight for it. In that way, all desires and activities will become meaningless and useless, and we will be stuck in indifference and cynicism.[67]

In a word, self-respect is extremely beneficial to the existence and development of society and thus, conforms to the ultimate purpose and standard of morality. Therefore, it is a kind of extremely important good: the stronger the self-respect, the greater the good it brings; the weaker the self-respect is, the smaller the good it brings.

Conversely, inferiority is a basic bad. If a person feels inferior and thinks that he is incapable of doing something, then he will obviously give up doing that something and abandon himself to despair, for no one will strive for what he thinks is impossible? The conclusion by American psychologist Kaplan's ten-year survey of 9,300 seventh-graders is as follows: inferiority is directly proportional to deviant behaviors (dishonesty, joining criminal gangs, unlawful acts, drug abuse, alcoholism, provocative behaviors, and various psychological abnormalities). For example, among the students with low-level inferiority, middle-level inferiority, and high-level inferiority, the rate of students who admitted to petty theft after one year or more was 8%, 11%, and 14%, respectively; the rate of students who were expelled from school was 5%, 7% and 9%, respectively, and the rate of students who thought of suicide or attempted suicide was 9%, 14%, and 23%, respectively. However, Adler believes that inferiority is the driving force of human progress. He writes:

> Senses of inferiority themselves are not abnormal. They are rather the reason why human status has been enhanced. For example, the rise of science resulted from humans' realization of their own ignorance and their need to predict the future. It is the result of human endeavors to improve their overall situation, to further explore the universe, and to better control nature. In fact, in my opinion, all our human cultures are based on inferiority. If we imagine a bored alien visiting our planet, he must have the following impressions: 'These people, look at their various societies and institutions, their efforts for safety, their roofs for rain protection, their clothes for warmth, and their streets for convenient transportation. Obviously, they all feel that they are the weakest group of all the inhabitants on the planet!'[68]

Apparently, the mistake by Adler lies in his misunderstanding of the concept of inferiority: his misconception is that a sense of inferiority is just feeling inferior. The hardly recognized truth is that feeling inferior can be either inferiority or self-respect: feeling inferior and believing that oneself is incapable of changing one's inferiority is called a sense of inferiority, whereas feeling inferior but striving to improve oneself is self-respect. The sense of inferiority that Adler refers to coincides obviously with the latter, rather than with the former. Therefore, the driving force of human progress is not the sense of inferiority that human beings feel when they believe themselves to be incapable of improving their inferior state, but the sense of self-respect in human beings who feel inferior but strive to improve their inferior state.

## *Principles of self-respect*

To achieve respect by oneself and others, one must achieve something: achievement is the only way to attain self-respect. However, one's achievements may be true or false. True achievements, as is generally understood, can only be attained through the exertion of hard work. False achievements are attained mainly through deceiving oneself and belittling others. At first, belittling others can make one feel successful. For example, I don't have any achievement, but if others achieve even less, then, won't I appear to have an achievement? I may not be good-looking, but if others are even less good-looking than I am, won't I appear good-looking? In this way, although I don't have any achievement at all, I can feel it by belittling others. This is, of course, false achievement. Besides, self-deception can make me seem to have achievement. For example, I am cowardly. However, if I brag about myself and deceive others into letting them believe that I am a warrior, then, in the eyes of others, won't I appear to have the achievement of being courageous? I have no talent for poetry, but if I deceive myself into believing in the greatness of my poetry, then in my own eyes, won't I appear to have the achievements of being a great poet? These are obviously false achievements.

In this sense, there are, in fact, two ways for a person to achieve his self-respect. One is a good way: a person truly tries to achieve great things through self-improvement, self-reliance, and exerting himself doing hard work to achieve self-respect. The other is a bad way: a person makes false achievements through deceiving himself and belittling others, to achieve self-respect. It is easy for a person, in pursuing his self-respect, to deviate from the good road of self-reliance, self-improvement, and the exertion of hard work, and slip into the bad road of deceiving himself and belittling others. Therefore, Maslow says,

> We become increasingly aware of the dangers of the self-respect that is based on others' evaluations—not on our true talents, abilities, and competence of our work. The most stable and thus the healthiest

self-respect is based on the respect earned naturally from others, not on external fame, reputation and baseless flattery.[69]

So, in summary, self-respect ought not to be based on deceiving oneself and belittling others; it ought to be based on one's own true achievements. This is the moral principle of self-respect.

Self-respect is respect for oneself. However, pride is also self-respect while modesty is self-humility. Self-respect is closely related to modesty and pride. Therefore, after a close study of self-respect, it is necessary to study modesty as well.

## Modesty

### Definitions of modesty

What is modesty? *Zhouyi* (*Book of Changes*) uses humility or humbleness to explain modesty: "The humble and courteous gentleman cultivates his moral character with humility."[70] In this regard, Zhu Xi explains: "Most people hold themselves superior and others inferior. A person with modesty restrains one's own height and holds himself inferior to others; this is equality."[71] Apparently, the so-called modesty refers to the psychology and behavior of holding oneself lower and others higher; it is the psychology and behavior of holding oneself inferior and others superior and treating others as one's teacher. On the contrary, pride is the psychology and behavior of holding oneself higher than others; it is the psychology and behavior of respecting oneself, humbling others, and acting as a teacher to others. As Spinoza says, "Pride can be defined as 'the feeling that a person, out of self-love or self-complacency, thinks too highly of himself'";[72] "the word pride refers to the feeling of holding others too low."[73]

However, if you are truly superior to others, is thinking this way according to the truth still considered pride? Yes.

> If you make achievements, you show off your achievements to others; if you are superior to others, you think you are superior and show off your superiority to others. The kind of behavior is pride. If you make achievements, you feel that your achievements are not inferior to others'; if you are superior to others, you feel that you are not inferior to others. This kind of behavior is pride.[74]

On the contrary, is it modest to think that you are inferior to others when you are actually superior to others, that you make no achievements when you have made achievements? Yes. Fung Yulan says: "If I have made achievements, but I do not think I have made achievements, then this is the so-called modesty."[75] Nevertheless, modesty is not deception. If a man holds others superior and himself inferior only in his speech and manners, but in his heart, he holds himself superior to others, then he is not a truly modest person yet. "A truly modest person is he who thinks that he himself has made no achievement when he has made achievements and thinks so both in his words and attitudes toward others and in his heart."[76]

As modesty means holding oneself inferior and others superior, doesn't modesty mean inferiority? Modesty and inferiority are, indeed, very much alike, for both modest people and people with inferiority who hold themselves inferior. The two may seem the same on the surface, but deep down they are fundamentally different. Modesty is the psychology and behavior of holding oneself inferior and others superior and taking others as one's teachers while the feeling of inferiority is the psychology and behavior of believing oneself incapable of changing one's inferior state. In this sense, in terms of one's attitude toward oneself, the feeling of inferiority is based on diffidence that one cannot change one's inferiority; on the contrary, modesty is based on treating others as one's teachers and on self-confidence that one can change one's inferior state. In terms of one's attitude toward others, modesty means one must respect people because what makes modesty what it is lies in holding oneself inferior and others superior; on the contrary, people with a feeling of inferiority tend to hold others low and belittle them. Spinoza puts it very well:

> The pain of a person with feeling of inferiority comes from his own weakness, which emerges through comparison with the achievements or virtue of others, so if he devotes his mind to criticize the shortcomings of others, his pain will be reduced and he even feels happy. This explains the adage: "Friendship in need reduces pain indeed." On the contrary, the more he feels inferior to others, the more painful he will be. Therefore, no one is more likely to be jealous than those with feeling of inferiority, so they prefer to try to see others' behavior with a critical rather than a corrective eye.[77]

As pride means holding oneself superior and others inferior, doesn't that mean pride is self-respect? In literal terms, they are, indeed, very similar, but they are actually not. The self-respect (*zi-zun*) in pride means holding oneself "high" (whose Chinese equivalent is *gao* 高). In this sense, pride means holding oneself higher than others; pride is the psychology and behavior of holding oneself superior and others inferior and enjoying being a teacher to others. In self-respect (*zi-zun*), the word "respect" means being worthy of respect from others (whose Chinese equivalent is *jing* 敬): self-respect means the psychology and behavior of making oneself respect-worthy by making valuable contributions. In this sense, self-respect is fundamentally different from pride: on the one hand, self-respect is one's own internal interest and ambition, while pride is one's external relationship with others; on the other hand, pride is bound to hold others inferior to oneself, while self-respect tends to hold others in respect. Those who respect others will always be respected, so if we want others to respect us, we must respect others.

## The value of modesty

*The Shangshu* (*The Book of Documents*) says: "Pride hurts while humility benefits." This saying can be understood in two ways. On the one hand, it can be understood in terms of my attitude toward others. If I am modest, I will hold others superior and myself inferior; thus, I will be able to take others as my teachers and learn from them.

> Any person must have some kind of good, so, if I can learn from the good of one hundred people, I will become a sage; any person must have some kind of opinion, so, if I can listen to the opinions of one hundred people, I will able to make decisions on major issues.[78]

In this way, I will continue to make progress. On the contrary, if I am proud, I will humble others and hold myself superior, and feel that others are inferior to me; I will be so self-complacent that I won't be able to learn from others. In this way, I will regress instead of making any progress. Therefore, Yang Jue says,

> If you think yourself good enough, then you will lose the ambition to pursue harder and further; you will be complacent with the one good you have had and allow no other good to influence you, eventually ending up in destruction or tragedy.[79]

On the other hand, it can be understood in terms of the attitude of others towards me. If I am modest, humble, and hold others superior, I will satisfy the self-respect of others and arouse their warmth; in return, others will recognize my strengths and help me overcome my weaknesses so that I can succeed. Therefore, Lao Zi says,

> If you don't boast about your own merits, then your merits will become even more conspicuous; if you are not self-righteous, your sense of right and wrong will become more noticed; if you do not brag about your achievements, your achievements will be granted more credit; if you do not hold yourself as virtuous and talented, you will earn respect from others.[80]

On the contrary, if I am proud and hold myself superior and others inferior, I will hurt others' self-respect and arouse jealousy in them; in return, instead of acknowledging my strength and helping me, they would oppose me and do me harm. Just imagine this: from ancient times to the present, among the many people who are proud of their merits, talents, and wealth who is the one who ends up well in his life? As Laozi says,

> He who stands on tiptoe to make himself look taller cannot stand for long; he who strides cannot walk for long; he who boasts about his

merits fails to make his merits conspicuous; he who thinks himself is always right fails to make his sense of right and wrong noticeable; he who brags about his achievements fails to get credit for his achievements; he who thinks highly of himself fails to win respect from others.[81]

It can thus be concluded that pride is extremely harmful to oneself and others, and violates the ultimate moral standard of "increasing the quantum of interests of everyone," so it is an extremely important bad. Wang Yangming even says, "Pride is a serious bad in life... pride is actually the greatest bad."[82] On the contrary, modesty is extremely beneficial to oneself and others and meets the ultimate standard of morality; it is, thus, a kind of extremely important good. "He who does not brag about his goodness earns respect from others."[83] *The Book of Changes* even says, "Modesty is the foundation of virtue."[84]

> The way of the heaven is that it takes away from the full to fill up the empty; the way of the earth is that it directs the overflow from the full toward the empty; the nature of gods and ghosts is to harm the proud so as to bless the humble; the way of humanity is to detest pride and favor humility. Humility brings respect and fame; humility is something a gentleman should abide by and should never violate his whole life.[85]

### *Cultivation of modesty*

Since modesty is the greatest good and pride is the greatest bad, how can one acquire the moral character of modesty and get rid of pride? The acquisition of this moral character proves rather difficult. Franklin even says,

> Of all the natural desires of man, perhaps the most difficult to overcome and control is pride. No matter how we try to hide it, suppress it, channel it, or destroy it, it still exists in the end and always comes out to show itself. Many readers could see its multifarious manifestations in an autobiography. Although I am confident that I have completely overcome my pride, I still can't help being proud of my modesty.[86]

The particular difficulty is in this: how can a person who is far superior to others feel sincerely inferior to them and be humble? Can self-deception work? Of course, not. In fact, there are two ways to make people—no matter how great they are—attain modesty.

One way is called "measuring others' strengths against one's own weaknesses." Sometimes a foot may prove short while an inch may prove too long. No matter how great you are, you will have some shortcomings and weaknesses; no matter how insignificant others are, they will have advantages and strengths. Therefore, Confucius says, "When three people walk together, among them there must be one person who can be my teacher."

In this way, if a great man can measure others' strengths by his own shortcomings, won't he sincerely feel inferior to others and feel modest? Gu Yanwu, a great scholar, is a model of modesty. He says,

> In the field of astronomy, I am not as good as Wang Yinxu; in terms of wise reading and keen observation, I am not as good as Yang Xuechen; I am not as versed as Zhang Jiruo in the three rituals; I am not as good as Li Zhongfu at working industriously without the guidance of a teacher; I am not as good as Wu Zhiyi in terms of extensive knowledge and strong memory; in terms of elegant writing, I am not as good as Zhu Xibi; in terms of tireless learning and devotion to friends, I am not as good as Wang Shanshi; I am not as good as Zhang Lichen in terms of expertise in the language.[87]

The other way is called "comparing oneself with the stronger." There is always a higher sky beyond the sky; there is always someone better than you. Therefore, everyone must have something inferior to others and something superior to others. In this way, if we are really better than others, we are simply comparing ourselves with those who are weaker than us; if we compare ourselves with people who are better than us, won't we sincerely feel inferior and thus modest? The ancients said, "If we aim for a high-level goal, we might get a mid-level result; if we aim for a mid-level goal, we might get a low-level result." If we aim at ideal virtues, then we might become as virtuous as Yan Hui; if we aim at being as virtuous as Yan Hui, then we might not be as virtuous as Yan Hui. Therefore, wise people always aim high and compare themselves with the stronger, so he will feel himself to be not good enough, inferior to others, and thus attain the virtue of modesty.[88]

It can be concluded that modesty is not self-depreciation or self-deception, but the result of "comparing oneself with the stronger" and "measuring others' strengths by one's own shortcomings." Modesty is holding oneself inferior to others, respecting others, and learning from others, so that one can achieve great things and achieve self-respect. So, what is the basic content of this kind of achievement and self-respect? It's wisdom. Therefore, after our close study of self-respect and modesty, we should study wisdom.

## Wisdom

### *The concept of wisdom*

There is no doubt that wisdom is a human faculty. The question is, what kind of human faculty is it? All human faculties display either mental or cerebral activities or physical or bodily activities; wisdom is of course the former kind of faculty. The so-called mental or cerebral ability is obviously the faculty of mental activity, psychological activity, thinking activity, and consciousness activity. These four terms are the same concept. Psychology, as we all know, is also divided into cognition, emotion, and will. Is wisdom the faculty of will? No. We cannot say that strong willpower is wisdom and weak will power is ignorance, as there is no wise or unwise will power. Is wisdom an emotional faculty? No. We can't say that a rich and sensitive emotional ability is wisdom and a poor and dull emotional ability is ignorance, as there is no wise or unwise emotional ability.

Therefore, wisdom can only be a cognitive ability, as only cognitive ability can distinguish wisdom from ignorance. So Mencius says, "The ability to distinguish right from wrong and advantage from disadvantage is wisdom."[89] Ban Gu says, "The wise man is he who perceives, he who develops his own perception of things around him without being confused by the illusions of things, he who can perceive the development of things from one small clue."[90] Zhang Dainian says, "Wisdom is the cognition of truth."[91] Fukuzawa Yukichi says, "Wisdom means the ability to think, analyze, and understand things."[92] According to *Cihai Dictionary* and *The Great Chinese Dictionary*, "wisdom is the ability to recognize, distinguish, judge, process, and invent and create things."

> *Zhi-hui* (智慧; the Chinese word for wisdom) is the Chinese equivalent for the term "prajnā" in Sanskrit, which means the highest wisdom. Buddhism considers wisdom as the ability to transcend the secular and illusory knowledge and grasp the truth.

So, what kind of cognitive ability is wisdom? To quote Malitan, "Wisdom reaches the level of perfection."[93] Piaget also believes that "wisdom is only an appellation for a species, which is used to signify the higher form of cognitive structure or balance"; "in this sense, wisdom is not only an adaptation, but also a perfection of continual expansion of the process of adaptation."[94] That is to say, wisdom is a relatively perfect cognitive ability, and, in more popular terms, a relatively perfect faculty of mental and thinking activity.

Wisdom is a relatively perfect cognitive faculty. On the one hand, wisdom is always time-bound and is always the wisdom of people belonging to certain times and places, so wisdom is relative only to certain times and places, but not to all times and places. Shipbuilding and netting are wisdom only for people in ancient times, but far from wisdom for modern people. Ancient sages have wisdom, which is wisdom relative only to ancient times, but not modern times. Fukuzawa Yukichi even says, "In terms of wisdom alone, ancient sages have wisdom that is no better than today's three-year-olds."[95]

On the other hand, it is because a person's wisdom and knowledge are always limited to certain areas, they cannot be complete. No one can have complete wisdom, but only wisdom in certain aspects, as complete wisdom is something that the entire humanity is incapable of. Therefore, the claim that a person has wisdom is true only when this wisdom is relative to his mental ability in certain areas, but not when wisdom is relative to all mental abilities. Han Xin has sufficient wisdom in military affairs, but no wisdom in politics. Zhuge Liang has wisdom both in military and political affairs, but no wisdom in preserving health.

Everyone's wisdom is relative and incomplete, so there are many kinds of wisdom, such as wisdom in relationships, wisdom in academics, wisdom in governing the country and the world, wisdom in farming the land, wisdom in building furniture, even wisdom in dating and attracting the opposite sex. In a few words, as long as one's cognitive ability achieves relative perfection in one aspect, we can consider it as wisdom.

It is widely acknowledged that Zhuge Liang has wisdom while Ma Su does not. In fact, Ma Su had no creative wisdom in the practical application of military strategies and tactics, but had wisdom in memorizing them, otherwise, Zhuge Liang would not often discuss military tactics with him. As far as the nature of the subjective psychological function of wisdom is concerned, there are five main types: wisdom in observation, that is, relatively perfect observation ability; wisdom in memory, that is, relatively perfect memory ability; wisdom in thinking, that is, relatively perfect thinking ability; wisdom in imagination, that is, relatively perfect imaginative ability; and fifth, creative wisdom, that is, relatively perfect creative ability.

According to *The Art of Worldly Wisdom* (*The Oráculo Manual*), sinners and wicked people have no wisdom.[96] In fact, sinners lack only moral wisdom, but they may have other types of wisdom, such as the creative wisdom of inventing some kind of instrument and so on. Based on the nature of the objective psychological content of wisdom, we can divide wisdom into moral wisdom and non-moral wisdom. Moral wisdom is the wisdom engaged in activities related to morality, that is, the relatively perfect cognitive ability of engaging in activities concerning interests of self and others; non-moral wisdom is the wisdom engaged in activities unrelated to morality, that is, the relatively perfect cognitive ability of engaging in activities unconcerned with interests of self and others. Mencius, for example, is full of moral wisdom because he has uttered wise maxims on how to deal with activities concerning interests of self and others: "*Ren* (Benevolence) is a gift from heaven and the most stable residence in the world; thus, it is unwise not to choose to dwell in benevolence when there is no hindrance."[97] On the contrary, Newton has non-moral wisdom, because Newton discovered the "law of gravity," which has nothing to do with activities concerning interests of self and others.

### Laws of wisdom

As wisdom belongs to the cognitive ability, moral wisdom belongs to the cognitive ability of morality, which is also a part of moral character, or more precisely, the guiding factor of moral character. "Virtue is the commander of wisdom."[98] Since moral wisdom is a part and a factor of moral character, it is thus obvious that the more moral wisdom a person has, the higher-level his moral character will be; the less moral wisdom he has, the lower-level his moral character will be. However, in fact, we can see that those with higher-level moral wisdom may have lower-level moral character, while those with higher-level moral character may have lower-level moral wisdom. Why is it so?

The reason is that although moral wisdom is a part and a factor of moral character, it is the guiding factor of moral character, but not the motive force factor of moral character, so it is not the determining factor of moral character. The motive force factor and determining factor of moral character is moral sentiment. The moral sentiment is the determining factor of moral character, so those with high-level moral sentiment will have high-level moral character. Moral wisdom is not the determining factor of moral character, so it is possible that those with high-level moral wisdom may have low-level moral character while those with high-level moral character may have low-level moral wisdom.

Thus, it can be concluded that the reason why a person with high moral wisdom has low-level moral character is not that he has high moral wisdom, but those other aspects of his moral character are low-level, such as his moral sentiment. On the contrary, the reason why a person with low-level moral wisdom has high-level moral character is not that he has low moral wisdom, but those other aspects of his moral character are high-level, such as his moral sentiment. When people's moral sentiments are at the same high-level as all other aspects of their moral character, then there is no doubt that those with high-level moral wisdom are bound to have high-level moral character, and those with high-level moral character are bound to have high-level moral wisdom.

Given this, as far as their relationship is concerned, moral wisdom and moral character are completely proportional to each other: the higher-level one's moral wisdom is, the higher-level one's moral character will be, the more beneficial actions and fewer harmful actions they will have; the lower-level one's moral wisdom is, the lower-level one's moral character will be, the fewer beneficial actions and the more harmful actions they will have. In short, moral wisdom is directly proportional to beneficial actions and inversely proportional to harmful actions. This is the law of moral wisdom.

Nevertheless, if a person has only moral wisdom, he may have good motives for wanting to benefit others, but may not be able to produce good results that benefit others. To produce good results that benefit others, he must also have non-moral wisdom. In ancient times when people used primitive methods of cultivation, if a person, with noble moral character and rich moral wisdom, sees a lot of fish in a river, he would have the good motive to catch the fish for others, however, if he did not have the non-moral wisdom of having a good netting, then he would not be able to produce the good result of catching the fish for others. Therefore, non-moral wisdom is a good means, method, and way to benefit people: the higher-level one's non-moral wisdom is, the more likely it is for him to benefit people; the lower-level the non-moral wisdom is, the less likely it is for him to benefit people.

However, if a person has only non-moral wisdom but no moral wisdom, the higher-level his non-moral wisdom is, the more beneficial he will be to others, but he may be equally harmful to some others. Numerous people in China and other countries, from ancient times till today, such as Qin Hui, Hitler, Mussolini, Yan Song, and Cai Jing, have done tremendous harm to their countries and their people because they had only non-moral wisdom, not moral wisdom. As Feuerbach says, "The greater a man is, the more beneficial he is to others, and of course the more harmful he is to others as well."[99]

Thus, the higher-level a person's non-moral wisdom, the more beneficial or harmful he will be to others; the lower-level a person's non-moral wisdom, the less beneficial or harmful he will be to others. Thus, non-moral wisdom may be in direct proportion to both beneficial behavior and harmful behavior. This is the law of non-moral wisdom.

A synthesis of both the law of moral wisdom and the law of non-moral wisdom reveals the following: a person should not have only moral wisdom, for, then he has only the motivation to benefit others but knows nothing about how to go about it; a person should not have only non-moral wisdom, because then he may benefit others and may also harm others; a person ought to have both moral wisdom and non-moral wisdom so that he will not harm others but only benefit others, and he will not only have good motivation for benefiting others, but also produce good results that benefit others. Therefore, wisdom is both an important social, external moral norm and a personal, internal moral quality. Ancient Greece regarded wisdom as one of the four main virtues, namely, wisdom, courage, continence, and justice. In the Chinese traditional morality, wisdom is regarded as the first of the three universal virtues and one of the five constant virtues: "Wisdom, benevolence, and courage are three universal virtues";[100] "the five constant virtues are benevolence, righteousness, courtesy, wisdom, and faith."[101] Then, how can one acquire wisdom?

### Acquisition of wisdom

He who wants to acquire wisdom, according to the ancients, must possess two conditions: talent and learning. The so-called talent is a gift inherited by birth while learning means acquisition through effort one makes after birth, a response activity through which organisms consciously acquire and develop their unique personality. Apparently, a person's talent is directly proportional to the amount of his wisdom: the higher-level his talent, the easier it is for him to acquire wisdom, and the greater the wisdom he will attain; the lower-level his talent, the more difficult it is for him to acquire wisdom, the lesser will be the wisdom he will attain; it is unlikely for a person with intelligence lower than average people, or a mentally challenged person to acquire wisdom.

Have you ever seen a person with low intelligence acquiring wisdom and becoming a wise person? Obviously, talent above what the average person has is a necessary condition for the acquisition of wisdom. This is because psychological tests show that persons who are mentally challenged and deficient, and whose intelligence is below average, have minimal intellectual plasticity. If they live in a deprived environment, their intelligence will be extremely low, but even if they live in a rich and favorable environment, their IQ can be only as high as 70 or 80. On the contrary, the intellectual plasticity of people with middle-level or high-level talents is tremendous. If they live in a deprived environment, their IQ could be between 50 and 60, but if they live in a rich and favorable environment, their IQ can reach above 180.[102]

It can be concluded that if a person has a talent that is above average, then whether he can acquire wisdom depends entirely on his learning. Evidently, the degree of one's efforts in learning is directly proportional to the amount of his wisdom: the harder one studies, the easier it is for him to acquire wisdom and the greater the wisdom he acquires; the less hard one studies, the more difficult it is for him to acquire wisdom, and the lesser the wisdom he acquires; if the effort one makes in learning is below a certain degree, he, though talented, is unlikely to acquire wisdom. Fang Zhongyong of the Song Dynasty is a case in point. At the age of five, he was able to write poems. His poetic talent was very high, but he never studied hard. As a result, he did not acquire the poet's wisdom and "ended up an average Joe." Therefore, Confucius says, "Learning moves one closer to wisdom."[103] A certain degree of hard learning is a necessary condition for acquiring wisdom.

It can be concluded that wisdom cannot be acquired only by talent or only by learning, but that wisdom is the child of their marriage: wisdom = talent + learning. However, the role of talent and learning in the acquisition of wisdom varies according to different types of wisdom. For the acquisition of moral wisdom, learning is obviously more important than talent: in terms of the total amount of wisdom acquired, acquisition through learning accounts for 70% and acquisition through talent accounts for 30%. Conversely, for the acquisition of non-moral wisdom, talent is more important than learning: in terms of the total amount of wisdom acquired, wisdom acquired through talent accounts for 70% and wisdom acquired through learning account for 30%. On this point, Zeng Guofan said some time ago,

> ancient saints, sages, and famous Confucian scholars have been universally glorified for their literary merits and achievements. However, in terms of literary achievements, talents account for 70% and learning no more than 30%; in terms of cultivation of moral character, effort to learn plays an important role and may alone take up 70%.[104]

Wisdom is a relatively perfect cognitive ability. Its significance and value lie entirely in controlling and realizing needs, desires, and emotions: if desires and emotions are governed by wisdom and reason, it is continence; otherwise, it is indulgence or incontinence. So, how can a person's wisdom and reason control his emotions? This is the object of the research on the moral rule of "continence."

256  *The system of moral rules*

## Continence

### *The concept of continence*

In *Mencius* there is a famous saying that everyone has "a big body" and "a small body." "The big body" is the heart and the reason; "the small body" refers to ears, eyes, and other senses, and is the emotion. If a person's behavior obeys reason, then it is moral and good and is, thus, the behavior of a gentleman. If a person's behavior obeys emotion, it is immoral and bad and is, thus, the behavior of an ordinary person. "Gongduzi asked, 'We are all human beings, but why some are gentlemen while some are ordinary people?' Mencius replied, 'He who obeys the big body is a gentleman; he who obeys the small body is an ordinary person.'"[105] So what kind of good is the act of subordinating emotion to reason? The ancient Greek philosopher answered, "continence and self-restraint."

First of all, Plato divides the human soul into two parts, reason and passion:

> Then we may fairly assume that they are two, and that they differ from one another; the one with which a man reasons, we may call the rational principle of the soul; the other, with which he loves, and hungers, and thirsts, and feels the flutterings of any other desire, may be termed as the irrational or appetitive.[106]

Second, Plato also believes that the rational part is the better part, while the passion is the worse part; if a person subordinates the worse part to the better part, then he has the virtue of continence and self-restraint: "The meaning, I believe, is that there is a better and there is also a worse principle; and when the better has the worse under control, and then a man is said to be master of himself."[107]

> Would you not say that he is temperate who has these same elements in friendly harmony, in whom the one ruling principle of reason, and the two subject ones of spirit and desire, are equally agreed that reason ought to rule, and do not rebel?[108]

Finally, Aristotle further points out that the fundamental characteristic of temperance and reason-governed behaviors is refraining from doing improper things knowingly; the fundamental characteristic of incontinence and passion-ruled behavior is doing improper things knowingly. "A man of Imperfect Self-Control does things at the instigation of his passions, knowing them to be wrong, while the man of Self-Control, knowing his lusts to be wrong, refuses, by the influence of reason, to follow their suggestions."[109]

Given this, human behaviors can be divided into two types: continence and indulgence. Continence is characterized by the rule of reason over emotion. When the person is governed by reason, he can do what he knows he ought to do and refrain from doing things he knows he ought not to do. On the contrary, the characteristic of indulgence is that emotion dominates reason. When a person is dominated by emotion, he does what he knows he ought not to do and does not do what he ought to do. For example, person A and person B, who have just recovered from hepatitis, are aware that drinking is harmful. A is governed by reason and does not do what he knows he ought not to do, so he stops drinking. B is dominated by passion and does things that he knows he should not do, so he does not stop drinking. In this case, A is a person of continence and B is a person of indulgence. Therefore, we can conclude that continence, that is, self-restraint is the behavior of a person who is governed by reason and who refrains from doing things that he knows he ought not to do. On the contrary, indulgence, that is, lack of continence or self-restraint, is the behavior of a person who is governed by emotion and does things he knows he ought not to do.

Continence is the behavior of reason dominating, controlling, and governing emotion, which means that the object of continence is emotion. Therefore, Cai Yuanpei said, "Self-restraint means moderation of emotion."[110] Passion (*qing yu* 情欲) is a combination of two words, also two things: desire (*yu* 欲) and emotion (*qing* 情). Desire includes material desire, such as the desire for wealth; social desire, such as the desire to be an official and achieve prestige; and spiritual desire, such as the desire to write books and establish schools of learning. Chinese traditional culture categorizes desires into six desires: eyes, ears, nose, tongue, body, and mind. Emotion is the feeling caused by the satisfaction of desires, such as bitterness and joy, love and hatred, etc. Chinese traditional culture categorizes emotions into seven emotions: joy, anger, melancholy, anxiety, sadness, fear, and fright.

In this sense, continence can be divided into two types: continence of desire and continence of emotion. Continence of desire is the act of reason governing desire. In other words, it means that in any case, one desires what he ought to desire and desires not what he ought not to desire. Of course, whether he ought to desire something or not depends entirely on his reason. This is what we call continence of desire. Continence of emotion is the act of reason governing emotion. In other words, in any case, one gets angry when he ought to be angry and shows no anger when he ought not to be angry, or one feels happy when he ought to feel happy and shows no joy when he ought not to show joy. In this way, the expression of one's anger and joy is tempered; this is what we call continence of emotion. Apparently, the key to continence is continence of desire, because emotion is nothing but the psychological response to the satisfaction or dissatisfaction of one's desire. The relationship between desire and emotion can be compared to a river: desire is the source while emotion is the flow. However, the fundamental question is, why should we practice continence—continence of desire and continence of emotion? Why should we let reason govern desire and emotion, but not vice versa? This question is a question concerning the value of continence.

258  *The system of moral rules*

### *The value of continence*

Fung Yulan once said, "Reason holds no power while passion has no eyes."[111] The reverse of this statement is also true: reason has eyes while passion holds power. This means that reason is the guide of action while passion is the motive force of action. That is to say, the purpose of every person's behavior is to satisfy his desire: material desire, spiritual desire, egoistic desire, or altruistic desire. The whole function of reason is to tell people how to behave in order to achieve their goals and satisfy their desires. So, as Hume says, "Reason is, and ought only to be the slave of passions and can never pretend to any other office than to serve and obey them."[112]

Since reason is the means to realize passions, it then seems that these two ought to be completely consistent rather than in conflict with each other. In fact, very often each person's reason and passion conflict with each together, however. This is because each person's passions are diverse and extremely complex. These passions can be classified into two categories according to the nature of interests concerning others and self. One kind of passion is beneficial to others and oneself and thus has a positive value, and is ought-to-be and rational; thus, it is called "rational passion," such as the desire for health, love for life, kindness, generosity, gratitude, and sympathy. The other kind of passion is harmful to others and oneself, and thus has a negative value, is ought-not-to-be and irrational, so it is called "irrational passion," such as indulgence in alcohol and sex, greed, stinginess, impetuosity, irritability, jealousy, and viciousness. Nonetheless, rational passions and irrational passions are not different passions; they are often of the same kind. They are nothing but fundamental desires, such as the desire for food, sex, fame, and material wealth, as well as basic emotions such as pleasure, anger, sadness, and joy. When these desires and emotions are moderate and opportune, then they are called rational passions; when these desires and emotions are excessive or inopportune, they are called irrational passions.

Thus, if a person's passion is rational, then reason and passion are entirely consistent; thus, obedience to reason is the same as obedience to desire, so there is no such thing as continence or indulgence. Continence and indulgence obviously exist only when a person has irrational passions. In this situation, reason and passion battle with each other: when passions submit to reason, then what we get is continence and suppression of passions; when reason submits to passions, we go against reason and indulge our passions. Given this, continence does not mean that all passions are tempered or suppressed but that only irrational passions, which are harmful to others and oneself, are tempered and suppressed. Conversely, indulgence does not mean that reason submits to all passions, but that reason submits only to irrational passions, which are harmful to others and oneself.

In this way, continence keeps people from doing things that they know they ought not to do, to avoid harming themselves and others; thus, continence conforms entirely to the ultimate moral standard of "increasing the

*The system of moral rules* 259

quantum of interests of everyone," and is thus a very important good. On the contrary, indulgence makes people do what they know they ought not to do and consequently harm themselves and others; indulgence ultimately does not meet the ultimate moral standard and thus is a very important bad. This explains why continence was one of the four main virtues of Greece: justice, courage, wisdom, and continence. In recalling Socrates, Xenophon said, "He used his words to persuade his men that continence was more important than anything else."[113] Spinoza also says, "The real virtue is to live purely under the guidance of reason."[114] Even Paulsen says: "The chief purpose of all moral culture is to fashion the rational will so that it may become the regulative principle of the entire sphere of conduct."[115] As continence is such an important virtue, then, how exactly should one acquire this virtue?

## *Principles of continence*

Since continence is to suppress irrational passions and obey rational passions, it is obvious that to achieve continence, we must, first of all, correctly understand our various passions and know which ones are rational and which ones are irrational. Otherwise, if reason makes mistakes and misreads rational passions as irrational passions or vice versa, then continence becomes something other than a virtue: the rational passions are suppressed while irrational passions are indulged. Therefore, to achieve continence, we, above all, ought to have a correct understanding of the value of passions: proper reasoning is the primary principle of continence. On this principle, Spinoza made an interesting comment a long time ago: "The more incorrect ideas we have in the mind, the more we are enslaved by passions; on the contrary, the more correct ideas we have in the mind, the more freedom we have."[116] "Therefore, we ought to work extremely hard to acquire knowledge as clear and unique as possible about various kinds of emotions."[117] "There is no more effective way to rectify our emotions than to have the right cognition about them."[118]

Nevertheless, exactly as Feuerbach says, the power of reason in an individual is extremely limited and always unreliable, while the same power in the entire humanity is infinite and reliable. Therefore, to make one's reason correct and reliable, the individual must inherit the legacy of the reason of the humanity. As is generally known, humanity's legacy of understanding the benefits and harms of passions, the rationality and irrationality of passions is mainly human ethics and legal thoughts, which are condensed into moral and legal norms. Hence the conclusion: reason is the primary principle of continence; the moral laws are the specific standards of continence. This point was made by Xunzi long time ago: "Li, namely rites, is the standard of continence." He wrote as follows:

> Humans are born with desires, so when desires are not met, we cannot give up pursuing these desires. When our pursuit of these desires goes

wild with no limit at all, then there will be contentions, which eventually lead to chaos and poverty. The late King detested such chaos, so he designed rites to demarcate desires so that people's desires can be satisfied and people's needs can be met.[119]

If the reason of a person is correct and his knowledge of his own passions is correct, can he suppress his irrational passions and attain the state of continence? For instance, can an alcoholic suppress his addictive passion for alcohol and stop drinking as long as he understands correctly that alcoholism is harmful? Apparently, he can't yet. On this point, Spinoza once quoted Arvid's poems and exclaimed: "Though I know what the reasonable path is and know the good of reason in my heart, I still choose the evil and do the evil thing, as if I have no self-defense before the evil."[120] However, why can't correct knowledge of passions restrain our desire? Liang Qichao answers, "Reason can only let people know what to do, how to do something, but cannot drive people to do it; only emotions can make people do things."[121] Reason itself has no power to suppress passion, but passion can only be suppressed by passion. This truth is well articulated by Spinoza: "reason cannot control emotion";[122] "one emotion can be controlled or eliminated only through another stronger emotion which is contrary to it."[123] That is to say, irrational passion can only be controlled or eliminated by a stronger rational passion.

Therefore, after a person has the right reason and knows what kind of passion is rational and what kind of passion is irrational, if he wants to control and restrain irrational passion, he must cultivate the rational passion revealed by reason. He can cultivate rational passions through repeated actions, which make them emerge from nothing, develop from weak to strong, from non-habitual to habitual. The time when rational passions become habitual or when rational passions are stronger than irrational passions is the time when irrational passions are restrained and eliminated, and thus the virtue of continence achieved. For example, if a person is addicted to playing cards and does not like reading, then just knowing that playing cards is harmful and reading is beneficial will not make him start reading and stop playing cards. How can he then achieve it? At first, he must make an attempt to read again and again, gradually cultivate the desire to read and continue to grow this desire. When the desire to read is stronger than the desire to play cards, he will read instead of playing cards. So, Locke says:

> Good things or greater good things, even if they are recognized and acknowledged, do not give us the will to pursue them; unless our desire for good things reaches a certain level, we will feel painful and uneasy without these good things.[124]

It can be concluded that a correct understanding of passion is indeed the primary principle of continence and that the cultivation of rational passion is the fundamental principle of continence. These principles demonstrate that continence is not so much reduction of passion as an increase of passion; it is more liberation than repression. The more virtuous a man is, the more rational passion he has, the less his irrational passion is, the less restraint and the more liberty he feels; on the contrary, the more he indulges in his passions, the more his irrational passion is, the less his rational passion is, the more restraint and the less liberty he feels. When one's virtue of continence reaches perfection, all of one's passions are rational, and one will be completely free from repression. It is, undoubtedly, very difficult to reach such a state. Confucius said that he did not reach this state until he was 70 years old:

> I am determined to learn at the age of 15; at the age of 30 I begin to have a clear goal to develop expertise in one area; at the age of 40 I am very sure about my life goal; at the age of 50 I begin to accept my destiny; at the age of 60 I can listen to criticism without getting angry; at the age of 70 I can follow my heart and do whatever I desire to do without violating norms.[125]

This holds true for everyone; as long as he follows these principles of continence, he will gradually approach this perfect state.

Continence is the rule of wisdom and reason over desire and emotion. Perhaps the most important continence in life is the rule of wisdom over courage. If a man wants to achieve great things, whether he pursues excellence in academics, career, or cultivation of virtues, he is bound to encounter hardships, sufferings, harms, and dangers in his life; therefore, if he lacks courage, he will never succeed. Hence, after wisdom and continence, we should study courage.

## Courage

### Definition of courage

Clearly, defining courage is no easy feat. But courage, as we all know, is related to things to be afraid of. Plato says, "Courage is a kind of salvation—the never-failing salvation of the opinions which law and education have prescribed concerning dangers."[126] Aristotle says, "He then may be most properly denominated Brave who is fearless in respect of objects inspiring boldness or fear."[127] The so-called objects inspiring fear are nothing but danger, injury, pain, hardship, loneliness, humiliation, poverty, disease, death, and so on. As Aristotle explains, "The objects of our fears are obviously things fearful or, in a general way of statement, evils.... Of course, we fear evils of all kinds: disgrace, for instance, poverty, disease, desolateness, and death."[128]

262  *The system of moral rules*

As shown, courage is a kind of psychological attitude and behavioral expression in response to fearful things. This kind of psychological attitude and behavioral expression is obviously this: no fearing anything. Therefore, Confucius says, "The brave fear nothing."[129] Aristotle says, "Brave who is fearless in respect of honorable death and such sudden emergencies as threaten death."[130] Sidgwick says, "For the sake of our understanding, it seems that the word 'courage' is appropriate to express the quality of not flinching in the face of any danger."[131] "Courage is the ability to resist painful, dangerous and terrible impressions by means of a rational will."[132] Cai Yuanpei says, "Courage is what can make people endure hardship."[133] In a word, courage is the behavior of not fearing terrible things; cowardice is the behavior of fearing terrible things.

### *Classification of courage*

According to *Master Zuo's Spring and Autumn Annals*, "Doing the righteous thing is courage";[134] "To die of unjust deeds is not courage."[135] Not doing the just thing and dying for unjust things are, in fact, also courage; it is only that they are not righteous courage but un-righteous courage. What is righteous courage? Cai Yuanpei answers, "To be brave in accordance with righteousness is called righteous courage."[136] Righteous courage means courage that conforms to righteousness, courage that conforms to the moral principles, and courage that benefits others and society, such as the courage of the hero Dong Cunrui, who carried the explosive and charged at the enemy, the courage of Huang Jiguang, who blocked the muzzle of enemy machine guns with his own body, or the courage of Liu Yingjun, who sacrificed his life to save children from being harmed by a frightened horse. Xunzi calls this kind of courage "the courage of gentlemen." He says, "Righteousness lies not in power or interests; people with righteousness focus on the benefits of the whole country and insist on justice until death. This is the courage of gentlemen."[137] Un-righteous courage is the courage that violates the moral principles, the courage that harms society and others, such as the courage of robbers who kill people and rob them of their goods in the dark, the courage of street hooligans who bravely throw themselves into a street fight. Xunzi calls this kind of courage "the courage of dogs and pigs":

> The courage of fighting for food with no sense of shame, no sense of what is right and wrong, no fear of death or injury, no fear of the power of the masses, but with resentful eyes cast only on food is the courage of dogs and pigs.[138]

The classification of courage into righteous courage and un-righteous courage is based on whether courage conforms to the nature of morality or not. Courage can also be divided into heroic courage and recklessness on the basis of whether courage conforms to the nature of wisdom or not. Aristotle believes that courage is a kind of mean state, above which is recklessness and below is cowardice:

> The coward, the rash, and the Brave man have exactly the same object-matter, but stand differently related to it: the two first-mentioned respectively exceed and are deficient, and the last is in a mean state and as he ought to be.[139]

Indeed, all three are related to the same object, that is, the fearful thing: courage means no fearing, and cowardice is not up to the degree of "no fearing" or is less than courage. But is recklessness an excess of no fearing? Is it a transition to courage? Is it courage that goes too far? Absolutely not.

Recklessness has nothing to do with the degree of courage, but with whether courage contains wisdom. Recklessness is unwise courage; it is courage against wisdom and not guided by wisdom; it is courage that brings losses than gains. For example, the courage of fighting with tigers empty-handed or wading across rivers with barefoot, the courage of rising rashly to a conflict without considering the consequences, the courage of the newborn calf ignorant of and thus not afraid of the tiger's power, etc. are all reckless; this recklessness is obviously not because it has excessive courage, but because it lacks wisdom or the guidance of the wisdom. The courage contrary to recklessness can be called heroic courage: "It is wisdom that distinguishes heroic courage… If you don't have the wisdom of a wise man, a brave man can't make achievements."[140] In this sense, heroic courage is the courage of wisdom, the courage in accordance with wisdom and under its guidance, the courage of "gaining" more than "losing." From this point of view, not only Zhuge Liang's empty-city stratagem for breaking the siege and Guan Yu's going single-handed to meet with his enemy are examples of heroic courage, but also Dong Cunrui carrying the explosive to charge at the enemy and Huang Jiguang's blocking the muzzle of the enemy's machine gun. These are all examples of heroic courage because they sacrificed themselves to save other human beings: more gains than losses.

### The value of courage

From the definition and classification of courage, we can understand why Confucians put courage on par with wisdom and benevolence and called them the three universal virtues: "Wisdom, benevolence, and courage are the three universal virtues of the world."[141] The courage that deviates from morality and wisdom is recklessness and un-righteous courage, which are harmful to society and others as well as to oneself and have a negative moral value; they are, therefore, ought-not-to-be, immoral, and bad. Only when courage is aligned with morality and wisdom can it be righteous courage and heroic courage, which are beneficial to society and others, as well as to oneself and have positive moral value, so they are ought-to-be, moral and good. That is to say, courage is only under certain condition, ought-to-be, moral, and good. Generally speaking, this condition is in line with morality and wisdom as mentioned above; specifically speaking, as described below, the condition is not fearing the fearful things that ought not to be feared and fearing the fearful things that ought to be feared.

We can, with the guidance of morality and wisdom, divide "the fearful things" into two kinds: the fearful things that "ought to be feared" and the fearful things that "ought not to be feared." For example, saving a person on a dark and windy night is a fearful thing, but it conforms to morality, so it is a thing that ought not to be feared; on the contrary, stealing on a dark and windy night is also a fearful thing, but as it does not conform to morality, it is something that ought to be feared. Mine clearance is a fearful thing; if the engineers go for mine clearance, which conforms to wisdom, then it will be something that ought not to be feared; on the contrary, if the laymen go for mine clearance, which goes against wisdom, then it will be something that ought to be feared.

Obviously, under the condition that those fearful things ought not to be feared, courage is ought-to-be, moral, and good while cowardice is ought-not-to-be, immoral, and bad. It is ought-to-be to save people on a dark and windy night, but it is ought-not-to-be to be too afraid to save people. It is ought-to-be for engineers to be brave in clearing mines, but it is ought-not-to-be for them to be too afraid to clear mines. On the contrary, under the condition that those fearful things ought to be feared, courage is ought-not-to-be, immoral, and bad while cowardice is ought-to-be, moral, and good. It is ought-to-be to be afraid of stealing, but it is ought-not-to-be to be brave in stealing. It is ought-to-be for laymen to be afraid of clearing mines, but it is ought-not-to-be for them to be brave in clearing mines. Therefore, Confucius says, "Confucius is both benevolent and cruel, both eloquent and inarticulate, but brave and cowardly."[142]

> Those who are willing to die in their wrestling with tigers empty-handed or wading in water without any device are not the kind of people I want to work with while those are afraid of things and thus are very cautious in planning and scheming will be successful.[143]

Cao Cao always says, "A good general has not only courage but also the sense about when to fear."[144]

Although the rule of courage is relative and premised on its conformity to morality and wisdom, it is indeed extremely important and basic for the moral norms of life. If a man wants to make achievements, no matter whether he wants to pursue success in academics, or a career, or cultivation of virtues, he is bound to encounter hardships, sufferings, and dangers in his life. If he does not have courage, he will never succeed. Therefore, Cai Yuanpei believes that courage is a necessary condition for success in life: "There is no one who can easily acquire success in learning and career. When we do not succumb to difficulties, we will succeed."[145] Courage is so important that it was listed as one of the "four major virtues" (wisdom, courage, continence, and justice) in ancient Greece, while in ancient China it was regarded as one of the "three universal virtues" (wisdom, benevolence, and courage).

So far, this research on normative ethics is about to bring its long and vast journey to an end. We have analyzed in detail all the universal moral principles (i.e. the principles of good, justice, equality, humanity, liberty, alienation, and happiness), and studied almost all the important and complex universal moral rules (i.e. the moral rules of courage, continence, wisdom, modesty, self-respect, cherishing-life, and honesty). Isn't normative ethics a scientific system about the universal moral norms—universal moral principles and universal moral rules? However, the question remains: is it that the more strictly, absolutely, extremely, and fixedly everyone follows these ethics, the better? How should we abide by ethics? This question concerns the last moral rule of the system of normative ethics, "the doctrine of the mean."

## The doctrine of the mean

### The concept of the doctrine of the mean

It is self-evident that infinite things, such as the universe, have no "middle" (*zhong* 中). On the contrary, every finite thing has a "middle." For example, on a six-foot-long line, three feet is the middle; for a circle, the center of the circle is the middle; between cold and hot, lukewarm is the middle. Although there are many forms of middle, generally speaking, as Yan Qun has seen, there are only two types of the middle. One is the "middle" in nature and the other is the "middle" in the human world: "The middle in the human world is called the golden mean."[146] However, strictly speaking, the "middle" of all human activities is not always the doctrine of the mean. For example, when you walk, the sixth step is "the middle" between the first step and the twelfth step, but it cannot be called "the doctrine of the mean."

So, what kind of human activity is the doctrine of the mean? Confucius says, "The doctrine of the mean is virtue."[147] Zhu Xi expounded on this point: "The middle in virtue and deeds, we call it the doctrine of the mean."[148] That is to say, the doctrine of the mean is a moral character and an ethical behavior: the doctrine of the mean is the "middle" of human ethical behavior. However, conversely, not all of the "middles" of ethical behaviors are the doctrine of the mean. For example, we can't call a lie which is neither too big nor too small the doctrine of the mean, just because it is the "middle" between a big lie and a small one.

Many people fail to see this point and mistake the "middle" in ethical behavior as the doctrine of the mean. Russell's opposition to the doctrine of the mean is precisely based on this misunderstanding:

> The doctrine of the mean is not entirely successful. For instance, how to define honesty? Honesty is regarded as a kind of morality, but it is

266  *The system of moral rules*

impossible for us to say that honesty is the middle way between telling big lies and telling no lies, though people may feel this idea not unwelcome in some ways. In any case, this definition does not apply to rational virtues.[149]

This kind of understanding of the doctrine of the mean is completely mistaken. Aristotle said a long time ago that neither the middle between bad and good nor the middle between big bad and small bad is the doctrine of the mean.[150] We can further add that the middle between big good and small good is not the doctrine of the mean, either. Then, what kind of middle of ethical behavior is the doctrine of the mean?

All human moral behaviors, in fact, can be divided into two fundamental categories and three kinds: one category is the behavior that fails to follow morality, that is, the so-called "below" behavior; the other category is the behavior that follows morality. Within the category of moral behavior, the behavior that follows moral principles too far is called the "over" behavior, and the behavior that follows moral principles properly is the so-called the doctrine of the mean. For example, if a person fails to keep his promise, he fails to follow the morality of faith; thus, his behavior is the "below" behavior. However, if a person tries to keep every promise he makes at any time and in any situation, his way of following the morality of faith is as stubborn and rigid as the way of Wei Sheng, who drowned while trying to keep his promise; this behavior is the "over" behavior. He keeps his promise when it is proper for him to keep it, and does not keep his promise when it is not proper for him to keep it, then in such a case, he aligns his decision on whether to follow the moral principle of faith or not with the virtue of righteousness. This behavior follows the virtue of faith properly, so it is the doctrine of the mean. This view can help understand why Wu Mi made the following diagram in his analysis of the doctrine of the mean and persistence (i.e., over and below):

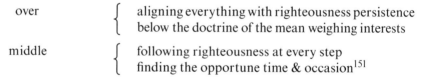

It can be concluded that the doctrine of the mean is neither the "middle" between the big bad and the small bad, nor the "middle" between the big good and the small good, nor the "middle" between the bad and the good; it is the "middle" of two special bads, namely, "the bad of not abiding by morality" and "the bad of excessively abiding by morality." In other words, the doctrine of the mean is the good act of properly abiding by morality; the "over" is the bad act of excessively abiding by morality and the "below" is the bad act of not abiding by morality. The "over" behavior and the "below" behavior can be summed into the category of persistence, which runs contrary to the golden mean.

## The value of the doctrine of the mean

It is self-evident that the "below" behavior or failure to follow morality is a bad, but why is it that only the doctrine of the mean—properly following morality—is considered the good while the "over" behavior or excessive following of morality is the bad? Isn't excessive following of morality more moral or a greater good? No! The truth is that things will develop in the opposite direction when they become extreme. If a thing varies within a certain range, the variation will not change the quality or nature of the thing, but if the variation goes beyond this range, then the opposite occurs and it becomes something else.

Morality is no exception to this truth. Following a certain moral principle within a certain range is moral and good; beyond this range, our behavior will go to the opposite side and become bad and immoral. Isn't too much self-respect pride? Isn't too much modesty inferiority? Isn't excessive continence abstinence? Isn't excessive benevolence indulgence of evils? Isn't excessive cherishing-life a lowly life? Obviously, only behavior of properly abiding by morality (the doctrine of the mean) is moral and good; excessive abiding by morality (the over) and not abiding by morality (the below) end up being the same thing: bad and immoral. Therefore, Confucius said, "Too much is as bad as too little,"[152] Aristotle says, "both excess and defect belong to Vice, and only the mean state to Virtue."[153]

Then, it can be concluded that these three types of moral behaviors cover all the ethical behaviors of humans: the behavior of not abiding by morality, the behavior of excessively abiding by morality, and the behavior of properly abiding by morality. Furthermore, all behaviors of the doctrine of the mean are good and vice versa, so the doctrine of the mean and the good overlap completely in their extension. Conversely, all "over" behaviors and all "below" behaviors are bad and all bad behaviors are either "over" or "below" the doctrine of the mean, so the extension of "over" and "below" is equal to the extension of "bad."

In this sense, Aristotle says, "Virtue is the nature of the state of the mean... Only the golden mean is a virtue."[154] Confucius says, "The gentleman is the doctrine of the mean while the small man is contrary to the doctrine of the mean."[155] Xunzi says, "What is middle? The answer is: rites and righteousness."[156] Wang Fu-zhi says, "The principle of the world is unified in one: the doctrine of the mean of benevolence, righteousness, rite, wisdom."[157] In a word, the doctrine of the mean is an extremely universal, fundamental, and important moral standard and moral quality of all good deeds and virtues: "The doctrine of the mean is the supreme virtue!"[158] So, how can we achieve the doctrine of the mean and avoid the below behavior or the over behavior?

## The method of the doctrine of the mean

How can we achieve the doctrine of the mean and avoid the below behavior and the over behavior? Confucians answer that the key is "adjusting the middle according to specific situation to find the right way to apply the moral principle." So, what does it mean? Zhu Xi explains, "There is no fixed standard for the doctrine of the mean, as it adjusts itself to time, location, and condition all the time."[159] "Weighing the situation just like the weight (the *Quan* 权) in the scale, so the best way is to choose the middle."[160] "The most important virtue is the doctrine of the mean and the most important thing in the doctrine of the mean is the weight (the *Quan* 权)."[161] Fung Yulan explains further:

> The 'middle,' the mean, is relative to the things and situations, so the 'middle' is changeable and cannot be fixed. 'The middle' adjusts to situation all the time, so Confucians say, 'Adjust the middle according to time.' Mencius says, 'Persistence without weighing the situation is insistence on one thing that is fixed all the time.' The so-called insistence on the one thing means that this one thing can be applied to everything in every situation.[162]

In other words, whether the way a person follows a certain moral principle is the doctrine of the mean and proper or not is not fixed, but varies from time to time, and from occasion to occasion. Specifically, when observing this moral principle does not conflict with observing other kinds of moral principles so that both kinds of moral principles can be followed, then following this moral principle is proper and is the doctrine of the mean, and not observing this moral principle is the "below" behavior. When observing a certain moral principle conflicts with observing other kinds of moral principles and they cannot be both observed at the same time, if the value of this moral principle is less than the value of other kinds of moral principle, then following this moral principle is the "over" behavior while following other kinds of moral principle rather than this moral principle is the doctrine of the mean. If the value of this moral principle is greater than that of other kinds of moral principles, then following this moral principle is the doctrine of the mean while not following this moral principle is the "below" behavior. The right way to follow a moral principle is that when two goods conflict, the greater good ought to be chosen, while when two bads conflict, the smaller bad ought to be chosen.

For example. Under normal circumstances, we should be honest, so honesty is the doctrine of the mean and lying is the below behavior. However, if there is a situation like the one described by Kant, when the murderer inquires whether the innocent who fled into our house after being pursued by him is in our house, the good of honesty conflicts with the good of saving people: honesty cannot save people and in this case saving means one cannot be honest; not telling lies will get the person killed while to save the person one must lie. However, honesty is a small good and saving the life of the person is a great good, so between these two goods, we ought to choose the great good, which is saving people. Lying is a small bad, and killing is a great bad, so between these two bads we ought to choose a small bad, which is lying. Therefore, in this situation we ought not to be honest and allow the innocent person to be killed; we ought to tell a lie to save this innocent person. In other words, "honesty" in this case is the "over" behavior and dishonesty is "the doctrine of the mean."

This example well proves the truth of Confucians' standing on this point: adjusting the middle according to specific situations to find the right way to apply morality is the basic method of achieving the doctrine of the mean. Wu Mi appropriately summarizes this method as "obeying the *jing* and always weighing the *Quan*":

> Obeying the *jing* (经) and weighing the *quan* (权) is equal to the doctrine of the mean, as *jing* (经) means the moral principle or the standard and the *quan* (权) means the proper application of the moral principle or the standard to specific situations.[163]

## Notes

1 Sima Guang, *A General Reflection for Political Administration,* (Guizhou: Guizhou People's Publishing House,1997), 198
2 John Rawls, *A Theory of Justice* (Belknap Press, 1999), 4.
3 Friedrich Paulsen, *System of Ethics*, Translated By Frank Thilly (New York: Charles Scribner's Sons, 1908), 668.
4 Sissela Bok, *Lying: Moral Choice in Public and Private Life* (New York: Vintage Books, 1989), 256.
5 Ibid., 257.
6 Sissela Bok. *Lying: Moral Choice in Public and Private Life*, 269.
7 Ibid., 268.
8 Ibid., 269.
9 *Mencius.*
10 *The Analects of Confucius,*"Governing."
11 Wang Fuzi, *Readings and Comments on Chinese History* (Beijing: China Book Bureau, 1975), 12.
12 Ibid., 12.
13 *Master Lü's Spring and Autumn Annals*, "Zhongji."
14 *Master Lü's Spring and Autumn Annals*, "Guisheng."
15 Jiang Sheng, *Lectures on the Taoist Ethics* (Chengdu: Sichuan University Press, 1995), 87.
16 *Mozi*, "Guiyi."
17 *Selected Works of Philosophy by Feuerbach*, Volume 2, Translated By Zhenhua Rong (Beijing: SDX Joint Publishing Company, 1962), 569.
18 Ibid., 775.
19 Ibid., 775.
20 Ibid., 545.
21 *Chuang-tzu*, "Zhile."
22 *Master Lü's Spring and Autumn Annals*, "Qingyi."
23 Ibid.
24 *Master Lü's Spring and Autumn Annals*, "Bensheng."
25 Shi Qi, *A Complete Book of Chinese Health Care* (Shanghai: Xue lin Publishing House, 1990), 3.

270  *The system of moral rules*

26 Ibid., 121.
27 Ibid.
28 Ibid., 97.
29 Zhang Qiwen, *Practical Health Care in Chinese Medicine* (Beijing: People's Medical Publishing House, 1989), 5.
30 Jingfeng, *Wisdom on Preserving Health*, 35.
31 Qiwen, *Practical Health Care in Chinese Medicine*, 8.
32 Bing. *On Living a Healthy and Easy Life in Old Age* (Knowledge Publishing House, 1991), 342.
33 Ibid., 35.
34 Qiwen, *Practical Health Care in Chinese Medicine*, 8.
35 Bing, *On Living a Healthy and Easy Life in Old Age*, 297.
36 Ibid., 292.
37 Ibid., 297.
38 Qiwen, *Practical Health Care in Chinese Medicine*, 156.
39 Bing, *On Living a Healthy and Easy Life in Old Age*, 197.
40 Ibid., 195
41 Ibid., 202.
42 Ibid., 297.
43 Bing, *On Living a Healthy and Easy Life in Old Age*, 297.
44 Ibid., 209.
45 Ibid., 226.
46 Ibid., 214.
47 Ibid., 219.
48 Bing, *On Living a Healthy and Easy Life in Old Age*, 2 8.
49 Qiwen, *Practical Health Care in Chinese Medicine*, 156.
50 Ibid., 109.
51 Ibid., 108.
52 Ibid., 109.
53 Bing, *On Living a Healthy and Easy Life in Old Age*, 276.
54 Qi, *A Complete Book of Chinese Health Care*, 169.
55 Ibid., 102.
56 Qiwen, *Practical Health Care in Chinese Medicine*, 18–120.
57 Qi, *A Complete Book of Chinese Health Care*, 102.
58 *Mencius*, "Jinxin".
59 Yulan, *Complete Works of Sansongtang*, Volume 4, 442.
60 John Rawls, *A Theory of Justice*, 386.
61 Yulan, *Complete Works of Sansongtang*, Volume 4, 442.
62 Adler, *Inferiority and Transcendence* (Beijing: Writers Publishing House, 1986), 42.
63 Maslow, *Motivation and Personality*, 45.
64 James, *Compendium of Psychology*, 23.
65 Maslow, *Motivation and Personality*, 45.
66 Liang Qichao, "On Self-Esteem," in *Theories on New Citizens* (Zhengzhou: Zhongzhou Ancient Books Publishing House, 1998).
67 John Rawls, *A Theory of Justice*, 386.
68 Adler, *Inferiority and Transcendence*, 50.
69 Maslow, *Motivation and Personality*, 46.
70 *Zhouyi*, "Modesty."
71 Zhu Xi, *Collections of Zhu Xi's Conversations*. Volume 70 (Shanghai: Shanghai Ancient Books Publishing House), 76.
72 Spinoza, *The Ethics and Selected Letters*, translated by Samuel Shirley; edited, with introduction, by Seymour Feldman (Indianapolis, IN: Hackett Pub. Co., 1982), 147.
73 Ibid., 186.

74 Tang Zhen, *The Hidden Book*, "Xushou."
75 Yulan, *Complete Works of Sansongtang*, Volume 4, 441.
76 Ibid., 441.
77 Spinoza. *The Ethics and Selected Letters*, 186–187.
78 Lv Kun, *Moaning*, "Self Cultivation."
79 Yang Jue, *Ming Confucianism*, Volume 9.
80 *Lao Tzu*, Chapter 22.
81 *Lao Tzu*, Chapter 24.
82 "Record of Study," *Complete Works of Wang Yangming*, Volume 3 (Shanghai: Shanghai Classics Publishing House, 1992).
83 Liu Shao, *Biography*, "Explanation and Debate."
84 Zhouyi, "The Great Appendix."
85 Zhouyi, "Modesty,"
86 Quoted in Adler, *Children Education* (Beijing: Commercial Press, 1937), 234.
87 Gu Yanwu, *Guang Shi*.
88 Yulan, *Complete Works of Sansongtang*, Volume 4, 450–451.
89 *Mencius*.
90 Ban Gu, "Tempermant," *Bai Hu Tong*.
91 Zhang Dainian, *Chinese Wisdom* (Shanghai: Shanghai People's Publishing House, 1989), 1.
92 Fukuzawa Yukichi, *Outline of Civilization* (Beijing: The Commercial Press, 1995), 73.
93 Jacque Maritain, *Science and Wisdom*, (Beijing: The Commercial Press, 1995), 20.
94 Jean Piaget, *Piaget's Genesis and Cognition Paper* (Shanghai: East China Normal University Press, 1991), 38.
95 Yukichi, *Outline of Civilization*, 81.
96 Baltasar Gracian, *Book of Wisdom*, translated by Chuanan Qin (Beijing: Beijing Library Press, 2004), 527.
97 *Mencius*.
98 Liu Shao, *Biography*, "Eight Views."
99 *Selected Works of Philosophy by Feuerbach*, 559.
100 *The Doctrine of the Mean*.
101 *Xunzi*.
102 Meng Zhaolan, *General Psychology* (Beijing: Peking University Press. 1994). 458.
103 *The Analects of Confucius*, "Governing."
104 Yulan, *Complete Works of Sansongtang*, Volume 4, 681.
105 *Mencius*.
106 Plato, *Republic*, translated by G.M.A. Grube (Indianapolis, IN: Hackett, 1974), 103.
107 Ibid., 96.
108 Ibid., 106.
109 *Aristotle's Nicomachean Ethics*, translated with commentaries and glossary by Hippocrates G. Apostle (Grinnell, IA: Peripatetic Press, 1984), 117.
110 *Cai Yuanpei's Complete Works*, Volume 2 (Beijing: China Book Company, 1980), 176.
111 Yulan, *Complete Works of Sansongtang*, Volume 4, 518.
112 David Hume, *A Treatise of Human Nature*, edited with an introduction by Ernest C. Mossner (New York: Penguin Books, c1969), 462.
113 Xenophon, *Memorabilia* (Beijing: Commercial Press, 1988), 171.
114 Spinoza, *The Ethics and Selected Letters*, 175.
115 Paulsen, *System of Ethics*, 483.
116 Spinoza, *The Ethics and Selected letters*, 105.
117 Ibid., 206.
118 Ibid., 207.

## 272  The system of moral rules

119 *Xunzi*, "Etiquette Theory."
120 Spinoza, *The Ethics and Selected Letters*, translated by Samuel Shirley; edited, with introduction, by Seymour Feldman (Indianapolis, IN: Hackett Pub. Co., c1982), 209.
121 Yulan, *Complete Works of Sansongtang*, Volume 4, 556.
122 Spinoza, *The Ethics and Selected Letters*, 176.
123 Ibid., 159.
124 John Locke, *An Essay Concerning Human Understanding*, abridged and edited with an introduction by A. D. Woozley. (New York: New American library, 1974), 173.
125 *The Analects*, "On Governing."
126 Plato's *Republic*, 94.
127 *Aristotle's Nicomachean Ethics*, 51.
128 Ibid., 46.
129 *The Analects of Confucius*, "On Virtues."
130 *Aristotle's Nicomachean Ethics*, 47.
131 Henry Sidgwick, *The Methods of Ethics* (London: Macmillan and Co. Limited, 1922), 309.
132 Paulsen, *System of Ethics*, 495.
133 *Cai Yuanpei's Complete Works*, Volume 2, 180.
134 *Master Zuo's Spring and Autumn Annals*.
135 Ibid.
136 *Cai Yuanpei's Complete Works*, 182.
137 *Xunzi*, "Honor."
138 Ibid.
139 *Aristotle's Nicomachean Ethics*, 48.
140 Pan Shu and Gao Juefu, *A Study of Ancient Chinese Psychological Thoughts* (Nanchang: Jiangxi People's Publishing House, 1983), 221.
141 *Liji*, "The Doctrine of the Mean."
142 *The Analects of Confucius*, "On Virtues."
143 *The Analects of Confucius*, "Shu Er."
144 *The Record of the Three Kingdoms*.
145 *Cai Yuanpei's Complete Works*, Volume 2, 182.
146 Yan Qun, *Aristotle's Ethics* (Beijing: Commercial Press, 1933), 26.
147 *The Analects of Confucius*.
148 Zhu Xi, "The Doctrine of the Mean," *Four Books*.
149 Russell, *Western Wisdom* (Shanghai: Shanghai People's Publishing House, 1992), 114.
150 *Aristotle's Nicomachean Ethics*, 29.
151 Wu Mi, *Literature and Life* (Beijing: Qinghua University Press, 1996), 120.
152 *The Analects of Confucius*.
153 *Aristotle's Nicomachean Ethics*, 29.
154 Ibid., 29.
155 *The Doctrine of the Mean*, Chapter 2.
156 *Xunzi*.
157 Wang Fuzi, *Complete Commentaries on the Four Books*, (Beijing: Zhonghua Press, 1975), 59.
158 *The Analects of Confucius*.
159 Zhu Xi, "The Doctrine of the Mean," *Four Books*.
160 Zhu Xi, "Meniscus," *Four Books*.
161 Ibid.
162 Yulan, *Complete Works of Sansongtang*, Volume 4, 435.
163 Mi, *Literature and Life*, 121.

# Index

ability and diligence, 203–204
abnormal and morbid happiness, 152–153
absolute contingency of despotism, 133–136
achievement, 201–202, 206, 207, 218, 245–250
action principle, 219–220
active body, 234–235
Acton, J.D., 26, 44–47, 77, 107
Adams, John, 46
Adler, A.W., 3, 67, 68, 242, 244, 245
*A Dream of the Red Mansion* (Jia Zhen), 182
adversity, 206, 207
Age of the Enlightenment, 2, 10
alienation: assimilation, 51; as basic concept of humanism, 52–54; definition, 53–56; elimination, 60; enslavement, 54–55; forced alienation, 56; as general scientific term, 51; Marx's analysis, 52; non-freedom, enslavement, and coercion, 52–53; positive and negative value, 58–60; self-enslavement, 55; self-realization and self-actualization, 59–60; slavery types, 54; types (*see* economic alienation; political alienation; religious alienation; social alienation); unconscious alienation, 57–58; value of, 58–60; voluntary alienation, 56–57
Annas, J., 166, 168, 171, 210
Aquinas, T., 113, 116, 118, 140–143, 161, 184–186, 226
Aristotle, 2, 21, 74, 105, 136, 138–141, 161–163, 167–169, 175, 184–186, 206, 256, 261, 262, 266, 267
Article I of the Bill of Rights of the United States, 40, 47

Article 2 of *The Declaration of Human Rights,* 28
*The Art of Worldly Wisdom* (*The Oráculo Manual*) 252
Arvid, 260
Asiatic mode of production: autocratic monarchical land ownership, 122; "chiefdom"/"chieftain territory," 121–122; classed society transition, 121; craftsmen and businessmen sponger official system, 124–125; despotism as inevitable product, 134; economic development, 134–135; enslavement in full monopoly, 129–130; extreme official ownership, 124; Marx claim, 122, 123; natural economy of kingly ownership, 122–123; official land ownership, 123–124; totalitarian despotism, 128–131
assimilation, 51
Athenian democracy, 76
authenticity and illusion of happiness, 179–181
autocratic monarchical land ownership, 122
average man theory, 80–81

Bain, 174
Ban Gu, 251
Bao hao, 192
Beethoven, 182
Belinsky, 216
Bentham, J., 42, 174, 208
Berlin, I., 12–20, 23, 43, 44, 46, 50, 57, 105
Bodin, J., 113, 116
Bosanquet, B., 42
Bradley, F.H., 42

Bronquil, 198
Bryce, J., 41
Buchanan, J.M., 43
Burke, E., 42
Bury, J.B., 38, 41, 140
Buyeva, 5

Cai Jing, 254
Cai Yuanpei, 257, 262, 264
cannibalism, 139
Cao Cao, 264
Cao Xueqin, 182, 183, 192, 193, 200–202, 216
Carneades, 212
Chambers, S., 78
Chen Duxiu, 115, 138, 139
Chen Sheng, 205
Chen Zhi, 234
cherishing-life: active body, 234–235; approaches, 233–241; concept of, 229–231; happiness, 232; kinetic movement, 235–236; life preservation, 233; living and fitness, 239–241; long-term pleasure, 232–233; moderate dieting, 236–238; morning routine, 238; quiet spirit, 233–234; regular daily routine, 238–239; rest in the evening, 239; self-interest, 231–232; sleep at night, 239; Taoist ideas, 229–230; "Ten Pleasures," 234; "Twelve Less," 235; value of, 231–233; work routine, 238
Chernyshevsky, N.G., 2, 192, 193, 198
choice of happiness, 217–219
Chuang Tzu, 85
*Cihai*, 152
coercion, 29–31, 46, 72
cognition of happiness, 215–217
Cohen, C., 33, 39
Collingwood, 50
communism, 9, 43
completeness, 169
Confucianism: kingly despotism, 114, 116; monarch, 114; people-centered theory, 116–117; ruling state as family, 146–148; theory, 114; "the Son of Heaven," 143; thought system, 138–139; "Three Cardinal Guides," 114–115
Confucius, 114, 115, 118, 119, 138, 139, 140, 143, 198, 207, 237, 249, 255, 261, 262, 264, 265, 267
Constant, B., 42, 108

constitutional democracy, 47–49, 77–78, 85–86
constitutionalism, 72
consumer happiness, 158
consumer needs, 196
continence: concept, 256–257; emotion and desire, 257; indulgence, 257; principles of, 259–261; rational and irrational passion, 258; and self-restraint, 256; types, 257; value of, 258–259
cooperative capitalism, 68, 70
Cooper, J.M., 169
courage: Brave, 262; classification, 262–263; definition, 261–262; heroic courage, 262–263; mine clearance, 264; objects of fears, 261–262; recklessness, 262–263; righteous and un-righteous courage, 262; salvation, 261; value of, 263–265
Cultural Revolution, 205

Dante, 25, 116, 140, 142
Danton, 206
Darwin, C., 175, 202
Da Vinci, L., 202
deception, 223–227
deity, 86, 87
deliberative/consultative democracy, 76–77
democracy, 47–49
Democritus, 2, 140, 174
desire *vs.* realization of happiness, 197–199, 213–214, 217–218
despotism, 74, 75; absolute contingency, 133–136; aristocracy, 136; aristocratic politics, 136; Asiatic mode of production, 121–125; autocratic rule, 112–113, 116, 118; cannibalism, 139; capitalist society of slavery, 131–132; classification, 113–119; concept, 112–113; Confucianism, 114–116, 144–148; democracy, 131–132; despotic monarchy, 131; dictatorship, 112; "divine rights of the monarch," 140; economic development, 134–136; emergence and existence of, 133–136; European and United States mode of production, 125–126; fallacies of, 136–139; feudal society, 132; feudal society with civil ownership, 125; free colony, 128; fundamental causes, 133; geographical environment,

126–128; hegemonic despotism, 115–116; hereditary despotism, 144–148; human-nature root of, 119–120; hydraulic society, 126; kingly despotism, 116–117; liberalism, 139–140; monarchy, 112; non-fundamental causes, 133–134; non- hydraulic society, 126–127; oriental official ownership, 121–125; Oriental societies, 126; people-centered theory, 116–118; political system, 136; serfdom feudal society, 125; social structure, 133–134; social structure, 120–121; state institution value, 136–137; supreme power of society/state, 119–120; theoretical basis, 139–148; theory of national unity, 141–143; theory of no two suns in the sky, 143–144; theory of rule by elites, 140–141; thought system, 138–139; Three Cardinal Guides, 138; totalitarian despotism, 128–131; universal origins of, 119–121; universal ownership, 126; value of, 136–139; value standards of state institutions, 137–138; western civil ownership, 125–126; *zhuan-zhi,* 112
destiny *vs.* realization of happiness, 205–208
Dewey, J., 24, 42
diligence, 203
doctrine of the mean: categories and kinds, 266; concept, 265–266; method, 267–269; value of, 267
Dong Cunrui, 262, 263
Dong Zhongshu, 114, 117
Dubroliv, 216
Dworkin, R., 43

economic alienation: capitalist stratum, 66, 70–71; class exploitation and oppression, 65, 67; concept, 60–61; constitutionalism, 72; cooperative capitalism, 68, 70; definition, 61; degree of power imbalance, 67; exploitation and oppression of strata, 65, 66; free competition capitalism, 67; labor exploitation, 61, 62; Marxist concept of exploitation, 64; monopoly of economic power, 62–63; monopoly of political power, 63–64; national capitalism/people capitalism, 70; neoliberalism, 66; non-equivalent exchange, 62; power imbalance, 65–67; public and private ownership, 67–70; public resources control, 63–64; real wage growth rate, 66–67; root causes of, 62–64; seller and buyer monopoly, 62–63; sortition election system, 71–72; state institutions, 67–72; universal suffrage democracy, 65–66, 71–72; working stratum, 71
economic freedom: and free competition, 36; government regulation, 35–37; human right, 36; market mechanisms, 35, 36; mixed economy, 37; natural freedom system, 35; planned economy, 37; state institutions, 35, 37
effort *vs.* realization of happiness, 202–204, 219–220
elements for success of life, 199
emotion (desire), 18–19
*The Emperor's Classic of Internal Medicine,* 237, 240
Engels, F., 52, 200
enslavement, 52–55
Epicurus, 163, 164, 168–170, 174, 208
equality principle of liberty, 27–28
*Essential Formulas Worth a Thousand in Gold to Prepare for Emergencies* (Qian Jin Yao Fang), 233
European and United States mode of production, 125–126
existentialism, 82, 83
extreme official ownership, 124

faithfulness, 224–225
Fang Zhongyong, 255
fatalism, 205
Faulkner, H.U., 127
Feinberg, J., 13, 14
Feng Tang, 206, 207
Ferguson, A., 28
Feuerbach, L.A., 2, 4, 51, 52, 93, 172, 230, 254, 259
Fichte, 17
Finner, S.E., 112
forced alienation, 56, 58
Fourier, C., 2
Franklin, Benjamin, 46, 172, 249
Frankl, V., 173
free competition capitalism, 67
freedom of thought: Article I of the Bill of Rights of the United States, 40; and behaviors, 38; concept, 37–38; culture development, 38; equality standard of liberty, 39; forbidden

thoughts, 41; freedom of press, 38, 40–41; freedom of speech, 38–40; French Declaration of Human Rights, 42; harmful consequences, 41–42; limit standard of liberty, 39; social progress, 40–41
free society, 27–28, 45, 49
Friedman, M., 35, 43
Fukuzawa Yukichi, 251
fundamental value standards, 100–101
Fung Yulan, 158, 168, 199, 200, 202–205, 207, 241, 246, 258, 268

Gao Lian, 236
gaze theory, 81
Goethe, 202
Gongduzi, 256
Gorjkoch, D., 7
Gotz, I.L., 158, 177, 199, 206
Green, T.H., 42
Guan Yu, 263
Guan Zhong, 238
Gu Guangyao, 219
Guo Xiang, 143
Gu Yanwu, 250

Hamilton, A., 42, 46
Han Fei, 115, 140
Han Xin, 205, 223, 251
happiness: abnormal and morbid happiness, 152–153; authenticity of, 179–181; avoidance of pain/misfortune, 169–170; behavior perspective of life, 171–172; *Cihai*, 152; completeness, 169; concepts, 161–162; consumer happiness, 158; creative and non-creative happiness, 158–159; definition, 151–154; development-based and survival-based happiness, 197; hedonism, 174–176; illusory happiness, 179–181; law of duration of happiness, 189–191; law of intensity of happiness, 187–189; law of succession of happiness, 191–194; laws of the realization of happiness, 197–214; laws of value of happiness, 194–197; life perspective, 172; lifetime behavior, 168–170; material happiness, 156, 157, 178, 183; meaningful and valuable life, 172–173; mental states, 165–166; misfortune, 167; net balance of life, 172–173; normal and healthy happiness, 152–153; objective essence of, 155; objective standard of, 154–155; objectivist happiness theory (objectivism), 184, 186–187; objectivity of, 178–179; particular happiness, 183–184; perfection theory, 161–162, 186; pleasure and pain values, 163–165; pleasure theory, 161–162; principle of action, 219–220; principle of choice, 217–219; principle of cognition, 215–217; principles of, 214–220; priority of needs vs. hierarchy level, 193; process happiness, 159–161; purpose of life, 167–170; qualitative and quantitative relativity of, 182–183; real happiness, 180–181; relativity and absoluteness of, 181–184; result happiness, 159–161; satisfaction degree of needs, 192–193; self-sufficiency, 169; social happiness, 156–157; spiritual happiness, 156, 157, 183; structure, 154–156; subjective perception of life, 173–174; subjectivist happiness theory (subjectivism), 184–186; subjectivity of, 154, 156, 176–178; success of life, 158; in survival and development, 153–154; theories on nature of happiness, 184–187; types of, 156–161; as ultimate good, 165–167; value of life and purpose of life, 171–174; value *vs.* nature and level of happiness, 196–197; void of existence, 173
Harveland and Ember, 121
Hayek, F.A., 22, 26, 27, 28, 30, 43–46, 48, 69
hedonism: definition, 174; extreme hedonism, 174, 175; moderate hedonism, 174–175; object of desire, 175–176; refutation of, 175–176
Hegel, 17, 18, 51, 52, 182
hegemonic despotism, 115–116
Heidegger, M., 79, 80, 85
Helda, 7, 8, 10
Heraclitus, 2, 140
Herder, J.G., 2
hereditary despotism: benevolent system, 144–145; Confucians, 146; despotism based on love, 147; hydraulic society, 145; preconditions, 147–148; pseudo-family/quasi-family state, 145–146; totalitarian despotism, 146–147
heroic courage, 262–263
Herzen, A.I., 2

Hitler, 254
Hobbes, T., 16, 17, 19, 28, 113, 116, 140, 161, 184, 185
Hobhouse, L.T., 28, 42, 45
honesty: ascendency of, 228–229; behavior, 224; concept, 223–225; and deception, 223–224; degree of benefits, 227; effects on others, 225; effects on society, 226; effects on themselves, 225–226; essence of, 229; goodwill, 225; language and action, 223–224; malicious, 225; moral value, 225–227; scope of application, 227–229; sincerity and faithfulness, 224–225; types of, 224–225; ultimate standard of morality, 226
Huang Jiguang, 262, 263
Hua Tuo, 236
humanism: of Age of Enlightenment, 2; basic needs of human, 6; creative potential, 6; definition, 3; human as highest value, 3–4; humanitarianism, 3; human society, 3–4; moral principle about human action, 6–7; origin of, 2–3; of Renaissance, 2; self-realization and self-perfection, 5–6; socialist humanism, 2; systematic theory, 2
humanity: capitalism, 10; cardinal guides, 1; concept, 1–2; definition, 1; ethical norms, 1; feudalism and theocracy, 10; fundamental principles of humanity, 11 (*see also* alienation; liberty); humanism of self-realization, 7–8; humanism of the Enlightenment, 10; ideal social system, 9, 10; inhumanity and un-humanity, 8–9; legal principles, 1; moral principle and immoral principle, 8, 9; philanthropic humanism, 7, 8; Prometheusian humanism, 7; Renaissance humanism, 10; socialist humanism, 10; state institutions, 9–10; sympathy, 8; virtues, 1; *see also* humanism
Humboldt, W. von, 23, 30, 31
Hume, D., 42, 161, 174, 184, 185, 258
Hu Shi, 11, 44
hydraulic society, 126, 145

Iakerton, L., 42
illusory happiness, 179–181
inferiority, 241–242, 244–245
inhumanity and un-humanity, 8–9
intelligence, 199–201

James, W., 157, 175, 243
Jefferson, T., 42, 46
Jevinsbo, J., 50
Jia Dao, 201
Jiang Yan, 183
Jia Zhen, 182
Jones, R., 123, 131
Jorge, A., 2
justice: and benevolence, 17; *vs.* humanity, 105–107; *vs.* liberty, 107–108

Kant, I., 2–4, 17, 18, 42, 151, 153, 175, 209, 210, 212, 227, 268
Kaplan, 244
Kautsky, 120, 134
Kelso, 67, 68
Kex, 154, 179, 185
kinetic movement, 235–236
kingly despotism, 116–117
knowledge, 251–252
Kraut, R., 154, 155, 186, 187
Kurtz, P., 25, 50

Lao Zi, 140, 248
Laski, H., 83
last man theory, 80
law of duration of happiness, 189–191
law of intensity of happiness, 187–189
law of succession of happiness, 191–194
laws of the realization of happiness: desire *vs.* realization of happiness, 197–199, 213–214; destiny *vs.* realization of happiness, 205–208; effort *vs.* realization of happiness, 202–204; sufficient and necessary conditions, 212–214; talent *vs.* realization of happiness, 199–202; "three immortality ideals," 212; virtue *vs.* realization of happiness, 208–212
laws of value of happiness, 194–197
Leibniz, G.W., 152
Lermontov, 192, 193
Liang Qichao, 244, 260
Liang Shuming, 91
Li Bai, 200, 201, 204
liberalism: constitutional democracy, 47–49; definition, 42–43; objects, 42–43; principles of liberty/free society, 45–47; theoretical categorization, 49–50; theoretical system, 43–49; value of liberty, 43–45
libertarianism, 44

liberty: advanced animal, 20; in ancient Chinese, 11; behavior, 12–13; concept, 12–17; condition to use liberty, 14–15; creativity, 22–24; definition, 12; emotion (desire), 18–19; equality principle, 27–28; extrinsic value, 21–26; in field of activity, 12; general principles of, 26–31; intrinsic value, 19–21; justice and benevolence, 17; limit principle, 29–31; need for, 20–21; negative liberty, 17, 18; non-liberty, 13, 16; obstacles/constraint, 13–15; personality, 22–23; positive liberty, 17–19; principle of economic freedom, 35–37; principle of freedom of thought, 37–42; principle of political liberty, 31–35; reason over desire, 18–19; rule-of-law principle, 26–27; self-determination, 11; self-realization, 22–25; as self-restraint, 17–19; social progress, 24–25; specific principles, 31–42; state institutions, 25–26; true liberty and non-liberty, 17–18; useless into useful liberty, 16; values of, 19–26; will (purpose), 12–14; *see also* liberalism
Li Dazhao, 114, 139
life preservation, 233
limit principle of liberty, 29–31, 45, 46
Lincoln, A., 12
Liu Bang, 205
Liu Mo, 181, 234
Liu Yingjun, 262
living and fitness, 239–241
Locke, J., 12, 22, 42, 174, 260
long-term pleasure, 232–233
luck/fortune, 206, 207
Lukacs, G., 59, 78, 84
Luo Rongqu, 128
Luther, 226
Lu Xun, 139, 192, 193

McFallon, 57
Machiavelli, N., 116, 140
Madison, James, 46
majority tyranny, 48
malicious deception, 225
Malitan, 251
Ma Qihua, 119
Marxist concept of exploitation, 64
Marx, K., 34, 52, 56, 61, 74, 75, 85, 121–123, 126, 128, 131, 134, 135, 145, 182, 191, 193, 198, 200

Maslow, A., 5, 6, 20, 22, 23, 59, 83, 157, 188, 191–196, 215, 242, 245
Ma Su, 252
material happiness, 156, 157, 178, 183, 194–195
material self-respect, 242
Ma Yongjun, 63, 64
Melotti, U., 123
Mencius, 116, 117, 119, 140, 208, 228, 251, 252, 256
Mill, J.S., 23, 24, 30, 31, 41, 42, 151, 161, 174, 184, 185, 190, 194–197, 215
Milton, J., 41, 42
mine clearance, 264
misfortune, 167
mixed economy, 37
Miyajima, 10
Miyashima, 7
moderate dieting, 236–238
modesty: "comparing oneself with the stronger," 250; cultivation of, 249–250; definition, 246–247; "measuring others," 249–250; pride, 246–249; value of, 248–249
Montesquieu, 2, 42, 129
Moore, T., 164, 174, 175, 176
morality and moral character, 208; *see also* virtue *vs.* realization of happiness
moral principle about human action, 6–9, 104
moral rules, 223 *see also* cherishing-life; continence; courage; doctrine of the mean; honesty; modesty; self-respect; wisdom
Mozi, 140, 142, 230
Mueller, M., 24, 40
Muller, J., 123
Müller, M., 86, 90
Mussolini, 254

Napoleon, 156, 157, 182, 206
national capitalism/people capitalism, 70
national unity theory, 141–143
natural economy of kingly ownership, 122–123
natural freedom system, 35
natural gift, 199
negative liberty, 17, 18
neoliberals, 30, 42
Newton, 252
Nietzsche, F., 79, 80, 85, 174
Nolan, R.T., 41
non-equivalent exchange, 62

non-liberty, 13, 16
non-moral happiness, 211
normal and healthy happiness, 152–153
no two suns in the sky theory, 143–144
Nozick, R., 43

Oakeshott, M., 43
official land ownership, 123–124
Olds, J., 163
*On Liberty* (Mill), 30
opportunity, 205–207
*Oriental Despotism* (Wittfogel), 134
Owen, R., 2

Paine, T., 42
pain of wisdom, 200
"paradox of freedom," 109–110
Parducci, A., 183
particular happiness, 183–184
Pascal, 4
Paulsen, F., 161, 175, 209, 259
Pavlov, 19, 20
Petofi, S., 19
Penn, 40, 42
people-centered theory, 116–118
perfection theory, 161–162, 186
Perry, 4, 6
Petofi, S., 19
philanthropic humanism, 7
Phillips, H.B., 22
Philma, 116
Piaget, J., 251
Picasso, 158
Pico, 5
Pius XI, 67
planned economy, 37
Plato, 17, 18, 25, 74, 109, 110, 136, 256, 261
pleasure theory, 161–162; *see also* happiness
Plekhanov, 206
Pojman, L.P., 179, 180
political alienation, 72–78; Athenian democracy, 76; behaviors of social importance, 72–73; concept, 72–73; constitutional democracy, 77–78; cultural behavior, 73; deliberative/consultative democracy, 76–77; democracy, 74–78; despotism, 74, 75; economic behavior, 73; monarchy, 74–75; monopoly of political power, 75; oligarchy, 74, 75; and political liberty, 72; principle of majority rule, 76; republic, 74; root causes of, 73–75;
social behavior, 73; universal suffrage democracy, 76–78
political liberty: definition, 31; democracy, 33; human right, 33–34; own will, 31, 32; people sovereignty/political equality principle, 34–35; rule and management, 32–33; social freedom, 34
Pope Leo XIII, 67
Popper, K.R., 40, 43, 46, 50, 109, 110
positive liberty, 17–19
Price, R., 27
pride, 246–249
principle of distribution, 105–106, 140
principle of economic equality, 101–102, 109
principle of equality, 106–107
principle of equal opportunities, 102
principle of majority rule, 76
principle of political equality, 101, 109–110
principles of alienation, 103
principles of humanity, 102, 105–107
Principles of Human Motivation, 191
principles of liberty, 45–47, 102–103, 107–108
process happiness, 159–161
Prometheusian humanism, 7
Pruyser, P.W., 91
public will, 27
purpose of life, 167–170
Pushkin, 200, 201

Qi Jing gong, 114
Qin Hui, 254
Qin Mugong, 117
Qin Shihuang, 205
Qoheleth, 200
quiet spirit, 233–234
Qu Yuan, 207

Rawls, J., 13, 28, 43, 77, 110, 111, 226, 241, 244
real happiness, 180–181
recklessness, 262–263
regular daily routine, 238–239
relativity and absoluteness of happiness, 181–184
religious alienation, 86–93; concept of the soul, 89–90; deity, 86, 87, 89, 90; duality, 88; elimination, 91–93; emotional yearning, 90–91; fear of death, 92; as humanistic concept,

88; misfortune and suffering, 90–91; origins of religions, 89–91; rational superstition, 89–91; religion definition, 86; as scientific term, 88; social oppression and misery, 93; spiritual entity, 86, 87; supernatural beings, 87; superstition, 89–90; voluntary alienation, 88–89
Renaissance humanism, 5–7, 10
result happiness, 159–161
righteous courage, 262
Robespierre, 40, 206
Robinson, 62
Roemer, J.E., 63
Roosevelt, 40, 47
Rousseau, J.-J., 27, 31, 42, 79, 213
Ruggiero, G. de, 50
rule by elites theory, 140–141
rule-of-law principle of liberty, 26–27, 45
Russell, 198
Ryan, A., 12

Saint-Just, 206
Saint-Simon, H. de, 2
Samuelson, P.A., 62, 63
Sapiro, 43
Sartori, G., 12, 34, 43, 49, 50
Sartre, J.-P., 21, 79, 81, 85
Schopenhauer, 160
*The Secrets of Longevity*, 238
self-achievement, 242–243
self-determination, 11
self-realization, 84–85, 195; humanity, 5–9; liberty, 22–25
self-realization theory *see* perfection theory
self-respect: categories, 242; concept, 241–243; inferiority, 241–242; internal and external self-respect, 242; material self-respect, 242; principles of, 245–246; self-achievement, 242–243; self-improvement and self-reliance, 243–244; social self-respect, 242–243; spiritual self-respect, 243; values of, 243–245
self-sufficiency, 169
*sheng-huo,* 168
Sidgwick, H., 164, 165, 174, 175, 262
Sima Qian, 1, 207
sincerity, 224–225
slavery, 54–56
Smith, A., 35, 36, 42, 47, 105
social alienation, 78–86; average man theory, 80–81; concept, 78–80; constitutional democracy, 85–86; *vs.* economic and political alienation, 85; existentialism, 82; gaze theory, 81; human rights, 83–84; last man theory, 80; root causes of, 80–86; rule of law and democracy, 82–83; secular loner, 81; self-realization, 84–85; socialization, 80; standard manifestation of, 80; types of, 78–79; will of leaders/senior officials, 79–80; will of the general public, 78–79
social coercion, 29–30
social freedom, 34
social happiness, 156–157
socialism, 9
socialist humanism, 2, 10
social oppression, 93
social self-respect, 242–243
Socrates, 17, 138, 139, 140, 259
sortition election system, 71–72
soul concept, 89–90
Spencer, H., 42, 174
Spinoza, B., 17, 18, 42, 153, 174, 192, 198, 216, 246, 247, 259, 260
spiritual entity, 86, 87
spiritual happiness, 156, 157, 183, 194–196
spiritual self-respect, 243
*Spring and Autumn Annals* (Master Lü), 233
Spitz, D., 44
sponger official system, 124–125
state institutions: economic freedom, 35, 37; humanity, 9–10; liberty, 25–26
Stoics, 166, 168, 169, 211
Streng, F.J., 89
subjectivity and objectivity of happiness, 176–179
Sun Simiao, 235–237
Sun Yat-sen, 40
supreme power of society, 48
supreme value standards, 102–103
sympathy, 8
system of natural freedom, 47
system of value standards: balance of value, 105; compatible values, 105; equality *vs.* liberty, 108–110; fundamental value standards, 100–101; general principle of equality, 101; justice *vs.* humanity, 105–107; justice *vs.* liberty, 107–108; moral principles, 104; Popper "paradox of freedom," 109–110; principle of distribution, 105–106; principle of economic

equality, 101–102, 109; principle of equality, 106–107; principle of equal opportunities, 102; principle of political equality, 101, 109–110; principles of alienation, 103; principles of humanity, 102, 105–107; principles of liberty, 102–103, 107–108; quantum of interests of everyone, 104; standards of morality, law, and politics, 100; supreme value standards, 102–103; ultimate value standards, 100, 105, 111; *see also* despotism

talent *vs.* realization of happiness, 199–202
Tao Hongjing, 238
Taoist ideas, 229–230
Taylor, E.B., 86, 89
Telfer, E., 151
"Ten Pleasures," 234
"three laws of fact" of happiness, 193–194
Tilley, 175
Tocqueville, A. de, 41, 42
Tolstoy, 200–202
totalitarian despotism, 128–131
Toynbee, 20
"Twelve Less," 235

ultimate value standards, 100, 105
ultra-liberals, 30
unconscious alienation, 57–58
universal human needs, 183
universal suffrage democracy, 65–66, 71–72, 76–78, 125, 132

value of liberty theory, 43–45
Veenhoven, R., 151
virtue *vs.* realization of happiness, 208–212
void of existence, 173
Voltaire, 2, 17
voluntary alienation, 56–57, 88–89

Wang Anshi, 202, 239
Wang Chuanshan, 228

Wang Fu-zhi, 267
Wang Yangming, 249
Wan Quan, 237
Wei Sheng, 266
Wen (Emperor), 207
western civil ownership, 125–126
will (purpose), 12–14
William, King, 129
Wilson, President, 33
wisdom: acquisition of, 254–255; cognitive ability, 251; concept, 250–252; and ignorance, 251; and knowledge, 251–252; laws of, 252–254; mental/cerebral ability, 250; moral and non-moral wisdom, 252–254; talent and learning, 254–255; types, 252; virtues, 254
Wittfogel, K.A., 134, 140
Wright, J.D., 64
Wu Guang, 206, 205
Wu Mi, 266, 269
Wu Yu, 139

Xenophon, 259
Xiang Yu, 205
Xunzi, 140, 259, 262, 267

Yan Fu, 112
Yang Changji, 129
Yang Jue, 248
Yang Zhu, 182
Yan Hui, 250
Yan Qun, 265
Yan Song, 254
Yan Zi, 129
Yuan Shikai, 139

Zeng Guofan, 212, 213, 255
Zeno, 211
Zhang Dainian, 251
Zhang Zai, 207
Zhongyong, 202
Zhuang Zi, 140, 172, 182, 205, 230, 235
Zhuge Liang, 199, 252, 263
Zhu Xi, 246, 265, 268
Zuoqiu Ming, 207

Printed in the United States
By Bookmasters